# THE HISTORY OF CORPORATE FINANCE

## DEVELOPMENT OF ANGLO-AMERICAN SECURITIES MARKETS, FINANCIAL PRACTICES, THEORIES AND LAWS

### *Volume 3*

Limited Liability

# THE HISTORY OF CORPORATE FINANCE

## DEVELOPMENT OF ANGLO-AMERICAN SECURITIES MARKETS, FINANCIAL PRACTICES, THEORIES AND LAWS

*Volume 3*

Limited Liability

*Edited by*
Robert E. Wright

*Advisory Editor*
Richard Sylla

Routledge
Taylor & Francis Group
LONDON AND NEW YORK

First published 2003 by Pickering & Chatto (Publishers) Limited

Published 2016 by Routledge
2 Park Square, Milton Park, Abingdon, Oxon OX14 4RN
605 Third Avenue, New York, NY 10017

*Routledge is an imprint of the Taylor & Francis Group, an informa business*



BRITISH LIBRARY CATALOGUING IN PUBLICATION DATA

The history of corporate finance : the development of Anglo-American securities markets, laws, and financial practices and theories
1. Stocks – Great Britain – History 2. Stocks – United States – History
3. Corporations – Great Britain – Finance – History – Sources 4. Corporations – United States – Finance – History – Sources
I. Wright, Robert E. II. Sylla, Richard
332'.0415'0941

LIBRARY OF CONGRESS CATALOGING-IN-PUBLICATION DATA

The history of corporate finance : the development of Anglo-American securities markets, laws, and financial practices and theories / edited by Robert E. Wright and Richard Sylla.
p. cm.
Compilation of excerpts from books previously published between 1677–1919.
Includes index.

1. Corporations – Finance – United States – History. 2. Corporations – Finance – Great Britain – History. 3. Corporations – Finance – Law and legislation – United States – History. 4. Corporations – Finance – Law and legislation – Great Britain – History. I. Wright, Robert E. (Robert Eric), 1969– II. Sylla, Richard Eugene.

HG4061 .H57 2002
332–dc21

2001059123

ISBN-13: 978-1-85196-749-0 (set)
ISBN- 13: 978-1-138-76069-1 (hbk)

Typeset by
P&C

# CONTENTS

# THE LIMITED LIABILITY ACT, TO WHICH ARE ADDED THE JOINT STOCK COMPANIES ACTS

David Gibbons
of the Middle Temple, Special Pleader.
*The Limited Liability Act, To Which Are Added the Joint Stock Companies Acts*
(London: John Weale, 1858–9)

THE

# LIMITED LIABILITY ACT,

18TH AND 19TH VICTORIA, CAP. 133.

TO WHICH ARE ADDED THE

# JOINT STOCK COMPANIES ACTS,

| | | | |
|---|---|---|---|
| CAP. | 110 | OF 7 & 8 | VICT. |
| — | 78 | 10 & 11 | — |
| — | 47 | 19 & 20 | — |
| — | 14 | 20 & 21 | — |
| — | 80 | 20 & 21 | — |
| — | 60 | 21 & 22 | — |
| — | 91 | 21 & 22 | — |

WITH NOTES AND AN INDEX

BY

DAVID GIBBONS, ESQ.,

OF THE MIDDLE TEMPLE, SPECIAL PLEADER.

LONDON:

JOHN WEALE, 59, HIGH HOLBORN.

1858-9.

# INTRODUCTION.

ANY man may limit his liability if he can agree with his Creditor that it shall be so. He may buy a horse on the terms that it shall be paid for out of a certain Legacy or a certain Dividend from a Railway; and if sold on those terms, the seller can only claim payment in the event of the buyer receiving the Legacy or Dividend. So a Partnership or a Company may contract to pay out of their Capital only; and if parties deal with them on those terms, their right to payment is gone when the Capital is exhausted. In the case of a Partnership or Company in which one person contracts for another, it is not enough that the authority of the Agent should be limited; the party dealing should also have notice of the Limitation, he being entitled to assume that the powers of a General Agent are general and unfettered by unusual restrictions. Limited Liability, though not impossible, is unusual, and not very practicable, except in the case of Insurance Companies, who usually, if not universally, insert in their Policies that the Assured shall look to the Capital Stock of the Company alone for the money assured; and in such cases, to render the Company liable, it must be stated and proved that their Capital Stock was sufficient to pay the claim; and a Shareholder of the Company who has paid up his Capital is not liable to the Assured. (Hallett *v.* Dowdall, 16 Jur. 462. *In re* The Sea Fire and Life Insurance Company, 18 Jur. 387.) Assurance Companies having proved themselves to be so well able to protect themselves in this respect, may be the reason why they are excepted from the Limited Liability Act.

This Act introduces no new principle into the law. It does not make that possible which formerly was impossible, but renders easy what was difficult. The term "limited," in the name of the Company constituted under the Act, is probably intended to operate as a notice to all persons dealing with it, that the authority of the Directors or Officers is restricted, and as a Clause in every Contract made with the Company that its Creditor shall look for payment to its property only.

In order to obtain Limited Liability under the recent Act of Parliament, a Company must be formed for a commercial purpose, or purpose of profit: it must be constituted by Deed of Settlement. The promoters, before advertising it, must obtain a Certificate of Provisional Registration from the Registrar of Joint Stock Companies. Whilst so provisionally registered, and before they are completely registered, it may be doubted whether they can receive more than 10*s.* per cent. on the amount of the Shares. Before a Certificate of Complete Registration with Limited Liability can be obtained, the Deed of Settlement of the Company must be executed by at least twenty-five Shareholders, holding Shares to the amount in the aggregate of at least three-fourths of the nominal Capital, on which Shares have been paid up by each of such Shareholders not less than £20 per cent. If this £20 per cent. cannot legally be paid until a Certificate of Complete Registration has been obtained, a Certificate of Complete Registration should precede a Certificate of Complete Registration with Limited Liability. The following steps should, it is suggested, be taken to establish a Company with Limited Liability:

1. A Certificate of Provisional Registration.
2. A Deed of Settlement.
3. A Certificate of Complete Registration.
4. Payment of £20 per cent. on at least three-fourths of the Capital, by at least twenty-five Shareholders.

5. A Certificate of Complete Registration with Limited Liability.

The whole of the provisions of 7 & 8 Vict. c. 110, and 10 & 11 Vict. c. 78, must be attended to, and relate to such Companies.

# THE LIMITED LIABILITY ACT.

---

18 & 19 VICTORIÆ REGINÆ, CAP. CXXXIII.

## An Act for limiting the Liability of Members of certain Joint Stock Companies. [14*th August*, 1855.]

WHEREAS it is expedient to enable Members of Joint Stock Companies to limit the Liability for the Debts and Engagements of such Companies to which they are now subject: Be it therefore enacted by the Queen's most Excellent Majesty, by and with the Advice and Consent of the Lords Spiritual and Temporal, and Commons, in this present Parliament assembled, and by the Authority of the same, as follows:

I. Any Joint Stock Company to be formed under the Act of the Eighth Year of Her Majesty, Chapter One hundred and ten[a] (other than an Assurance Company), with a Capital to be divided into Shares of a nominal Value not less than Ten Pounds each, may obtain a Certificate of Complete Registration with Limited Liability upon complying with the Conditions following, in addition to doing all other Matters and Things now required in order to obtain a Certificate of Complete Registration; that is to say,

[a] See 7 & 8 Vict. c. 110, s. 2, and note.

(1.) The Promoters shall state on their Returns to the Office for Provisional Registration that such Company is proposed to be formed with Limited Liability:

(2.) The Word "Limited" shall be the last Word of the Name of the Company:[b]

(3.) The Deed of Settlement shall contain a Statement to the Effect that the Company is formed with Limited Liability:

(4.) The Deed of Settlement shall be executed by Shareholders, not less than Twenty-five in number, holding Shares to the Amount in the aggregate of at least Three Fourths of the nominal Capital of the Company, and there shall have been paid up by each of such Shareholders on account of his Shares not less than Twenty Pounds *per Centum*:[c]

(5.) The Payment of the above Per-centage shall be acknowledged in or endorsed on the Deed of Settlement, and the Fact of the same having been *bonâ*

[b] The word "Limited" should perhaps come after the word "Registered," see 7 & 8 Vict. c. 110, s. 25; as, for instance, The Universal Chimney Sweeping and Soot Collecting Association, "Registered Limited."

[c] The promoters of a Company provisionally registered cannot receive on the Shares more than 10*s.* per cent. (7 & 8 Vict. c. 110, s. 23); and it is illegal for a Company to act otherwise than provisionally before it has obtained a Certificate of Complete Registration (s. 7). Perhaps, therefore, a Company should obtain a Certificate of Registration before this £20 per Cent. can be lawfully paid into its funds, and must afterwards apply for a Certificate for Limited Liability. See also s. 7 of 7 & 8 Vict. c. 110, as to the Signature of the Deed necessary for obtaining a Certificate of Complete Registration.

*fide* so paid shall be verified by a Declaration of the Promoters, or any Two of them, made in pursuance of the Act made in the Sixth Year of the Reign of His late Majesty King *William* the Fourth, Chapter Sixty-two:

And upon such Conditions being complied with, and such other Matters and Things done, the Registrar of Joint Stock Companies shall grant a Certificate of Complete Registration with Limited Liability to such Company.

II. Any Joint Stock Company, except as aforesaid, now or hereafter completely registered under the said Act of the Eighth Year of Her Majesty, may obtain a Certificate of Complete Registration with Limited Liability, in manner and subject to the Condition following; that is to say,

The Directors of such Company may, with the Consent of at least Three Fourths in Number and Value of its Shareholders who may be present, personally or by Proxy, at any General Meeting summoned for that Purpose, make such Alteration in the Name, nominal Value of Shares, and Deed of Settlement of the Company as may be necessary for enabling it to comply with the Conditions herein-before mentioned with respect to Joint Stock Companies seeking to obtain Certificates of Complete Registration with Limited Liability; and upon Compliance with such Conditions the Registrar, after the Affairs of the Company shall at the Expense of the Company have been audited by some Person appointed by the Board of Trade, and on Certificate from the said Board that the complete Solvency thereof has been established on such Audit to its Satisfaction, shall grant to such Company, by its new Name, a Certificate of Complete Registration with Limited Liability, and thereupon all Privileges and Obligations hereby attached to Companies with Limited Liability, their Shareholders, Directors, and Officers, shall attach to the Company named in such Certificate, its Shareholders, Directors, and Officers.

III. Any Joint Stock Company, except as aforesaid, constituted under any Private Act of Parliament, whereof it shall be proved to the Satisfaction of the Board of Trade, after the Affairs of the Company shall, at the Expense of the Company, have been audited by some Person appointed by the Board of Trade, that the said Company is perfectly solvent, and that not less than Twenty *per Centum* of Three Fourths of the nominal Capital of such Company has been paid up, may obtain a Certificate of Complete Registration with Limited Liability, in manner and subject to the Condition following; that is to say,

The Directors of such Company may, with the Consent of at least Three Fourths in Number and Value of its Shareholders who may be present, personally or by Proxy, at any General Meeting summoned for that Purpose, make such Alteration in the Name and nominal Value of Shares as may be necessary for enabling it to comply with the Condition in that Behalf herein-before mentioned with respect to Joint Stock Companies seeking to obtain Certificates of Complete Registration with Limited Liability; and upon

Compliance with such Condition the Registrar, on Receipt of a Certificate of the Solvency of the Company, and of the Payment of Capital as before mentioned, shall grant to such Company, by its new Name, a Certificate of Complete Registration with Limited Liability; and thereupon all Privileges and Obligations hereby attached to Companies with Limited Liability, their Shareholders, Directors, and Officers, shall attach to the Company named in such Certificate, its Shareholders, Directors, and Officers.

IV. Every Company that has obtained a Certificate of Complete Registration with Limited Liability shall paint or affix, and shall keep painted or affixed, its Name on the Outside of every Office or Place in which the Business of the Company is carried on, in a conspicuous Position, in Letters easily legible, and shall have its Name engraven in legible Characters on its Seal, and shall have its Name mentioned in legible Characters in all Notices, Advertisements, and other official Publications of such Company, and in all Bills of Exchange, Promissory Notes, Cheques, Orders for Money, Bills of Parcels, Invoices, Receipts, Letters, and other Writings used in the Transaction of the Business of the Company.

V. If such Company do not paint or affix, and keep painted or affixed, its Name, in the Manner aforesaid, each of the Directors thereof shall be liable to a Penalty not exceeding Five Pounds for not so painting or affixing its Name, and for every Day during which such Name is not so kept painted or affixed; and if any Director or other Officer of the Company, or any Person on its Behalf, use any Seal purporting to be a Seal of the Company whereon its Name is not so engraven as aforesaid, or issue or authorize the Issue of any Notice, Advertisement, or other official Publication of such Company, or of any Bill of Exchange, Promissory Note, Cheque, Order for Money, Bill of Parcels, Invoice, Receipt, Letter, and other Writing used in the Transaction of the Business of the Company, wherein its Name is not mentioned in the Manner aforesaid, he shall be liable to a Penalty of Fifty Pounds, and shall further be personally liable to the Holder of any such Bill of Exchange, Promissory Note, Cheque, or Order for Money, for the Amount thereof, unless the same shall be duly paid by the Company.

VI. No Increase to be made in the nominal Capital of any Company that has obtained a Certificate of Complete Registration with Limited Liability shall be advertised or otherwise treated as Part of the Capital of such Company, until it has been registered with the Registrar of Joint Stock Companies; and no such Registration shall be made unless a Deed is produced to the Registrar, executed by Shareholders holding Shares of the nominal Value of not less than Ten Pounds to the Amount in the aggregate of at least Three Fourths of the proposed increased Capital of the Company, nor unless it is proved to the Registrar, by such acknowledgment and Declaration as herein-after mentioned, that upon each of such Shares there has been paid up by the Holder thereof an Amount of not less than Twenty Pounds *per Centum;* and if any such Increase of Capital as aforesaid be advertised or otherwise treated as Part of the Capital of the Company before the same has been so registered, every Director of such Company shall incur a Penalty of Fifty Pounds; and the Payment of the above Per-centage shall be acknowledged in or endorsed on the Deed so produced, and the Fact of the same having been bonâ fide so paid shall be verified by a Declaration of the Directors, or any Two of them, made in pursuance of the said Act made in the Sixth Year of the Reign of His late Majesty King *William* the Fourth, Chapter Sixty-two.

VII. The Members of a Joint Stock Company which has so obtained a Certificate of Complete Registration with Limited Liability, after such Certificate is granted, notwithstanding the Provisions contained in the said Act of the Eighth Year of Her present Majesty, shall not be liable, under any Judgment, Decree, or Order which shall be obtained against such Company, or for any Debt or Engagement of such Company, further or otherwise than is herein-after provided.

VIII. If any Execution, Sequestration, or other Process in the Nature of Execution, either at Law or in Equity, shall have been issued against the Property or Effects of the Company, and if there cannot be found sufficient whereon to levy or enforce such Execution, Sequestration, or other Process, then such Execution, Sequestration, or other Process may be issued against any of the Shareholders to the Extent of the Portions of their Shares respectively in the Capital of the Company not then paid up, but no Shareholder shall be liable to pay in satisfaction of any One or more such Execution, Sequestration, or other Process a greater sum than shall be equal to the Portion of his Shares not paid up: Provided always, that no such Execution shall issue against any Shareholder except upon an Order of the Court, or of a Judge of the Court, in which the Action, Suit, or other Proceeding shall have been brought or instituted, and such Court or Judge may order Execution to issue accordingly, with the reasonable Costs of such Application and Execution, to be taxed by a Master of the said Court; and for the Purpose of ascertaining the Names of the Shareholders, and the Amount of Capital remaining to be paid upon their respective Shares, it shall be lawful for any Person entitled to any such Execution, at all reasonable Times, to inspect the Register of Shareholders without Fee.[a]

IX. If the Directors of any such Company shall declare and pay any Dividend when the Company is known by them to be insolvent, or any Dividend the Payment of which would to their Knowledge render it insolvent, they shall be jointly and severally liable for all the Debts of the Company then existing, and for all that shall be thereafter contracted, so long as they shall respectively continue in Office; provided that the Amount for which they shall all be so liable shall not exceed the Amount of such Dividend, and that if any of the Directors shall be absent at the Time of making the Dividend, or shall object thereto, and shall file their Objection in Writing with the Clerk of the Company, they shall be exempted from the said Liability.

X. No Note or Obligation given by any Shareholder to the Company whereof he is a Shareholder, whether secured by any Pledge or

(a) As to execution against Shareholders of Registered Companies, see 7 & 8 Vict., cap. 110, ss. 66, 67, 68.

otherwise, shall be considered as Payment of any Money due from him on any Share held by him, and no Loan of Money shall be made by any such Company to any Shareholder therein; and if any such Loan shall be made to a Shareholder, the Directors who shall make it, or who shall assent thereto, shall be jointly and severally liable to the extent of such Loan. and Interest for all the Debts of the Company contracted before the Repayment of the Sum so lent.

XI. Where any Company completely registered under the said Act of the Eighth Year of Her present Majesty, or any Company constituted under any Act of Parliament, shall obtain a Certificate of Complete Registration with Limited Liability, the Grant of such Certificate shall not prejudice or affect any Right which previously to the Grant of such Certificate has accrued to any Creditor or other Person against the Company in its Corporate Capacity, or against any Person then being or having been a Member of such Company, but every such Creditor or other Person shall be entitled to all such Remedies against the Company in its Corporate Capacity, and against every Person then being or having been a Member of such Company, as he would have been entitled to in case such Certificate had not been obtained.

XII. No Alteration made by virtue of this Act in the Name of any Company shall prejudice or affect any Right which previously to such Alteration has accrued to such Company as against any other Company or Person, or which has accrued to any other Company or Person as against such Company, but every such Company as against any other Company or Person, and every other Company or Person as against such Company and the Members thereof, shall be entitled to all such Remedies as they or he would have been entitled to if no such Alteration had been made; and no such Alteration shall abate or render defective any legal Proceeding pending at the Time when such Alteration is made.

XIII. In the Case of any Company which has obtained a Certificate of Limited Liability, whenever, on taking the yearly Accounts of such Company, or by any Report of the Auditors thereof, it appears that Three Fourths of the subscribed Capital Stock of the Company has been lost, or has become unavailable in the Course of Trade, from the Insolvency of Shareholders, or from any other Cause, the Trading and Business of such Company shall forthwith cease, or shall be carried on for the sole Purpose of winding up its affairs; and the Directors of such Company shall forthwith take proper Steps for the Dissolution of such Company, and for the winding up of its affairs, either by Petition to the Court of Chancery, or by Exercise of the Powers of the Deed of Settlement, or by such other lawful Course as they may think most fit.

XIV. In cases where a Certificate of Registration with Limited Liability has been obtained, when One Auditor only shall have been appointed under the Thirty-eighth Section of the Act of the Eighth of *Victoria*, Chapter One hundred and ten, that single Auditor, and when Two or more such Auditors shall have been so appointed then One of such Auditors, shall be subject to the Approval of the Board of Trade, and such Board in case the Auditor submitted to them for approval shall for any Reason appear unfit or objectionable shall appoint another in his Place.

XV. Every pecuniary Penalty imposed in pursuance of this Act shall be deemed a debt due to the Crown, and shall be recoverable accordingly.

XVI. This Act shall, so far as is consistent with the Contents and Subject Matter thereof, be taken as Part of and construed with the said Act of the Eighth Year of Her present Majesty, Chapter One hundred and ten, and the Act of the Eleventh Year of Her Majesty, Chapter Seventy-eight, and all the Provisions of the said Acts, save in so far as they are varied by this Act, shall apply to Persons and Companies applying for or obtaining a Certificate of Complete Registration with Limited Liability.

XVII. The Provisions of the Act of the Eighth Year of Her present Majesty, Chapter One hundred and eleven, and of the Joint Stock Companies Winding-up Act, 1848, and of the Joint Stock Companies Winding-up Amendment Act, 1849, shall apply to Persons and Companies obtaining a Certificate of Complete Registration with Limited Liability, subject only to such Variations as may be occasioned by the Provisions of this Act.

XVIII. This Act shall not apply to *Scotland.*

XIX. This Act may be cited for all Purposes as "The Limited Liability Act, 1855."

# JOINT STOCK COMPANIES ACT.

---

## 7 & 8 VICTORIÆ REGINÆ, CAP. CX.

An Act for the Registration, Incorporation, and Regulation of Joint Stock Companies. [*5th September*, 1844.]

WHEREAS it is expedient to make Provision for the due Registration of Joint Stock Companies during the Formation and Subsistence thereof; and also after such complete Registration as is herein-after mentioned, to invest such Companies with the Qualities and Incidents of Corporations, with some Modifications, and subject to certain Conditions and Regulations; and also to prevent the Establishment of any Companies which shall not be duly constituted and regulated according to the Provisions of this Act: Now be it enacted by the Queen's most Excellent Majesty, by and with the Advice and Consent of the Lords Spiritual and Temporal, and Commons, in this present Parliament assembled, and by the Authority of the same, That this Act shall come into operation at the following Times; that is to say, as to the Officers to be appointed in pursuance hereof for the Registration of Companies, and the Regulation of the Office hereby provided for that Purpose, immediately on the passing hereof; and as to all Companies to which this Act is to apply, and all other the Provisions herein-after contained, except such as relate to such Officers and Office as aforesaid, on the First Day of *November* in the Year One thousand eight hundred and forty-four.

II. And be it enacted, That this Act shall apply to every Joint Stock Company, as herein-after defined, established in any Part of the United Kingdom of *Great Britain* and *Ireland* except *Scotland,* or established in *Scotland* and having an Office or Place of Business in any other Part of the United Kingdom, for *any commercial Purpose, or for any Purpose of Profit,*[a] or for the Purpose of Assurance or Insurance (except Banking Companies, Schools, and Scientific and Literary Institutions, and also Friendly Societies, Loan Societies, and Benefit Building Societies, respectively duly certified and enrolled under the Statutes in force respecting such Societies, other than such Friendly Societies as grant Assurances on Lives to the Extent herein-after specified;) and that the Term "Joint Stock Company" shall comprehend,—

Every Partnership whereof the Capital is divided or agreed to be divided into Shares, and so as to be transferable without the express Consent of all the Co-partners; and also,

Every Assurance Company or Association for the Purpose of Assurance or Insurance on Lives, or against any Contingency in-

[a] It has been decided that a Land Society established for the purpose of purchasing land, and dividing it amongst its members, is not established for a commercial purpose, or purpose of profit, within the meaning of this Act, and therefore cannot claim to be registered. (Reg. *v.* Whitmarsh, 15 G. R. 600.) The like decision was come to in the case of a Loan Society, which lent its funds only to its members (Bear *v.* Bromley, 16 Jur. 450). It would seem to follow that such societies cannot claim the privilege of limited liability.

volving the Duration of Human Life, or against the Risk of Loss or Damage by Fire, or by Storm or other Casualty, or against the Risk of Loss or Damage to Ships at Sea or on Voyage, or to their Cargoes, or for granting or purchasing Annuities on Lives; and also every Institution enrolled under any of the Acts of Parliament relating to Friendly Societies, which Institutions shall make Assurances on Lives, or against any Contingency involving the Duration of Human Life to an Extent upon One Life or for any One Person to an Amount exceeding Two hundred Pounds, whether such Companies, Societies, or Institutions shall be Joint Stock Companies or Mutual Assurance Societies, or both; and also,

Every Partnership which at its Formation, or by subsequent Admission (except any Admission subsequent on Devolution or other Act in Law), shall consist of more than Twenty-five Members:

And that, except where the Provisions of this Act are expressly applied to Partnerships existing before the said First Day of *November*, it shall be held to apply only to Partnerships the Formation of which shall be commenced after that Date: Provided nevertheless, that, except as herein-after specially provided, this Act shall not extend to any Company for executing any Bridge, Road, Cut, Canal, Reservoir, Aqueduct, Waterwork, Navigation, Tunnel, Archway, Railway, Pier, Port, Harbour, Ferry, or Dock which cannot be carried into execution without obtaining the Authority of Parliament: Provided also, that, except as herein-after is specially provided, this Act shall not extend to any Company incorporated or which may be hereafter incorporated by Statute or Charter, nor to any Company authorized or which may be hereafter authorized by Statute or Letters Patent to sue and be sued in the Name of some Officer or Person.

III. And be it declared, That the following Words and Expressions are intended to have the Meanings hereby assigned to them respectively, so far as such Meanings are not excluded by the Context or by the Nature of the Subject Matter; that is to say,

The Word "Company" to mean any Joint Stock Company or other Institution, as before defined:

The Expression "Assurance Company" to mean any Assurance Company, Association, or Institution, as before defined:

The Word "Directors" to mean the Persons having the Direction, Conduct, Management, or Superintendence of the Affairs of a Company:

The Expression "Promoter," or "Promoter of a Company," to apply to every Person acting by whatever Name in the forming and establishing of a Company at any Period prior to the Company obtaining a Certificate of comple Registration as herein-after mentioned:

The Word "Subscriber" to mean any Person who shall have agreed in Writing to take or have taken any Share in a proposed Company or in a Company formed, and who shall not have executed the Deed of Settlement, or a Deed referring thereto:

The Word "Shareholder" to mean any Person entitled to a Share in a Company, and who has executed the Deed of Settlement, or a Deed referring to it, or, in the Case of Mutual Assurance Societies, any Person who shall be an assured Member thereof:

The Word "Person" to apply to Bodies Politic or Corporate, whether sole or aggregate:

The Expression "Commissioners of the Treasury" to apply to the Lord High Treasurer for the Time being, or the Commissioners of Her Majesty's Treasury for the Time being, or any Three or more of them:

The Expression "Committee of Privy Council for Trade" to mean the Lords of the Committee of Her Majesty's Privy Council for the Consideration of all Matters of Trade and Plantations:

The Expression "Secretary of the Committee" to mean One of the Joint Assistant Secretaries of the said Committee of Privy Council for Trade:

The Word "Justice" to mean a Justice of the Peace for the County, City, Borough, Liberty, or Place where the Matter requiring the Cognizance of any Justice shall arise, and who shall not be interested in the matter:

The Expression "special Authority" to mean any Deed of Settlement, Bye Laws, Letters Patent, Charter, or Local and Personal Act of Parliament, by which Powers are conferred or Regulations prescribed with reference to any individual Company:

The Word "prescribed" to mean provided for by special Authority:

The Word "Month" to mean Calendar Month:

The Expression "Superior Courts" to mean Her Majesty's Superior Courts of Law or Equity in *England* or *Ireland*:

The Word "Occupation," when applied to any Person, to mean his Trade or Following, and, if none, then his Rank or usual Title, as Esquire, Gentleman:

The Expression "Place of Residence" to include the Street, Square, or Place where the Party shall reside, and the Number (if any) or other Designation of the House in which he shall so reside:

The Word "Oath" to include Affirmation or other Declaration lawfully substituted for an Oath:

And generally, whensoever, with regard to any Matter or to any Function in respect thereof, the Name of an Officer (whether a public Officer or an Officer of a Company) ordinarily having Cognizance of such Matter, or ordinarily exercising such Function, is mentioned, such Reference is to be understood to apply as well to any other Person or Officer who may have Cognizance of such Matter, or exercise such Function in respect of such Matter:

And, subject as aforesaid to the Context and to the Nature of the Subject Matter, Words denoting the Singular Number are to be understood to apply also to a Plurality of Persons or Things, and Words denoting the Masculine Gender are to be understood to apply also to Persons of the Feminine Gender.

IV. And be it enacted, That before proceeding to make public, whether by way of Prospectus, Handbill, or Advertisement, any Intention or Proposal to form any Company for any Purpose within the Meaning of this Act, whether for executing any such Work as aforesaid under the Authority of Parliament, or for any other Purpose, it shall be the Duty of the Promoters of such Company and they or some of them are hereby required to make to the Office hereby provided for the Registration of Joint Stock Companies (and herein-after called the Registry Office) Returns of the following Particulars according to the Schedule (C.) hereunto annexed; that is to say,

1. The proposed Name of the intended Company; and also,
2. The Business or Purpose of the Company; and also,
3. The Names of its Promoters, together with their respective Occupations, Places of Business (if any), and Places of Residence;

And also the following Particulars, either before or after such Publication as aforesaid, when and as from Time to Time they shall be decided on; viz.,

4. The Name of the Street, Square, or other Place in which the provisional Place of Business or Place of Meeting shall be situate, and the Number (if any) or other Designation of the House or Office; and also,
5. The Names of the Members of the Committee or other Body acting in the Formation of the Company, their respective Occupations, Places of Business (if any), and Places of Residence,

together with a written Consent on the Part of every such Member or Promoter to become such, and also a written Agreement on the Part of such Member or Promoter, entered into with some One or more Persons as Trustees for the said Company, to take One or more Shares in the proposed Undertaking, which must be signed by the Member or Promoter whose Agreement it purports to be (but such Agreements need not be on a Stamp); and also,

6. The Names of the Officers of the Company and their respective Occupations, Places of Business (if any), and Places of Residence; and also,

7. The Names of the Subscribers to the Company, their respective Occupations, Places of Business (if any), and Places of Residence; and also, before it shall be circulated or issued to the Public,

8. A Copy of every Prospectus or Circular, Handbill, or Advertisement, or other such Document at any Time addressed to the Public, or to the Subscribers or others, relative to the Formation or Modification of such Company:

9. And afterwards, from Time to Time, until the complete Registration of such Company, a Return of a Copy of every Addition to or Change made in any of the above Particulars:

And that upon such Registration of at the least the Three Particulars first before mentioned the Promoters of such Company shall be entitled to a Certificate of provisional Registration.[a]

[a] 10 & 11 Vict. c. 78, ss. 5, 6, 7.

V. And be it enacted, That if for a Period of One Month after the Particulars hereby required to be registered, or any of them, shall have been ascertained or determined, the Promoters of any Company fail to register such Particulars, then, on Conviction thereof, any Promoter as aforesaid shall be liable to forfeit for every such Offence a sum not exceeding Twenty Pounds.

VI. Provided always, and be it enacted, That if the Promoters of a proposed Company appoint a Person, being an Attorney or Solicitor of One of Her Majesty's Superior Courts of Law or Equity, to be Solicitor for the Promoters of such Company, and return to the said Registry Office a Duplicate of such Appointment in Writing, signed by some One or more of such Promoters, together with a Duplicate of the Acceptance of such Appointment, signed by the Person so appointed, then, until a Duplicate of the Revocation or of the Resignation of such Appointment be returned in like Manner, so signed as aforesaid, or until the Decease of such Solicitor, all Returns by this Act required to be made by such Promoters shall be made by such Solicitor in their Behalf, and the Penalty herein-before imposed in respect of any Failure to make such Returns shall not be incurred by them; and that if within the Period of One Month after the Particulars hereby required to be registered, or any of them, shall have been ascertained, or determined, such Solicitor fail to make such Returns, then he shall be liable to forfeit for every such Offence a Sum not exceeding Twenty Pounds; and that if it be made to appear to the Court to which he shall belong that he fraudulently omitted to make a Return of any such Particulars, then he shall be liable to be suspended from Practice for any Time to be appointed by the said Court, or to be struck off the Rolls of the said Court.

VII. And be it enacted, That it shall not be lawful for any Joint Stock Company hereafter to be formed for any Purpose within the Meaning of this Act, whether for executing any such Work as aforesaid under the Authority of Parliament, or for any other purpose, to act otherwise than provisionally in accordance with this Act until such Company shall have obtained a Certificate of complete Registration as herein-after provided; and no Joint Stock Company shall be entitled to receive a Certificate of complete Registration unless it be formed by some Deed or Writing under the Hands and Seals of the Shareholders therein; and in or by such Deed there must be appointed not less than Three Directors, and also One or more Auditors; and such Deed must set forth in a Schedule thereto, in a tabular Manner, according to the Order herein-after mentioned, the following Particulars; that is to say,

1. The Name of the Company; and also,
2. The Business or Purpose of the Company; and also,
3. The principal or only Place for carrying on such Business, and every Branch Office (if any); and also,
4. The Amount of the proposed Capital, and of any proposed additional Capital, and the Means by which it is to be raised; and where the Capital shall not be Money, or shall not consist entirely of Money, then the Nature of such Capital and the Value thereof shall be stated; and also,

5. The Amount of Money (if any) to be raised or authorized to be raised by Loan; and also,
6. The total Amount of the Capital subscribed or proposed to be subscribed at the Date of such Deed; and also,
7. The Division of the Capital (if any) into equal Shares, and the total number of such Shares, each of which is to be distinguished by a separate Number in a regular Series; and also,
8. The Names and Occupations and (except Bodies Politic) the Places of Residence of all the then Subscribers, according to the Information possessed by the Officers of the Company in respect of such Names and Occupations and Places of Residence; and also,
9. The Number of the Shares which each Subscriber holds, and the distinctive Numbers thereof, distinguishing the Numbers of the Shares on which the Deposit has been paid from those on which it has not been paid; and also,
10. The Names of the then Directors of the Company, and of the then Trustees of the Company (if any), and of the then Auditors of the Company, together with their respective Places of Business (if any), Occupations, and Places of Residence; and also,
11. The Duration of the Company, and the Mode or Condition of its Dissolution:

And that such Deed must contain a Covenant on the Part of every Shareholder, with a Trustee on the Part of the Company, to pay up the Amount of the Instalments on the Shares taken by such Shareholder, and to perform the several Engagements in the Deed contained on the Part of the Shareholders; and that such Deed must also make Provision for such of the Purposes set forth in Schedule (A.) to this Act annexed as the Nature and Business of the Company may require, and either with or without Provision for such other Purposes (not inconsistent with Law) as the Parties to such Deed shall think proper; and that every such Deed of Settlement must be signed by at least One Fourth in Number of the Persons who at the Date of the Deed have become Subscribers, and who shall hold at least One Fourth of the maximum Number of Shares in the Capital of the Company; and that every such Deed must be certified by Two Directors of the Company, by Writing endorsed thereon in the Form contained in the Schdule (B.) to this Act annexed; and that on the Production of such Deed, setting forth such Matters and making such Provisions as are hereby required to be provided for, and being so signed and certified, together with a complete Abstract or Index thereof, to be previously approved by the Registrar of Joint Stock Companies, and also a Copy of such Deed, for the Purpose of registering the same, or as soon after such Production as conveniently may be, the Registrar of Joint Stock Companies shall grant a Certificate of complete Registration, according to the Provisions of this Act in that Behalf; and unless such Deed and other Matters be so produced, and such Conditions be so performed, it shall not be lawful for him to grant such Certificate; and that after such Certificate shall be granted, it shall be taken as Evidence of the proper Provisions being inserted in such Deed, and of the Performance of the Conditions hereby required previously to the granting such Certificate of complete Registration; and that any Defect or Omission as regards the Matters hereby required in any Deed of Settlement may from Time to Time be supplied by a supplementary Deed or Deeds; and that if any such supplementary Deed be not inconsistent with or repugnant to this Act, or any Act respecting Joint Stock Companies, and if it be duly registered, then it shall have the same Effect as if there were only One Deed for the Purposes of this Act; and that unless the same shall be registered it shall be of no Force or Effect.

VIII. And be it enacted, That if any Deed of Settlement or supplementary Deed of Settlement, whether made before or after the granting of the Certificate of complete Registration, appear to such Registrar of Joint Stock Companies to be insufficient by reason of the Omission or Incompleteness of any of the Provisions therein contained for the Purposes set forth in the said Schedule (A.), or if the Deed contain Provisions which appear to such Registrar to be inconsistent with or repugnant to this Act, or any Act for the Time being in force respecting Joint Stock Companies, then as soon thereafter as conveniently may be such Registrar shall notify the same in Writing to the Persons or to the Company by whom the Deed shall have been presented for Registration, specifying in such Notification the Particulars wherein such Deed of Settlement or supplementary Deed of Settlement is incomplete, or inconsistent with or repugnant to any such Act as aforesaid.

IX. Provided always, and be it enacted, That if any Company for executing any Bridge, Road, Cut, Canal, Reservoir, Aqueduct, Waterwork, Navigation, Tunnel, Archway, Railway, Pier, Port, Harbour, Ferry, or Dock, which cannot be carried into execution without the Authority of Parliament, deposit at the proper Offices of the Two Houses of Parliament, in compliance with the Standing Orders of such Houses respectively, and at or within the Time required by such Standing Orders, such Deeds of Partnership or Subscription Contracts as shall be required to be deposited by such Standing Orders, and also return to the said Registry Office a Copy of such Deeds of Partnership or Subscription Contracts, together with such Certificate of the Receipt of such Plans, Sections, and Books of Reference as shall be appointed by the said Committee of Privy Council for Trade, then it shall be lawful for the Registrar of Joint Stock Companies and he is hereby required to accept the same instead of the Deed of Settlement by this Act required to be returned for the Purpose of obtaining a Certificate of complete Registration; and thereupon such Company shall be entitled to a Certificate of complete Registration accordingly.

X. And be it enacted, That throughout the Continuance of any Joint Stock Company completely registered under this Act, except such Companies as shall have been incorporated by Act of Parliament after complete Registration and within One Month after the Date of any new or supplementary Deed of Settlement, there shall be transmitted by the Directors of every such Company to the Registrar of Joint Stock Companies a Copy of such new or supplementary Deed of Settlement, together with a complete Abstract thereof so approved of as aforesaid; and within Six Months after any Change shall have taken place in any of the Particulars herein-before required to be set forth in the Schedule to the Deed of Settlement, except so far as respects the Shareholders thereof and their respective. Shares, there shall be transmitted Returns of such Particulars, so far as the same shall have been changed; and if within such Period any such Return be not made, then, on Conviction thereof, every Director of such Company shall be liable to pay a Sum not exceeding Twenty Pounds.

XI. And be it enacted, that in the Months of *January* and *July* in every Year the Directors of every Joint Stock Company completely registered under this Act, except Companies which shall have been incorporated by Act of Parliament after complete Registration, shall make or cause to be made the following Returns to the Registrar of Joint Stock Companies; namely,

A Return according to the Schedule (E.) hereunto annexed, and containing the Particulars therein set forth, of every Transfer of any Share in such Company which shall have have been made since the preceding half-yearly Return (or, in the Case of the first of such Returns made by such Company since the complete Registration thereof), and which shall have come to the Knowledge of the Directors:

And also a Return according to the Schedule (F.) hereunto annexed, and containing the Particulars therein set forth, of the Names and Places of Abode of all Persons who shall either have ceased to be Shareholders of such Company, or have become Shareholders of such Company otherwise than by a Transfer as aforesaid, since the preceding half-yearly Return, or since the complete Registration of the Company, as the Case may require, and also of the Changes in the Names of all Shareholders of such Company whose Names shall have been changed by Marriage or otherwise since the last preceding half-yearly Return, or since the complete Registration of the Company, as the Case may require:

And if within any such Period any such Return be not made, then, on Conviction thereof, every Director of such Company shall be liable to pay a Sum not exceeding Twenty Pounds.

XII. And be it enacted, That if at any Time any Party to a Transfer of a Share request in Writing the Directors of any such Company to make a Return thereof, then forthwith on such Request the Directors shall make the same accordingly; and that on Proof of such Transfer and such Request to the Satisfaction of the Registrar of Joint Stock Companies it shall be lawful for any such Party to make a Return of such Transfer, which shall be received, marked, and registered, and with the same Effect as hereby provided in the Case of Returns made by such Companies.

XIII. And be it enacted, That until the Return of the Transfer or other Fact or Event whereby a Person becomes the Holder of any Shares be made, pursuant to the Provisions herein-before contained, it shall not be lawful for such Company, its Directors or Officers, if such Fact or Event be known to them respectively, to pay to any such Person any Part of the Profits of the Concern, nor for any such Person to sue for or recover any part of the Profits arising in respect of such Share, or in anywise to act as a Shareholder; and that until the Return of the Transfer of any Share shall have been made pursuant to the Provisions herein-before contained the Person whose Share shall have been thereby transferred shall, so far as respects his Liability to the Debts and Engagements of the Company, and also as respects the Reimbursement of any Loss, Damages, Costs, and Charges he may incur thereby, be deemed to continue a Shareholder of such Company.

XIV. And be it enacted, That annually in the Month of *January* in every Year every Company completely registered under this Act, except Companies which shall have been incorporated by Act of Parliament after complete Registration, shall make to the said Registry Office a Return of the Name and Business of the Company; and that on the Receipt of such Return the Registrar of Joint Stock Companies shall give a Certificate thereof; and that if within the further Period of One Month such Return be not made, then on Conviction thereof such Company shall be liable to pay a Sum not exceeding Twenty Pounds: Provided always, that it shall be lawful for the Lords of the said Committee, on the Application of any Company, to appoint any other Period of the Year for the making of such annual Return as aforesaid.

XV. And be it enacted, That when the Particulars and Documents severally by this Act required to be returned to the said Registry Office shall have been so returned, it shall be the Duty of the said Registrar of Joint Stock Companies and he is hereby required to cause to be written on every such Document and Return of Particulars brought to him for Registration the Day of the Receipt thereof, and to cause to be marked on every such Return and Document, in Writing or otherwise, a Number denoting the Order in which the same was received, and also, upon Demand, to cause an Acknowledgment of the Receipt of such Return or Document to be given to the Person by whom the same shall be so brought; and that if such Returns or Documents be conformable to the Provisions of this Act, or of any Regulations in that Behalf, then it shall be the Duty of the Registrar and he is hereby required forthwith to register the same, and, on Demand, to grant to such Company a Certificate of provisional or complete Registration, as the Case may require, signed by him, and sealed with the Seal of his Office; which Certificate must set forth whether the Company has been constituted provisionally or completely; and that, in the Absence of Evidence to the contrary, any such Certificate, or a Copy of any such Return as aforesaid, shall be received in Evidence, without Proof of the Signature thereto, or of the Seal of Office affixed thereto.

XVI. And be it enacted, That until the Company shall have obtained its Certificate of complete Registration the Promoters of the Company or their Solicitor as aforesaid, shall make or cause to be made every Return by this Act required to be made; and after such Company shall have obtained a Certificate of complete Registration the Directors of the Company shall make or cause to be made every such Return; and One or more of such Promoters, or their Solicitor, or such Directors, as the Case may be, shall sign such Return; and every such Return which shall be made after complete Registration of the Company shall be sealed with the Seal of the Company.

XVII. And be it enacted, That if the Committee of Privy Council for Trade shall deem it expedient, then it shall be lawful for the said

Committee and they are hereby authorized from Time to Time to make Regulations respecting the Form of any such Returns as are hereby directed to be made, and the Manner and Time of making them, and for those Purposes to alter and vary the Schedules annexed to this Act, and to dispense with any of the Returns hereby made necessary, or any of the Forms of Returns prescribed by this Act; and that every such Regulation shall be published in the *London Gazette*, and thereupon shall be of the like Force as if the same were contained in this Act: Provided always, that nothing herein contained shall be construed to permit the said Committee to make any such Regulations which shall not apply alike to all such Companies as may be registered under the Authority of this Act, so far as the same may be applicable to them.

XVIII. And be it enacted, That every Person shall be at liberty to inspect the Returns, Deeds, Registers, and Indexes which shall be made to or kept by the said Registrar of Joint Stock Companies; and that there shall be paid for such Inspection such Fees as may be appointed by the Commissioners of Her Majesty's Treasury in that Behalf, not exceeding One Shilling for each such Inspection; and that any Person shall be at liberty to require a Copy or Extract of any such Return or Deed, to be certified by the said Registrar; and there shall be paid for such certified Copy or Extract such Fee as the Commissioners of Her Majesty's Treasury may appoint in that Behalf, not exceeding Sixpence for each Folio of such Copy or Extract: and that in all Courts of Law and Equity and elsewhere every such Copy or Extract so certified shall be received in Evidence, without Proof of the Signature thereto, or of the Seal of Office affixed thereto.

XIX. And be it enacted, That it shall be lawful for the Committee of Privy Council for Trade and they are hereby empowered to appoint a Person to be and to be called the Registrar of Joint Stock Companies, and, if the said Committee see fit, an Assistant Registrar, Clerks, and other necessary Officers and Servants; and that every such Registrar and Assistant Registrar, Clerks, and Officers shall be entitled to hold their offices during the Pleasure only of the said Committee; and that from Time to Time it shall be lawful for the Commissioners of Her Majesty's Treasury and they are hereby authorized to fix the Salary or Remuneration of such Registrar, Assistant Registrars, Clerks, Officers, and Servants; and that, subject to the Provisions of this Act, it shall be lawful for the said Committee of Privy Council for Trade and they are hereby authorized to make Rules for regulating the Execution of the Office of the said Registrar; and that such Registrar shall have a Seal of Office to be by him used in the Authentication of all Matters relating to his said Office in respect of which such Authentication is by this Act required; and that such Assistant Registrar shall, in the absence of the Registrar, be competent to do all Things which the Registrar is authorized or empowered, directed, or required to do, as fully and effectually, to all Intents and Purposes, as the Registrar himself may do; and all Provisions in this Act relating to the Signature and Seal of Office of the said Registrar shall apply to the said Assistant Registrar: Provided always, that the Registrar shall not be absent from the Duties of his Office, except on Account of ill Health or other urgent Cause, without express Leave in Writing of the said Committee of Privy Council for Trade for that Purpose previously obtained.

XX. And be it enacted, That from the Hour of Ten of the Clock in the Morning until Five of the Clock in the Afternoon, and at such other Times as the said Committee of Privy Council for Trade shall appoint, such Registrar, or in the unavoidable, or, as aforesaid, permitted Absence of the Registrar, then such Assistant Registrar, shall give his Attendance at the said Office every Day throughout the Year, except *Sundays, Good Friday, Christmas Day*, and any other general Holiday or Fast Day appointed by Her Majesty in Council.

XXI. And be it enacted, That every Company shall pay the following Fees; (that is to say,)

For a Certificate of provisional Registration the Sum of Five Pounds:

For a Certificate of complete Registration the Sum of Five Pounds; and One Shilling additional in respect of every Thousand Pounds Value of Capital, as declared on the Formation of the Company in the Deed of Settlement, or by any other special Authority:

For an annual Certificate the Sum of One Pound:

And also such other Fees as shall be appointed to be paid in respect of any other Services to be performed by the said Registrar; and that from Time to Time it shall be lawful for the Commissioners of Her Majesty's Treasury, and they are hereby authorized, in addition to the Fees herein-before required to be paid in respect of such Certificates, to fix such other Fees to be paid for the Services to be performed by the Registrar of Joint Stock Companies as they shall deem requisite to defray both the Expenses of the said Office, and the Salaries or other Remuneration of the said Registrar and of any other Persons employed under him, with the Sanction of the said Commissioners of Her Majesty's Treasury, in the Execution of this Act; and that the Balance, if any, shall be carried to the Consolidated Fund of the United Kingdom of *Great Britain* and *Ireland*, and be paid accordingly into the Receipt of Her Majesty's Exchequer at *Westminster;* and that it shall be lawful for the said Commissioners of Her Majesty's Treasury to regulate the Manner in which such Fees are to be received, and in which they are to be kept, and in which they are to be accounted for: Provided always, that if within Two years after a Company shall have obtained a Certificate of complete Registration such Company shall obtain an Act for the Incorporation thereof, then Three Fourths of the Fee paid by or on behalf of such Company on such complete Registration in respect of the Capital of the Company shall be reimbursed and repaid to the said Company, and that it shall be lawful for the said Commissioners of Her Majesty's Treasury and they are hereby authorized and empowered to repay the same accordingly.

XXII. And be it enacted, That if either the said Registrar of Joint Stock Companies, or any Person employed under him, either demand or receive any Gratuity or Reward in respect of any Service performed by him, other than the Fees aforesaid, then for every such Offence every such Registrar or Person shall be guilty of a Misdemeanor.

XXIII. And be it enacted, That on the provisional Registration of any Company being certified by the Registrar of Joint Stock Companies it shall be lawful for the Promoters of any Company so registered to act provisionally, but not for any longer Period than Twelve Months from the Date of the Certificate, unless such Certificate shall be renewed, which may be done on Application for that Purpose; and no such renewed Certificate shall be in force for a longer Period than Twelve Months from the Date thereof; and it shall be lawful for the Promoters of such Company,—

To assume the Name of the intended Company, but coupled with the Words "Registered provisionally;" and also,

To open Subscription Lists; and also,

To allot Shares, and receive Deposits by way of Earnest thereon, at a Rate not exceeding Ten Shillings for every One hundred Pounds on the Amount of every Share in the Capital of the intended Company; and also, in the Case of Companies for executing any Bridge, Road, Cut, Canal, Reservoir, Aqueduct, Waterwork, Navigation, Tunnel, Archway, Railway, Pier, Port, Harbour, Ferry, or Dock, which cannot be carried into execution without the Authority of Parliament, in addition to and exclusive of such Sum of Ten Shillings *per* Hundred Pounds, such further Sum *per* Hundred Pounds on the Amount of every such Share as may be required by the Standing Orders of either House of Parliament to be deposited before the obtaining of an Act of Parliament for enabling the Company to execute such Work; and also,

To perform such other Acts only as are

necessary for constituting the Company, or for obtaining Letters Patent, or a Charter, or an Act of Parliament;

But not to make Calls, nor to purchase, contract for, or hold Lands, nor to enter into Contracts for any Services, or for the Execution of any Works, or for the Supply of any Stores, except such Services and Stores or other Things as are necessarily required for the establishing of the Company, and except any Purchase or other Contract to be made conditional on the Completion of the Company, and to take effect after the Certificate of complete Registration, Act of Parliament, or Charter or Letters Patent, shall have been obtained, and, except in the Case of Companies for executing such Works as aforesaid, Contracts for Services in making Surveys and performing all other Acts necessary for obtaining an Act of Incorporation or other Act for enabling the Company to execute such Works.[d]

XXIV. And be it enacted, That if before a Certificate of provisional Registration shall be obtained the Promoters or any of them, or any Person employed by or under them, take any Moneys in consideration of the Allotment either of Shares or of any Interest in the Concern, or by way of Deposit for Shares to be granted or allotted; or issue, in the Name or on behalf of the Company, any Note or Scrip, or Letter of Allotment, or other Instrument or Writing to denote a Right or Claim, or Preference or Promise, absolute or conditional, to

[d] A contract contrary to this clause is illegal, and the individual making it is not liable upon it. (Bull *v.* Chapman, 8 Gr. 444.) But on a contract allowed by this clause, the Company, after it has been completely registered, may be sued. (Taylor *v.* Crowland Gas Company, in the Exchequer.)

any Shares; or advertise the Existence or proposed Formation of the Company; or make any Contract whatsoever for or in the Name or on behalf of such intended Company; then every such Person shall be liable to forfeit for every such Offence a Sum not exceeding Twenty-five Pounds; and that it shall be lawful for any Person to sue for and recover the same by Action of Debt.

XXV. And be it enacted, That on the complete Registration of any Company being certified by the Registrar of Joint Stock Companies, such Company and the then Shareholders therein, and all the succeeding Shareholders, whilst Shareholders, shall be and are hereby incorporated as from the Date of such Certificate by the Name of the Company as set forth in the Deed of Settlement, and for the Purpose of carrying on the Trade or Business for which the Company was formed, but only according to the Provisions of this Act, and of such Deed as aforesaid, and for the Purpose of suing and being sued, and of taking and enjoying the Property and Effects of the said Company; and thereupon any Covenants or Engagements entered into by any of the Shareholders or other Persons with any Trustee on the Behalf of the Company, at any Time before the complete Registration thereof, may be proceeded on by the said Company and enforced in all respects as if they had been made or entered into with the said Company after the Incorporation thereof; and such Company shall continue so incorporated until it shall be dissolved, and all its Affairs wound up; but so as not in anywise to restrict the Liability of any of the Shareholders of the Company, under any Judgment, Decree, or Order for the Payment of Money which shall be obtained against such Company, or any of the Members thereof, in any Action or Suit prosecuted by or against such Company in any Court of Law or Equity; but every such Shareholder shall, in respect of such Moneys, subject as after mentioned, be and continue liable as he would have been if the said Company had not been incorporated; and thereupon it shall be lawful for the said Company, and they are hereby empowered as follows; that is to say,

1. To use the registered Name of the Company, adding thereto "Registered;" and also,
2. To have a Common Seal (with Power to break, alter, and change the same from Time to Time), but on which must be inscribed the Name of the Company; and also,
3. To sue and be sued by their registered Name in respect of any Claim by or upon the Company upon or by any Person, whether a Member of the Company or not, so long as any such Claim may remain unsatisfied; and also,
4. To enter into Contracts for the Execution of the Works, and for the Supply of the Stores, or for any other necessary Purpose of the Company; and also,
5. To purchase and hold Lands, Tenements, and Hereditaments in the Name of the said Company, or of the Trustees or Trustee thereof, for the Purpose of occupying the same as a Place or Places of Business of the said Company, and also (but nevertheless with a Licence, general or special, for that Purpose, to be granted by the Committee of the

Privy Council for Trade, first had and obtained,) such other Lands, Tenements, and Hereditaments as the Nature of the Business of the Company may require; and also,

6. To issue Certificates of Shares; and also,
7. To receive Instalments from Subscribers in respect of the Amount of any Shares not paid up; and also,
8. To borrow or raise Money within the Limitations prescribed by any special Authority; and also,
9. To declare Dividends out of the Profits of the Concern; and also,
10. To hold General Meetings periodically, and extraordinary Meetings upon being duly summoned for that Purpose; and also,
11. To make from Time to Time, at some General Meeting of Shareholders specially summoned for the Purpose, Bye Laws for the Regulation of the Shareholders, Members, Directors, and Officers of the Company, such Bye Laws not being repugnant to or inconsistent with the Provisions of this Act or of the Deed of Settlement of the Company; and also,
12. To perform all other Acts necessary for carrying into effect the Purposes of such Company, and in all respects as other Partnerships are entitled to do:

And the said Company are hereby empowered and required,—

13. To appoint from Time to Time, for the Conduct and Superintendence of the Execution of the Affairs of the Com-

pany, a Number of Directors, not less than Three, for a Period not greater than Five Years, with or without Eligibility to be re-elected at the Expiration of the Term, as may be prescribed by any Deed of Settlement or Bye Law; and also,

14. To appoint and remove One or more Auditors, and such other Officers as the Deed of Settlement under which the Company shall be constituted may authorize:

Subject nevertheless, with respect to all such Powers and Privileges, to the Provisions of this Act, and subject also to the Provisions of the Deed of Settlement of the Company or any other special Authority: Provided always, with regard to any Company for executing any Bridge, Road, Cut, Canal, Reservoir, Aqueduct, Waterwork, Navigation, Tunnel, Archway, Railway, Pier, Port, Harbour, Ferry, or Dock, which cannot be carried into execution without obtaining the Authority of Parliament, that on the complete Registration of any such Company, and before such Company shall have obtained its Act of Incorporation or other Act whereby the Authority of Parliament shall be granted for executing such Work, it shall not be lawful for any such Company or the Directors or Officers thereof to exercise the hereinbefore mentioned Power to enter into Contracts, otherwise than conditionally upon obtaining such Act, or to exercise the Power to purchase and hold Lands as aforesaid, or to exercise the Power to receive Instalments from Shareholders beyond the Sum or Per-centage necessary to be deposited in compliance with the Standing Orders of either House of Parliament, or such other Sum as may be requisite for obtaining the Act of Incorporation or other Act for granting the Authority of Parliament to execute such Work, or to exercise the Power to borrow Money, as aforesaid, or to exercise the Power to declare Dividends as aforesaid; and, subject to these last-mentioned Exceptions, all the Powers by this Enactment herein-before given to any Company completely registered, except the general Power to perform all Acts necessary for carrying on the Business of the Company, may be exercised as fully by any such Company so completely registered as by any other Company so completely registered: Provided always, that it shall be lawful for any such Company to perform all Acts which may be necessary for obtaining an Act of Incorporation or other Act for obtaining the Authority of Parliament to execute its Works as aforesaid, anything herein contained to the contrary notwithstanding; and that upon obtaining such Act of Incorporation or other such Act as aforesaid, or at the Time of the coming into operation of such Act, as shall be thereby appointed, all the Powers which any such Company shall obtain by virtue of this Act, and all the Provisions and Regulations of this Act which shall apply to such Company, shall cease and determine, except so far as shall be otherwise provided by such Act of Incorporation or other such Act as aforesaid.

XXVI. And be it enacted, That no Shareholder of any Joint Stock Company completely registered under this Act shall be entitled to receive any Dividends or Profits, or be entitled to the Remedies or Powers hereby given to Shareholders, until he he shall have executed the Deed of Settlement of the said Company, or some Deed referring thereto, and also have paid up all Instalments or Calls due from him, and shall have been registered in the Registry Office aforesaid; and further, that it shall be lawful for every Shareholder who shall have signed such Deed, and paid up such Instalments or Calls, and shall have been registered, and he is hereby entitled—

To be present at all General Meetings of the Company; and also,

To take part in the Discussions thereat; and also,

To vote in the Determination of any Question thereat, and that either in Person or by Proxy, unless the Deed of Settlement shall preclude Shareholders from voting by Proxy; and also,

To vote in the Choice of Directors, and of every Auditor to be elected by the Shareholders;

Subject nevertheless to the Provisions of this Act, and of the Deed of Settlement of the Company or other special Authority, so far as such Provisions shall either regulate or restrict the Exercise of such Powers, but not so as to deprive such Shareholders thereof; and further, with regard to Subscribers and every Person entitled or claiming to be entitled to any Share in any Joint Stock Company the Formation of which shall be commenced after the First Day of *November* One thousand eight hundred and forty-four, that until such Joint Stock Company shall have obtained a Certificate of complete Registration, and until any such Subscriber or Person shall have been duly registered as a Shareholder in the said Registry Office, it shall not be lawful for such Person to dispose, by Sale or Mortgage, of such Share, or of any Interest therein, and that every Contract for or Sale or Disposal of such Share or Interest shall be void, and that every Person entering into such Contract shall forfeit a Sum not exceeding Ten Pounds; and that for better protecting Purchasers it shall be the Duty of the Directors of the Company by whom Certificates of Shares are issued to state on every such Certificate the Date of the first complete Registration of the Company, as before provided; and that if any such Director or Officer knowingly make a false Statement in that respect then he shall be liable to the Pains and Penalties of a Misdemeanor.

XXVII. And be it enacted, That with regard to the Powers and Duties of Directors it shall be lawful for the Directors of any Joint Stock Company registered under this Act,—

1. To conduct and manage the Affairs of the Company according to the Provisions and subject to the Restrictions of this Act, and of the Deed of Settlement, and of any Bye Law, and for that Purpose to enter into all such Contracts and do and execute all such Acts and Deeds as the Circumstances may require; and also,
2. To appoint the Secretary, if any; and also,
3. To appoint the Clerks and Servants; and also from Time to Time, as they see fit,
4. To remove such Secretary, Clerks, and Servants, and to appoint others, as Occasion shall require; and also,
5. To appoint other Persons for special Services as the Concerns of the Com-

pany may from Time to Time require; and also,

6. To hold Meetings periodically and from Time to Time as the Concerns of the Company shall require; and also,

7. To appoint a Chairman to preside at all such Meetings, and in his Absence to appoint a Chairman at each such Meeting;

Subject nevertheless to the Provisions and Restrictions of this Act, and to the Provisions of the Deed of Settlement of the Company or other special Authority, but not so as to enable the Shareholders to act in their own Behalf in the ordinary Management of the Concerns of the Company otherwise than by means of Directors: Provided always, that it shall not be lawful for the Directors to purchase any Shares of the Company, nor to sell any such Shares, except Shares forfeited on the Non-payment of Calls or Instalments, nor to lend to any one of their Number, or to any Officer of the Company, any Money belonging to the Company without the Authority and Sanction of a General Meeting of Shareholders duly convened.

XXVIII. And be it enacted, That henceforth, notwithstanding anything to the contrary in any Deed of Settlement or other Instrument by which a Joint Stock Company shall be constituted or regulated, it shall not not be lawful to appoint any Person to be or to act as a Director, whether honorary or otherwise, or to hold the Office of Patron or President, or any other Office of the like Description; nor shall it be lawful for any Person to act in any such Capacity unless at the Time of such his Appointment or of such his acting he hold in his own Right at least one Share in the Capital of such Company; and that if, without having such Share, any Person be or become or act as Director, Patron, or President of such Company, or in any Office of such or the like Nature, then he shall forfeit for every such Offence a Sum not exceeding Twenty Pounds; and that if any Person be announced or held out by or on behalf of the Company as a Director, Patron, or President, or as holding any Office of such or the like Description, without having so consented or acted, then each Director of such Company knowingly concurring in such Representation shall forfeit a Sum not exceeding Twenty Pounds.

XXIX. And be it enacted, That if any Director of a Joint Stock Company registered under this Act be either directly or indirectly concerned or interested in any Contract proposed to be made by or on behalf of the Company, whether for Land, Materials, Work to be done, or for any Purpose whatsoever, during the Time he shall be a Director, he shall, on the Subject of any such Contract in which he may be so concerned or interested, be precluded from voting or otherwise acting as a Director; and that if any Contract or Dealing (except a Policy of Assurance, Grant of Annuity, or Contract for the Purchase of an Article or of Service, which is respectively the Subject of the proper Business of the Company, such Contract being made upon the same or the like Terms as any like Contract with other Customers or Purchasers), shall be entered into, in which any Director shall be interested, then the Terms of such Contract or Dealing shall be submitted to the next General or Special Meeting of the Shareholders to be summoned for that Purpose; and that no such Contract shall have Force until approved and confirmed by the Majority of Votes of the Shareholders present at such Meeting; and that if at any Time any Director cease to be a Holder of the Prescribed Number of Shares in the Company, or shall become a Bankrupt or Insolvent, or shall have suspended Payment, or compromised with his Creditors, or be declared a Lunatic, then it shall be unlawful for any such Director to continue as a Director, or to act as such, and the Office of such Director shall be and is hereby declared to be vacant.

XXX. And be it enacted, That notwithstanding it may be afterwards discovered that there was some Defect or Error in the Appointment of any Person acting or who may have acted as a Director of a Joint Stock Company registered under this Act, or that such Person was disqualified, yet all Acts done by him as such Director before the Discovery of such Defect or Error, either solely or with other Directors, shall be as binding on him, and on the Company, and the Directors and Officers thereof, as if such Person had been duly appointed or qualified, and, if such Acts were done *bonâ fide*, shall be as binding on all Persons whomsoever as if such Person had been duly appointed or qualified.

XXXI. And be it enacted, That if any such Director or other Officer of any Joint Stock Company registered under this Act wrongfully do or omit any Act, with Intent to defraud the Company or any Shareholder therein, or falsify or fraudulently mutilate or fraudulently make any Erasure in the Books of Account or Books of Register, or any Document belonging to the Company, then such Director or Officer shall be deemed to be guilty of a Misdemeanor.

XXXII. And be it enacted, That if the Entry of the Proceedings of any Meeting of the Shareholders or of the Directors of any Joint Stock Company registered under this Act purport to be signed by the Chairman duly presiding at such Meeting, and sealed with the Seal of the Company, then it shall be the Duty of all Courts of Justice, Justices, and others, and they are hereby required, to receive the Book in which such Entry shall be made as *primâ facie* Evidence, not only of the Proceedings of the Meeting of which Entry shall be so made, but of such Meetings having been duly convened, and of the Persons making or entering such Orders or Proceedings being Shareholders or Directors, and of the Signature of the Chairman.

XXXIII. And be it enacted, That the Books of any such Company wherein the Proceedings of the Company are recorded shall be kept at the principal or only Place of Business of the Company, and at all reasonable Times such Books shall be open to the Inspection of any Shareholder of the Company; subject nevertheless to the Provisions of the Deed of Settlement or of any Byelaw.

XXXIV. And be it enacted, that the Directors shall cause the Accounts of such Company to be duly entered in Books to be provided for the Purpose.

XXXV. And be it enacted, That Fourteen Days at the least before the Period at which the Accounts are required to be delivered to the Auditors as herein-after provided the Directors of such Company shall cause the Books of the Company to be balanced, and a full and fair Balance Sheet to be made up; and that previously to such Balance Sheet being delivered to the Auditors as herein-after provided, the Directors, or any Three of their Number, shall examine such Balance Sheet, and sign it as so examined; and that when the Balance Sheet shall have been so examined the Chairman of the Directors shall sign such Balance Sheet, and that thereupon the Directors shall cause the same to be recorded in the Books of the Company.

XXXVI. And be it enacted, That at each ordinary Meeting of the Shareholders the Directors shall produce such Balance Sheet to the Shareholders assembled thereat.

XXXVII. And be it enacted, That during the Space of Fourteen Days previously to such ordinary Meeting, and also during One Month thereafter, every Shareholder of the Company may, subject to the Provisions of the Deed of Settlement, or of any Byelaw, inspect the Books of Account and the Balance Sheet of the Company, and take Copies thereof and Extracts therefrom; and that if at any other Time Three Directors authorize in Writing any Shareholder to make such Inspection, then at such other Time the Shareholder so authorized may make such Inspection.

XXXVIII. And be it enacted, That every Joint Stock Company completely registered under this Act shall annually at a General Meeting appoint One or more Auditors of the Accounts of the Company (One of whom at least shall be appointed by the Shareholders present at the Meeting in Person or by Proxy), and shall return the Names of such Auditors to the Registrar of Joint Stock Companies; and that if an Auditor be not appointed on behalf of the Shareholders, or if he shall die, or become incapable of acting, or shall decline to act at the prescribed Period, or if such Return be not made, then on the Application of any Shareholder of the Company it shall be the Duty of the Committee of Privy Council for Trade and they are hereby authorized to appoint an Auditor on behalf of the Shareholders; and that such Auditor shall continue to act till the next General Meeting; and the due Appointment of such Auditor shall be returned to the Registrar of Joint Stock Companies, and that thereupon it shall be his Duty to register the same; and that it shall be lawful for the Commissioners of the Treasury and they are hereby empowered to appoint that the Company shall pay to such Auditor such Salary or Remuneration as to the said Commissioners shall appear suitable, having regard to the Duties of his Office, and that thereupon such Auditor shall be entitled to recover such Salary from the Company as and when it shall become due, according to the Terms of the Appointment thereof.

XXXIX. And be it enacted, That Twenty-eight Days at least before the ensuing ordinary Meeting at which such Balance Sheet is required to be produced to the Shareholders the Directors shall deliver to the Auditors the half-yearly or other periodical Accounts and the Balance Sheet required to be presented to the Shareholders; and that the Auditors shall receive from the Directors such Accounts and Balance Sheet, and examine the same.

XL. And be it enacted, That throughout the Year and at all reasonable Times of the Day it shall be lawful for the Auditors and they are hereby authorized to inspect the Books of Account and Books of Registry of such Company; and that the Auditors may demand and have the Assistance of such Officers and Servants of the Company and such Documents as they shall require for the full Performance of their Duty in auditing the Accounts.

XLI. And be it enacted, That within Fourteen Days after the Receipt of such Balance Sheet and Accounts the Auditors shall either confirm such Accounts, and report generally thereon, or shall, if they do not see proper to confirm such Accounts, report specially thereon, and deliver such Accounts and Balance Sheet to the Directors of the Company.

XLII. And be it enacted, That Ten Days before the ordinary Meeting of such Company the Directors shall, subject to the Provisions of any Deed of Settlement or Byelaw in that Behalf, send or cause to be sent a printed Copy of the Balance Sheet and Auditors' Report to every Shareholder, according to his registered Address, and shall at such Meeting of the Company cause such Report to be read, together with the Report of the Directors.

XLIII. And be it enacted, That within Fourteen Days after such Meeting it shall be the Duty of such Directors and they are hereby required to return to the said Registry Office a Copy of the Balance Sheet, and of the Report of the Auditors thereon; and that thereupon it shall be the Duty of the Registrar of Joint Stock Companies and he is hereby required to register or file the same with the other Documents relating to such Company.

XLIV. And for the Purpose of regulating Contracts entered into on behalf of any Joint Stock Company completely registered under this Act (except Contracts for the Purchase of any Article the Payment or Consideration of which doth not exceed the Sum of Fifty Pounds, or for any Service the Period of which doth not exceed Six Months, and the Consideration for which doth not exceed Fifty Pounds, and except Bills of Exchange and Promissory Notes), be it enacted, That every such Contract shall be in Writing, and signed by Two at least of the Directors of the Company on whose Behalf the same shall be entered into, and shall be sealed with the Common Seal thereof, or signed by some Officer of the Company on its Behalf, to be thereunto expressly authorized by some Minute or Resolution of the Board of Directors applying to the particular Case; and that in the Absence of such Requisites or of any of them any such Contract shall be void and ineffectual (except as against the Company on whose Behalf the same shall have been made);[a] and that every such Contract for the Purchase of any Article the Consideration of which doth not exceed the Sum of Fifty Pounds, or for any Services the Period of which doth not exceed Six Months, and the Consideration for which doth not exceed Fifty Pounds, entered

[a] The contract, if made within the authority conferred by the Deed of Settlement, is binding on the Company (Ridley *v.* Plymouth and Stonehouse Grinding and Baking Company, 2 Ex. 711). These lateral contracts, i. e. contracts by which only one party obliges himself to do an act, as covenants to pay money, are not within this clause (British Empire Mutual Life Assurance Company *v.* Browne, 16 Jurisp. 1157).

into on Behalf of any Joint Stock Company completely registered under this Act, may be entered into by any Officer authorized by a general Byelaw in that Behalf; and that every such Contract, whether under Seal or not, shall immediately after the same shall have been entered into be reported to the Secretary or other appointed Officer of the Company on whose Behalf the same shall have been entered into, who shall enter the same in proper Books to be kept for that Purpose; and that if any such Contract be not so reported and entered, then the Officer by whose Default such Contract shall not be so reported or entered shall be liable to repay to the Company on whose Behalf such Contract may be made the Amount of the Consideration agreed to be paid by or on Behalf of such Company in respect of such Contract.

XLV. And be it enacted, with regard to Bills of Exchange and Promissory Notes made, accepted, or endorsed on the Behalf or Account of any such Company, so far as relates to the Mode of making, accepting, or endorsing the same, and to the Liability of any such Company thereon, That if the Directors of the Company be authorized by Deed of Settlement or Bye Law to issue or accept Bills of Exchange or Promissory Notes, then every such Bill of Exchange or Promissory Note shall be made or accepted (as the Case may be) by and in the Names of Two of the Directors of the Company on whose Behalf or Account the same may be so made or accepted, and shall be by such Directors expressed to be made or accepted by them on behalf of such Company;[b] and that

[b] Any words in the making or acceptance, showing that the Bill is made or accepted on behalf of the Company will suffice to bind them. It is not essential to use the words on behalf of the Company. (Hulford *v.* Cameron Company, 16 G. R. 442.)

every such Bill of Exchange and Promissory Note so made or accepted as aforesaid shall be countersigned by the Secretary or other appointed Officer of the Company in whose Behalf the same is expressed to be made or accepted; and that every Bill of Exchange so made as aforesaid, or received by or on behalf of the Company, may be endorsed in the Name of the Company by any Officer authorized by Deed of Settlement or Bye Law in that Behalf; and that every such Bill of Exchange or Promissory Note so made, accepted, or endorsed as aforesaid shall, immediately after the making, accepting, or endorsing of the same, be reported to the proper Officer of the Company on whose Behalf the same shall have been made, accepted, or endorsed, and such last-mentioned Officer shall enter the same in proper Books to be kept for that Purpose; and that if any such Bill of Exchange or Promissory Note be not so reported and entered, then the Officer by whose Default such Bill or Note shall not be so reported or entered shall be liable to repay to the Company the Amount which the Company shall pay or be liable to pay in respect of such Bill or Note: Provided always, that nothing herein contained shall be deemed to make any such Secretary or Officer personally liable upon any such Bill of Exchange or Promissory Note, nor be deemed to make any such Directors personally liable thereon, except as Shareholders of the Company; and that every such Company on whose Behalf or Account any Bill of Exchange or Promissory Note shall be made, accepted, or endorsed, in manner and form aforesaid, shall and may sue and be sued thereon, as fully and effectually, and in the same Manner, as in the Case of any Contract made and entered into under their Common Seal.

XLVI. And be it enacted, That all Deeds

and Instruments bearing the Seal of the Company shall be signed by Two at the least of the Directors of the Company.

XLVII. And be it enacted, That all Bye Laws made by any Joint Stock Company completely registered under this Act, in pursuance of the Power hereinbefore given, must be reduced into Writing, and must have affixed thereto the Common Seal of the Company; and that such Bye Laws must be registered at the Office for registering Joint Stock Companies, and until they be so registered they shall not be of any Force; and that such Bye Laws must be printed and circulated for the Use of the Shareholders, and a Copy thereof must be given to every Officer of the Company, and to every Shareholder who shall require the same.

XLVIII. And be it enacted, That in all Actions, Suits, and other legal Proceedings for the Enforcement of such Bye Laws, or other Penalties for the Breach thereof, the Production of a written or printed Copy of the Bye Laws of the Company, having the Seal of Office of the Registrar of Joint Stock Companies affixed thereto, shall be sufficient Evidence of such Bye Laws.

XLIX. And be it enacted, That it shall be the Duty of the Directors of every Joint Stock Company registered under this Act to keep or cause to be kept a Book, to be called the "Register of Shareholders," and from Time to Time in such Book to enter the following Particulars; that is to say,

The Names and Addresses of all Persons or Corporations being Shareholders of the Company; and also,

The Number of Shares to which such Shareholders shall be respectively entitled, distinguishing each Share by its Number; and also,

The Amount of the Instalments paid on such Shares.

L. And be it enacted, That it shall be lawful for every Shareholder, or if such Shareholder be a Corporation then the Clerk or principal Officer of such Corporation, at all convenient Times to search the Register of Shareholders gratis, and to require a Copy thereof or of any Part thereof; and that the Company may demand a Sum not exceeding Sixpence for every One hundred Words so required to be copied.

LI. And be it enacted, That, on Demand of the Holder of any Share in any Joint Stock Company completely registered under this Act, the Company shall cause a Certificate of the Proprietorship of such Share to be delivered to such Shareholder, specifying the Share in the Undertaking to which such Shareholder is entitled, and the Amount paid up in respect of such Share at the Date of such Certificate, and shall have the Common Seal of the Company affixed thereto; and for such Certificate the Company may demand any Sum not exceeding One Shilling; and that such Certificate must be according to the Form in the Schedule (I.) to this Act annexed, or to the like Effect.

LII. And be it enacted, That it shall be the Duty of all Courts of Justice, Judges, Justices, and others, to admit such Certificate as *primâ facie* Evidence of the Title of the Shareholder to the Share therein specified; nevertheless the Want of such Certificate shall not prevent the Holder of any Share from disposing thereof.

LIII. And be it enacted, That if any such Certificate be worn out or damaged, then, upon such Certificate being produced at some Meeting of the Directors, it shall be lawful for them to order such Certificate to be cancelled; and that thereupon another similar Certificate shall, if he require the same, be given to the Party in whom the Property of such Certificate and of the Share therein mentioned shall at the Time be vested; or if such Certificate be lost or destroyed, then, upon Proof thereof, a similar Certificate shall, if he require the same, be given to the Party entitled to the Certificate so lost or destroyed; and that in either Case it shall be the Duty of the Secretary and he is hereby required to make a due Entry of the substituted Certificate in the Register of Shareholders; and for every such Certificate so given or exchanged the Company may demand any Sum not exceeding the Sum of One Shilling.

LIV. And be it enacted, That, subject to the Regulations herein contained, and to be contained in any Deed of Settlement of any Joint Stock Company completely registered under this Act, it shall be lawful for every Shareholder of such Company and he is hereby entitled to sell and transfer his Shares therein by Deed duly stamped, in which the full Amount of the pecuniary Consideration for such Sale shall be truly expressed, and which Instrument of Transfer must be according to the Form in the Schedule (K.) to this Act annexed, or to the like Effect; and that the Directors of the Company shall cause a Memorial of such Instrument of Transfer, when produced at the

Office of the Company, to be entered in a Book to be called "The Register of Transfers," and the Entry thereof to be endorsed on the Instrument of Transfer; and for every such Entry and Endorsement the Company may demand any Sum not exceeding One Shilling; and that until such Instrument of Transfer shall have been so produced at the Office of the Company the Purchaser of the Share shall not be entitled to receive any of the Profits of the Company, or to vote in respect of such Share: Provided always, that if at the Time of such Transfer the Shareholder shall not have paid the full Amount due and payable to the Company on every Share held by him, then he shall not be entitled to transfer any Share, unless there be a Provision to the contrary in the Deed of Settlement.

LV. And be it enacted, That if any Shareholder fail to pay any Instalment of Capital due upon or in respect of any Share held by him, when the same shall become due, it shall be lawful for any such Company and they are hereby authorized to sue such Shareholder for the Amount in an Action of Debt in any Court having competent Jurisdiction in respect of the same: and that in the Declaration in any such Action it shall be sufficient to state only that at the Time of the Commencement of the Suit the Defendant, as the Holder of certain Shares (stating how many) in a certain Company or Undertaking, as the Case may be, (naming it,) was indebted to the Company in a certain Sum (stating the Amount of the Instalments, or so much thereof as is sought to be recovered,) for certain Instalments of Capital then due and payable in respect of the said Shares, and that the Defendant hath not paid the same; and that if upon the Trial of any such Action it shall be proved that the Defendant was the Holder of any Share when such Instalments, or any of them, in respect of the same, and for which the Action is brought, became due, then such Company shall recover such Instalments, or so much thereof as is due, together with Interest for the same at the Rate of Five Pounds *per Centum per Annum*, to be computed from the Day on which such Instalment shall have become due.

LVI. And be it enacted, That if any Share be held jointly by several Persons, then any Notice required to be given shall be given to such of the said Persons whose Name shall stand first on the Register of Shareholders, and Notice so given shall be sufficient Notice to all the Proprietors of such Share, and the Person so standing first shall be entitled to vote, and to have all the Privileges hereby conferred on Shareholders.

LVII. And be it enacted, That at every principal Place of Business of any Joint Stock Company completely registered under this Act it shall be the Duty of the Directors and Officers of the Company and they are hereby respectively required to have written or printed Copies of an Index or Abstract of the Deed of Settlement, approved by the Registrar of Joint Stock Companies, and a List of the Shareholders of the Company, and the Number of Shares held by each, and also a List of the Directors and Officers thereof, and a Copy of the Bye Laws sealed with the Seal of the Company, as returned to the said Registry Office; and that if at any reasonable Time any Shareholder, or any Person authorized in Writing by him, apply at any such Place of Business of the Company, to inspect the same, then, on

Demand thereof made during the usual Hours of Business, it shall be the Duty of the Directors or Officers and they respectively are hereby required to permit such Inspection; and that if on such Demand any Director or Officer to whom such Demand is made do not thereupon permit such Inspection, then, on Conviction thereof, he shall be liable to pay for every such Offence a Sum not exceeding Forty Shillings.

LVIII. And be it enacted, with regard to all Joint Stock Companies to which this Act is herein-before made to apply, and which shall exist on the First Day of *November* One thousand eight hundred and forty-four, whether incorporated by Act of Parliament, or by Charter, or privileged by Letters Patent, or established by virtue of a Deed of Settlement, or of any other Instrument, or by virtue of any Authority whatever, or in any other Way whatever, That within Three Months from the said First Day of *November* the Directors, Managers, Officers, or others having the Direction, Management, Conduct, Superintendence, or Execution of the Affairs of any such Company, shall register such Company at the Office for the Registration of Joint Stock Companies, and for that Purpose shall make or cause to be made a Return of the following Particulars, according to the Schedule (I.) hereunto annexed; that is to say,

1. The Name or Style of the Company; and also,
2. The Purpose of the Company; and also,
3. The principal or only Place for carrying on its Business:

And that on such Registration every such Company shall be entitled to have a Certificate of Registration, without paying any Fee either for such Registration or for such Certificate, but such Certificate shall be for the Purpose of showing that such Company had registered, and shall not be considered as a Certificate of complete Registration, so as to confer on any such Company the Powers and Privileges of this Act; and that if within the said Period the Persons hereby required to register any such Company fail so to do, then, on Conviction thereof, every such Company so failing shall forfeit for every such Offence a Sum not exceeding Fifty Pounds.

LIX. And be it enacted, with regard to such existing Companies as aforesaid (except Assurance Companies), That if any such existing Company be so constituted as is by this Act required with regard to any future Company, or if the Deed or Deeds of Settlement of such existing Company contain the Particulars by this Act required to be contained in some one or other Deed of Settlement of such future Company, and if any other Conditions required to be fulfilled by or in respect of any such future Company, in order to obtain a Certificate of complete Registration, be fulfilled in respect of any such existing Company, then such existing Company shall be entitled to obtain a Certificate of complete Registration; but if such existing Company be not so constituted, or if such Deed of Settlement do not contain such Particulars, or if such other Conditions be not fulfilled, then, on such existing Company returning a Deed or Deeds according to the Provisions of this Act, and also, in addition to any other Matters by this Enactment required to be returned by such existing

Company, such other Matters as are by this Act required to be returned by any future Company in order to obtain or before obtaining a Certificate of complete Registration as aforesaid, or such Modification of the said Deeds or Returns, or of any of them, as the Committee of Privy Council for Trade shall direct by any Regulation to be made in that Behalf, either on the Part or in respect of any One Company or of any Class of Companies, and signed by One of the Secretaries of the said Committee, such existing Company shall be entitled to a Certificate of complete Registration; and on such Certificate of complete Registration being granted by the Registrar of Joint Stock Companies it shall be lawful for such existing Company, its Shareholders, its Directors, and its Officers, and they are respectively hereby empowered, to have and exercise all such Powers and Privileges as are by this Act conferred upon Joint Stock Companies to be hereafter formed, subject nevertheless with respect to all such Powers and Privileges to the Provisions of this Act, or of any other Act to be hereafter passed for regulating the same; and that every such Company not incorporated shall be incorporated for the Purposes of this Act, as from the Date of the Certificate of complete Registration, in such Manner as hereinbefore provided with regard to Companies to be formed after the First Day of *November* next; and that any Directors or other Managers of any such Company as last aforesaid, with the Consent of at least Three Fourths in Number and Value of the Shareholders of such Company present at a General Meeting summoned for that Purpose, may at any Time or Times hereafter make any Alterations in the Constitution of the said Company or otherwise as shall be necessary for enabling such Company to come within the Provisions of this Act, so as the same shall be approved of by the said Committee of Privy Council for Trade; and the Order of such Committee, signed as aforesaid, shall be sufficient Evidence of such Provisions having been complied with, and that any such Company has come within the Provisions of this Act: Provided always, with regard to existing Companies, that in the event of any such Company becoming entitled to a Certificate of Complete Registration as aforesaid, it shall not be necessary to pay in respect of such Certificate any higher Fee than the Sum of Five Pounds, and also the Sum of Sixpence additional in respect of every Thousand Pounds Value of Capital, as declared on the Formation of the Company in the Deed of Settlement, or by any other special authority.

LX. And be it enacted, That so much of the Provisions of this Act as are applicable to Companies formed after the First Day of *November* next shall apply to Companies begun or formed since the passing of this Act, so far as such Provisions shall on or after the First Day of *November* be applicable to such last-mentioned Companies.

LXI. Provided always, and be it enacted, That, notwithstanding the Incorporation of any existing Company in pursuance of this Act, every such Company, and the Members and Officers of every such Company, shall be liable to be sued in respect of any valid Obligation incurred before such Incorporation, in the same Manner and with the same legal Consequences as if such Company had not been incorporated.

LXII. And be it enacted, That if at any

Time during the Period of Five Years from the said First Day of *November* a Memorial be presented to the Committee of Privy Council for Trade, by or on the Part of any Company, whether now existing or hereafter formed, except Assurance Companies, making Application that any of the Conditions and Regulations prescribed by this Act be dispensed with or modified, and setting forth the special Grounds of such Application, and if such Application be registered at the Office of the Registrar of Joint Stock Companies, and if, before such Application be granted, the same be Three Times advertised, at Intervals not less than One Week, in the *London Gazette*, then from Time to Time during the said Period of Five Years, and Six Months after the Expiration thereof, it shall be lawful for the said Committee and they are hereby empowered, both as regards Companies formed before this Act shall come into operation and afterwards, either to dispense with or modify such of the Conditions by this Act required to be fulfilled by any future Company for the Purpose of obtaining a Certificate of complete Registration, and such of the Regulations by this Act made for the Government or Management of such Companies, as to the said Committee shall seem fit for facilitating the Application of this Act to the Constitution and Arrangements of any such Company, but so that nevertheless the Order or Instrument by which such Dispensation or such Modification shall be made in Writing, and be registered at the Office for registering Joint Stock Companies; and this Act shall be construed as if such Modifications or Alterations were herein contained; and further, that annually it shall be the Duty of the said Committee to cause to be laid before both Houses of Parliament a

Return of all such Applications for such Dispensation or Modification, and of the Orders made on such Applications.

LXIII. Provided always, and be it enacted, That nothing in this Act contained shall extend or be construed to extend to any Partnership formed for the working of Mines, Minerals, and Quarries, of what Nature soever, on the Principle commonly called the Cost Book Principle.

LXIV. Provided always, and be it enacted, That nothing in this Act contained shall extend or be construed to extend to Partnerships in *Ireland* commonly called "Anonymous Partnerships," formed under and by virtue of an Act passed in the Parliament of *Ireland* in the Twenty-first and Twenty-second Years of the Reign of His late Majesty King *George* the Third, intituled *An Act to promote Trade and Manufactures by regulating and encouraging Partnerships.*

LXV. And forasmuch as great Injury has been inflicted upon the Public by Companies falsely pretending to be patronized or directed or managed by eminent or opulent Persons; now for the Purpose of preventing such false Pretences, be it enacted, with regard to every Company or pretended Company whatsoever, whether registered or not, and whether now existing or not, That if any Person shall make any such false Pretences, knowing the same to be false, in any Advertisement or other Paper, whether printed or written, and whether published in any Newspaper, or Handbill, or Placard, or Circular, then every such Person shall forfeit for every such Offence a Sum not exceeding Ten Pounds.

LXVI. Provided always, and be it enacted, That every Judgment and every Decree or Order which shall be at any Time after the passing of this Act obtained against any Company completely registered under this Act, except Companies incorporated by Act of Parliament or Charter, or Companies the Liability of the Members of which is restricted by virtue of any Letters Patent, in any Action, Suit, or other Proceeding prosecuted by or against such Company in any Court of Law or Equity, shall and may take effect and be enforced, and Execution thereon be issued, not only against the Property and Effects of such Company, but also, if due Diligence shall have been used to obtain Satisfaction of such Judgment, Decree, or Order, by Execution against the Property and Effects of such Company, then against the Person, Property, and Effects of any Shareholder for the Time being, or any former Shareholder of such Company, in his natural or individual Capacity, until such Judgment, Decree, or Order shall be fully satisfied; provided, in the Case of Execution against any former Shareholder, that such former Shareholder was a Shareholder of such Company at the Time when the Contract or Engagement for which such Judgment, Decree, or Order may have been obtained was entered into, or became a Shareholder during the Time such Contract or Engagement was unexecuted or unsatisfied, or was a Shareholder at the Time of the Judgment, Decree, or Order being obtained; provided also, that in no Case shall Execution be issued on such Judgment, Decree, or Order against the Person, Property, or Effects of any such former Shareholder of such Company after the Expiration of Three Years next after the Person sought to be charged shall have ceased to be a Shareholder of such Company.

LXVII. Provided always, and be it enacted, That every Person against whom, or against whose Property or Effects, Execution upon any Judgment, Decrec, or Order obtained as aforesaid shall have been issued as aforesaid shall be entitled to recover against such Company all Loss, Damages, Costs, and Charges which such Person may have incurred by reason of such Execution: and that, after due Diligence used to obtain Satisfaction thereof against the Property and Effects of such Company, such Person shall be entitled to Contribution for so much of such Loss, Damages, Costs, and Charges as shall remain unsatisfied, from the several other Persons against whom Execution upon such Judgment, Decree, or Order, obtained against such Company, might also have been issued under the Provision in that Behalf aforesaid; and that such Contribution may be recovered from such Persons as aforesaid in like Manner as Contribution in ordinary Cases of Copartnership.

LXVIII. And be it enacted, That in the Cases provided by this Act for Execution on any Judgment, Decree, or Order in any Action or Suit against the Company, to be issued against the Person or against the Property and Effects of any Shareholder or former Shareholder of such Company, or against the Property and Effects of the Company, at the Suit of any Shareholder or former Shareholder, in satisfaction of any Moneys, Damages, Costs, and Expenses paid or incurred by him as aforesaid in any Action or Suit against the Company, such Execution may be issued by Leave of the Court, or of a Judge of the Court, in which such Judgment, Decree, or Order shall have been obtained, upon Motion or Summons to show Cause, or other Motion or Summons consistent with the Practice of the Court, without any Suggestion or Scire facias in that behalf; and that it shall be lawful for such Court or Judge to make absolute or discharge such Rule, or allow or dismiss such Motion (as the Case may be), and to direct the Costs of the Application to be paid by either Party, or to make such other Order therein as to such Court or Judge shall seem fit; and in such Cases such Form of Writs of Execution shall be sued out of the Courts of Law and Equity respectively for giving effect to the Provision in that Behalf aforesaid as the Judges of such Courts respectively shall from Time to Time think fit to order; and the Execution of such Writs shall be enforced in like Manner as Writs of Execution are now enforced: Provided that any Order made by a Judge as aforesaid may be discharged or varied by the Court, on Application made thereto by either Party dissatisfied with such Order: Provided also, that no such Motion shall be made, nor Summons granted, for the Purpose of charging any Shareholder or former Shareholder, until Ten Days' Notice thereof shall have been given to the Person sought to be charged thereby.

LXIX. And be it enacted, That all Penalties and Forfeitures inflicted or authorized to be imposed by this Act, and all Costs and Expenses for which any Person may be liable under this Act or by virtue of any Bye Law, and the Recovery of which has not been otherwise specially herein-before provided, shall and may be recovered, by any Person who shall proceed for the same, before any Two of Her Majesty's Justices of the Peace of the County,

City, or Place where the Offender or Person liable to pay such Costs or Expenses shall reside, or where the Offence shall be committed.

LXX. Provided always, and be it enacted, That all Penalties and Forfeitures recovered under this Act, and not otherwise specially appropriated, shall be applied as follows: one Half thereof shall be paid to the Person who shall sue or proceed for the same, and the other Half to Her Majesty's Use, and shall be paid to the Sheriff of the County, City, or Town where the same shall have been imposed; and that all Convictions before Justices shall be returned to the Court of Quarter Sessions under the Provisions of an Act passed in the Third Year of the Reign of His late Majesty King *George* the Fourth, intituled *An Act for the more speedy Return and levying of Fines, Penalties, and Forfeitures, and Recognizances estreated*, and shall be paid to the Sheriff of the County, City, or Town, and shall be duly accounted for by him.

LXXI. And be it enacted, That in all Cases in which any Penalty or Forfeiture or any Costs or Expenses are recoverable before Two Justices of the Peace under this Act, it shall and may be lawful for any One Justice of the Peace to whom Complaint shall be made of any such Offence to summon the Party complained of, and the Witnesses on each Side, before any Two such Justices, and at the Time and Place mentioned in such Summons, or at any Adjournment of such Summons, the said Two Justices may hear and determine the Matter of such Complaint, and upon due Proof thereof, either by Confession of the Party or by the Oath of One or more credible Witness or Witnesses, give Judgment or Sentence on such

Complaint, with Costs, to be allowed by such Justices, although no Information in Writing shall have been exhibited or taken; and all such Proceedings by Summons without Information shall be as good, valid, and effectual to all Intents and Purposes as if an Information in Writing had been exhibited; and all Penalties, Forfeitures, and Costs so adjudged may be levied by Distress and Sale of the Goods and Chattels of the Party offending, by Warrant under the Hand and Seal of any one Justice; and in default of such Distress the Offender may be committed to Prison by any One Justice, by Warrant under his Hand and Seal, there to remain for any Time not exceeding Three Months, unless such Penalties, Forfeitures, and Costs shall be sooner paid.

LXXII. And be it enacted, That if any Person shall be summoned as a Witness to give Evidence before such Justices of the Peace touching any Matter which such Justices are hereby authorized to inquire into, and shall neglect or refuse to appear at the Time and Place for that Purpose appointed, without a reasonable Excuse for such Neglect or Refusal, to be allowed by such Justices, or appearing shall refuse to be examined on Oath and give Evidence before such Justices, then every such Person shall forfeit for every such Offence a Sum not exceeding Five Pounds, to be levied and paid in such Manner and by such Means as are herein-before directed as to other Penalties recoverable before Justices under this Act.

LXXIII. And be it enacted, That every Proceeding for any Offence punishable on summary Conviction by virtue of this Act shall be commenced within Six Months after the Commission of the Offence, and not after.

LXXIV. And be it enacted, That if any Person shall think himself aggrieved by the Judgment of such Justices, he may, within One Month next after such Conviction, and upon giving Ten Days' Notice of Appeal in Writing to the Party in whose Favour such Judgment shall have been given, stating the Nature and Grounds of Appeal, and upon entering into Recognizances with Two sufficient Sureties to the Amount of the Value of such Penalty and Costs, together with such further Costs as shall be awarded in case such Judgment shall be affirmed, appeal to the next General Quarter Sessions of the Peace for the County, City, or Place where such Conviction shall have been made; and the Justices at such Sessions are hereby empowered to summon and examine Witnesses on Oath, and to hear and finally determine the Matter of such Appeal, and to award such Costs as the Court shall think reasonable to the Party in whose Favour such Appeal shall be determined.

LXXV. And be it enacted, That no Conviction or other Proceeding before Justices under this Act shall be set aside for Want of Form, nor be removed by Certiorari or otherwise into any of Her Majesty's Superior Courts of Record.

LXXVI. And be it enacted, That in any Case to which a Penalty is annexed by this Act the Whole or any Part of such Penalty may be recovered by Action of Debt in any Court now or hereafter having competent Jurisdiction, by any Person who shall sue for the same; and that in every such Action for the Recovery of such Penalty, so much of such Penalty as is sought to be recovered shall be endorsed on the Writ of Summons, and the

Plaintiff shall not be entitled to recover a greater Sum than the Sum so endorsed; and if the Party suing for any such Penalty recover the same or any Part as aforesaid, he shall be entitled to full Costs of Suit.

LXXVII. And be it enacted, That it shall not be lawful for any Person to commence or prosecute any Action, Bill, Plaint, Information, or Prosecution in any of Her Majesty's Superior Courts, for the Recovery of any Penalty or Forfeiture incurred by reason of any Offence committed against this Act, unless the same be commenced or prosecuted in the Name and with the Consent of Her Majesty's Attorney General; and that if any Action, Bill, Plaint, Information, or Prosecution, or any Proceeding before any Justices as aforesaid, shall be commenced or prosecuted in the Name of any other Person than is in that Behalf before mentioned, the same shall be and are hereby declared to be null and void.

LXXVIII. And be it enacted, That with regard to every Act, Instrument, or Writing by this Act required or authorized to be done or to be made or executed by the Committee of Privy Council for Trade, that if the same purport to be so done, made, or executed by or on behalf of the said Committee, and be signed by One of the Secretaries of the said Committee, and (if it require the Seal) be sealed by the Seal of the said Committee, then it shall be deemed to be sufficiently done, made, or executed, to all Intents and Purposes.

LXXIX. And be it enacted, That it shall be the Duty of the Registrar of Joint Stock Companies to make a Report annually to the said Committee of Privy Council for Trade, setting forth,—

1. A List of Companies provisionally registered during the past Year:
2. A List of Companies completely registered during the past Year:
3. A List of Cases in which Application shall have been made for the Enforcement of Penalties of Failure to register, and the Proceedings, whether by Prosecution or otherwise, taken in consequence of such Applications, and the Results of such Proceedings:
4. A List of Companies which shall have been provisionally registered, but which have not obtained complete Registration:
5. A Return of the Regulations made by the said Committee with regard to the Returns required to be made by Companies:
6. A Return of Persons appointed to the Office of Registrar of Joint Stock Companies, and other Officers and Clerks, and of their Salaries or other Remuneration, and of the Rules made for the Regulation of the said Office:
7. A Return of the Amount of all Fees paid for Certificates of provisional or complete Registration, and for every other Purpose:
8. A Return of the Scale of Fees appointed by the Commissioners of Her Majesty's Treasury for the Services to be performed by the Registrar, and of the respective Amounts of such Fees:
9. A Return of the Cases in which the Companies had failed to appoint Auditors, and of the Proceedings taken thereon:
10. A Return of Prosecutions under this Act

for any Offences not herein-before specified:

11. A Return of the Number of Bankruptcies of Joint Stock Companies, and of the Amount of the Debts and Assets of such Companies respectively:

12. A Return of Modifications made by the Committee of Privy Council for Trade, in pursuance of this Act, in the Conditions and Regulations to be observed by Companies, whether existing or future:

And that, within Six Weeks after the Meeting of Parliament next after the First Day of *January* in every Year, such Report shall be laid before both Houses of Parliament.

LXXX. And be it enacted, That this Act may be amended or repealed by any Act to be passed in this present Session of Parliament.

# SCHEDULES to which this Act refers.

## SCHEDULE (A.)—See § 7.

LIST of PURPOSES for which Provision is required to be made by the Deed of Settlement of a Company before such Company can obtain a Certificate of complete Registration.

I.—*For the holding of Meetings, and the Proceedings thereat; viz.*

1. For holding ordinary General Meetings of the Company once at the least in every Year, at some appointed Place and Time.
2. For holding extraordinary Meetings, either upon the convening of the Directors of the Company, or upon the Requisition of not less than Five Shareholders.
3. For the Adjournment of Meetings.
4. For the Advertisement and Notification of Meetings, and the Business to be transacted thereat.
5. For defining the Business which may be transacted at Meetings, ordinary and extraordinary, or at Adjournments thereof.
6. For the Appointment of the Chairman at any Meeting of the Company.
7. For ensuring that each Shareholder shall have a Vote; and where it is not provided that each Shareholder is to have a Vote in respect of

each Share, the Appointment of the Number of Votes to be given by Shareholders in respect of any Number of Shares held by them.

8. For enabling Guardians, Trustees, and Committees to vote in respect of the Interests of Infants, Cestuique Trusts, Lunatics, and Idiots.
9. For ascertaining what shall be the Majorities or Numbers of Votes requisite to carry all or any Questions, and where a simple Majority is to decide.
10. For prescribing the Mode and Form of the Appointment of Proxies to vote in the Place of absent Shareholders, and for limiting the Number of Proxies which may be held by any one Person.
11. For determining Questions where the Votes are equally divided, whether by the casting Vote of the Chairman or otherwise.

II.—*For the Direction of the Execution of the Affairs of the Company, and the Registration of its Proceedings; viz.*

12. For prescribing the maximum Number of Directors to be appointed; the Number of Shares or the Amount of Interest by which they are to be qualified; the Period for which they are to hold Office, so that at least One Third of such Directors, or the nearest Number to One Third, shall retire annually, subject to Re-election if thought fit; and for the Determination of the Persons who shall so retire in each Year.
13. For filling up Vacancies in the Office of the Directors as they occur; but not so as to enable the Board of Directors (if the filling up be assigned to them) to fill up such Vacancy for a longer Period than until the next General Meeting of the Company.
14. For the continuance in Office of Directors in default of Election of new Directors.
15. For regulating the Meetings of Directors, the

Quorum thereof, the Proceedings thereat, and the Adjournment thereof.

16. For recording the Attendance of Directors, and reporting the same to the Shareholders.
17. For the Determination of Questions upon which the Votes of the Directors may be equally divided.
18. For the Appointment of a Person to take the Chair of the Directors, and for supplying any Vacancy in the Office of Chairman.
19. For the Appointment of the Chairman of the Directors at Meetings at which the permanent Chairman may not be present.
20. For regulating the Appointment by the Directors of Officers, Clerks, and Servants.
21. For recording the Proceedings of the Directors.
22. For keeping and entering of Minutes of such Proceedings.
23. For ensuring the safe Custody of the Seal of the Company, and for regulating the Authority under which it is to be used.
24. For providing for the Remuneration of the Auditors of the Accounts of the Company.
25. For providing for the Appointment of a Secretary or Clerk (if any) of the Directors.
26. For providing for the Receipt, Custody, and Issue of Monies belonging to the Company.
27. For providing for the keeping of Books of Account, and for periodically balancing the same.
28. For keeping the Records and Papers of the Company.
29. For prescribing and regulating the Duties and Qualifications of Officers.
30. For determining what Books of Accounts, Books of Registry, and other Documents may be inspected by the Shareholders of the Company, and for regulating such Inspection.

III.—*For the Distribution of the Capital of the Company into Shares, or for the Apportionment of the Interest in the Property of the Company; viz.*

31. For determining whether Calls or Instalments of Payments (if any) are to be made in certain Amounts and at fixed Periods, and, if so, what Amounts and at what Periods.
32. For determining whether, on Failure to pay any Instalments or Calls, the Share shall or shall not be forfeited, and, if forfeited, whether and on what Conditions the Property in such Share may be recovered by the Shareholder.
33. For determining whether, and under what Circumstances, and on what Conditions, the Capital of the Company may be augmented, by the Conversion of Loans into Capital or otherwise, or by the Issue of new Shares or otherwise.
34. For determining whether the Amount of new Capital shall or shall not be divided so as to allow such Amount to be apportioned amongst the existing Shareholders.

IV.—*For the Borrowing of Money; viz.*

35. For determining whether the Company may borrow Money, and, if so, whether on Bond, or Mortgage, or any other and what Security.
36. For determining whether the Directors may contract Debts in conducting the Affairs of the Company, and, if so, whether to any definite Extent.
37. For determining whether and to what Extent the Directors may make or issue Promissory Notes.
38. For determining whether and to what Extent the Directors may accept Bills of Exchange.

## SCHEDULE (B).—See § 7.

CERTIFICATE required to be endorsed on the Deed of Settlement and signed by Two Directors.

We do hereby certify, That the within-written Deed is the Deed of Settlement of
Company, and that to the best of our Knowledge the Particulars therein contained are correctly set forth.

## SCHEDULE (C).—See § 4.

RETURN made pursuant to the JOINT STOCK COMPANIES REGISTRATION and REGULATION ACT, 7 & 8 Vict. c. 110, 1844.

FOR PROVISIONAL REGISTRATION.

Name and Business of the Company.

| Name of the proposed Company. | Business or Purpose. | Place of Business (if any). |
| --- | --- | --- |
| | | |

Promoters of the Company.

| Names. | Occupations. | Places of Business (if any) | Places of Residence. |
| --- | --- | --- | --- |
| | | | |

*⁎* The Names of the Provisional Officers may be added to this Return under a separate Head, and the Subscribers may be given in a similar Manner.

## Provisional Committee or Provisional Directors.

| Names. | Occupations. | Places of Business (if any). | Places of Residence. | Signature of Consent to act on Committee or as a Director. |
|---|---|---|---|---|
| | | | | |

Dated this Day of 18

[*Signature.*]

## SCHEDULE (D).

RETURN made pursuant to the JOINT STOCK COMPANIES REGISTRATION and REGULATION ACT, Vict. c. , 1844.

### Change of Place of Business.

| Name of Company. | Business or Purpose. | Former Place [*or* principal Place, *if more than One,*] of Business. | Present Place [*or* principal Place] of Business. |
|---|---|---|---|
| | | | |

[*Date.*] [*Signature.*]

## SCHEDULE (E.)—See § 11.

RETURN made pursuant to the JOINT STOCK COMPANIES REGISTRATION and REGULATION ACT, Vict. c. , 1844.

Transfer of Shares.

| Name of Company. | Business or Purpose. | Place [*or* principal Place, *if more than One*,] of Business. | |
|---|---|---|---|
| | | | |
| Name and Place of Abode of Person by whom Transfer is made. | Name and Place of Abode of Person to whom Transfer is made. | Distinctive Numbers of the Shares transferred. | Date of Transfer. |
| | | | |

[*Date.*] [*Signature.*]

## SCHEDULE (F.)—See § 12.

RETURN made pursuant to the JOINT STOCK COMPANIES REGISTRATION and REGULATION ACT, Vict. c. , 1844.

Change of Shareholders.

| Name of Company. | Business or Purpose. | Place [*or* principal Place, *if more than One*,] of Business. |
|---|---|---|

Persons known to have ceased to be Shareholders (except by Transfer) since the last Return, dated the Day of

| Name. | Place of Abode. | Distinctive Number of Shares. |
|---|---|---|
| | | |

Persons known to have become Members (except by Transfer) since the last Return dated the Day of

| Name. | Place of Abode. | Distinctive Number of Shares. |
|---|---|---|
| | | |

Persons whose Names have become changed by Marriage or otherwise.

| Former Name. | Former Place of Abode. | Present Name. | Present Place of Abode. | Distinctive Number of Shares. |
|---|---|---|---|---|
| | | | | |

[*Date.*] [*Signature.*]

## SCHEDULE (G.)—See § 56.

RETURN made pursuant to the JOINT STOCK COMPANIES REGISTRATION and REGULATION ACT, Vict. c. , 1844.

For Registration of existing Companies, Name of the Company, Business, &c.

| Name of the Company. | Business or Purpose. | Place of Business, with the Branches (if any). |
|---|---|---|
| | | |

## SCHEDULE (H.)

RETURN made pursuant to the JOINT STOCK COMPANIES REGISTRATION and REGULATION ACT, Vict. c. , 1844.

CORRECTED RETURN.

[*Copy of former incorrect Return.*]

Copy.

Amended Return, with correct Names and Description [*in such of the preceding Forms as are applicable to the Case under the Provisions of the Foregoing Act*].

[*Date.*] [*Signature.*]

## SCHEDULE (I.)—See § 50.

### CERTIFICATE of SHARE.

The Company, first completely Registered on the Day of 18 .

Number

This is to certify, that *A.B.* of is the Proprietor of the Share, Number , of the Company, subject to the Regulations of the said Company, and that up to this Day there has been paid up in respect of such share the Sum of

Given under the Common Seal of the said Company, the Day of in the Year 18

[*Signature of Secretary.*] (L.S.)

## SCHEDULE (K.)—See § 53.

### TRANSFER OF SHARES.

I *A.B.* of in consideration of the Sum of paid to me by *C.D.* of do hereby transfer to the said Share [*or* Shares], numbered , in the Undertaking called the Company, to hold unto the said his Executors, Administrators, and Assigns, [*or* Successors and Assigns,] subject to the several Conditions on which I hold the same at the Time of the Execution hereof. And I the said do hereby agree to take the said Share [*or* Shares], subject to the same Conditions, and to the Provisions of the Deed or Deeds of Settlement of the said Company. As witness our Hands and Seals, the Day of .

[*Signature.*]

# JOINT STOCK COMPANIES ACT AMENDMENT ACT.

---

10 & 11 VICTORIÆ REGINÆ, CAP. LXXVIII.

## An Act to amend an Act for the Registration, Incorporation, and Regulation of Joint Stock Companies.

[*22nd July*, 1847.]

WHEREAS by an Act passed in the Session of Parliament holden in the Seventh and Eighth Years of the Reign of Her present Majesty, intituled *An Act for the Registration, Incorporation, and Regulation of Joint Stock Companies*, it is amongst other things enacted, that on the complete Registration of any Company being certified in the Manner prescribed in the said Act, it shall be lawful for such Company, amongst other things, to purchase and hold Lands, Tenements, and Hereditaments in the Name of such Company, or of the Trustees or Trustee thereof, for the Purpose of occupying the same as a Place or Places of Business of the said Company, and also (but nevertheless with a Licence, general or special, for that Purpose, to be granted by the Committee of Privy Council for Trade, first had and obtained,) such other Lands, Tenements, and Hereditaments as the Nature of the Business of the Company may require:

And whereas Doubts have in certain Cases arisen as to the Meaning of the said Provision, and it is expedient that such Doubts should be removed, and that further Provision should be made as to the granting of such Licences as aforesaid by the said Committee of Privy Council: Be it therefore enacted by the Queen's most Excellent Majesty, by and with the Advice and Consent of the Lords Spiritual and Temporal, and Commons, in this present Parliament assembled, and by the Authority of the same, That whenever any Company, having obtained a Certificate of complete Registration under the said Act, is desirous of purchasing or holding, taking on Lease, holding on Mortgage, or in any other Manner acquiring an Interest such as Bodies Politic or Corporate are by Law incapacitated from acquiring in any Lands, Tenements, or Hereditaments, other than such as it is under the said Act entitled to purchase and hold, as a Place or Places of Business, it shall be lawful for such Company to make Application to the Lords of the said Committee of Privy Council for Trade for a Licence to purchase, take, or hold the same, and the Lords of the said Committee shall thereupon take such Application into their Consideration, and may, if they see fit, grant a Licence to such Company accordingly; and in such Licence the Lords of the said Committee may either authorize such Company to purchase, take, and again let, sell, or otherwise dispose of such Lands, Tenements, or Hereditaments as may in the Licence be particularly described, and to hold the same for such Time as may be specified in such Licence, or in any Licence to be subsequently and from Time to Time granted by the said Committee of Privy Council for Trade on the Application of such Company, or may authorize them from Time to Time to acquire, dispose of, and again acquire such Lands, Tenements, or Hereditaments as the Company may from Time to Time desire, or may authorize them to hold Lands, Tenements, or Hereditaments on Mortgage, and may frame such Licence in such Manner, and insert in the same such Conditions, as with reference to the special Circumstances of each Case they may deem expedient; and such Licence shall be held to confer upon such Company the Rights and Powers therein expressed to be given in respect of purchasing, holding, and disposing of Lands, Tenements, or Hereditaments as aforesaid.

II. And be it enacted, That there shall be presented to both Houses of Parliament, in each Year, within Fourteen Days after the Commencement of the Session, an Account of the several Licences, and Renewals or Extensions of Licences, so granted by the Committee of the Privy Council for Trade, specifying the Nature and Extent of the Powers contained in each of such Licences, and of the Lands so authorized to be held, and also, in the Case of any Renewal or Extension of such Licences, an Account of the Extent of Land actually held by the Company at the Time of such Renewal or Extension, and the Counties within which such Lands are situate.

III. And whereas certain Licences have from Time to Time been granted by the Lords of the said Committee in pursuance of the said Act: Be it enacted, That in case any Doubt arise as to the Effect thereof, it shall be held that any Licence so granted before the passing of this Act is valid and effectual for the Purposes therein expressed, and shall be deemed sufficient Evidence that the Lands, Tenements, or Hereditaments therein described or referred to, or which have been purchased, taken, held, or disposed of under the Authority thereof, are such as the Nature of the Business of the Company requires.

IV. And whereas by the said recited Act the Promoters of any Company formed for any Purpose within the Meaning of the said Act are, amongst other things, required to return to the Office for the Registration of Joint Stock Companies a Copy of every Prospectus or Circular, Handbill or Advertisement, or other such Document, at any Time addressed to the Public, or to the Subscribers or others, relative to the Formation or Modification of such Company: And whereas the Registration of such Prospectuses and Advertisements has been found to be very burdensome to the Promoters of such Companies, and it is desirable to relieve such Promoters from the Necessity thereof, and in lieu thereof to substitute the Provisions herein-after contained: Be it therefore enacted, That so much of the said Act as is lastly herein-before recited shall be and the same is hereby repealed.

V. And be it enacted, That in addition to the Particulars which the Promoters of every such Company as aforesaid are by the said Act required to return to the said Office for the Registration of Joint Stock Companies, when and as from Time to Time they shall be decided on, such Promoters shall also return, and they are hereby required to return, to the said Office, the following additional Particulars, so soon as the same shall be decided on; (that is to say,)

First. the Amount of the proposed Capital of the Company;

Second. The Amount and Number of the Shares into which the same is to be divided:

And if the said Company be dissolved, or be incorporated by Act of Parliament, or by Royal Charter, or by the Queen's Letters Patent, or be in any way withdrawn or supposed to be withdrawn from the Operation of the said Act, the Promoters of the Company shall forthwith give Notice thereof to the Registrar of Joint Stock Companies.[a]

VI. And be it enacted, That in case of any Alteration being made in any of the Particulars registered by the Promoters of any Company in pursuance of the said recited Act or of this Act, such Alteration shall forthwith be returned to the Registrar of Joint Sstock Companies; and if such Return be not made within one Month after such Alteration has been made and decided upon, any Promoter of the Company shall be liable to forfeit for each and every Alteration not returned as aforesaid any Sum not exceeding Twenty Pounds.

VII. And be it enacted, That it shall not be lawful for the Promoters of any Company, or for any Person connected with any Company, at any Time before such Company has obtained a Certificate of complete Registration under the said recited Act, to issue or publish or in any Manner address or cause or suffer to be addressed to the Public, or to the Subscribers or others, any Prospectus or Circular, Handbill or Advertisement, or other such

[a] 7 & 8 Vict., cap. 110, s. 4.

Document relative to the Formation or Modification of the Company, containing any Statement at variance with the Particulars which may have been returned to the Registrar of Joint Stock Companies under the said recited Act or this Act, nor to issue, publish, or in any Manner address or cause or suffer to be addressed to the Public, or to the Subscribers or others, any such Prospectus, Circular, Handbill, or Advertisement, containing any Statements of Particulars which are by the said recited Act or by this Act directed to be returned to the Registrar of Joint Stock Companies, until such Particulars have been so returned; and if any Prospectus or Circular, Handbill or Advertisement, be issued, published, or addressed to the Public, or to the Subscribers or others, contrary hereto, any Promoter of the Company shall be liable for each and every such Issue or Publication to forfeit any sum not exceeding Twenty Pounds.

VIII. And be it enacted, That the Penalties imposed by this Act shall be sued for, recovered, and applied in the same Manner as Penalties imposed by the said recited Act are therein directed to be sued for, recovered, and applied respectively.

IX. And be it enacted, That this Act may be amended or repealed by any Act to be passed in the present Session of Parliament.

# JOINT STOCK COMPANIES ACT.

19 & 20 VICTORIA, Cap. 47.

## An Act for the Incorporation and Regulation of Joint Stock Companies and other Associations. [14*th July*, 1856.]

WHEREAS it is expedient that the Law relating to the Incorporation and Regulation of Joint Stock Companies and other Associations should be consolidated and amended: Be it therefore enacted by the Queen's most Excellent Majesty, by and with the Advice and Consent of the Lords Spiritual and Temporal, and Commons, in this present Parliament assembled, and by the Authority of the same, as follows:

I. This Act may be cited for all Purposes as "The Joint Stock Companies Act, 1856."

II. This Act shall not apply to Persons associated together for the Purpose of Banking or Insurance.

## PART I.

### CONSTITUTION AND INCORPORATION OF COMPANIES AND ASSOCIATIONS.

*Registry.*

III. Seven or more Persons, associated for any lawful Purpose, may, by subscribing their Names to a Memorandum of Association, and otherwise complying with the Requisitions of this Act in respect of Registration, form themselves into an Incorporated Company, with or without Limited Liability.

IV. Not more than Twenty Persons shall, after the Third Day of *November* One thousand eight hundred and fifty-six, carry on in Partnership any Trade or Business having Gain for its Object, unless they are registered as a Company under this Act, or are authorized so to carry on Business by some Private Act of Parliament or by Royal Charter or Letters Patent, or are engaged in working Mines within and subject to the Jurisdiction of the Stannaries; and if any Persons carry on Business in Partnership contrary to this Provision, every Person so acting shall be severally liable for the Payment of the whole Debts of the Partnership, and may be sued for the same without the Joinder in the Action or Suit of any other Members of the Partnership.

V. The Memorandum of Association shall contain the following Things; (that is to say,)

1. The Name of the proposed Company;
2. The Part of the United Kingdom, whether *England, Scotland,* or *Ireland,* in which the registered Office of the Company is to be established;
3. The Objects for which the proposed Company is to be established;
4. The Liability of the Shareholders, whether it is to be limited or unlimited;
5. The Amount of the nominal Capital of the proposed Company;
6. The Number of Shares into which such Capital is to be divided, and the Amount of each Share; subject to the following Restriction:

That in the Case of a Company formed with

Limited Liability, and herein-after called a Limited Company, the Word "Limited" shall be the last Word in the Name of the Company.

VI. No Company shall be registered under a Name identical with that by which a subsisting Company is already registered, or so nearly resembling the same as to be calculated to deceive; and if any Company, through Inadvertence or otherwise, is registered by a Name identical with that by which a subsisting Company is registered, or so nearly resembling the same as to be calculated to deceive; such first-mentioned Company may, with the Sanction of the Registrar, change its Name, and upon such Change being made the Registrar shall enter the new Name on the Register in the Place of the former Name, but no such Alteration of Name shall affect any Rights or Obligations of the Company, or render defective any legal Proceedings instituted or to be instituted by or against the Company, and any legal Proceedings may be continued or commenced against the Company by its new Name that might have been continued or commenced against the Company by its former Name.

VII. The Memorandum of Association shall be in the Form marked A. in the Schedule hereto, or as near thereto as Circumstances admit, and it shall, when registered, bind the Company and the Shareholders therein to the same Extent as if each Shareholder had subscribed his Name and affixed his Seal thereto or otherwise duly executed the same, and there were in such Memorandum contained, on the Part of himself, his Heirs, Executors, and Administrators, a Covenant to conform to all the Regulations of such Memorandum, subject to the Provisions of this Act.

VIII. Every Subscriber of the Memorandum of Association shall take One Share at the least in the Company: The Number of Shares taken by each Subscriber shall be set opposite his Name in such Memorandum of Association, and upon the Incorporation of the Company he shall be entered in the Register of Shareholders herein-after mentioned as a Shareholder to the Extent of the Shares he has taken.

IX. The Memorandum of Association may be accompanied by or have annexed thereto or endorsed thereon Articles of Association, signed by the Subscribers to the Memorandum of Association, and prescribing Regulations for the Company; but if no such Regulations are prescribed, or so far as the same do not extend to modify the Regulations contained in the Table marked B. in the Schedule hereto, such last-mentioned Regulations shall, so far as the same are applicable, be deemed to be the Regulations of the Company, and shall bind the Company and the Shareholders therein to the same Extent, as if they had been inserted in Articles of Association, and such Articles had been registered.

X. The Articles of Association shall be in the Form marked C. in the Schedule hereto, or as near thereto as Circumstances admit: They shall, when registered, bind the Company and the Shareholders therein to the same Extent as if each Shareholder had subscribed his Name and affixed his Seal thereto or otherwise duly executed the same, and there were in such Articles contained, on the Part of himself, his Heirs, Executors, and Administrators, a Covenant to conform to all the Regulations of such Articles, subject to the Provisions of this Act.

XI. The Memorandum of Association and

the Articles of Association shall respectively bear the same Stamps as if they were Deeds: Any Person signing a printed Copy of the Memorandum of Association or Articles of Association shall be deemed to have signed such Memorandum and Articles respectively, and where the proper Stamp has been duly fixed on such Memorandum of Association or Articles of Association it shall not be necessary to stamp any printed Copy so signed: The Execution by any Person of the Memorandum of Association or Articles of Association shall be attested by One Witness at the least; and Attestation by One Witness shall be sufficient Attestation in *Scotland* as well as in *England* and *Ireland.*

XII. The Memorandum of Association and Articles of Association shall be delivered to the Registrar of Joint Stock Companies, who shall retain and register the same: There shall be paid to the Registrar of Joint Stock Companies, in respect of the several Matters mentioned in the Table marked D. in the Schedule hereto, the several Fees therein specified, or such smaller Fees as the Board of Trade may from Time to Time direct; and all Fees so paid shall be paid into the Receipt of her Majesty's Exchequer, and be carried to the Account of the Consolidated Fund of the United Kingdom of *Great Britain* and *Ireland.*

XIII. Upon any such Memorandum of Association, either with or without Articles of Association as aforesaid, being registered, the Registrar shall certify under his Hand that the Company is incorporated, and in the Case of a Limited Company that the Company is limited: The Subscribers of the Memorandum of Association, together with such other Persons as may from Time to Time become Shareholders of the Company, shall thereupon be a Body Corporate by the Name prescribed in the Memorandum of Association, having a perpetual Succession and a Common Seal, with Power to hold Lands; but with such pecuniary Liability on the Part of the Shareholders as is herein-after mentioned: The Certificate of Incorporation given by the Registrar shall be conclusive Evidence that all the Requisitions of this Act in respect of Registration have been complied with; and the Date of such Certificate shall be deemed to be the Date of the Incorporation of the Company.

XIV. If the Directors of any such Company shall declare and pay any Dividend when the Company is known by them to be insolvent, or any Dividend the Payment of which would to their Knowledge render it insolvent, they shall be jointly and severally liable for all the Debts of the Company then existing, and for all that shall be thereafter contracted, so long as they shall respectively continue in office: Provided always, that the Amount for which they shall all be so liable shall not exceed the Amount of such Dividend; and that if any of the Directors shall be absent at the Time of making the Dividend or Dividends so declared or paid, or shall object thereto, and shall file their Objection in Writing with the Clerk of the Company, they shall be exempted from the said Liability.

XV. As soon as a Certificate of Incorporation has been granted by the Registrar of Joint Stock Companies, the Company may issue Certificates of Shares to the Subscribers to the Memorandum of Association, and to all other Persons to whom Shares may be allotted, of such Number and Amount as may be prescribed by the Memorandum of the Association, but not of any greater Number or Amount: The Shares so issued shall be Personal Estate, and shall not be of the Nature of Real Estate: And each Share shall be distinguished by its appropriate Number.

*Register of Shareholders.*

XVI. Every Company registered under this Act, herein-after referred to as "the Company," shall cause to be kept in One or more Books a Register of Shareholders, and there shall be entered therein the following Particulars:

1. The Names, Addresses, and Occupations, if any, of the Shareholders in the Company, and the Shares held by each of them, distinguishing each Share by its Number:
2. The Amount paid on the Shares of each Shareholder:
3. The Date at which the Name of any Person was entered in the Register as a Shareholder:
4. The Date at which any Person ceased to be a Shareholder in respect of any Share.

XVII. Once at the least in every Year a List shall be made of all Persons who on the Fourteenth Day succeeding the Day on which the Ordinary General Meeting of the Company, or, if there is more than One Ordinary Meeting in each Year, the First of such Ordinary General Meetings is held, are Holders of Shares in the Company; and such List shall state the Names, Addresses, and Occupations of all the Persons therein mentioned, and the Number of Shares held by each of them, and shall contain a Summary specifying the following Particulars:

1. The Amount of the nominal Capital of

the Company, and the Number of Shares into which it is divided:

2. The Number of Shares taken from the Commencement of the Company up to the Date of the Summary:
3. The Amount of Calls made on each Share:
4. The Total Amount of Calls that have been received:
5. The total Amount of Calls unpaid:
6. The total Amount of Shares forfeited.

The above List and Summary shall be contained in a separate Part of the Register, and shall be in the Form marked E. in the Schedule hereto, or as near thereto as Circumstances admit; such List and Summary shall be completed within Seven Days after such Fourteenth Day as is mentioned in this Section, and a Copy thereof authenticated by the Seal of the Company shall forthwith be forwarded to the Registrar, and any Person may inspect and take Copies of the same, subject to the Regulations under which a Person is herein-after declared to be entitled to inspect and take Copies of any Documents kept by the Registrar.

XVIII. If any Company registered under this Act makes default in keeping a Register of Shareholders, or in sending a Copy of such List and Summary as aforesaid to the Registrar, in compliance with the foregoing Rules, such Company shall incur a Penalty not exceeding Five Pounds for every Day during which such Default continues.

XIX. No Notice of any Trust, express or implied or constructive, shall be entered on the Register or receivable by the Company; and every Person who has accepted any Share in a Company registered under this Act, and whose

Name is entered in the Register of Shareholders, and no other Person (except a Subscriber to the Memorandum of Association in respect of the Shares subscribed for by him) shall for the Purposes of this Act be deemed to be a Shareholder.

XX. The Transfer of any Share in the Company shall be in the Form marked F. in the Schedule hereto, or to the like Effect, and shall be executed both by the Transferror and Transferree: The Transferror shall be deemed to remain a Holder of such Share until the Name of the Transferree is entered in the Register Book in respect thereof.

XXI. A Certificate, under the Common Seal of the Company, specifying any Share or Shares held by any Shareholder, shall be *primâ facie* Evidence of the Title of the Shareholder to the Share or Shares therein specified.

XXII. The Amount of Calls for the Time being unpaid on any Share shall be deemed to be a Debt due from the Holder of such Share to the Company.

XXIII. The Register of Shareholders commencing from the Incorporation of the Company shall be kept at the registered Office of the Company herein-after mentioned; except when closed as herein-after mentioned, it shall during Business Hours, but subject to such reasonable Restrictions as the Company in General Meeting may impose, so that not less than Two Hours in each Day be appointed for Inspection, be open to the Inspection of any Shareholder *gratis,* and to the Inspection of any other Person on the Payment of One Shilling, or such less Sum as the Company may prescribe for each Inspection; and every such Shareholder or other Person may require a Copy of such Register, or of any Part thereof, on Payment of Sixpence for every One hundred Words required to be copied; if such Inspection or Copy is refused, the Company shall incur for each Refusal a Penalty not exceeding Two Pounds, and a further Penalty not exceeding Two Pounds, for every Day during which such Refusal continues.

XXIV. The Company may, upon giving Notice by Advertisement in some Newspaper circulating in the District in which the registered Office of the Company is situated, close the Register of Shareholders for any Time or Times not exceeding on the whole Twenty-one Days in each Year, and the Period during which the Books are closed shall not be reckoned as Part of the Time within which a Transfer is to be registered.

XXV. If the Name of any Person is without sufficient Cause entered or omitted to be entered in the Register of Shareholders of any Company, such Person, or any Shareholder of the Company, may, as respects Companies registered in *England* or *Ireland*, by Motion in any of Her Majesty's Superior Courts of Law or Equity, and as respects Companies registered in *Scotland* by Summary Petition to the Court of Session, apply to such Court for an Order that the Registry may be rectified, and the Court may either refuse such Application, with or without Costs, to be paid by the Applicant, or it may, if satisfied of the Justice of the Case, make an Order for the Rectification of the Register, and may direct the Company to pay all the Costs of such Motion or Petition, and any Damages the Party aggrieved may have sustained; and if the Company makes default or is guilty of unnecessary Delay in registering any Transfer of Shares, they shall be responsible to any Person injured by such Default or Delay for the Amount of Damage he may thereby have sustained.

XXVI. The Register of Shareholders shall be Evidence of any Matters by this Act directed or authorized to be inserted therein.

XXVII. Copies of the Memorandum of Association and Articles of Association shall be forwarded to every Shareholder, at his Request, on Payment of the Sum of One Shilling for each Copy, or such less Sum as may be prescribed by the Company.

---

## PART II.

### Management and Administration of Companies.

*General.*

XXVIII. The Company shall have a registered Office to which all Communications and Notices may be addressed: If any Company registered under this Act carries on Business without having such an Office, it shall incur a Penalty not exceeding Five Pounds for every Day during which Business is so carried on.

XXIX. Notice of the Situation of such registered Office, and of any Change therein, shall be given to the Registrar of Joint Stock Companies, and recorded by him: Until such Notice is given the Company shall not be deemed to have complied with the Provisions of this Act with respect to having a registered Office.

XXX. Every Limited Company registered under this Act shall paint or affix, and shall keep painted or affixed, its Name on the Outside of every Office or Place in which the Business of the Company is carried on, in a conspicuous Position, in Letters easily legible, and shall have its Name engraven in legible Characters on its Seal, and shall have its Name mentioned in legible Characters in all Notices, Advertisements, and other official Publications of such Company, and in all Bills of Exchange, Promissory Notes, Endorsements, Cheques, and Orders for Money or Goods, purporting to be signed by or on behalf of such Company, and in all Bills of Parcels, Invoices, Receipts, and Letters of Credit of the Company.

XXXI. If any Limited Company registered under this Act does not paint or affix, and keep painted or affixed, its Name in manner aforesaid, it shall be liable to a Penalty not exceeding Five Pounds for not so painting or affixing its Name, and for every Day during which such Name is not kept painted or affixed; and if any Officer of such Company, or any Person on its Behalf, uses any Seal purporting to be a Seal of the Company whereon its Name is not so engraven as aforesaid, or issues or authorizes the Issue of any Notice, Advertisement, or other official Publication of such Company, or signs or authorizes to be signed on behalf of such Company any Bill of Exchange, Promissory Note, Endorsement, Cheque, Order for Money or Goods, or issues or authorizes to be issued any Bill of Parcels, Invoice, Receipt, or Letter of Credit of the Company, wherein its Name is not mentioned in manner aforesaid, he shall be liable to a Penalty of Fifty Pounds, and shall further be personally liable to the Holder of any such Bill of Exchange, Promissory Note, Cheque, or Order for Money or Goods, for the Amount thereof, unless the same is duly paid by the Company.

XXXII. A General Meeting of the Company shall be held once at the least in every Year.

XXXIII. Any Company registered under this Act may in General Meeting, from Time to Time, by such Special Resolution as is hereinafter mentioned, alter and make new Provisions in lieu of or in addition to any Regulations of the Company contained in the Articles of Association of the Table marked B. in the Schedule.

XXXIV. A Resolution shall be deemed to be a Special Resolution of the Company whenever the same has been passed by Three Fourths in Number and Value of such Shareholders of the Company for the Time being entitled to vote as may be present in Person or by Proxy (in Cases where, by the Regulations of the Company, Proxies are allowed) at any Meeting of which Notice specifying the Intention to propose such Resolution has been duly given, and such Resolution has been confirmed by a Majority of Shareholders for the Time being entitled to vote as may be present in Person or by Proxy at a subsequent Meeting, of which Notice has been duly given, and held at an Interval of not less than One Month, nor more than Three Months, from the Date of the Meeting at which such Special Resolution was first passed; Unless a Poll is demanded by at least Five Shareholders a Declaration of the Chairman of any such Meeting as is mentioned in this Section, that a Special Resolution has been carried, shall be deemed conclusive Evidence of the Fact, without Proof of the Number or Proportion of the Votes recorded in favour of or against the same: Notice of any Meeting shall, for the Purposes of this Section, be deemed to be duly given, and the Meeting to be duly held, whenever such Notice is given and Meeting held in manner prescribed by the Regulations of the Company.

XXXV. A Copy of any Special Resolution that is passed by any Company registered under this Act shall be forwarded to the Registrar of Joint Stock Companies, and recorded by him: If such Copy is not so forwarded within Fifteen Days from the Date of the passing of the Resolution, the Company shall incur a Penalty not exceeding Two Pounds for every Day after the Expiration of such Fifteen Days during which such Copy is omitted to be forwarded.

XXXVI. A Copy of any Special Resolution shall be given to any Shareholder on Payment of One Shilling, or of such less Sum as the Company may direct.

XXXVII. The Company if authorized so to do by its Regulations, may increase its nominal Capital in manner directed by such Regulations, but Notice of any Increase so made shall be given to the Registrar of Joint Stock Companies within Fifteen Days from the Date of the passing of the Resolution by which such Increase has been authorized, and the Registrar shall forthwith record the Amount of such Increase: If such Notice is not given within the Period aforesaid the Company shall incur a Penalty not exceeding Five Pounds for every

Day during which such Neglect to give Notice continues.

XXXVIII. No Company that is not for the Time being carrying on a Trade or Business having Gain for its Object shall be entitled, without the Sanction of the Board of Trade, to hold more than Two Acres of Land, but the Board of Trade may empower any such Company to hold Lands in such Quantity and subject to such Conditions as they think fit, and may for that Purpose grant a Licence in the Form marked G. in the Schedule hereto, or to the like Effect.

XXXIX. If any Company registered under this Act carries on Business when the Number of its Shareholders is less than Seven, for a Period of Six Months after the Number has been so reduced, then every Person who is a Shareholder in such Company during the Time that it so carries on Business after such Period of Six Months shall be severally liable for the Payment of the whole Debts of the Company contracted during such Time, and may be sued for the same without the Joinder in the Action or Suit of any other Shareholder.

XL. The Company shall cause Minutes of all Resolutions and Proceedings of General Meetings of the Company to be duly entered in Books to be from Time to Time provided for the Purpose, and any such Minute as aforesaid, if signed by any Person purporting to be the Chairman of such Meeting, shall be receivable in Evidence in all legal Proceedings, and until the contrary is proved every General Meeting in respect of the Proceedings of which Minutes have been so made shall be deemed to have been duly held and convened.

*Legal Instruments of Company.*

XLI. Contracts on behalf of any Company registered under this Act may be made as follows; (that is to say,)

1. Any Contract which if made between private Persons would be by Law required to be in Writing, and if made according to *English* Law to be under Seal, may be made on behalf of the Company in Writing under the Common Seal of the Company, and such Contract may be in the same Manner varied or discharged:
2. Any Contract which if made between private Persons would be by Law required to be in Writing, and signed by the Parties to be charged therewith, may be made on behalf of the Company in Writing signed by any Person acting under the express or implied Authority of the Company, and such Contract may in the same Manner be varied or discharged:
3. Any Contract which if made between private Persons would by Law be valid although made by Parol only, and not reduced into Writing, may be made by Parol on behalf of the Company by any Person acting under the express or implied Authority of the Company, and such Contract may in the same Way be varied or discharged:

And all Contracts made according to the Provisions herein contained shall be effectual in Law, and shall be binding upon the Company and their Successors, and all other Parties thereto, their Heirs, Executors, or Administrators, as the Case may be.

*Deeds.*

XLII. Any Company registered under this Act may, by Instrument or Writing under their Common Seal, empower any Person, either generally or in respect of any specified Matters, as their Attorney, to execute Deeds on their Behalf in any Place not situate in the United Kingdom; and every Deed signed by such Attorney, on behalf of the Company, and under his Seal, shall be binding on the Company to the same Extent as if it were under the Common Seal of the Company.

XLIII. A Promissory Note or Bill of Exchange shall be deemed to have been made, accepted, or endorsed on behalf of any Company registered under this Act, if made, accepted, or endorsed in the Name of the Company by any Person acting under the express or implied Authority of the Company.

XLIV. In any Mortgage made according to *English* Law by any Company registered under this Act there shall be implied the following Covenants (unless Words expressly negativing such Implication are contained therein); that is to say, a Covenant on the Part of the Company to pay the Money thereby secured, and Interest thereon, at the Time and Rate therein mentioned; a Covenant that they have Power to convey or assure the Property declared to be conveyed or assured to the Mortgagee free from Incumbrances; and a Covenant for further Assurance of such Property, at the Expense of the Company, to the Mortgagee or any Person claiming through, under, or in trust for him; and if a Power of Sale is thereby given such Power shall imply an Authority to sell by Public Auction or Private Contract, altogether or in Parcels, and to make, rescind, or vary Contracts for Sale or Resale without being liable for Loss, and also an Authority to give effectual Receipts for Purchase Monies, and such Mortgage may be in the Form marked H. in the Schedule hereto, or as near thereto as Circumstances admit.

XLV. In any Bond and Disposition in Security made according to *Scotch* Law by any Company registered under this Act there shall be implied the following Obligations and Undertakings (unless Words expressly negativing such Implication are contained therein); that is to say, an Obligation on the Part of the Company to pay the Mouey thereby secured, and Interest thereon, at the Time and Rate therein mentioned; an Undertaking that they have Power to convey the Property declared to be conveyed to the Heritable Creditor free from Incumbrances; and an Obligation to make and execute, at the Expense of the Company, in favour of the Heritable Creditor, or any Person claiming through, under, or in trust for him, any further Deed necessary to give Effect and Validity to the Security; and if a Power of Sale is thereby given, such Power shall imply an Authority to sell by Public Auction or Private Contract, altogether or in Parcels, and to make, rescind, or vary Contracts of Sale or Resale, without being liable for Loss, and also an Authority to give effectual Receipts for Purchase Monies; and such Bond and Disposition in Security may be in the Form marked I. in the Schedule hereto, or as near thereto as Circumstances admit, and shall be registered in the General or Particular or Burgh Register of Sasines, as the Case may be, and being so registered shall be equivalent to a Bond and Disposition in Security in ordinary Form, containing Power of Sale, with Sasine thereon, duly recorded in the Register of Sasines.

XLVI. In any Conveyance or Assurance made according to *English* Law by any Company registered under this Act there shall be implied (unless Words expressly negativing such Implication are contained therein) the following Covenants on the Part of the Company; (that is to say,)

A Covenant that, notwithstanding any Act or Default done by the Company, they were at the Time of the Execution of such Conveyance or Assurance seized or possessed of the Lands or Premises thereby conveyed or assured for an indefeasible Estate of Inheritance in Fee Simple, free from Incumbrances occasioned by them, or otherwise for such Estate or Interest as therein expressed to be assured, free from Incumbrances occasioned by them:

A Covenant that the Person to whom such Lands or Premises are conveyed or assured, his Heirs, Successors, Executors, Administrators, and Assigns, (as the Case may be,) shall quietly enjoy the same against the Company and their Successors, and all other Persons claiming under them, and be indemnified and saved harmless by the Company and their Successors from all Incumbrances occasioned by the Company:

A Covenant for further Assurance of such Lands or Premises at the Expense of the Person to whom the same are conveyed or assured, his Heirs, Successors, Executors, Administrators, or Assigns, (as the Case may be,) by the Company or their Successors, and all other Persons claiming under them.

XLVII. In any Disposition of Heritable Property granted according to *Scotch* Law by any Company registered under this Act there shall be implied, unless Words expressly excluding such Implication are contained therein, an Obligation of absolute Warrandice, and an Obligation to complete the Company's Title at its own Expense so far as necessary to validate or give full Effect to such Disposition, and an Obligation to grant also at its own Expense any further Deeds which may be necessary to render such Disposition effectual.

*Examination of Affairs of Company.*

XLVIII. Upon the Application of One Fifth in Number and Value of the Shareholders of any Company registered under this Act, the Board of Trade may appoint One or more competent Inspectors to examine into the Affairs of the Company, and to report thereon in such Manner as the Board of Trade directs.

XLIX. It shall be the Duty of all Officers and Agents of the Company to produce for the Examination of the Inspectors all Books and Documents in their Custody or Power: Any Inspector may examine upon Oath the Officers and Agents of the Company in relation to its Business, and may administer such Oath accordingly: If any Officer or Agent refuses to produce any such Book or Document, or to answer any Question relating to the Affairs of the Company, he shall incur a Penalty not exceeding Five Pounds in respect of each Offence.

L. Upon the Conclusion of the Examination the Inspectors shall report their Opinion to the Board of Trade: Such Report shall be written or printed, as the Board of Trade directs: A Copy shall be forwarded by the Board of Trade to the registered Office of the Company, and a further Copy shall, at the Request of the Shareholders upon whose Application the Inspection was made, be delivered to them or to any One or more of them: All Expenses of and incidental to any such Examination as aforesaid shall be defrayed by the Shareholders upon whose Application the Inspectors were appointed.

LI. Any Company registered under this Act may in General Meeting appoint Inspectors for the Purpose of examining into the Affairs of the Company: The Inspectors so appointed shall have the same Powers and perform the same Duties as Inspectors appointed by the Board of Trade, with this Exception, that, instead of making their Report to the Board of Trade, they shall make the same in such Manner and to such Persons as the Company in General Meeting directs, and the Officers and Agents of the Company shall incur the same Penalties, in case of any Refusal to produce any Book or Document to such Inspectors, or to answer any Question, as they would have incurred if such Inspectors had been appointed by the Board of Trade.

LII. A Copy of the Report of any Inspectors appointed under this Act, authenticated by the Seal of the Company into whose Affairs they have madc Inspection, shall be admissible as Evidence in any legal Proceeding.

*Notices.*

LIII. Any Summons or Notice requiring to be served upon the Company may, except in

Cases where a particular Mode of Service is directed, be served by leaving the same, or sending it through the Post addressed to the Company, at their registered Office, or by giving it to any Director, Secretary, or other principal Officer of the Company.

LIV. Notice by Letter shall be posted in such Time as to admit of the Letter being delivered in the due Course of Delivery within the Period (if any) prescribed for the giving of such Notice; and in proving such Service it shall be sufficient to prove that such Notice was properly directed, and that it was put into the Post Office at such Time as aforesaid.

LV. Any Summons, Notice, Writ, or Proceeding requiring Authentication by the Company may be signed by any Director, Secretary, or other authorized Officer of the Company, and need not be under the Common Seal of the Company, and the same may be in Writing or in Print, or partly in Writing and partly in Print.

*Legal Proceedings.*

LVI. All Offences under this Act made punishable by any Penalty may be prosecuted summarily before Two or more Justices, as to *England* in manner directed by an Act passed in the Session holden in the Eleventh and Twelfth Years of the Reign of Her Majesty Queen *Victoria*, Chapter Forty-three, intituled *An Act to facilitate the Performance of the Duties of Justices of the Peace out of Sessions within* England *and* Wales *with respect to summary Convictions and Orders;* and as to *Scotland,* before Two or more Justices or the Sheriff of the County, in the Manner directed by the

Act passed in the Session of Parliament holden in the Seventeenth and Eighteenth Years of the Reign of Her Majesty Queen *Victoria*, Chapter One hundred and four, intituled *An Act to amend and consolidate the Acts relating to Merchant Shipping*, as regards Offences in *Scotland* against that Act, not being Offences by that Act described as Felonies and Misdemeanours; and as to *Ireland*, in the Manner directed by the Act passed in the Session holden in the Fourteenth and Fifteenth Years of the Reign of Her Majesty Queen *Victoria*, Chapter Ninety-three, intituled *An Act to consolidate and amend the Acts regulating the Proceedings of Petty Sessions and the Duties of Justices of the Peace and of Quarter Sessions in* Ireland, or any Act passed for the Amendment of the above-mentioned Act.

LVII. The Justices or Sheriff imposing any Penalty under this Act may direct the whole or any Part thereof to be applied in or towards Payment of the Costs of the Proceedings, or in or towards the rewarding the Person upon whose Information or at whose Suit such Penalty has been recovered; and subject to such Direction, all Penalties shall be paid into the Receipt of Her Majesty's Exchequer, in such Manner as the Treasury may direct, and shall be carried to and form Part of the Consolidated Fund of the United Kingdom.

### *Alteration of Forms.*

LVIII. The Board of Trade may from Time to Time make such Alterations in the Forms and Tables contained in the Schedule hereto as they deem requisite: They shall publish any Form or Table when altered in the *London Gazette*, and upon such Publication being made, it shall have the same Form as if it were included in the Schedule to this Act.

---

## PART III.

### WINDING-UP.

#### *Preliminary.*

LIX. The Provisions of this Act relating to the Winding-up of Companies shall apply to all Companies registered under this Act, and to all Companies registered under the Act passed in the Eighth Year of the Reign of Her present Majesty, Chapter One hundred and ten, and intituled *An Act for the Registration, Incorporation, and Regulation of Joint Stock Companies* from and after the Date at which they have obtained Registration under this Act in manner herein-after mentioned, but not any other Companies.

LX. The Expression "the Court," as used in the Third Part of this Act, shall mean the following Authorities; (that is to say,)

In the Case of a Company engaged in working any Mine within and subject to the Jurisdiction of the Stannaries,—the Court of the Vice-Warden of the Stannaries:

In the Case of a Limited Company registered in *England* that is not engaged in working any such Mine as aforesaid,—the Court of Bankruptcy having Jurisdiction in the Place in which the registered Office of the Company is situate:

In the Case of a Limited Company registered in *Ireland*, whose registered nominal Capital does not exceed Five thousand Pounds, —the Commissioners of Bankruptcy in *Ireland.*

In all Cases not herein-before provided for, the Court shall mean as respects Companies registered in *England* the High Court of Chancery of *England,* as respects Companies registered in *Scotland* the Court of Session in either Division thereof, and as respects Companies registered in *Ireland* the Court of Chancery of *Ireland.*

And any Court to which Jurisdiction is given by the Third Part of this Act, not being the Court of Chancery or the Court of Session, shall, in addition to its ordinary Powers, have the same Power of enforcing any Orders made by it in pursuance of this Act, if in *England,* as the Court of Chancery has, if in *Ireland,* as the Court of Chancery in *Ireland* has, in relation to Matters within the Jurisdiction of such Courts respectively.

LXI. In the event of any Company being wound-up by the Court or voluntarily, the existing Shareholders shall be liable to contribute to the Assets of the Company to an Amount sufficient to pay the Debts of the Company, and the Costs, Charges, and Expenses of winding-up the same, with this Qualification, that if the Company is limited no Contribution shall be required from any Shareholder exceeding the Amount, if any, unpaid on the Shares held by him.

LXII. In the event of any Company other than a Limited Company being wound-up by the Court or voluntarily, any Person who has ceased to be a Shareholder within the Period of Three Years prior to the Commencement of the Winding-up shall be deemed, for the Purposes of Contribution towards Payment of the Debts of the Company, and the Costs, Charges, and Expenses of winding-up the same, to be an existing Shareholder, and shall have in all respects the same Rights, and be subject to the same Liabilities to Creditors, as if he had not so ceased to be a Shareholder, with this Exception, that he shall not be liable in respect of any Debt of the Company contracted after the Time at which he ceased to be a Shareholder.

LXIII. In the event of any Limited Company being wound-up by the Court or voluntarily, any Person who has ceased to be a Holder of any Share or Shares within the Period of One Year prior to the Commencement of the Winding-up shall be deemed, for the Purposes of Contribution towards Payment of the Debts of the Company, and the Costs Charges, and Expenses of winding-up the same, to be an existing Holder of such Share or Shares, and shall have in all respects the same Rights and be subject to the same Liabilities to Creditors as if he had not so ceased to be a Shareholder.

LXIV. The Winding-up shall, if the Company is wound-up by the Court, be deemed to commence at the Time of the Presentation of such Petition as is herein-after required to be presented to the Court, and if the Company is wound-up voluntarily, be deemed to commence at the Time of the passing of the Resolution authorizing such Winding-up.

LXV. Any existing or former Shareholder upon whom Calls are authorized to be made by the Third Part of this Act is herein-after called "a Contributory," and the Representatives of any deceased Contributory shall be liable in a due Course of Administration to the same Extent as such Contributory would be liable under the Third Part of this Act, if alive.

LXVI. For the Purpose of ascertaining the Liability of existing and former Shareholders as between themselves, the following Rule shall be adopted; (that is to say,)

1. In the Case of a Company other than a Limited Company every Transferree of Shares shall, in a Degree proportioned to the Shares transferred, indemnify the Transferror against all existing and future Debts of the Company:

2. In the Case of a Limited Company every Transferree shall indemnify the Transferror against all Calls made or accrued due on the Shares transferred subsequently to the Transfer.

### *Winding-up by Court.*

LXVII. A Company may be wound-up by the Court under the following Circumstances; (that is to say,)

1. Whenever the Company in General Meeting has passed a Special Resolution requiring the Company to be wound-up by the Court:

2. Whenever the Company does not commence its Business within a Year from its Incorporation, or suspends its Business for the Space of a whole Year.

3. Whenever the Shareholders are reduced in Number to less than Seven:

4. Whenever the Company is unable to pay its Debts :
5. Whenever Three Fourths of the Capital of the Company have been lost or become unavailable.

LXVIII. A Company shall be deemed to be unable to pay its Debts,

1. Whenever a Creditor to whom the Company is indebted in a Sum exceeding Fifty Pounds then due has served on the Company, by leaving the same at their registered Office, a Demand under his Hand requiring the Company to pay the Sum so due, and the Company have for the Space of Three Weeks succeeding the Service of such Demand neglected to pay such Sum, or to secure or compound for the same to the Satisfaction of the Creditor.
2. Whenever, in *England* and *Ireland*, Execution issued on a Judgment, Decree, or Order obtained in any Court in favour of any Creditor in any Suit or other legal Proceeding instituted by such Creditor against the Company is returned unsatisfied, in whole or in part, by the Sheriff of the County in which the registered Office of the Company is situate :
3. Whenever, in *Scotland*, the Induciæ of a Charge for Payment on an Extract, Decree, or an Extract registered Bond, or an Extract registered Protest, have expired without Payment being made.

LXIX. Any Application for the winding-up of a Company shall be by Petition, and there shall be filed or lodged at the Time when such Petition is presented an Affidavit verifying the same: Such Petition may, in Cases where the Company is unable to pay its Debts, be presented either by a Creditor or a Contributory, but where any other Ground is alleged for winding-up the Company a Contributory alone is entitled to present the Petition.

LXX. Upon the Hearing of any Petition presented by a Creditor, the Court may dismiss such Petition, with or without Costs, to be paid by the Petitioner, or it may make an Order or pronounce an Interlocutor directing the Company, by a Day to be named in the Order or Interlocutor, to pay or secure Payment to the Creditor of all Monies that may be proved due to him, together with such Costs as the Court may direct; or the Court may, if it so thinks fit, on the Hearing of such Petition, make an Order or Decree for winding-up the Company in the first instance, or such other Order as it deems just.

LXXI. If at the Expiration of the Time named in such Order or Interlocutor such Payment is not made, or Security given, the Court may thereupon make an Order or Decree for winding-up the Company.

LXXII. Upon the Hearing of a Petition presented by a Contributory, the Court may dismiss such Petition, with or without Costs, to be paid by the Petitioner, or it may make an Order or Decree directing the Company to be wound-up, or such other Order or Decree as it deems just.

LXXIII. After the Date of such Order or Decree for winding-up the Company, all Suits and Actions against the Company shall, if the

Court so orders, be stayed. No Director or other Officer of the Company shall, without the Sanction of the Court, dispose of any of the Property, Effects, or Things in Action of the Company, and no Transfer of any Shares shall be valid without the Sanction of the Court: A Copy of such Order or Decree shall forthwith be reported by the Company to the Registrar of Joint Stock Companies, who shall make a Minute thereof in his Books relating to the Company.

LXXIV. In Cases where the Court of Chancery in *England* or *Ireland* makes an Order for winding-up a Company, it may, if it thinks fit, direct all or any subsequent Proceedings for winding-up the same to be had in the Court of Bankruptcy having Jurisdiction in the Place in which the registered Office of the Company is situate, or if the Company is formed for the Purpose of working any such Mine as is within and subject to the Jurisdiction of the Stannaries, in the Court of the Vice-Warden of the Stannaries; and upon such Order being made the Court therein named shall have the same Jurisdiction and exercise the same Powers with respect to winding-up such Company as it would have and exercise in a Case by this Act declared to be within its Jurisdiction.

LXXV. As soon as may be after making an Order or Decree for winding-up the Company the Court shall cause the Assets of the Company to be collected, and applied in discharge of its Liabilities in a due Course of Administration.

LXXVI. Any such Conveyance, Mortgage, Delivery of Goods, Payment, Execution, or other Act relating to Property, as would, if made or done by or against any individual Trader, be deemed in the event of his Bankruptcy to have been made or done by way of undue or fraudulent Preference of any Creditor of such Trader, shall, if made or done by or against any Company registered under this Act, be deemed, in the event of an Order being made for winding-up such Company, to have been made or done by way of undue or fraudulent Preference of such Creditor of such Company, and shall be invalid accordingly; and for the Purposes of this Section the Presentation of a Petition for winding-up a Company shall be deemed to correspond with the filing of a Petition for Adjudication of Bankruptcy in the Case of an individual Trader; and any Conveyance or Assignment made by any Company registered under this Act of all its Estate and Effects to Trustees for the Benefit of all its Creditors shall be void to all Intents.

LXXVII. The Court may, after it has made an Order or Decree for winding-up the Company, summon before it any Person known or suspected to have in his Possession any of the Estate or Effects of the Company, or supposed to be indebted to the Company, or any Person whom the Court may deem capable of giving Information concerning the Trade, Dealings, Estate, or Effects of the Company; and the Court may require any such Person to produce any Books, Papers, Deeds, Writings, or other Documents in his Custody or Power which may appear to the Court requisite to the full Disclosure of any of the Matters which the Court thinks necessary to be inquired into for the Purpose of winding-up the Company; and if any Person so summoned refuses to come before the Court at the Time appointed, having no lawful Impediment (made known to the

Court at the Time of its sitting, and allowed by it), the Court may by Warrant authorize and direct the Persons therein named for that Purpose to apprehend such Person, and bring him before the Court for Examination.

LXXVIII. The Court may examine upon Oath, either by Word of Mouth or upon written Interrogatories, any Person appearing or brought before them in manner aforesaid, concerning the Trade, Dealings, Estate, or Effects of the Company, and may reduce into Writing the Answers of every such Person, and require him to sign and subscribe the same.

LXXIX. If any Director, or Contributory of any Company for the winding-up of which an Order or Decree has been made under this Act destroys, mutilates, alters, or falsifies any Books, Papers, Writings, or Securities, or makes or is privy to the making of any false or fraudulent Entry in any Register, Book of Account, or other Document belonging to the Company, with Intent to defraud the Creditors or Contributories of such Company or any of them, every Person so offending shall be deemed to be guilty of a Misdemeanor, and upon being convicted shall be liable to Imprisonment for any Term not exceeding Two Years, with or without Hard Labour.

LXXX. If any Attachment, Sequestration, or Execution is issued against any Company, by virtue whereof the Estate and Effects of the Company, or any of them, may be attached, sequestered, or taken in Execution, at any Time within Three Months next before the Filing or Presentation of the Petition for winding-up the Company, such Attachment, Sequestration, or taking in Execution shall be void in favour of the Liquidators of the Company, as against the attaching, sequestrating, or Execution Creditor, whether the same has been completely executed or not, except that such Creditor shall, if the Attachment, Sequestration, or Execution would have been valid but for this Provision, be entitled to retain out of any Money already realized, his Costs of Suit, and of the Attachment, Sequestration, or Execution, or to proceed with the Attachment, Sequestration, or Execution for the Purpose of realizing such Costs; but on Satisfaction of such Costs, or on Tender of the Amount thereof by the Liquidators to the Creditor, it shall be lawful for the Liquidators to recover from such Creditor the Property so attached, sequestrated, and taken in Execution, and the Proceeds of such Property, or the Residue thereof, as the Case may be.

LXXXI. All Books, Accounts, and Documents of the Company, and of the Liquidators herein-after mentioned, shall, as between the Contributories of the Company, be *primâ facie* Evidence of the Truth of all Matters therein contained, and purporting to be therein recorded.

LXXXII. The Court may, at any Time after making an Order or Decree for winding-up a Company, and before it has ascertained the Sufficiency of the Assets of the Company, or the Debts in respect of which the several Classes of Contributories are liable, make Calls on all or any of the Contributories, to the Extent of their Liability, for Payment of all or any Sums it deems necessary to satisfy the Debts of the Company and the Costs of winding it up, and it may, in making a Call, take into consideration the Probability that some of the Contributories upon whom the same is made may partly or wholly fail to pay their respective Portions of the same.

LXXXIII. All Monies received under the Direction of the Court on account of the Sale or Conversion of any of the Assets of the Company, or in respect of Calls made on any Contributories, or of any other Matter, with the Exception of such Balance, if any, as the Official Liquidators may, with the Sanction of the Court, retain in their Hands for the Payment of current Expenses, shall in *England* be paid into the Bank of *England* or some Branch thereof, and in *Ireland* into the Bank of *Ireland* or some Branch thereof, and in *Scotland* into One of the incorporated or chartered Banks in *Scotland*, to the Credit of such Account as the Court may direct; and no Money standing to such Account shall be paid out by the Bank except upon Cheques signed in such Manner as the Court directs.

LXXXIV. The Court may, at any Time after the Presentation of a Petition for winding up a Company, and either before or after making an Order for winding-up the same, upon the Application by Motion of any Creditor or Contributory of such Company, restrain further Proceedings in any Action or Suit against the Company, or appoint a Receiver of the Estate and Effects of the Company; it may also, by Notice or Advertisement require all Creditors to present and prove their Claims within a certain Time, or be precluded from the Benefit of any Distribution which may be made before such Claim is proved.

LXXXV. The Court may, at any Time after an Order or Decree has been made for winding up a Company, upon the Application by Motion of any Creditor or Contributory of the Company, and upon Proof to the Satisfaction of the Court that all Proceedings in relation to such Winding-up ought to be stayed, make an Order staying the same, either altogether or for a limited Time, on such Terms and subject to such Conditions as it deems fit.

LXXXVI. As soon as the Creditors are satisfied, the Court shall proceed to adjust the Rights of the Contributories amongst themselves; and to distribute any Surplus that may remain amongst the Parties entitled thereto, and for the Purposes of such Adjustment it may make Calls on the Contributories to the Extent of their Liability for Payment of such Sums as it deems necessary; and it may, in making a Call, take into consideration the Probability that some of the Contributories upon whom the same is made may partly or wholly fail to pay their respective Portions of the same.

LXXXVII. The Court may make such Order as to the Priority and Payment out of the Estate of the Company of the Costs, Charges, and Expenses incurred in winding-up any Company as it thinks just.

*Official Liquidators.*

LXXXVIII. For the Purpose of conducting the Proceedings in winding-up a Company, and assisting the Court therein, there shall be appointed a Person or Persons to be called an Official Liquidator or Official Liquidators; and such Appointment shall be made as follows; that is to say,

In Cases within the Jurisdiction of the Court of Chancery in *England* or *Ireland*, or of the Court of Session in *Scotland*, or of the Court of the Stannaries, the Court having

Jurisdiction may, after requiring the Security, appoint such Persons or Person, either provisionally or otherwise, as he thinks fit, to the Office of Official Liquidators: it may from Time to Time remove any Person or Persons so appointed, and fill up any Vacancy occasioned by such Removal or by the Death or Resignation of any such Appointee or Appointees; if One Person only is appointed, he shall have all the Powers hereby given to several Liquidators; if more Persons than One are appointed, the Court shall declare whether any Act hereby required or authorized to be done by the Official Liquidators may be done by all or any One or more of such Persons:

In Cases within the Jurisdiction of any Court of Bankruptcy, the Official Assignee to be named by the Court shall be the Official Liquidator; but it shall be lawful, in Cases where the Winding-up takes place at the Suit of a Creditor, for the major Part in Value of the Creditors assembled at a Meeting to be held for the Purpose, and in Cases where the Winding-up takes place at the Suit of a Contributory, for the major Part in Value of the Contributories assembled at a Meeting to be held for the Purpose, to appoint an Official Liquidator to act concurrently with the Official Liquidator so named by the Court.

LXXXIX. The Official Liquidators or Liquidator shall be described by the Style of the Official Liquidators or Official Liquidator of the particular Company in respect of which they or he are or is appointed, and not by their or his individual Names or Name; they or he shall take into their or his Custody all the Property, Effects, and Things in Actions of the Company, and shall perform such Duties in reference to the winding-up of the Company as may be imposed by the Court.

XC. The Official Liquidators shall have Powers, with the Sanction of the Court, to do the following Things:

To bring or defend any Action, Suit, or Prosecution, or other legal Proceeding, Civil or Criminal, in the Name and on behalf of the Company:

To carry on the Business of the Company, so far as may be necessary for the beneficial Winding-up of the same:

To sell the Real and Personal and Heritable and Moveable Property, Effects, and Things in Action of the Company by Public Auction or Private Contract, with Power, if they think fit, to transfer the whole thereof to any Person or Company, or to sell the same in Parcels:

To execute, in the Name and on behalf of the Company, all Deeds, Receipts, and other Documents they may think necessary, and for that Purpose to use, when necessary, the Company's Seal:

To refer Disputes to Arbitration, and compromise any Debts or Claims:

To prove, claim, rank, and draw a Dividend, in the Matter of the Bankruptcy or Insolvency or Sequestration of any Contributory, for any Balance against the Estate of such Contributory, and to take and receive Dividends in respect of such Balance, in the Matter of Bankruptcy or Insolvency or Sequestration, as a separate Debt due from such Bankrupt or Insolvent, and rateably with the other separate Creditors:

To draw, accept, make, and endorse any Bill

of Exchange or Promissory Note, and also to raise upon the Security of the Assets of the Company from Time to Time any requisite Sum or Sums of Money; and the drawing, accepting, making, or endorsing of every such Bill of Exchange or Promissory Note as aforesaid on behalf of the Company shall have the same Effect with respect to the Liability of such Company as if such Bill or Note had been drawn, accepted, made, or endorsed by such Company in the course of carrying on the Business thereof:

To do and execute all such other Things as may be necessary for winding-up the Affairs of the Company and distributing its Assets.

XCI. The Official Liquidators may, with the Approval of the Court, appoint a Solicitor or Law Agent, and such Clerks or Officers as may be necessary to assist them in the Performance of their Duties: There shall be paid to such Solicitor or Law Agent, Clerks and Officers, such Remuneration by way of Fees or otherwise as may be allowed by the Court.

XCII. There shall be paid to the Official Liquidators such Salary or Remuneration, by way of Per-centage or otherwise, as the Court directs.

XCIII. When the Affairs of the Company have been completely wound-up, the Court shall make an Order or Decree declaring the Company to be dissolved from the Date of such Order or Decree, and the Company shall be dissolved accordingly.

XCIV. Any Order or Decree so made shall

be reported by the Official Liquidators to the Registrar of Joint Stock Companies, who shall make a Minute accordingly in his Books of the Dissolution of such Company.

XCV. In *England*, the Lord Chancellor of *Great Britain*, with the Advice and Consent of the Master of the Rolls and any One of the Vice-Chancellors for the Time being, or with the Advice and Consent of any Two of the Vice-Chancellors, may, as often as Circumstances require, make such Rules concerning the Mode of proceeding to be had for winding-up a Company in the Court of Chancery as may from Time to Time seem necessary; but, until such Rules are made, the general Practice of the Court of Chancery, including the Practice hitherto in use in winding-up Companies, shall, so far as the same is applicable, and not inconsistent with this Act, apply to all Proceedings for winding-up a Company, and Official Liquidators shall be considered as occupying in all respects the Place of an Official Manager.

XCVI. In *Ireland*, the Lord Chancellor of *Ireland* may, as respects the winding-up of Companies in *Ireland*, with the Advice and Consent of the Master of the Rolls in *Ireland*, exercise the same Power of making Rules as is by this Act herein-before given to the Lord Chancellor of *Great Britain*; but, until such Rules are made, the general Practice of the Court of Chancery in *Ireland*, including the Practice hitherto in use in *Ireland* in winding-up Companies, shall, so far as the same is applicable, and not inconsistent with this Act, apply to all Proceedings for winding-up a Company, and Official Liquidators shall in all respects be considered as occupying the Place of an Official Manager.

XCVII. In *Scotland* the Court of Session may, by Act of Sederunt, exercise the same Power of making Rules of Practice as is hereinbefore given to the Lord Chancellor of *Great Britain* as regards *England,* but, until such Rules are made, the general Practice of the Court of Session in Suits pending in such Court shall, so far as the same is applicable, and not inconsistent with this Act, apply to all Proceedings for winding-up a Company, and Official Liquidators shall in all respects be considered as possessing the same Powers as any Trustee on a Bankrupt Estate.

XCVIII. The Vice-Warden of the Stannaries may from Time to Time, with the Approval of the Lord Chancellor of *Great Britain,* make such General Rules as may be necessary or expedient for the Purpose of carring into execution the Powers conferred by this Act upon the Court of the said Vice-Warden; but, subject to such Rules, the general Practice of the said Court in Cases within the Jurisdiction thereof shall, so far as the same is applicable, and not inconsistent with this Act, apply to all Proceedings under this Act, and any Order made by the Vice-Warden of the Stannaries may be enforced in the same Manner in which Orders made in Proceedings within the ordinary Jurisdiction of such Court are enforced; and for the Purpose of Jurisdiction any Company registered under this Act engaged in working any Mine within and subject to the Jurisdiction of the Stannaries shall be deemed to be resident within the Stannaries, and at the Place where such Mine is situate: It shall be competent for the Vice-Warden in any Suit instituted against any Shareholder or Contributory of a Company so registered to authorize the Service of Process on such Shareholder or Contributory in any Part of *England* or *Wales*; provided, that it shall be lawful for the Lord Warden to remit at once any Cause or Matter pending before him on Appeal against any Decree or Order of the Court made in pursuance of the Power conferred upon it by this Act for the winding-up of such a Company to the Court of Appeal in Chancery, which shall thereupon have Power to hear and determine such Appeal and to make such Order or Orders therein as may seem fit.

XCIX. Any Two Commissioners of Bankruptcy appointed by the Lord Chancellor of *Great Britain* may, as respects the Courts of Bankruptcy in *England*, and the Commissioners of Bankrupt in *Ireland* may, as respects the Courts of Bankruptcy in *Ireland*, make Rules as they respectively from Time to Time, but subject to the Approval of the Lord Chancellors of *Great Britain* and *Ireland* respectively, think fit, for the Purpose of regulating the Proceedings in such Courts for winding-up Companies, but, subject to such Rules, the general Practice of the Courts of Bankruptcy in *England* and *Ireland* respectively, in Cases within the ordinary Jurisdiction of such Courts, shall, so far as the same is applicable, and not inconsistent with this Act, apply to all Proceedings under this Act; and any Order made by any Commissioner of Bankruptcy in such Proceedings may be enforced in the same Manner in which Orders made in Proceedings within the ordinary Jurisdiction of such Court are enforced.

C. The Lord Chancellor of *Great Britain* as respects the Courts of Chancery and Bankruptcy in *England*, the Lord Chancellor of *Ireland* as respects the Courts of Chancery and Bankruptcy in *Ireland*, the Court of Session in

*Scotland* by Act of Sederunt as respects Proceedings in such Court, may make Rules specifying the Fees to be paid in respect of Proceedings taken under the Third Part of this Act for winding-up a Company in such Courts respectively, and the Fees so paid in any Court of Chancery or Bankruptcy shall be applied in the Manner in which Fees taken in such Courts in ordinary Proceedings are applied; and as respects Fees to be paid in like Proceedings in the Court of the Vice-Warden of the Stannaries, it shall be lawful for the Vice-Warden to authorize Fees to be taken not exceeding in Number or Amount the Fees so authorized from Time to Time by the Lord Chancellor of *Great Britain* to be paid in Courts of Bankruptcy, and the Council of the Prince of *Wales*, or the Special Commissioners for managing the Affairs of the Duchy of *Cornwall*, as the Case may be, may direct in what Manner the Monies arising from such Fees are to be applied towards the Annual Expenses of the Court of Stannaries or towards the Payment or in augmentation of the present official Salaries.

CI. The District Commissioners of the Court of Bankruptcy and the Judges of the County Courts in *England* who sit at Places more than Twenty Miles from the General Post Office, and the Commissioners of Bankrupt and the Assistant Barristers and Recorders in *Ireland*, and the Sheriffs of Counties in *Scotland*, shall be Commissioners for the Purpose of taking Evidence under the Third Part of this Act in Cases where any Company is wound-up by the Courts of Chancery in *England* or *Ireland* or by the Court of Session in *Scotland;* and it shall be lawful for such Court to refer the whole or any Part of the Examination of any Witnesses under the Third Part of this Act to any such Commissioner, although such Commissioner is out of the Jurisdiction of the Court by which the Order or Decree for winding-up the Company was made; and every such Commissioner shall, in addition to any Power of summoning and examining Witnesses, and requiring the Production or Delivery of Documents, and certifying or punishing Defaults by Witnesses, which he might lawfully exercise as a District Commissioner of the Court of Bankruptcy, Judge of a County Court, Commissioner of Bankrupt, Assistant Barrister, or Recorder, or as a Sheriff of a County, have in the Matter so referred to him all the same Powers of summoning and examining Witnesses, and requiring the Production or Delivery of Documents, and punishing Defaults by Witnesses, and allowing Costs and Charges and Expenses to Witnesses, as the Court which made the Order for winding-up the Company has; and the Examination so taken shall be returned or reported to such last-mentioned Court in such Manner as it directs.

*Voluntary Winding-up of Company.*

CII. A Company may be wound-up voluntarily,

1. Whenever the Period, if any, fixed for the Duration of the Company by the Articles of Association expires, or whenever the Event, if any, occurs upon the Occurrence of which it is provided by the Articles of Association that the Company is to be dissolved:
2. Whenever the Company in General Meeting has passed a Special Resolution requiring the Company to be wound-up voluntarily.

Whenever a Company is wound-up voluntarily the Company shall, from the Date of the Commencement of such Winding-up, cease to carry on its Business, except so far as may be required for the beneficial Winding-up thereof, but its Corporate State and all its Corporate Powers shall, notwithstanding any Provision to the contrary in its Articles of Association, continue until the Affairs of the Company are wound-up.

CIII. Notice of any Special Resolution to wind-up a Company voluntarily shall be given, as respects Companies registered in *England* in the *London Gazette*, as respects Companies registered in *Scotland* in the *Edinburgh Gazette*, and as respects Companies registered in *Ireland* in the *Dublin Gazette*.

CIV. The following Consequences shall ensue upon the voluntary Winding-up of a Company:

1. The Property of the Company shall be applied in satisfaction of its Liabilities, and, subject thereto, shall, unless it be otherwise provided by the Articles of Association, be distributed amongst the Shareholders in proportion to their Shares:
2. Liquidators shall be appointed for the Purpose of winding-up the Affairs of the Company and distributing the Property:
3. The Company in General Meeting may appoint such Person or Persons as it thinks fit to be a Liquidator or Liquidators, and may fix the Remuneration to be paid to them:
4. If One Person only is appointed, all the

Provisions herein contained in reference to several Liquidators shall apply to him:

5. When several Liquidators are appointed, every Power hereby given may be exercised by any Two of them:

6. The Liquidators may at any time after the passing of the Resolution for winding up the Company, and before they have ascertained the Sufficiency of the Assets of the Company, or the Debts in respect of which the several Classes of Contributors are liable, call on all or any of the Contributories to the Extent of their Liability to pay all or any Sums they deem necessary to satisfy the Debts of the Company and the Costs of winding it up, and they may in making a Call take into Consideration the Probability that some of the Contributories upon whom the same is made may partly or wholly fail to pay their respective Portions of the same:

7. The Liquidators shall have all Powers herein-before vested in Official Liquidators, and may exercise the same without the Intervention of the Court:

8. All Books, Papers, and Documents in the Hands of the Liquidators shall at all reasonable Times be open to the Inspection of the Shareholders:

9. When the Creditors are satisfied, the Liquidators shall proceed to adjust the Rights of the Contributories amongst themselves, and for the Purposes of such Adjustment they may make Calls on all the Contributories to the Extent of their Liability for any Sums they may deem necessary, and they may in making a Call take into Consideration the Proba-

bility that some of the Contributories upon whom the same is made may partly or wholly fail to pay their respective Portions of the same:

10. As soon as the Affairs of the Company are fully wound-up, the Liquidators shall make up an Account showing the Manner in which such Winding-up has been conducted, and the Property of the Company disposed of; and such Account, with the Vouchers thereof, shall be laid before such Person or Persons as may be appointed by the Company to inspect the same; and upon such Inspection being concluded the Liquidators shall proceed to call a General Meeting of the Shareholders for the Purpose of considering such Account; but no such Meeting shall be deemed to be duly held unless One Month's previous Notice, specifying the Time, Place, and Object of such Meeting, has been published, as respects Companies registered in *England* in the *London Gazette,* and as respects Companies registered in *Scotland* in the *Edinburgh Gazette,* and as respects Companies registered in *Ireland* in the *Dublin Gazette.*

11. Such General Meeting shall not enter npon any Business except the Consideration of the Account; but the Meeting may proceed to the Consideration thereof, notwithstanding the Quorum required by any Regulation of the Company to be present at General Meetings, is not present thereat; and if, on Consideration, the Meeting is of opinion that the Affairs of the Company have been fairly wound-up, they shall pass a Resolution to that

Effect, and thereupon the Liquidators shall publish a Notice of such Resolution, as respects Companies registered in *England* in the *London Gazette,* and as respects Companies registered in *Scotland* in the *Edinburgh Gazette,* and as respects Companies registered in *Ireland* in the *Dublin Gazette,* aad shall also make a Return to the Registrar of Joint Stock Companies of such Resolution, and on the Expiration of One Month from the Date of the Registration of such Return the Company shall be deemed to be dissolved :

12. If within One Year after the passing of a Resolution for a winding-up the Affairs of the Company such Affairs are not wound-up, the Liquidators shall immediately thereafter make up an Account showing the State of the Affairs and the Progress which has been made in winding-up down to that Date, and they shall add thereto a Report stating the Reason why the Winding-up has not been completed, and a General Meeting shall be called to consider the same, and so on from Year to Year until the Winding-up of the Affairs of the Company is completed :

All Costs, Charges, and Expenses properly incurred in the voluntary Winding-up of a Company, including the Remuneration of the Liquidators, shall be payable out of the Assets of the Company in priority to all other Claims.

CV. The voluntary Winding-up of a Company shall not prejudice the Right of any Creditor of such Company to institute Proceedings for the Purpose of having the same wound-up by the Court.

## PART IV.

### REGISTRATION OFFICE.

CVI. The Registration of Companies shall be conducted as follows; (that is to say)

1. The Board of Trade may from Time to Time appoint such Registrars, Assistant Registrars, Clerks and Servants as they may think necessary for the Registration of Companies under this Act, and remove them at pleasure:
2. The Board of Trade may make such Regulations as they think fit with respect to the Duties to be performed by any such Registrars, Assistant Registrars, Clerks, and Servants as aforesaid.
3. The Board of Trade may from Time to Time determine the Place or Places at which Offices for the Registration of Companies are to be established: Provided always, that there shall be at all Times maintained in each of the Three Parts of the United Kingdom at least One such Office, and that no Company shall be registered except at an Office within that Part of the United Kingdom in which by the Memorandum of Association the registered Office of the Company is declared to be established:
4. The Board of Trade may from Time to Time direct a Seal or Seals to be prepared for the Authentication of any Documents required for or connected with the Registration of Companies.
5. Every Person may inspect the Documents kept by the Registrar of Joint Stock

Companies; and there shall be paid for such Inspection such Fees as may be appointed by the Board of Trade, not exceeding One Shilling for each Inspection; and any Person may require a Copy or Extract of any Document or any Part of any Document, to be certified by the Registrar; and there shall be paid for such certified Copy or Extract such Fee as the Board of Trade may appoint, not exceeding Sixpence for each Folio of such Copy or Extract, or in *Scotland* for each Sheet of Two hundred Words; and such certified Copy shall be *primâ facie* Evidence of the Matters therein contained in all legal Proceedings whatever:

6. The existing Registrar, Assistant Registrars, Clerks, and other Officers and Servants in the Office for the Registration of Joint Stock Companies, shall, during the Pleasure of the Board of Trade, hold the Offices and receive the Salaries hitherto held and received by them, but they shall in the Execution of their Duties conform to any Regulations that may be issued by the Board of Trade:

7. There shall be paid to any Registrar, Assistant Registrar, Clerk, or Servant that may hereafter be employed in the Registration of Joint Stock Companies such Salary as the Board of Trade may, with the Sanction of the Commissioners of the Treasury, direct:

8. Whenever any Act is herein directed to be done to or by the Registrar of Joint Stock Companies, such Act shall, until the Board of Trade otherwise directs, be

done in *England* to or by the existing Registrar of Joint Stock Companies, or in his Absence by the Assistant Registrar, in *Scotland* to or by such Officer as the Board of Trade may appoint, and in *Ireland* to or by the existing Assistant Registrar of Joint Stock Companies for *Ireland;* but, in the event of the Board of Trade altering the Constitution of the existing Registry Office, such Act shall be done to or by such Officer or Officers and at such Place or Places with reference to the local Situation of the registered Offices of the Companies to be registered as the Board of Trade may appoint.

---

## PART V.

### REPEAL OF FORMER ACTS, AND TEMPORARY PROVISIONS

*Repeal.*

CVII. There shall be repealed,—

1. The Act passed in the Eighth Year of the Reign of Her present Majesty, Chapter One hundred and ten:
2. An Act passed in the Eleventh Year of the Reign of Her present Majesty, Chapter Seventy-eight, intituled *An Act to amend an Act for the Registration, Incorporation, and Regulation of Joint Stock Companies.*
3. The Limited Liability Act, 1855:

But such Repeal shall not take effect with respect to any Company completely registered under the said Act of the Eighth Year of

Her present Majesty until such Company has obtained Registration under this Act, as herein-after mentioned.

CVIII. The following Acts, that is to say,

1. An Act passed in the Eleventh Year of the Reign of Her present Majesty, Chapter Forty-five, and intituled *An Act to amend the Acts for facilitating the Winding-up of the Affairs of Joint Stock Companies unable to meet their pecuniary Engagements, and also to facilitate the Dissolution and Winding-up of Joint Stock Companies and other Partnerships:*

2. An Act passed in the Thirteenth Year of the Reign of Her present Majesty, Chapter One hundred and eight, and intituled *An Act to amend the Joint Stock Companies Winding-up Act,* 1848.

3. An Act passed in the Eighth Year of Her present Majesty, Chapter One hundred and eleven, and intituled *An Act for facilitating the Winding-up the Affairs of Joint Stock Companies unable to meet their pecuniary Engagements:*

4. An Act passed in the Ninth Year of the Reign of Her present Majesty, Chapter Ninety-eight, and intituled *An Act for facilitating the Winding-up the Affairs of Joint Stock Companies in* Ireland *unable to meet their pecuniary Engagements:*

shall not apply to Companies registered under this Act, nor to Companies registered under the said Act of the Eighth Year of the Reign of Her present Majesty, Chapter One hundred and ten, from and after the Date at which they have obtained Registration under this Act, as herein-after mentioned.

CIX. No Repeal hereby enacted shall affect,

1. Anything duly done under any Acts hereby repealed before such Repeal comes into operation:
2. Any Right acquired or Liability incurred under any such Acts before such Repeal comes into operation:
3. Any Penalty, Forfeiture, or other Punishment incurred or to be incurred in respect of any Offence against any such Acts committed before such Repeal comes into operation:
4. Any Proceeding to be taken in the Prosecution of any Order for winding-up a Company made before such Repeal comes into operation.

*Temporary Provisions.*

CX. Every Company completely registered under the said Act of the Eighth Year of the Reign of Her present Majesty, Chapter One hundred and ten, shall on or before the Third Day of *November* One thousand eight hundred and fifty-six, and any other Company duly constituted by Law previously to the passing of this Act, and consisting of Seven or more Shareholders, may at any Time hereafter, register itself as a Company under this Act, with or without Limited Liability, subject to this Proviso that no Company shall be registered under this Act as a Limited Company unless either a Certificate of Complete Registration with Limited Liability under the "Limited Liability Act, 1855," has been obtained by it, or an Assent to its being so registered has been given by Three Fourths in Number and Value of such of its Shareholders as may have been present, personally or by Proxy, in Cases where

Proxies are allowed by the Regulations of the Company, at some General Meeting summoned for that Purpose

CXI. Previously to the Registration under this Act of any existing Company, there shall be delivered to the Registrar of Joint Stock Companies the following Documents; that is to say,

1. In the Case of a Company completely registered under the said Act of the Eighth Year of Her present Majesty, Chapter One hundred and ten, if such Company is not intended to be registered as a Limited Company, a List showing the Names, Addresses, and Occupations of all Persons who on the Day of Registration are Holders of Shares in the Company, with the Addition of the Shares held by such Persons respectively, distinguishing each Share by its Number:

2. If such Company as last aforesaid has obtained a Certificate of Complete Registration with Limited Liability under the Limited Liability Act, 1855, or if it has not obtained such a Certificate, but is intended to be registered as a Limited Company under the Provisions of this Act, the above List shall be accompanied with a Statement specifying the following Particulars:

   The nominal Capital of the Company, and the Number of Shares into which it is divided:

   The Number of Shares taken, and the Amount paid on each Share:

   Such Statement shall also contain, in

case the Company has not previously obtained a Certificate of Limited Liability, but is intended to be registered as a Limited Company under this Act,

The Name of such Company, with the Addition of the Word "Limited" as the last Word thereof:

3. In the Case of any other Company duly constituted by Law previously to the passing of this Act, and consisting of Seven or more Shareholders, if it is not intended to be registered as a Limited Company, there shall be delivered to the Registrar of Joint Stock Companies such List of Shareholders as is hereinbefore mentioned, and also a Copy of any Act of Parliament, Royal Charter, Letters Patent, Deed of Settlement, or other Instrument constituting or regulating the Company:

4. If any such Company as last aforesaid is intended to be registered as a Limited Company, the above List and Copy shall be accompanied by a Statement specifying the following Particulars; that is to say,

The nominal Capital of the Company, and the Number of Shares into which it is divided;

The Number of Shares taken, and the Amount paid on each Share;

The Name of the Company, with the Addition of the Word "Limited" as the last Word thereof.

CXII. The List of Shareholders and any other Particulars relating to the Company hereby required to be delivered to the Registrar shall be verified by a Declaration of the Directors of the Company delivering the same, or any Two of them, or of any Two other principal Officers of the Company, made in pursuance of the Act passed in the Sixth Year of the Reign of His late Majesty King *William* the Fourth, Chapter Sixty-two; but no Fees shall be charged in respect of the Registration under this Act of any Company completely registered under the said Act of the Eighth Year of the Reign of Her present Majesty, Chapter One hundred and ten, in Cases where the Liability of the Shareholders is not intended to be limited, or where such Company has already obtained a Certificate of Complete Registration with Limited Liability.

CXIII. Upon Compliance with the foregoing Requisitions, the Registrar of Joint Stock Companies shall certify under his Hand that the Company so applying for Registration is incorporated as a Company under this Act, and in the Case of a Limited Company, that it is limited, and thereupon such Company shall be incorporated accordingly, and all Provisions contained in any Deed of Settlement, Act of Parliament, Royal Charter, or Letters Patent, or other Instrument constituting or regulating the Company, shall be deemed to be Regulations of the Company within the Meaning of this Act, and all the Provisions of this Act shall apply to such Company in the same Manner in all respects as if it had been originally incorporated under this Act; subject, nevertheless, to the Reservations herein-after contained with respect to the existing Rights of Creditors and other Persons; and subject to this Proviso, that, except in so far as is herein-after permitted, no Company constituted by Act of Parliament shall have Power to alter any of the Provisions contained in such Act of Parliament, and no Company constituted by Royal Charter or Letters Patent shall have Power, by Special Resolution or otherwise, to alter any of the Provisions contained in such Charter or Letters Patent, without the Sanction of the Board of Trade.

CXIV. Any existing Company may, for the Purpose of obtaining Registration with Limited Liability, change its Name by adding thereto the Word "Limited," or do any other Act that may be necessary.

CXV. The Certificate of Incorporation given to any existing Company, in pursuance of this Act, shall be conclusive Evidence that all the Requisitions herein contained in respect of Registration under this Act have been complied with, and the Date of such Certificate shall be deemed to be the Date at which the Company is incorporated under this Act.

CXVI. The Registration of any existing Company under this Act shall not, nor shall any Act of the Company subsequent to such Registration, prejudice any Right which previously to such Registration has, or which would, if no such Registration had taken place, have accrued to any Creditor or other Person against the Company in its Corporate Capacity, or against any Person then being or having been a Member of such Company, but every such Creditor or other Person shall be entitled to all such Remedies against the Company in its Corporate Capacity, and against every Person then being or having been a Member of such Company, as he would have been entitled to in case such Registration had not taken place.

# SCHEDULE.

## FORM A.—Section 7.

Memorandum of Association of the " Eastern Steam Packet Company, Limited."

1st. The name of the Company is " The Eastern Steam " Packet Company, Limited."

2d. The registered Office of the Company is to be established in England.

3d. The Objects for which the Company is to be established are, " the Conveyance of Passengers and Goods in Ships or Boats between such Places as the Company may from Time to Time determine, and the doing all such other Things as are incidental or conducive to the Attainment of the above Object."

4th. The Liability of the Shareholders is " Limited."

5th. The nominal Capital of the Company is Two hundred thousand Pounds, divided into One thousand Shares of Two hundred Pounds each.

WE, the several Persons whose Names and Addresses are subscribed, are desirous of being formed into a Company, in pursuance of this Memorandum of Association, and we respectively agree to take the Number of Shares in the Capital of the Company set opposite our respective Names.

| Names and Addresses of Subscribers. | | Number of Shares taken by each Subscriber. |
|---|---|---|
| " 1. John Jones of | in the County of - | 200 |
| " 2. John Smith of | in the County of - | 25 |
| " 3. Thomas Green of | in the County of - | 30 |
| " 4. John Thompson of | in the County of - | 40 |
| " 5. Caleb White of | in the County of - | 15 |
| " 6. Andrew Brown of | in the County of - | 5 |
| " 7. Cæsar White of | in the County of - | 10 |
| | Total Shares taken - - . | 325 |

Dated the 22nd Day of November 1856.

Witness to the above Signatures,

A.B., No. 13, Hute Street, Clerkenwell, Middlesex.

## TABLE B.—See § 9.

### REGULATIONS FOR MANAGEMENT OF THE COMPANY.

### SHARES.

1. No Person shall be deemed to have accepted any Share in the Company unless he has testified his Acceptance thereof by Writing under his Hand, in such Form as the Company from Time to Time directs.
2. The Company may from Time to Time make such Calls upon the Shareholders in respect of all Monies unpaid on their Shares as they think fit, provided that Twenty-one Days Notice at least is given of each Call, and each Shareholder shall be liable to pay the Amount of Calls so made to the Persons and at the Times and Places appointed by the Company.
3. A Call shall be deemed to have been made at the Time when the Resolution authorizing such Call was passed.
4. If before or on the Day appointed for Payment any Shareholder does not pay the Amount of any Call to which he is liable, then such Shareholder shall be liable to pay Interest for the same at the Rate of Five Pounds per Cent. per Annum from the Day appointed for the Payment thereof to the Time of the actual Payment.
5. The Company may, if they think fit, receive from any of the Shareholders willing to advance the same all or any Part of the Monies due upon their respective Shares beyond the Sums actually called for; and upon the Monies so paid in advance, or so much thereof as from Time to Time exceeds the Amount of the Calls then made upon the Shares in respect of which such Advance has been made, the Company may pay Interest at such Rate as the Shareholder paying such Sum in advance and the Company agree upon.
6. If several Persons are registered as joint Holders of any Share, any One of such Persons may give effectual Receipts for any Dividend payable in respect of such Share.
7. The Company may decline to register any Transfer of Shares made by a Shareholder who is indebted to them.
8. Every Shareholder shall, on Payment of such Sum, not exceeding One Shilling, as the Company may prescribe, be entitled to a Certificate, under the Common Seal of the

Company, specifying the Share or Shares held by him, and the Amount paid up thereon.

9. If such Certificate is worn out or lost, it may be renewed, on Payment of such Sum, not exceeding One Shilling, as the Company may prescribe.

9*a*. The Transfer Books shall be closed during the Fourteen Days immediately preceding the Ordinary General Meeting in each Year.

## TRANSMISSION OF SHARES.

10. The Executors or Administrators of a deceased Shareholder shall be the only Persons recognized by the Company as having any Title to his Share.

11. Any Person becoming entitled to a Share in consequence of the Death, Bankruptcy, or Insolvency of any Shareholder, or in consequence of the Marriage of any Female Shareholder, or in any way other than by Transfer, may be registered as a Shareholder upon such Evidence being produced as may from Time to Time be required by the Company.

12. Any Person who has become entitled to a Share in any way other than by Transfer may, instead of being registered himself, elect to have some Person to be named by him registered as a Holder of such Share.

13. The Person so becoming entitled shall testify such Election by executing to his Nominee a Deed of Transfer of such Share.

14. The Deed of Transfer shall be presented to the Company accompanied with such Evidence as they may require to prove the Title of the Transferror, and thereupon the Company shall register the Transferree as a Shareholder.

## FORFEITING OF SHARES.

15. If any Shareholder fails to pay any Call due on the appointed Day, the Company may, at any Time thereafter, during such Time as the Call remains unpaid, serve a Notice on him, requiring him to pay such Call, together with any Interest that may have accrued by such Nonpayment.

16. The Notice shall name a further Day, and a Place or Places being a Place or Places at which Calls of the Company are usually made payable, on and at which such Call is

to be paid: It shall also state that in the event of Nonpayment at the Time and Place appointed the Shares in respect of which such Call was made will be liable to be forfeited.

17. If the Requisitions of any such Notice as aforesaid are not complied with, any Share in respect of which such Notice has been given may be forfeited by a Resolution of the Directors to that effect.

18. Any Share so forfeited shall be deemed to be the Property of the Company, and may be disposed of in such Manner as the Company thinks fit.

19. Any Shareholder whose Shares have been forfeited shall notwithstanding be liable to pay to the Company all Calls owing upon such Shares at the Time of the Forfeiture.

### INCREASE IN CAPITAL.

20. The Company may, with the Sanction of the Company previously given in General Meeting, increase its Capital.

21. Any Capital raised by the Creation of New Shares shall be considered as Part of the original Capital, and shall be subject to the same Provisions in all respects, whether with reference to the Payment of Calls, or the Forfeiture of Shares on Nonpayment of Calls, or otherwise, as if it had been Part of the original Capital.

### GENERAL MEETINGS.

22. The First General Meeting shall be held at such Time, not being more than Twelve Months after the Incorporation of the Company, and at such Place, as the Directors may determine.

23. Subsequent General Meetings shall be held at such Time and Place as may be prescribed by the Company in General Meeting; and if no other Time or Place is prescribed, a General Meeting shall be held on the First Monday in February in every year, at such Place as may be determined by the Directors.

24. The above-mentioned General Meetings shall be called Ordinary Meetings; all other General Meetings shall be called Extraordinary.

25. The Directors may, whenever they think fit, and they shall upon a Requisition made in Writing by any Number of Shareholders holding in the aggregate not less than One

Fifth Part of the Shares of the Company, convene an Extraordinary General Meeting.

26. Any Requisition so made by the Shareholders shall express the Object of the Meeting proposed to be called, and shall be left at the registered Office of the Company.

27. Upon the Receipt of such Requisition the Directors shall forthwith proceed to convene a General Meeting: If they do not proceed to convene the same within Twenty-one Days from the Date of the Requisition, the Requisitionists, or any other Shareholders holding the required Number of Shares, may themselves convene a Meeting.

28. Seven Days Notice at the least, specifying the Place, the Time, the Hour of meeting, and the Purpose for which any General Meeting is to be held, shall be given by Advertisement, or in such other Manner, if any, as may be prescribed by the Company.

29. Any Shareholder may, on giving not less than Three Days previous Notice, submit any Resolution to a Meeting beyond the Matters contained in the Notice given of such Meeting.

30. The Notice required of a Shareholder shall be given by leaving a Copy of the Resolution at the registered Office of the Company.

31. No Business shall be transacted at any Meeting except the Declaration of a Dividend, unless a Quorum of Shareholders is present at the Commencement of such Business; and such Quorum shall be ascertained as follows; that is to say, if the Shareholders belonging to the Company at the Time of the Meeting do not exceed Ten in Number, the Quorum shall be Five; if they exceed Ten there shall be added to the above Quorum One for every Five additional Shareholders up to Fifty, and One for every Ten additional Shareholders after Fifty, with this Limitation, that no Quorum shall in any Case exceed Forty.

32. If within One Hour from the Time appointed for the Meeting the required Number of Shareholders are not present, the Meeting, if convened upon the Requisition of the Shareholders, shall be dissolved: In any other Case it shall stand adjourned to the following Day, at the same Time and Place; and if at such adjourned Meeting the required Number of Shareholders is not present, it shall be adjourned *sine die*.

33. The Chairman (if any) of the Board of Directors shall preside as Chairman at every Meeting of the Company.

34. If there is no such Chairman, or if at any Meeting he is not present at the Time of holding the same, the Shareholders present shall choose some One of their Number to be Chairman of such Meeting.

35. The Chairman may, with the Consent of the Meeting, adjourn any Meeting from Time to Time and from Place to Place, but no Business shall be transacted at any adjourned Meeting other than the Business left unfinished at the Meeting from which the Adjournment took place.

36. At any General Meeting, unless a Poll is demanded by at least Five Shareholders, a Declaration by the Chairman that a Resolution has been carried, and an Entry to that effect in the Book of Proceedings of the Company, shall be sufficient Evidence of the Fact, without Proof of the Number or Proportion of the Votes recorded in favour of or against such Resolution.

37. If a Poll is demanded in manner aforesaid the same shall be taken in such Manner as the Chairman directs, and the Result of such Poll shall be deemed to be the Resolution of the Company in General Meeting.

## VOTES OF SHAREHOLDERS.

38. Every Shareholder shall have One Vote for every Share up to Ten; he shall have an additional Vote for every Five Shares beyond the first Ten Shares up to One hundred, and an additional Vote for every Ten Shares held by him beyond the First Hundred Shares.

39. If any Shareholder is a Lunatic or Idiot he may vote by his Committee Curator bonis, or other legal Curator; and if any Shareholder is a Minor he may vote by his Guardian, Tutor, or Curator, or any One of his Guardians, Tutors, or Curators, if more than One.

40. If One or more Persons are jointly entitled to a Share or Shares the Person whose Name stands first in the Register of Shareholders as One of the Holders of such Share or Shares, and no other, shall be entitled to vote in respect of the same.

41. No Shareholder shall be entitled to vote at any Meeting unless all Calls due from him have been paid, nor until he shall have been possessed of his Shares Three Calendar Months, unless such Shares shall have been acquired or shall have

come by Bequest, or by Marriage, or by Succession to an Intestate's Estate, or by the Custom of the City of London, or by any Deed of Settlement after the Death of any Person who shall have been entitled for Life to the Dividends of such Shares.

42. Votes may be given either personally or by Proxies: A Proxy shall be appointed in Writing under the Hand of the Appointor, or, if such Appointor is a Corporation, under their Common Seal.

43. No Person shall be appointed a Proxy who is not a Shareholder, and the Instrument or Mandate appointing him shall be deposited at the registered Office of the Company not less than Forty-eight Hours before the Time of holding the Meeting at which he proposes to vote; but no Instrument or Mandate appointing a Proxy shall be valid after the Expiration of One Month from the Date of its Execution.

## DIRECTORS.

44. The Number of the Directors, and the Names of the First Directors, shall be determined by the Subscribers of the Memorandum of Association.

45. Until Directors are appointed, the Subscribers of the Memorandum of Association shall for all the Purposes of this Act be deemed to be Directors.

## POWERS OF DIRECTORS.

46. The Business of the Company shall be managed by the Directors, who may exercise all such Powers of the Company as are not by this Act or by the Articles of Association, if any, declared to be exercisable by the Company in General Meeting, subject nevertheless to any Regulations of the Articles of Association, to the Provisions of this Act, and to such Regulations, being not inconsistent with the aforesaid Regulations or Provisions, as may be prescribed by the Company in General Meeting; but no Regulation made by the Company in General Meeting shall invalidate any prior Act of the Directors which would have been valid if such Regulation had not been made.

## DISQUALIFICATION OF DIRECTORS.

47. The Office of Director shall be vacated,—

If he holds any other Office or Place of Profit under the Company;

If he becomes bankrupt or insolvent;
If he is concerned in or participates in the Profits of any Contract with the Company;
If he participates in the Profits of any Work done for the Company:

But the above Rules shall be subject to the following Exceptions: That no Director shall vacate his Office by reason of his being a Shareholder in any incorporated Company which has entered into Contracts with or done any Work for the Company of which he is Director; nevertheless he shall not vote in respect of such Contract or Work; and if he does so vote his Vote shall not be counted, and he shall incur a Penalty not exceeding Twenty Pounds.

ROTATION OF DIRECTORS.

48. At the First Ordinary Meeting after the Incorporation of the Company the whole of the Directors shall retire from Office; and at the First Ordinary Meeting in every subsequent Year One Third of the Directors for the Time being, or if their Number is not a Multiple of Three, then the Number nearest to One Third, shall retire from Office.
49. The One Third or other nearest Number to retire during the First and Second Years ensuing the Incorporation of the Company shall, unless the Directors agree among themselves, be determined by Ballot: In every subsequent Year the One Third or other nearest Number who have been longest in Office shall retire.
50. A retiring Director shall be re-eligible.
51. The Company at the General Meeting at which any Directors retire in manner aforesaid shall fill up the vacated Offices by electing a like Number of Persons.
52. If at any Meeting at which an Election of Directors ought to take place no such Election is made, the Meeting shall stand adjourned till the next Day, at the same Time and Place; and if at such adjourned Meeting no Election takes place, the former Directors shall continue to act until new Directors are appointed at the First Ordinary Meeting of the following Year.
53. The Company may from Time to Time, in General Meeting, increase or reduce the Number of Directors, and may also determine in what Rotation such increased or reduced Number is to go out of Office.
54. Any casual Vacancy occurring in the Board of Directors may

be filled up by the Directors, but any Person so chosen shall retain his Office so long only as the vacating Director would have retained the same if no Vacancy had occurred.

### PROCEEDINGS OF DIRECTORS.

55. The Directors may meet together for the Despatch of Business, adjourn, and otherwise regulate their Meetings as they think fit, and determine the Quorum necessary for the Transaction of Business: Questions arising at any Meeting shall be decided by a Majority of Votes: In case of an Equality of Votes the Chairman, in addition to his original Vote, shall have a Casting Vote: A Director may at any Time summon a Meeting of the Directors.

56. The Directors may elect a Chairman of their Meetings, and determine the Period for which he is to hold Office; but if no such Chairman is elected, or if at any Meeting the Chairman is not present at the Time appointed for holding the same, the Directors present shall choose some One of their Number to be Chairman of such Meeting.

57. The Directors may delegate any of their Powers to Committees consisting of such Member or Members of their Body as they think fit: any Committee so formed shall, in the Exercise of the Powers so delegated, conform to any Regulations that may be imposed on them by the Directors.

58. A Committee may elect a Chairman of their Meetings: If no such Chairman is elected, or if he is not present at the Time appointed for holding the same, the Members present shall choose One of their Number to be Chairman of such Meeting.

59. A Committee may meet and adjourn as they think proper: Questions at any Meeting shall be determined by a Majority of Votes of the Members present; and in case of an equal Division of Votes the Chairman shall have a Casting Vote.

60. All Acts done by any Meeting of the Directors, or of a Committee of Directors, or by any Person acting as a Director, shall, notwithstanding that it be afterwards discovered that there was no Defect in the Appointment of any such Directors or Persons acting as aforesaid, or that they or any of them were disqualified, be as valid as if every such Person had been duly appointed and was qualified to be a Director.

61. The Directors shall cause Minutes to be made in Books provided for the Purpose,—

1. Of all Appointments of Officers made by the Directors;
2. Of the Names of the Directors present at each Meeting of Directors and Committees of Directors;
3. Of all Orders made by the Directors and Committees of Directors; and,
4. Of all Resolutions and Proceedings of Meetings of the Company, and of the Directors and Committees of Directors.

And any such Minute as aforesaid, if signed by any Person purporting to be the Chairman of any Meeting of Directors, or Committee of Directors, shall be receivable in Evidence without any further Proof.

62. The Company, in General Meeting, may, by a special Resolution, remove any Director before the Expiration of his Period of Office, and appoint another qualified Person in his Stead: The Person so appointed shall hold Office during such Time only as the Director in whose Place he is appointed would have held the same if he had not been removed.

### DIVIDENDS.

63. The Directors may, with the Sanction of the Company in General Meeting, declare a Dividend to be paid to the Shareholders in proportion to their Shares.
64. No Dividend shall be payable except out of the Profits arising from the Business of the Company.
65. The Directors may, before recommending any Dividend, set aside out of the Profits of the Company such Sum as they think proper as a reserved Fund to meet Contingencies, or for equalizing Dividends, or for repairing, or maintaining the Works connected with the Business of the Company, or any Part thereof; and the Directors may invest the Sum so set apart as a reserved Fund upon such Securities as they, with the Sanction of the Company, may select.
66. The Directors may deduct from the Dividends payable to any Shareholder all such Sums of Money as may be due from him to the Company on account of Calls or otherwise.
67. Notice of any Dividend that may have been declared shall be given to each Shareholder, or sent by Post or otherwise to his registered Place of Abode, and all Dividends unclaimed for Three Years, after having been declared,

may be forfeited by the Directors for the Benefit of the Company.

68. No Dividend shall bear Interest as against the Company.

## ACCOUNTS.

69. The Directors shall cause true Accounts to be kept,—

Of the Stock in Trade of the Company;

Of the Sums of Money received and expended by the Company, and the Matter in respect of which such Receipt and Expenditure takes place; and

Of the Credits and Liabilities of the Company:—

Such Accounts shall be kept, upon the Principle of Double Entry, in a Cash Book, Journal, and Ledger: The Books of Account shall be kept at the principal Office of the Company, and, subject to any reasonable Restrictions as to the Time and Manner of inspecting the same that may be imposed by the Company in General Meeting, shall be open to the Inspection of the Shareholders during the Hours of Business.

70. Once at the least in every Year the Directors shall lay before the Company in General Meeting a Statement of the Income and Expenditure for the past Year, made up to a Date not more than Three Months before such Meeting.

71. The Statement so made shall show, arranged under the most convenient Heads, the Amount of gross Income, distinguishing the several Sources from which it has been derived, and the Amount of gross Expenditure, distinguishing the Expense of the Establishment, Salaries, and other like Matters: Every Item of Expenditure fairly chargeable against the Year's Income shall be brought into Account, so that a just Balance of Profit and Loss may be laid before the Meeting; and in Cases where any Item of Expenditure which may in Fairness be distributed over several Years has been incurred in any One Year the whole Amount of such Item shall be stated, with the Addition of the Reasons why only a Portion of such Expenditure is charged against the Income of the Year.

72. A Balance Sheet shall be made out every Year, and laid before the General Meeting of the Company, and such Balance Sheet shall contain a Summary of the Property

and Liabilities of the Company arranged under the Heads appearing in the Form annexed to this Table, or as near thereto as Circumstances admit.

73. A printed Copy of such Balance Sheet shall, Seven Days previously to such Meeting, be delivered at or sent by Post to the registered Address of every Shareholder.

AUDIT.

74. The Accounts of the Company shall be examined and the Correctness of the Balance Sheet ascertained by One or more Auditor or Auditors to be elected by the Company in General Meeting.

75. If not more than One Auditor is appointed, all the Provisions herein contained relating to Auditors shall apply to him.

76. The Auditors need not be Shareholders in the Company: No Person is eligible as an Auditor who is interested otherwise than as a Shareholder in any Transaction of the Company; and no Director or other Officer of the Company is eligible during his Continuance in Office.

77. The Election of Auditors shall be made by the Company at their Ordinary Meeting, or, if there are more than One, at their First Ordinary Meeting in each Year.

78. The Remuneration of the Auditors shall be fixed by the Company at the Time of their Election.

79. Any Auditor shall be re-eligible on his quitting Office.

80. If any casual Vacancy occurs in the Office of Auditor, the Directors shall forthwith call an Extraordinary General Meeting for the Purpose of supplying the same.

81. If no Election of Auditors is made in manner aforesaid the Board of Trade may, on the Application of One Fifth in Number of the Shareholders of the Company, appoint an Auditor for the current Year, and fix the Remuneration to be paid to him by the Company for his Services.

82. Every Auditor shall be supplied with a Copy of the Balance Sheet, and it shall be his Duty to examine the same, with the Accounts and Vouchers relating thereto.

83. Every Auditor shall have a List delivered to him of all Books kept by the Company, and he shall at all reasonable Times have Access to the Books and Accounts of the Company: He may, at the Expense of the Company, employ Accountants or other Persons to assist him in investigating such Accounts, and he may in relation to

such Accounts examine the Directors or any other Officer of the Company.

84. The Auditors shall make a Report to the Shareholders upon the Balance Sheet and Accounts, and in every such Report they shall state whether, in their Opinion, the Balance Sheet is a full and fair Balance Sheet, containing the Particulars required by these Regulations, and properly drawn up so as to exhibit a true and correct View of the State of the Company's Affairs, and in case they have called for Explanations or Information from the Directors, whether such Explanations or Information have been given by the Directors, and whether they have been satisfactory; and such Report shall be read, together with the Report of the Directiors, at the Ordinary Meeting.

## NOTICES.

85. Notices requiring to be served by the Company upon the Shareholders may be served either personally, or by leaving the same or sending them through the Post in a Letter addressed to the Shareholders at their registered Places of Abode.

86. All Notices directed to be given to the Shareholders shall, with respect to any Share to which Persons are jointly entitled, be given to whichever of the said Persons is named first in the Register of Shareholders; and Notice so given shall be sufficient Notice to all the Proprietors of such Share.

87. All Notices required by this Act to be given by Advertisement shall be advertised in a Newspaper circulating in the District in which the registered Office of the Company is situate.

FORM OF BALANCE SHEET REFERRED TO IN TABLE B.

Dr. BALANCE SHEET of the Co. made up to 18 Cr.

| CAPITAL AND LIABILITIES. | | | £ s. d. | £ s. d. | PROPERTY AND ASSETS. | | | £ s. d. | £ s. d. |
|---|---|---|---|---|---|---|---|---|---|
| I. CAPITAL. | 1. | *Showing:*<br>*The total Amount received from the Shareholders; showing also:*<br>*(a.) The Number of Shares -*<br>*(b.) The Amount paid per Share -*<br>*(c.) If any Arrears of Calls, the Nature of the Arrear, and the Names of the Defaulters. - -*<br>*Any Arrears due from any Director or Officer of the Company to be separately stated.*<br>*(d.) The Particulars of any forfeited Shares.* | | | III. PROPERTY held by the Company. | 4. | *Showing:*<br>*Immovable Property, distinguishing -*<br>*(a.) Freehold Land - -*<br>*(b.) ,, Buildings - -*<br>*(c.) Leasehold ,, - -* | | |
| | | | | | | 5. | *Movable Property, distinguishing -*<br>*(d.) Stock in Trade - -*<br>*(e.) Plant - - -*<br>*The Cost to be stated with Deduction for Deterioration in Value as charged by the Reserve Fund or Profit and Loss.* | | |
| II. DEBTS and LIABILITIES of the Company. | 2. | *Showing:*<br>*The Amount of Loans on Mortgage or Debenture Bonds.* | | | IV. DEBTS owing to the Company - | 6. | *Showing:*<br>*Debts considered good for which the Company hold Bills or other Securities.* | | |
| | 3. | *The Amount of Debts owing by the Company, distinguishing—*<br>*(a.) Debts for which Acceptances have been given.*<br>*(b.) Debts to Tradesmen for Supplies of Stock in Trade or other Articles.*<br>*(c.) Debts for Law Expenses.*<br>*(d.) Debts for Interest on Debentures or other Loans.*<br>*(e.) Unclaimed Dividends.*<br>*(f.) Debts not enumerated above.* | | | | 7. | *Debts considered good for which the Company hold no Security.* | | |
| | | | | | | 8. | *Debts considered doubtful and bad -*<br>*Any Debt due from a Director or other Officer of the Company to be separately stated.* | | |
| VI. RESERVE FUND. | | *Showing:*<br>*The Amount set aside from Profits to meet Contingencies.* | | | V. CASH AND INVESTMENTS. | 9. | *Showing:*<br>*The Nature of Investment and Rate of Interest.* | | |
| VII. PROFIT AND LOSS. | | *Showing:*<br>*The disposable Balance for Payment of Dividend, &c.* | | | | 10 | *The Amount of Cash, where lodged, and if bearing Interest.* | | |
| CONTINGENT LIABILITIES. | | *Claims against the Company not acknowledged as Debts.*<br>*Monies for which the Company is contingently liable.* | | | | | | | |

## FORM C.

Memorandum of Association of the "Patent Stereotype Company, Limited," with Articles of Association annexed—Sec. 10.

### Memorandum of Association.

1st. The Name of the Company is "The Patent Stereotype Company."

2d. The registered Office of the Company is to be established in Ireland.

3d. The Objects for which the Company is established are "the working of a Patent Method of founding and casting Stereo-"type Plates, of which Method John Smith of "is the sole Patentee."

4th. The Liability of the Shareholders is "Limited."

5th. The Capital of the Company is Two Thousand Pounds, divided into Twenty Shares of One hundred Pounds each.

We, the several Persons whose Names are subscribed, are desirous of being formed into a Company, in pursuance of this Memorandum of Association, and we respectively agree to take the Number of Shares in the Capital of the Company set opposite our respective Names.

| Names and Addresses of Subscribers. | | Number of Shares taken by Subscribers. |
|---|---|---|
| "1. John Jones of | in the County of - | 1 |
| "2. John Smith of | in the County of - | 5 |
| "3. Thomas Green of | in the County of - | 2 |
| "4. John Thompson of | in the County of - | 2 |
| "5. Caleb White of | in the County of - | 3 |
| "6. Andrew Brown of | in the County of - | 4 |
| "7. Abel Brown of | in the County of - | 1 |
| Total Shares taken - - | | 18 |

Witness to the above Signatures,
A.B., No. 29, Bond-street, Middlesex.

## Articles of Association of the Patent Stereotype Company, Limited.

"It is agreed as follows:—

"1st. No Shareholder shall transfer his Shares without the Consent of the Directors expressed in Writing.

"2d. If any Shareholder feels aggrieved with the Refusal of the Directors to allow him to transfer his Shares, the Matter shall be settled by Arbitration.

"3d. Calls on the Shares of the Company not considered as paid-up Shares shall be made at such Time as the Directors think fit; but no Call shall exceed Ten Pounds per Share.

"4th. The Company shall not be obliged to register the Transferree, under the Regulations numbered Twelve and Thirteen in the said Table, unless he is approved by the Directors, but in the event of their disapproving the Matter may be decided by Arbitration.

"5th. The Regulations of Table D. as to General Meetings numbered 22, 23, and 25 shall not apply.

"6th. The First General Meeting of the Company shall be held on the First of July next, and subsequent General Meetings shall be held on the First of July on every succeeding Year, or if that Day is a Sunday on the succeeding Monday.

"7th. An Extraordinary General Meeting may be summoned at any Time by any Two Shareholders of the Company.

"8th. All Matters in question between the Shareholders shall be decided by an Arbitrator appointed by the Manchester Chamber of Commerce.

"9th. The Regulation of Table B. as to Votes of Shareholders, numbered Thirty-eight, shall not apply, and every Shareholder shall have One Vote in respect of every Share that he holds.

"The several Persons herein-after named, Subscribers to the Memorandum of Association, shall be the First Directors of the Company; that is to say, John Jones, Thomas Green, John Thompson, Caleb White, Andrew Brown, and Abel Brown.

### Names and Addresses of Subscribers.

"1. John Jones of in the County of
"2. John Smith of in the County of
"3. Thomas Green of in the County of
"4. John Thomson of in the County of

"5. Caleb White of in the County of
"6. Andrew Brown of in the County of
"7. Abel Brown of in the County of

Witness to the above Signatures,
A.B.,
No. 20, Bond-street, Middlesex.

---

## TABLE D.

### TABLE OF FEES.

| | £ | s. | d. |
|---|---|---|---|
| For Registration of a Company whose nominal Capital does not exceed £1,000 - - - | 5 | 0 | 0 |
| For every £1,000 of nominal Capital, or Part of 1,000, after the First £1,000, and up to £100,000, an additional Fee of - - - - | 0 | 5 | 0 |
| For every £1,000 or Part of £1,000 after the First £100,000, an additional Fee of - - | 0 | 1 | 0 |
| For Registration of any Increase in the Capital of a Company for every £1,000 or Part of £1,000, up to £100,000 in the whole - - - | 0 | 5 | 0 |
| For every £1,000 or Part of £1,000 beyond the First £100,000, an additional Fee of - - | 0 | 1 | 0 |
| For Registration of any existing Company, except such Companies as are by this Act exempted from Payment of Fees in respect of Registration under this Act, the same Fee as is charged for registering a new Company | | | |
| For registering any Document hereby required or authorized to be registered, other than the Memorandum of Association - - - - | 0 | 5 | 0 |
| For making a Record of any Fact hereby authorized or required to be recorded by the Registrar of Companies, a Fee of - - - - | 0 | 5 | 0 |

Section XVI.

# FORM E.

*Summary of Capital and Shares of the Company, made up to the Day of*

Nominal Capital £ divided into Shares of £ each
Number of Shares taken up to the Day of
There has been called up on each Share £
Total Amount of Calls received £
Total Amount of Calls unpaid £
Total Amount of Shares forfeited £

LIST of Persons holding Shares in the Company on the Day of , and of Persons who have held Shares thereon at any Time during the Year immediately preceding the said Day of , showing their Names and Addresses, and an Account of the Shares so held.

| Folio in Register Ledger containing Particulars. | NAMES, ADDRESSES, AND OCCUPATIONS. | | | | ACCOUNT OF SHARES. | | | | | Remarks. |
|---|---|---|---|---|---|---|---|---|---|---|
| | Surnames. | Christian Name. | Address. | Occupation. | Shares held by existing Shareholders on the Day of | Additional Shares held by existing Shareholders during preceding Year. | | Shares held by Persons no longer Shareholders. | | |
| | | | | | | Number. | Date of Transfer. | Number. | Date of Transfer. | |
| | | | | | | | | | | |

## FORM F.—Sec. 19.

*Form of Transfer of Shares.*

I of (a) in consideration of the Sum of paid to me by of do hereby transfer to the said Share [*or* Shares], numbered in "The Company" standing in my Name in the Books of the Company, to hold unto the said his Executors, Administrators, and Assigns, [*or* Successors and Assigns,] subject to the several Conditions on which I held the same at the Time of the Execution hereof; and I the said do hereby agree to take the said Share [*or* Shares] subject to the same Conditions. As witness our Hands the Day of

(*a*) *These Words will be omitted if no Consideration is paid.*

## FORM G.—Sec. 38.

*Licence to hold Lands.*

The Lords of the Committee of Privy Council appointed for the Consideration of Matters relating to Trade and Foreign Plantations hereby license the " Association, Limited," to hold the Lands hereunder described [*insert Description of Lands*]. The Conditions of this Licence are [*insert Conditions if any*].

## FORM H.—Sec. 42.

*For England and Ireland.*

Indenture of Mortgage made between the "London Gas Company, Limited," of the one Part, and "John Smith" of the other Part.

Whereas the said "John Smith" has advanced to the said Company the Sum of One thousand Pounds, on condition that the Company will repay the same to him on the First Day of

January next, with Interest thereon in the meantime at the Rate of Five Pounds per Centum; and in the event of their not repaying the same on the said First of January will, so long as the same remains unpaid, pay Interest thereon at the Rate of Five Pounds per Centum by equal half-yearly Payments on the First Day of July and the First Day of January in every Year:

Now it is hereby witnessed, that for securing the said Advance and Interest the Company hereby grant to the said "John Smith" and his Heirs all the Lands described in the Schedule hereto, with all their actual and reputed Appurtenances; and it is hereby declared, that if the Company fails in paying the whole of the Principal and Interest Monies hereby secured on the said First of January, the said "John Smith," or any Person for the Time entitled to such Monies, may, at any Time thereafter, upon giving to the Company Three Months Notice, sell the said Mortgaged Lands, and reimburse himself out of the Monies arising from the Sale all Sums due on this Security, and all Expenses incurred by him in respect of such Sale, rendering the Surplus, if any, to the Company or their Assigns. The Condition as to Notice shall apply only between the Parties to this Indenture, and shall not affect a Purchaser, a Sale to whom shall be valid notwithstanding such Notice may not have been given.

In witness, &c.

---

## FORM I.—Sec. 43.

---

*For Scotland.*

Bond and Disposition in Security by the "Edinburgh Gas Company, Limited," to "John Smith."

Whereas the said "John Smith" has advanced to the said Company the Sum of One thousand Pounds, on condition that the Company will repay the same to him on the First Day of January next, with Interest thereon in the meantime at the Rate of Five Pounds per Centum; and in the event of their not repaying the same on the said First of January will, so long as the same remains unpaid, pay Interest thereon at the Rate of Five Pounds per Centum by equal half-yearly Payments on the First Day of July and the First Day of January in every Year:

Therefore, for securing the said Advance and Interest, the said Company hereby dispone to the said "John Smith," and his

Heirs and Assignees whomsoever, all and whole (describe the Lands); and it is hereby declared that if the Company fails in paying the whole of the Principal and Interest Monies hereby secured on the said First of January, the said "John Smith," or any Person for the Time entitled to such Monies, may, at any Time thereafter, upon giving to the Company Three Months Notice, sell the said Lands, and reimburse himself out of the Monies arising from the Sale all Sums due on this Security, and all Expenses incurred by him in respect of such Sale, rendering the Surplus, if any, to the Company or their Assigns: The Condition as to Notice shall apply only between the Parties to this Indenture, and shall not affect a Purchaser, a Sale to whom shall be valid notwithstanding such Notice may not have been given.

In witness whereof.

(To be tested and signed in common Form.)

# JOINT STOCK COMPANIES ACT.

## 20 & 21 VICTORIA, Cap. 14.

An Act to amend the Joint Stock Companies Act, 1856. [13*th July*, 1857.]

---

WHEREAS it is expedient that further Provision should be made for the Incorporation and Regulation of Joint Stock Companies, and that for that Purpose the Joint Stock Companies Act, 1856, should be amended: Be it therefore enacted by the Queen's most Excellent Majesty, by and with the Advice and Consent of the Lords Spiritual and Temporal, and Commons, in this present Parliament assembled, and by the Authority of the same, as follows:

### *Preliminary.*

I. This Act may be cited for all Purposes as "The Joint Stock Companics Act, 1857."

II. "The Joint Stock Companies Act," 1856," herein-after called "the Principal Act," and this Act, shall, so far as is consistent with the Context and Objects of such Acts, be construed as One Act, and this Act and the Principal Act may be cited together for all Purposes as "The Joint Stock Companies Acts, 1856, 1857."

### *Registry* (*Part I. of Principal Act*).

III. The Fourth Section of the Principal Act shall be repealed, and in lieu thereof be it enacted as follows:

If after the passing of this Act more than Twenty Persons carry on, in Partnership, any Trade or Business, having for its Object the Procurement of Gain to the Partnership, then, unless such Persons are included within One or more of the Classes following, (that is to say,)

1. Are registered as a Company under the Principal Act;
2. Are a Company incorporated or otherwise legally constituted, by or in pursuance of some Act of Parliament, Royal Charter, or Letters Patent; or
3. Are engaged in working Mines within and subject to the Jurisdiction of the Stannaries:

Each one of the Persons so carrying on Business in Partnership together contrary to this Provision shall be severally liable for the Payment of the whole Debts of the Partnership, and may be sued for the same without the Joinder in the Action or Suit of any other Member of the Partnership.

IV. The Registrar shall on Payment of Five Shillings issue a Certificate of Incorporation of any Company to any Person applying for the same, and such Certificate shall be admissible in Evidence in like Manner as the Certificate of Incorporation directed to be given by the principal Act.

*Register of Shareholders (Part I. of Principal Act).*

V. Any Limited Company may by special Resolution convert into Stock any Shares which have been fully paid up; and upon such Conversion being made all the Provisions of the

Principal Act or of this Act which require or imply that the Capital of the Company is divided into Shares of any fixed Amount, and distinguished by Numbers, and all the Provisions of the Principal Act that require the Company to keep a Register of Shareholders, or to make an annual List of Shareholders in the Register, shall cease as to so much of the Capital as has been so converted into Stock.

VI. Any Company that has converted any Portion of its Capital into Stock shall give Notice of such Conversion, specifying the Shares so converted, to the Registrar of Joint Stock Companies, within Fifteen Days from the Date of the last of the Meetings at which the Resolution was passed by which such Conversion was authorized, and the Registrar shall forthwith record the Fact of such Conversion: If such Notice is not given within the Period aforesaid, the Company shall incur a Penalty not exceeding Five Pounds for every Day during which such Neglect to give Notice continues.

VII. Any Company that has converted any Portion of its Capital into Stock shall keep at the registered Office of the Company a Register of the Names and Addresses of the Persons for the Time being entitled to such Stock, and such Register shall be open to Inspection in the Manner and subject to the Penalties in and subject to which the Register of Shareholders is by the Principal Act directed to be kept open.

VIII. If the Name of any Person is without sufficient Cause entered or omitted to be entered in the Register of Stock of any Company, such Person, or any Holder of Stock in the Company, may apply to have the Register rectified in manner directed by the Twenty-fifth Section of the Principal Act.

IX. The Court may in any Proceeding under the Twenty-fifth Section of the Principal Act decide on any Question relating to the Title of any Person who is a Party to such Proceeding, to have his Name entered in or erased from the Register, whether such Question arises between Two or more Holders or alleged Holders of the Shares or Stock, or between any Holders or alleged Holders of Shares or Stock and the Company, and generally the Court may in any such Proceeding decide any Question that it may be necessary or expedient to decide for the Rectification of the Register.

X. If any Company makes default in forwarding Copies of the Memorandum of Association and Articles of Association to Shareholders, in pursuance of Section Twenty-seven of the Principal Act, the Company so making default shall for each Offence incur a Penalty not exceeding One Pound.

*Winding up by Court (Part III. of Principal Act).*

XI. Where an Order has been made for winding up a Company under the Third Part of the Principal Act, if upon the Application of the official Liquidator it appears to the Court having Jurisdiction in the Matter of such Winding-up that there is probable Cause for believing that any Contributory to such Company is about to quit the United Kingdom, or otherwise abscond, or to remove or conceal any of his Goods or Chattels, for the Purpose of evading Payment of Calls, or for avoiding Examination in respect of the Affairs of the

Company, the Court may, by Warrant directed to such Person or Persons as it thinks fit, cause such Contributory to be arrested, and his Books, Papers, Monies, Securities for Monies, Goods and Chattels, to be seized, and him and them to be safely kept until such Time as the Court may order.

XII. Any Contributory who has been arrested or whose Goods or Chattels have been seized under any such Warrant as aforesaid may, at any Time after such Arrest or Seizure, apply to the Court that issued the Warrant to discharge him from Custody, or to direct the Delivery to him of any Books, Papers, Monies, Securities for Money, Goods or Chattels, that may have been seized; and the Court shall take such Application into consideration, and shall make such Order thereon as it thinks just.

XIII. All Calls that are authorized by the Third Part of the Principal Act to be made on a Contributory, in the event of the Company to which he belongs being wound up by the Court or voluntarily, shall be deemed in *England* and *Ireland* to be Speciality Debts due from such Contributory to the Company.

*Official Liquidators* (*Part III. of Principal Act*).

XIV. In Cases within the Jurisdiction of the Court of Chancery in *England* or *Ireland*, or of the Court of Session in *Scotland*, or of the Court of the Stannaries, the Court having Jurisdiction shall, in the Appointment of an Official Liquidator or Official Liquidators, consult the Interests of both the Creditors and Contributories, and hear such Creditors or Contributories as it thinks fit to hear with respect to such Appointment. It may, unless both the Creditors and Contributories concur in the Appointment of a single Liquidator, appoint One or more Liquidator or Liquidators to act on behalf of each of such Parties. It may declare that, in case of Difference, any Act may be done by a Majority of Liquidators; or it may require the Liquidators in all Cases of Difference to apply to the Court. It may do anything hereby authorized to be done, either upon the First Appointment of a Liquidator or at any subsequent Stage of the Winding-up; but, notwithstanding anything herein contained, it shall not be obligatory on the Court to appoint more than One Liquidator, if in its Discretion it thinks that such Appointment will be most conducive to Justice.

XV. In Cases within the Jurisdiction of any Court of Bankruptcy the Official Assignee shall, where a Liquidator is appointed by the Creditors, be considered as appointed as the Representative of the Contributories, and where a Liquidator is appointed by the Contributories be considered as appointed as the Representative of the Creditors.

XVI. The Power of compromising Debts and Claims given by the Principal Act to the Liquidators therein mentioned shall be deemed to extend to the Compromise of any Calls or Debts due from any Contributory or alleged Contributory to the Company on Receipt of a smaller Sum in lieu of a greater, or upon such Terms as may be agreed upon, with Power to the Liquidators to take any Security for any Calls or Debts so due, and to give effectual Discharges on Completion of such Compromise, subject to this Proviso, that no such Compromise shall be made by any Official Liquidator except with the Sanction of the Court, and after giving such Notice to Creditors, and subject to such Conditions as to obtaining the Consent of Creditors or any Portion of them, as the Court may direct, and that no such Compromise shall be made by the Liquidators appointed on the voluntary Winding-up of a Company, except with the Sanction of a special Resolution.

XVII. Where a Company is being wound up voluntarily, and the whole or a Portion of its Property is about to be sold to another Company, registered under this Act, the Liquidators of the first-mentioned Company may, with the Sanction of a special Resolution of the Company by whom they were appointed, receive, in Compensation or part Compensation for such Sale, Shares in such other Company, for the Purpose of Distribution amongst the Shareholders of the Company being wound up, or may enter into any other Arrangement whereby the Shareholders of the Company being wound up may, in lieu of receiving Cash or Shares, or in addition thereto, participate in the Profits of or receive any other Benefit from the purchasing Company; and any Sale made or Arrangement entered into by the Liquidators in pursuance of this Section shall be binding on the Shareholders of the Company being wound up, subject to this Proviso, that if any Shareholder in the Company being wound up who has not voted in favour of the special Resolution passed by his Company at either of the Meetings held for passing the same expresses his Dissent from any such special Resolution, in Writing addressed to the Liquidators or One of them, and left at the registered Office of the Company, not later than Seven Days after the Date of the last of the Meetings at which such special Resolution was passed, such dissentient Shareholder may require the Liquidators to do such One of the following Things as they may prefer ; that is to say, either to abstain from carrying such Resolution into effect, or to purchase the Shares held by the dissentient Shareholders or Shareholder, at such Price as may be agreed upon or settled by Arbitration, such Purchase Money to be paid before the Company is dissolved, and to be raised by the Liquidators in such Manner as may be determined by special Resolution.

XVIII. In the Case of a Company being wound up voluntarily, the Liquidators may, from Time to Time, during the Continuance of such Winding-up, summon General Meetings of the Company for the Purpose of obtaining the Sanction of the Company by a special Resolution, or for such other Purposes as they think fit.

XIX. Where a Company is in course of being wound up voluntarily, and Proceedings are taken for the Purpose of having the same wound up by the Court, the Court may, if it thinks fit, notwithstanding that it makes an Order directing the Company to be wound up by the Court, provide in such Order or in any other Order for the Adoption of all or any of the Proceedings taken in the course of the voluntary Winding-up: It may also, instead of making an Order that the Company should be altogether wound up by the Court, direct that the voluntary Winding-up should continue, but subject to such Supervision of the Court, and with such Liberty for Creditors, Contributories, or others to apply to the Court, and generally upon such Terms and subject to such Conditions as the Court thinks just.

XX. If the Liquidators make default in

reporting to the Registrar, in the Case of a Company being wound up by the Court, the Decree declaring the Company to be dissolved, and in the Case of a Company being wound up voluntarily, the Resolution declaring the Company to have been fairly wound up, they shall be liable to a Penalty not exceeding Five Pounds for every Day during which they are so in default, and moreover shall not, while so in default, be entitled to recover any Compensation for their Services as Liquidators.

XXI. If at the Expiration of Twelve Months from the Date of the Dissolution of any Company that has been wound up there remain in the Hands of the Liquidators any Money, Shares, or other Property which they have been unable, by reason of the Absence or Death of any Person entitled thereto, or for any other Reason, to distribute amongst the Parties so entitled, the Liquidators shall be deemed to be Trustees of such Monies, Shares, or other Property, within the Meaning of an Act passed in the Eleventh Year of the Reign of Her present Majesty, Chapter Ninety-six, and intituled *An Act for better securing Trust Funds, and for the Relief of Trustees*, and of any Act amending the same, and may pay or transfer such Monies, Shares, or other Property into the Court of Chancery accordingly.

*Alteration of Forms (Part III. of Principal Act).*

XXII. No Alteration made by the Board of Trade in the Table marked B. contained in the Schedule to the Principal Act shall affect any Company registered prior to the Date of such Alteration, or repeal as respects such Company any Portion of such Table, unless such Alteration is adopted by special Resolution.

*Repeal (Part V. of Principal Act).*

XXIII. The 107th Section of the Principal Act shall be repealed, and in lieu thereof be it enacted, That,—

1. An Act passed in the Eighth Year of the Reign of Her present Majesty, Chapter One hundred and ten, and intituled *An Act for the Registration, Incorporation, and Regulation of Joint Stock Companies;* and
2. An Act passed in the Eleventh Year of the Reign of Her present Majesty, Chapter Seventy-eight, intituled *An Act to amend an Act for the Registration, Incorporation, and Regulation of Joint Stock Companies;* and
3. The Limited Liability Act, 1855,

Shall be deemed to have been and still to remain unrepealed as to any Company completely registered which has not obtained Registration under the Principal Act, until such Time as such Company obtains Registration under the Joint Stock Companies Acts, 1856, 1857, but from and after such Time, and not before, shall be repealed as to such last-mentioned Company; and, subject as aforesaid, all the Acts mentioned in this Section shall be repealed.

*Costs by Limited Companies.*

XXIV. Where a Limited Company is Plaintiff or Pursuer in any Action, Suit, or other legal Proceeding, any Judge having Jurisdiction in the Matter may, if it be proved to his Satisfaction that there is Reason to believe that if the Defendant be successful in his Defence the Assets of the Company will be insufficient to pay his Costs, require sufficient Security to be givenfor such Costs, and may stay all Proceedings until such Security be given.

*Temporary Provisions (Part V. of Principal Act.)*

XXV. Where any Company completely registered under the said Act passed in the Eighth Year of the Reign of Her present Majesty, Chapter One hundred and ten, has obtained Registration under the Principal Act after the Third of *November* One thousand eight hundred and fifty-six, but before the passing of this Act, such Registration shall be as effectual to all Intents as if it had taken place on or before the said Third Day of *November* One thousand eight hundred and fifty-six,

XXVI. The One hundred and tenth Section of the Principal Act shall be repealed.

XXVII. Every Company completely registered under the said Act of the Eighth Year of the Reign of Her present Majesty, Chapter One hundred and ten, including any Company that has obtained a Certificate of Complete Registration under "The Limited Liability Act, 1855," but excluding any Company formed for the Purpose of Insurance, shall, if it has not already registered under the Principal Act, register under the Joint Stock Companies Acts, 1856, 1857, on or before the Second Day of *November* One thousand eight hundred and fifty-seven, or incur such Penalty as is hereinafter mentioned.

XVIII. If any Company hereby required to register under the Joint Stock Companies Acts makes default in registering on or before the said Second Day of *November* One thousand eight hundred and fifty-seven, then, from and after such Day until the Day on which such Company is registered under the Joint Stock

Companies Acts, 1856, 1857, the following Consequences shall ensue; (that is to say),

1. The Company shall be incapable of suing either at Law or in Equity, but shall not be incapable of being made a Defendant to a Suit either at Law or in Equity:
2. No Dividend shall be payable;
3. Each Director or Manager of the Company shall for each Day during which the Company is in default incur a Penalty of Five Pounds, and such Penalty may be recovered by any Person, and be applied by him to his own Use.

Nevertheless such Default shall not render the Company so being in default illegal, nor subject it to any Penalty or Disability other than as specified in this Section.

XXIX. Every Company consisting of Seven or more Shareholders, having a Capital of fixed Amount, divided into Shares, also of fixed Amount, duly constituted by Law prior to the passing of this Act, and not being a Company hereby required to be registered, may at any Time hereafter, upon Compliance with the Provisions of the Joint Stock Companies Acts, 1856, 1857, register itself as a Company under such Acts, with or without Limited Liability; subject to this Proviso, that no Company shall be registered as a Limited Company unless either the Liability of the Shareholders is already limited to the Amount of the unpaid Calls on their Shares, or an Assent to its being so registered has been given by Three Fourths in Number and Value of such of its Shareholders as may have been present, personally or by Proxy, in Cases where Proxies are allowed by the Regulations of the Company, at some General Meeting summoned for that Purpose.

XXX. Where an existing Company, authorized to register under the Joint Stock Companies Acts, 1856, 1857, has had the whole or any Portion of its Capital converted into Stock, such Company shall, as to the Capital so converted, instead of delivering to the Registrar the Statement of Capital and Shares required by the Principal Act, deliver to the Registrar a Statement of the Amount of Stock belonging to the Company, and the Names of the Persons who were Holders of such Stock, on some Day to be named in the Statement, not more than Six Days before the Day of Registration.

XXXI. The List of Shareholders required by Section One hundred and eleven of the Principal Act to be delivered to the Registrar need not be made up to the Day of the Registration of the Company, but may be made up to any Day not more than Six Days before such Day of Registration.

XXXII. No Fees shall be charged in respect of the Registration under the Joint Stock Companies Acts, 1856, 1857, of any Company existing at the Date of this Act, and required or authorized to be registered by the said Joint Stock Companies Acts or either of them, in Cases where such Company is not registered as a Limited Company, or where previously to its being registered as a Limited Company, the Liability of the Shareholders was limited by some other Act of Parliament or by Letters Patent.

XXXIII. The Hundred and thirteenth Section of the Principal Act shall be repealed; and in lieu thereof be it enacted as follows: Upon Compliance with the Requisitions of the Joint

Stock Companies Acts, 1856, 1857, respecting Registration, the Registrar of Joint Stock Companies shall certify under his Hand that the Company applying for Registration is incorporated as a Company under the Joint Stock Companies Acts, 1856, 1857, and in the Case of a Limited Company that it is limited, and thereupon such Company shall be incorporated accordingly; and all Provisions contained in any Act of Parliament, Deed of Settlement, Letters Patent, or other Instrument constituting or regulating any Company that has been registered under the Provisions of the said One hundred and thirteenth Section, or any Company that may hereafter be registered under this Section, shall be deemed to be Regulations of the Company, in the same Manner as if they were contained in a registered Memorandum of Association and Articles of Association; and all the Provisions of the Joint Stock Companies Acts, 1856, 1857, shall apply to such Company, in the same Manner in all respects as if it had been originally incorporated under such Acts, subject to the Reservation in favour of Creditors contained in the Principal Act, and to the following Provisoes:

1. That Table B. shall not, unless adopted by Special Resolution, apply to any such Company as is mentioned in this Section:
2. That no Company shall have Power to alter any Provision contained in any Act of Parliament relating to the Company:
3. That no Company shall have Power, without the Sanction of the Board of Trade, to alter any Provision contained in any Letters Patent relating to the Company:

4. That nothing herein contained shall authorize any Company to alter any such Provisions contained in any Deed of Settlement, Letters Patent, or other Instrument constituting or regulating the Company, as would, if such Company had originally been incorporated under the Joint Stock Companies Acts, 1856, 1857, have been contained in the Memorandum of Association, and are not authorized to be altered by such last-mentioned Acts:

But nothing herein contained shall derogate from any Power of altering its Constitution or Regulations which may be vested in any existing Company by virtue of any such Act of Parliament, Deed of Settlement, Letters Patent, or other Instrument constituting or regulating the Company: Moreover the Repeal of the said One hundred and thirteenth Section of the Principal Act shall not affect any Right acquired under the Section so repealed.

# JOINT STOCK COMPANIES ACT.

## 20 & 21 VICTORIA, Cap. 80.

An Act to amend "The Joint Stock Companies Act, 1856." [25*th August*, 1857.]

---

WHEREAS it is expedient that a further Amendment should be made in "The Joint Stock Companies Act, 1856:" Be it enacted by the Queen's most Excellent Majesty, by and with the Advice and Consent of the Lords Spiritual and Temporal, and Commons, in this present Parliament assembled, and by the Authority of the same, as follows:

I. The Joint Stock Companies Acts, 1856, 1857, shall not, nor shall either of them, be deemed to have repealed, as respects Companies already formed for the Purpose of carrying on the Business of Insurance, under the Act passed in the Eighth Year of Her present Majesty, Chapter One hundred and ten, or as respects Companies hereafter to be formed for the said Purpose, the said Act passed in the Eighth Year of Her present Majesty, Chapter One hundred and ten, or any other Act amending the same or relating to such Companies: Provided that if any Insurance Company, formed under the said Act of the Eighth Year of Her present Majesty, or the Directors of or Shareholders in any such Company have, during the Interval between the passing of the said Joint Stock Companies Act, 1856, and of this Act, acted as if the said Act of the Eighth Year of Her present Majesty had, as to such Company, been repealed by the said Joint Stock Companies Act, 1856, then so far as affects the Mutual Rights and Relations of the said Company, its Directors and Officers, and late or present Shareholders, and so far as affects any Penalties which the said Company or its Directors, Officers, or Shareholders, may have incurred by Non-observance of the said Act of the Eighth Year of her present Majesty, the said Act of the Eighth Year of Her present Majesty shall, as regards the Actions of the said Company, its Directors and Shareholders, during such Interval as aforesaid, be deemed to have been repealed.

# JOINT STOCK COMPANIES ACTS AMENDMENT.

## 21 & 22 VICTORIA, Cap. 60.

An Act to amend the Joint Stock Companies Acts, 1856 and 1857, and the Joint Stock Banking Companies Act, 1857. [23d *July*, 1858.]

---

WHEREAS by the Nineteenth Section of "The Joint Stock Companies Act, 1857," it is amongst other things provided that where a Company is in course of being wound up voluntarily, and Proceedings are taken for having the same wound up by the Court, the Court may, instead of making an Order that the Company should be altogether wound up by the Court, direct that the voluntary Winding-up should continue, but subject to such Supervision of the Court, and with such Liberty for Creditors, Contributories, and others to apply to the Court, and generally upon such Terms and subject to such Conditions as the Court thinks just: And whereas it is expedient to make further Provision for enabling Companies to be wound up in manner directed by the said Nineteenth Section: And whereas it is expedient to explain and amend the Acts hereinafter referred to as the Joint Stock Companies Acts, that is to say, "The Joint Stock Companies Act, 1856," "The Joint Stock Companies Act, 1857," and "The Joint Stock Banking Companies Act, 1857:" Be it enacted by the Queen's most Excellent Majesty, by and with the Advice and Consent of the Lords Spiritual and Temporal, and Commons, in this present Parliament assembled, and by the Authority of the same, as follows:

I. This Act may be cited for all Purposes as "The Joint Stock Companies Amendment Act, 1858," and it shall be included in the Expression "Joint Stock Companies Acts," as herein-after used, unless there is something in the Context inconsistent with its being so included.

II. A Petition praying wholly or in part that a voluntary Winding-up may continue, subject to the Supervision of the Court, shall, for the Purpose of giving Jurisdiction to the Court over Suits and Actions, and over the Appointment of a Receiver, be deemed to be a Petition for winding up the Company by the Court; and in determining whether the Company is to be wound up altogether compulsorily or under the Provisions of the said Nineteenth Section, the Court may have regard to the Wishes of the Majority in Number and Value of the Creditors as proved to it by any sufficient Evidence.

III. Where any Order is made by the Court, in pursuance of the said Nineteenth Section, for the Continuance of a voluntary Winding-up, the Court may in such Order or in any subsequent Order appoint any additional Liquidator or Liquidators; and any Liquidator or Liquidators so appointed by the Court shall have the same Powers, be subject to the same Obligations, and in all respects stand in the same Position as if they had been appointed by the Company: The Court may from Time to Time remove any Liquidator or Liquidators so appointed by the Court, and fill up any Vacancy occasioned by such Removal, or by the Death or Resignation of any such Liquidator or Liquidators: The Court shall in the Appointment of a Liquidator or Liquidators under this Section consult any Creditor or Classes of Creditors it may think expedient to consult for the Purpose of ascertaining what Appointments are most for the Interest of the Creditors.

IV. Where an Order is made by the Court, in pursuance of the said Nineteenth Section, for the Continuance of a voluntary Winding-up, the Liquidators appointed to conduct such Winding-up may, subject to any Order made by the Court, exercise all Powers given to them, without the Intervention of the Court, in the same Manner as if the Company were being wound up altogether voluntarily; but, save as aforesaid, any Order made by the Court, in pursuance of the said Nineteenth Section, for the Continuance of a voluntary Winding-up, shall for all Purposes, including the Application of any Provision relating to fraudulent Preference, be deemed to be an Order of the Court for winding up the Company by the Court, and shall confer full Authority on the Court to make Calls, or to enforce Calls made by the Liquidators, and to exercise all other Powers which it might have exercised of its own Motion, or on the Application of the official Liquidators, if an Order had been made for winding up the Company altogether by the Court.

V. Where an Order, Interlocutor, or Decree has been made in *Scotland* for winding up a Company compulsorily, or where an Order, Interlocutor, or Decree has been made in pursuance of the said Nineteenth Section for the Continuance of a voluntary Winding-up, it shall be competent to the Court in *Scotland* during

Session, and to the Lord Ordinary on the Bills during Vacation, on Production by the Liquidators of a List certified by them of the Names of the Contributories liable in Payment of any Calls which they may wish to enforce, and of the Amount due by each Contributory respectively, and of the Date when the same became due, to pronounce forthwith a Decree against such Contributories for Payment of the Sums so certified to be due by each of them respectively, with Interest from the said Date till Payment at the rate of Five Pounds *per Centum per Annum*, in the same Way and to the same Effect as if they had severally consented to Registration for Execution, on a Charge of Six Days, of a legal Obligation to pay such Calls and Interest; and such Decree may be extracted immediately, and no Suspension thereof shall be competent, except on Caution or Consignation, unless with special Leave of the Court or Lord Ordinary.

VI. Where an Order has been made for winding up a Company compulsorily, or where an Order has been made, in pursuance of the said Nineteenth Section, for the Continuance of a voluntary Winding-up, no Suit, Action, or other legal Proceeding shall be proceeded with or commenced against the Company or the Public Officer thereof, or any Member of the Company in respect of a Debt of the Company, except with the Leave of the Court, and subject to such Terms as the Court may impose.

VII. Where an Order has been made for winding up a Company compulsorily, or where an Order has been made, in pursuance of the said Nineteenth Section, for the Continuance of a voluntary Winding-up, the Court may make such Order as it thinks just as to the Inspection by the Creditors and Contributories of Books and Papers of the Company, and such Books and Papers may be inspected by Creditors or Contributories, in conformity with such Order of the Court, but not further or otherwise.

VIII. Where an Order has been made in pursuance of the said Nineteenth Section for the Continuance of a voluntary Winding-up, and such Order is afterwards superseded by an Order directing the Company to be wound-up compulsorily, the Court may in such last-mentioned Order, or in any subsequent Order, appoint the voluntary Liquidators or any of them, either provisionally or permanently, and either with or without the Addition of any other Persons, to be official Liquidators.

IX. Where the Court makes an Order for winding up a Company compulsorily, it may, if it thinks fit, provide by that or any subsequent Order that the official Liquidators may exercise any specified Powers without the Intervention of the Court.

X. Where an Order has been made for winding up a Company compulsorily, or where an Order has been made, in pursuance of the said Nineteenth Section, for the Continuance of a voluntary Winding-up, the Liquidators may, with the Sanction of the Court, and upon such Notice of Creditors as to the Court shall seem fit, at any Stage of the Winding-up, pay any Classes of Creditors in full, or make such other Arrangements with Creditors as the Court may sanction; and any general or partial Scheme of Liquidation, if approved of by the Court, shall be binding on all the Creditors and Contributories of the Company.

XI. The Practice hitherto in use in the Court of Chancery in *England* in winding up Companies, under "The Joint Stock Companies Winding-up Act, 1848," and "The Joint Stock Companies Winding-up Act, 1849," including the Service of Summonses, Notices, and other Documents by Post, and including the Payment of a Per-centage in lieu of Fees to the Suitors Fee Fund, the Non-entry of Orders at the Registry Office, and all Powers and Jurisdictions given to the said Court of Chancery by the said Acts, and not conferred by the Joint Stock Companies Acts, shall be applicable to the winding up under the said Joint Stock Companies Acts of Companies by the Court of Chancery and Courts of Bankruptcy in *England*, until Rules for regulating such Winding-up are made in pursuance of the Powers for that Purpose given by the said Joint Stock Companies Acts; and the Courts of Chancery and Courts of Bankruptcy in *England* may adopt such Practice, Powers, and Jurisdictions to the same Extent as if the Companies were being wound up under "The Joint Stock Companies Winding-up Act, 1848," and "The Joint Stock Companies Winding-up Act, 1849;" and in the Case of Companies engaged in working any Mines within and subject to the Jurisdiction of the Stannaries, and registered under the Joint Stock Companies Acts, 1856, 1857, the like Practice, Powers, and Jurisdiction may, by Rules to be made under the Ninety-eighth Section of "The Joint Stock Companies Act, 1856," be adopted and exercised by the Court of the Vice-Warden of the Stannaries, so far as such Practice, Powers, and Jurisdiction are or can be made applicable to that Court.

XII. Any Order made by the Court in *England* for or in the Course of the Winding-up of a Company under the Joint Stock Companies Acts shall be enforced in *Scotland* and *Ireland* in the Courts that would respectively have had Jurisdiction in respect of such Company if the registered Office of the Company had been established in *Scotland* or *Ireland,* and in the same Manner in all respects as if such Order had been made by the Courts that are hereby required to enforce the same; and in like Manner Order, Interlocutors, and Decrees made by the Court in *Scotland* for or in the Course of the Winding-up of a Company shall be enforced in *England* and *Ireland,* and Orders made by the Court in *Ireland* for or in the Course of winding up a Company shall be enforced in *England* and *Scotland,* by the Courts which would respectively have had Jurisdiction in the Matter of such Company if the registered Office of the Company were established in the Division of the United Kingdom where the Order is required to be enforced, and in the same Manner in all respects as if such Order had been made by the Court required to enforce the same in the Case of a Company within its own Jurisdiction.

XIII. Where any Order, Interlocutor, or Decree made by one Court is required to be enforced by another Court, as herein-before provided, an Office Copy of the Order, Interlocutor, or Decree so made shall be produced to the proper Officer of the Court required to enforce the same, and the Production of such Office Copy shall be sufficient Evidence of such Order, Interlocutor, or Decree having been made, and thereupon such last-mentioned Court shall cause such Order, Interlocutor, or Decree to be registered, or shall take such other Steps in the Matter as may be requisite for enforcing such Order, Interlocutor, or Decree, in the same Manner as if it were the Order, Interlocutor, or Decree of the Court enforcing the same.

XIV. Where a Company is being wound up altogether voluntarily, the Liquidators may apply to the Court, or to the Lord Ordinary on the Bills in *Scotland* in Time of Vacation, by Petition, Motion, the Presentation of a Special Case, or in such other Manner as the Court may direct, to determine any Question arising in the Matter of such Winding-up, or to exercise, as respects the enforcing any Calls, or in respect of any other particular Matter, all or any of the Powers which the Court might exercise if the Company were being wound up compulsorily; and the Court, or Lord Ordinary in the Case aforesaid, if satisfied that the Determination of such Question or the required Exercise of Power will be just and beneficial, may accede, wholly or partially, to such Application, upon such Terms and subject to such Conditions as the Court thinks fit, or it may make such other Order, Interlocutors, or Decree on such Application as the Court thinks just.

XV. Where any Company is being wound up altogether voluntarily, or is being wound up subject to the Provisions of the said Nineteenth Section, the Company in General Meeting may fill up any Vacancy occasioned by the Death or Resignation of any Liquidator or Liquidators appointed by the Company.

XVI. In case of any Company being wound up compulsorily, the Liquidators may invest any Monies for the Time being in their Hands, or standing to their Credit in the Bank of *England*, arising from such Winding-up, in Government Securities, including Exchequer Bills.

XVII. In fixing the Amount payable by any Contributory, in pursuance of the Joint Stock Companies Acts or any of them, he shall be debited with the Amount of all Debts due from him to the Company, including the Amount of the Call, and shall be credited with all Sums due to him from the Company on any independent Contract or Dealing between him and the Company, and the Balance, after making such Debit and Credit as aforesaid, shall be deemed to be the Sum due.

XVIII. All Calls made or to be made on any Shareholder or Contributory, in pursuance of any of the Joint Stock Companies Acts, shall, in the event of such Shareholder or Contributory becoming bankrupt or insolvent, be proveable against his Estate.

XIX. The Sixteenth Section of "The Joint Stock Companies Act, 1857," shall be repealed; and in lieu thereof be it enacted as follows: The Liquidators shall have Power to compromise all Calls and Liabilities to Calls, Debts and Liabilities capable of resulting in Debts, and all Claims, whether present or future, certain or contingent, ascertained, or sounding only in Damages, subsisting or supposed to subsist between the Company and any Contributory or alleged Contributory, or other Debtor or Person apprehending Liability to the Company, upon the Receipt of such Sums, payable at such Times, and generally upon such Terms as may be agreed upon, with Power for the Liquidators to take any Security for the Discharge of such Debts or Liabilities, and to give complete Discharges in respect of all or any such Calls, Debts, or Liabilities; subject to the Proviso, that where an Order has been made by the Court for winding-up a Company compulsorily, or when an Order has been made, in pursuance of a said Nineteenth Section, for the Continuance of a voluntary Winding-up, no such Compromise shall be made, except in accordance with the Directions of the Court, as expressed generally in any Order made by the Court, or as given in each particular Case, and after giving such Notice to Creditors, or any Portion of them, as the Court shall direct; and that where a Company is being wound up altogether voluntarily no such Compromise shall be effected, except with the Sanction of a special Resolution of the Company, or of a general or particular Power delegated to the Liquidators by a special Resolution.

XX. Where any Order is made for winding up a Company compulsorily, or for the Continuance of a voluntary Winding-up, subject to the Provisions of the said Nineteenth Section, if it appear in the Course of such Winding-up that any past or existing Director, Manager, Public Officer, or Member of such Company has been guilty of any Offence in relation to the Company for which he is criminally responsible, the Court may, on the Application of any Person interested in such Winding-up, or of its own Motion, direct the official Liquidators, or the Liquidators, (as the Case may be,) to institute and conduct a Prosecution or Prosecutions for such Offence, and to order the Costs and Expences to be paid out of the Assets of the Company.

XXI. Where a Company is being wound-up altogether voluntarily, if it appear to the Liquidators conducting such Winding-up that any past or existing Director, Manager, Public Officer, or Member of such Company has been guilty of any Offence in relation to the Company for which he is criminally responsible, it shall be lawful for the Liquidators, with the previous Sanction of the Court, to prosecute such Offender, and all Expences properly incurred by them in such Prosecution shall be payable out of the Assets of the Company in Priority to all other Liabilities.

XXII. This Act shall apply in Cases where an Order has been already made for winding up a Company compulsorily, or where an Order has been made, in pursuance of the Nineteenth Section, for the Continuance of a voluntary Winding-up, or where a Company is in the Course of being wound up altogether voluntarily.

XXIII. Any Company or Copartnership, consisting of seven or more Persons, having by its Constitution a Capital of fixed Amount, divided into Shares, also of fixed Amount, if it legally carried on the Business of Banking previously to "The Banking Company Act, 1857," is entitled to register itself or to continue registered under "The Joint Stock Companies Act, 1857," for the Purpose of winding up under that Act, and if it legally carried on any other Business than Banking, except that of Insurance, previously to the passing of "The Joint Stock Companies Act, 1856," is entitled to register itself or to continue registered under "The Joint Stock Companies Act, 1856," or the Joint Stock Companies Acts, 1856, 1857, for the Purpose of winding up under those Acts.

XXIV. This Act shall extend to the Provisions of the Joint Stock Companies Acts, 1856, 1857, incorporated with "The Joint Stock Banking Companies Act, 1857."

# JOINT STOCK BANKING COMPANIES.

## 21 & 22 VICTORIA, Cap. 91.

An Act to enable Joint Stock Banking Companies to be formed on the Principle of Limited Liability. [*2nd August*, 1858.]

---

WHEREAS it is expedient to enable Banking Companies to be formed on the Principle of Limited Liability; Be it enacted by the Queen's most Excellent Majesty, by and with the Advice and Consent of the Lords Spiritual and Temporal, and Commons, in this present Parliament assembled, and by the Authority of the same, as follows:

1. So much of the Joint Stock Banking Companies Act, 1857, as prohibits a Banking Company from being formed under that Act with limited Liability, or prohibits an existing Banking Company from being registered under that Act with limited Liability, shall be repealed, subject to the following Proviso, that no Banking Company claiming to issue Notes in the United Kingdom shall be entitled to limited Liability in respect of such Issue, but shall continue subject to unlimited Liability in respect thereof, and that, if necessary, the Assets shall be marshalled for the Benefit of the general Creditors, and the Shareholders shall be liable for the whole Amount of the Issue, in addition to the Sum for which they would be liable as Shareholders of a Limited Company.

II. The Registration of a Banking Company under the Joint Stock Banking Companies Act, 1857, or under any other Act, shall not prejudice the Right of such Company to register itself again as a Limited Company under the said Joint Stock Banking Companies Act, 1857, and the Acts incorporated therewith.

III. Provided, That every Company so registering itself again as a limited Company, and every existing Banking Company which shall register itself as a Limited Banking Company, shall, at least Thirty Days previous to obtaining a Certificate of Registration with Limited Liability, give Notice that it is intended so to register the same to every Person and Partnership Firm who shall have a Banking Account with the Company, and such Notice shall be given either by delivering the same to such Person or Firm, or leaving the same or putting the same into the Post addressed to him or them at such Address as shall have been last communicated or otherwise become known as his or their Address to or by the Company; and in case the Company shall omit to give any such Notice as is herein-before required to be given, then as between the Company and the Person or Persons only who are for the Time being interested in the Account in respect of which such Notice ought to have been given, and so far as respects such Account and all Variations thereof down to the Time at which such Notice shall be given, but not further or otherwise, the Certificate of Registration with Limited Liability shall have no operation.

IV. Every Limited Joint Stock Banking Company shall before it commences Business, or, if a Banking Company at the Time carrying on Business with unlimited Liability, before it avails itself of the Provisions of this Act, and also on the First Day of *February* and the First Day of *August* in every Year during which it carries on Business, make a Statement in the Form contained in the Schedule hereto, or as near thereto as Circumstances will admit, and a Copy of such Statement shall be put up in a conspicous Place in the registered Office of the Company, and in every Branch Office or Place where the

Banking Business of the Company is carried on; and if Default is made in due Compliance with the Provisions of this Section, each Director shall be liable to a Penalty not exceeding Five Pounds for every Day during which such Default continues, and such Penalties shall be recovered in a summary Manner.

V. Limited Joint Stock Banking Companies shall be wound up in the same Manner and under the same Jurisdiction as that in and under which Joint Stock Banking Companies other than Limited are required to be wound up by the Joint Stock Banking Companies Act, 1857.

---

## SCHEDULE referred to in the foregoing Act.

*Form of Statement to be published by a Limited Joint Stock Banking Company.*

The Liability of the Shareholders is limited.

The Capital of the Company is One million, divided into Ten thousand Shares of One hundred Pounds each.

The Number of Shares issued is Ten thousand.

Calls to the Amount of Twenty Pounds per Share have been made, under which the Sum of One hundred and eighty thousand Pounds has been received.

| The Liabilities of the Company on the First Day of January (*or* July) were, | £ *s.* *d.* |
|---|---|
| Notes issued - - - - - - - | |
| Deposits not bearing Interest - - - - | |
| Deposits bearing Interest - - - - - | |
| Seven Day and other Bills - - - - - | |
| Total | |

| The Assets of the Company on that Day were, | |
|---|---|
| Government Securities - - - - - - | |
| Bills of Exchange - - - - - - | |
| Loans on Mortgage - - - - - - | |
| Other Loans - - - - - - - | |
| Bank Premises - - - - - - - - | |
| Other Securities, exclusive of unpaid Calls on Shares | |
| Total | |

Dated the First Day of February *or* August One Thousand eight hundred and fifty-nine.

# LIMITED LIABILITY MADE PRACTICAL. REDUCTION OF CAPITAL OF COMPANIES AND THE SUBDIVISION OF SHARES

Loftus Fitz-Wigram
of Lincoln's Inn, Barrister-at-Law.
*Limited Liability Made Practical.*
*Reduction of Capital of Companies and the Subdivision of Shares*
(London: Effingham Wilson, 1867)

LIMITED LIABILITY MADE PRACTICAL.

# REDUCTION

OF

# CAPITAL OF COMPANIES

AND THE

## Subdivision of Shares;

WITH REMARKS ON THE

## 12th SECTION OF "THE COMPANIES ACT, 1862,"

AND SUGGESTIONS AS TO

## "SHARES TO BEARER."

BY

LOFTUS FITZ-WYGRAM, Esq.,

OF LINCOLN'S INN, BARRISTER-AT-LAW.

LONDON:

EFFINGHAM WILSON, ROYAL EXCHANGE.

1867.

*One Shilling.*

# PREFACE.

THE questions which are brought forward in this short treatise are at the present moment much discussed in the legal as well as the commercial world.

The fact that a measure referring to the principal object of these pages was only defeated by a very narrow majority in the House of Lords last year, and that a similar Bill will, I understand, be brought forward in the present Session, will, I trust, be some excuse for my thus venturing to trespass on public attention.

LOFTUS FITZ-WYGRAM.

5, KING'S BENCH WALK, TEMPLE,
*January*, 1867.

# THE REDUCTION

OF THE

# NOMINAL CAPITAL OF COMPANIES.

THE principle of limited liability may be regarded as established, and, as the late Parliamentary Returns of Joint Stock Companies include, I believe, only seven which are registered as "unlimited," the probability is, that few such Companies will be formed hereafter except on that basis.

Where legislation on a new and important subject is comprised in a single Act, as is the case with "The Companies Act, 1862," it is hardly possible that an Act, however ably framed, must not be susceptible of some improvement, or that some mistaken view must not be taken therein, or some *casus omissus* arise. But the defects which undoubtedly exist are defects more in the carrying out of the principle than in the principle itself.

The object of these pages is to suggest an amendment of the 12th section of the Act of 1862.

We are all, as the public, now familiar—perhaps too familiar—with the form of a Prospectus, with the array of names of Directors, and the assurances of the certainty of the success of the undertaking, and the well-known reference to "the Articles of Association to be seen at office of the Solicitor of the Company." Attention, however, is rarely specially invited to the Memorandum of Association, the true basis of the intents of the Company, and of which the Articles are but the amplification, and to which they are in law subservient; for it cannot be too earnestly borne in mind that Articles of Association, however wide and extensive, cannot confer power to do any acts, or justify the pursuit of any business not included in or incidental to the Memorandum of Association.

Now, by the 8th section of the Act, which runs as given below,* it will be seen that the Promoters of

* VIII. Where a Company is formed on the principle of having the liability of its Members limited to the amount unpaid on their Shares, hereinafter referred to as a Company limited by Shares, the Memorandum of Association shall contain the following things, that is to say,—

(1.) The name of the proposed Company, with the addition of the word "limited," as the last word in such name.

(2.) The part of the United Kingdom—whether *England*, *Scotland*, or *Ireland*—in which the Registered Office of the Company is proposed to be situate.

(3.) The objects for which the proposed Company is to be established.

any undertaking under the Act must, *inter alia*, define the nominal amount of the Shares into which the capital of the Company is to be divided, and probably no point ought to be more anxiously weighed. The nominal capital itself may be small, or, as happily described by Mr. Dickens, "a figure of two and as many cyphers as the printer can get into the same line;" but the question still remains, into what Shares of what nominal value ought the capital to be divided?

When the Act first came into operation, it was more usual to divide the capital of the new Limited Liability Companies into Shares of large amounts, for the reason principally that, when they were placed in good hands, the necessary capital was more easily raised. Experience is now in favour of the opposite system, which affords equal security to the creditor, and greater convenience to the Shareholders and the general public.

We shall more easily understand why opinion has thus changed if we take the case of a Company perfectly sound in itself, but whose capital was originally in Shares of a large nominal value. What has followed? As soon as a time of finan-

(4). A declaration that the liability of the Members is limited.

(5.) The amount of capital with which the Company proposes to be registered, divided into Shares of a certain fixed amount.

cial difficulties arose, other Companies, based on the principle of large Shares, failed, and heavy calls were made.* The public at once conceived an abhorrence of large Shares, and awoke to the fact (now painfully clear) that nominal limited liability is in many cases practically unlimited. If, as in a recent instance, the Shareholder who paid up £10 on each of his £50 Shares, fully expecting never to be asked for more, is suddenly called upon by legal compulsion to pay at once the remaining £40 per Share, his ruin (unless he be a capitalist) is equally complete as if he were not under the protecting shadow of so-called limited liability.

But the position of the supposed Company continues sound, and confidence in it would be undiminished save for the incubus of the nominal liability attached to the holdings. The step to be taken is obvious: the Directors say at once, "Our large nominal capital is not and cannot be required; let us assist our constituents, and as we should in due form increase our capital had more been required, so let us now reduce it to the amount which we find will be actually necessary, and in lieu of every £50 Share we will issue to the holder thereof a £25 Share."

If, however, as often happens, a considerable

* At this present time a call of £30 per Share has been made by the liquidators of one Company, and of £40 per Share by those of another.

portion of the nominal capital should be really required as each call is made, the market value of the Shares sinks, purchasers are not to be found, and the larger the Share sought to be transferred, the more cumbrous, inconvenient, and unnegotiable it becomes, until in hard times it cannot be practically transferred except at a ruinous discount. The Directors again argue,—"There is no market for our £50 Shares; let us issue five Shares of £10 each, with a proportionate amount marked as paid thereon, for each £50 Share. Where an intending transferor cannot find one purchaser of a £50 Share, he will probably find five purchasers each of a £10 Share; we will call in the old £50 Shares, and exchange them each for five £10 Shares. The aggregate amount of the capital of our Company will be the same for the security of creditors, and our Shareholders will possess Shares more easily transferable."

Both these schemes, however, viz.,—

1. The reduction of nominal Capital.

2. The reduction of nominal amount of Shares.

although apparently very practical and simple in themselves, cannot be carried into effect, and for this reason, that the Act of 1862 here intervenes. The course proposed may be, and is in fact, fair, simple, and just, but it is not included in, and therefore is contrary to, the provisions of the 12th section, which bestows only the following powers:—

XII. Any Company limited by Shares may so far modify the conditions contained in its Memorandum of Association, if authorized to do so by its regulations, as originally framed, or as altered by Special Resolution, in manner hereinafter mentioned, as to increase its Capital, by the issue of new Shares, of such amount as it thinks expedient, or to consolidate and divide its Capital into Shares of larger amount than its existing Shares, or to convert its paid-up Shares into Stock; but, save as aforesaid, and save as hereinafter provided, in the case of a change of name, no alteration shall be made by any Company in the conditions contained in its Memorandum of Association.

Some have supposed the powers of this section to be extended by the 50th section of the Act. But it is clear by the words, "Subject to the powers," &c., that the powers contained in the last-mentioned section are limited to those sanctioned by the 12th section.

There are but two ways of doing that which is forbidden by law—

1. By private legislation.
2. By altering the general law on the subject.

The necessity of diminishing the nominal amount of Shares was experienced long before the recent commercial panic, and from time to time, with that view, Private Bills were deposited for the purposes of individual Companies. As far as my recollection serves me, only one of these Bills, and that under very exceptional circumstances, ever passed into a law. I do not remember if any Bill ever came to a formal discussion in either House, but my impression is, that all were withdrawn, it being understood that the Chairman of

Committees of the House of Lords refused his assent in each case. At the same time it is right to state that his Lordship was not, I believe, opposed to the principle involved in such bills, but only objected to exceptional legislation in particular instances.

The private redress for particular grievances—although it was owing to the notices to be given, and the expenses to be incurred, both tedious and costly—having thus failed, many applications were made to the then Board of Trade, to introduce a general measure on the subject. These applications were favourably received by the then President, and the Companies who had given notice of Private Bills last Session were informed that steps would be taken for the passing of a Public Act. Finally a Bill was brought in intituled, "The Companies Act (1862) Amendment Act." This measure ran thus:—

A BILL TO AMEND THE COMPANIES ACT, 1862.

Be it enacted by the Queen's most Excellent Majesty, by and with the Advice and Consent of the Lords Spiritual and Temporal, and Commons, in this present Parliament assembled, and by the Authority of the same, as follows:—

1. In addition to the Powers conferred by Section Twelve of The Companies Act, 1862, on a Company limited by Shares to modify to the extent therein mentioned the Conditions contained in its Memorandum of Association, any Company limited by Shares (incorporated either before or after the passing of this Act) may so far modify the Conditions contained in its Memorandum of Association, if authorized to do so by its Regulations as originally framed or as altered by

Special Resolution in manner in the said Act provided, as to divide its Capital or any Part thereof into Shares of a less Amount than that fixed in the Memorandum of Association, but not of a less Amount in any Case than *Ten Pounds*, and may for that Purpose subdivide its several existing Shares, or any of them, into Two or more Shares, but so that any Share created by such Subdivision be not in any Case of a less Amount than *Ten Pounds*.

2. Every Company that alters the Division of its Capital under the Authority of this Act shall give notice of such Alteration to the Registrar of Joint Stock Companies.

3. The Subdivision of an existing Share, under the Authority of this Act, shall not operate to relieve a Member of the Company from any Liability to which he was subject in respect of that Share before its Subdivision.

4. This Act shall be construed as One Act with The Companies Act, 1862, and may be cited as The Companies Act Amendment Act, 1866.

This Bill, brought in as a Government measure, passed through all its stages in the House of Commons without any serious dispute, and having been read according to custom a first time in the House of Lords, came on for the second reading thereof on the 8th day of June, 1866.

It might have been fairly expected that a Government measure which had passed without a division through the House of Commons, and with which many Members of that House were practically conversant, and more especially as the second reading was moved and the general principle of the Bill was approved by the Chairman of Committees, (perhaps the highest living authority on legislation relating to Companies,) would have met with but little opposition. Lord Redesdale was, however, followed by Lord Overstone, who "contended that the returns obtained by himself in two former years showed a great increase in the number of Shares in Companies in existence; that the Bill would tend to the further multiplication thereof; that many commercial failures were daily occurring; that by any such increase of the number of Shares more and more persons would be affected by any such subsequent failures; that small Shares would but allure people of humble means to embark in speculations leading to a like disastrous result:" and who finally implored their Lordships "not to give additional liberty or further existence to a system (*i.e.*, limited liability) fraught with such dangerous failures."

His Lordship was answered by Lord Stanley of Alderley, who justly observed that "Lord Overstone's speech was simply that of an opponent of limited liability *ab initio*, without reference to the Bill in question; that the failures alluded to by him were not brought about by limited liability; and that even if a Company failed, the creditors thereof would be better secured by having as their debtors 10 Shareholders each of a £10 Share, than one such of a £100 Share."

The debate was continued by Earl Grey and Lord Teynham respectively, against and for the measure, and on the division the Bill was lost by a majority of three, the numbers being seventeen to fourteen.

There are but few of Lord Overstone's observations that might not be questioned, if the case is, as it should be, viewed and argued on public grounds. If the basis of smaller Shares (not under £10) is, as remarked by a recent writer on the subject, quite as secure as the narrower one of larger Shares, and if it be advisable, of which there has been no question, not to exclude the middle classes from investing their savings in Joint Stock Companies, there can be no doubt that the Shares should be so framed that they may be at once within the reach and suitable to the circumstances of this class of investors. The Joint Stock system, in the present gigantic state of mercantile operations, prevents what may be termed the middle classes of commerce from being out-bought, out-sold, and out-financed by the great capitalists. And to the Joint Stock system limited liability is a necessary, an imperatively necessary, adjunct and accessory.

The consequences of this vote of the House of Lords were soon visible: the existing depression of Companies was enhanced; Shares in sound and unsound undertakings became equally unsaleable, the promises of the Government had not been realized, and Companies were driven to do for themselves, in a costly, roundabout, and inconvenient way, that which they had trusted to Parliament to enable them to effect by an easy and inexpensive process. Various and complex were the schemes that ensued. Some Companies dissolved, liquidated their affairs, and then obtained certificates of incorporation, under slightly varying names, with a capital divided into Shares of less nominal value; and this is now the usual course. A Company winds itself up, and transfers its business to a newly-formed undertaking, which is, in fact, but the old Company itself, with the desired changes effected in the constitution thereof. Some have pursued the beaten track of private legislation, and given notice to deposit Bills for the coming Session. Some have availed themselves of powers in their Articles of Association to accept surrenders of Shares, and then re-issued the same, sub-divided, as new Shares.

This is the state of things at this moment. Where reforms of any Act are imperatively required, legal ingenuity will always find a way, roundabout it may and must be, but still a way to do indirectly that which an accidental omission in the Act forbids to be done directly.

But why is this ingenuity required? Simply because the wording of the 12th section stands in the way, and, while commercial sense and public feeling point out the course to be pursued, prevents its adoption. Those interested in the change proposed, and they are nearly the whole investing public, can only hope that, even amid the throes of political reform and the intricacies of railway debenture legislation, the Bill of last year may be again brought forward *melioribus opto auspiciis*, and that it may not be again interdicted to do, generally and simply, that which individual Companies now effect in tortuous and complex fashion. By such a measure alone can the commercial status of many Companies be restored.

Thus far we have only advocated that which was contained in the Government Bill of last year. May we advance further, and hope the Bill of the pending Session may include not only the reduction of the nominal value of Shares, but also the reduction of the nominal capital of Companies. Here I am aware that I am treading on somewhat doubtful ground, and am free to confess that to such reduction it may be necessary that the consent of the Board of Trade may be required in each particular instance. But application to and the assent of that Board, after due inquiry, would be a sufficient guarantee to the creditors. I should also recommend that notice of any such application should be obliged to be served on each individual creditor, by the usual advertisements, and that every creditor should be at liberty to appear in opposition.

I venture to add a few remarks on the existing system of registration of Shares. The object of registering each Share in a particular name is two-fold :—

1st. To enable the Company to know who is responsible to them for the unpaid amount on each Share.

2ndly. To enable those interested as creditors or otherwise in the Company to see at a glance the constituent body with whom they have dealings.

So long as liability is still attached to the Shares, this system of registration works well, and, I may venture to say, is necessary. But a time arises (and very early in some Companies, where Shares, or a considerable portion thereof, are permitted to be paid up in full) when this liability ceases, or practically ceases, to exist. When this is so, the object of registration is fulfilled; the Company cease to have an interest, as far as further demands on those Shares are concerned; the creditors of the Company care but little in whose names the Shares stand, for even the highest names are but of trivial moment when those names are no longer responsible.

But although the objects of registration in a particular name thus cease to exist, still in this country the transfer of a fully paid-up Share remains fenced around with the self-same legal formalities as were attached to such Share before it became fully paid-up. Yet the object and aim of those formalities is gone; it is a matter of total indifference to the creditors of a Company, and to the Company itself, whether the Share is registered in any particular name, or if, indeed, it is registered at all, but still the same ceremonies must be gone through on each successive transfer as if the original amount of liability remained attached thereto. In other words, whether the Share is burdened with the whole weight of its original liability, or whether all such is discharged, it cannot be transferred except by deed and registration. On the Continent Shares paid-up in full, and I believe also Shares marked with a certain amount as paid, pass from hand to hand by delivery, or as it is technically termed, as "Shares to bearer." Here alone it is otherwise. I am here in this place bound to anticipate an objection which will probably be made, that, as at present, every transfer deed ought to bear an *ad valorem* stamp according to the amount of the consideration expressed on the face of the deed, the Government would lose such duty if the existing system of transfer was abolished in the case of fully paid-up Shares. I might fairly contend that although it is enacted that the consideration in a transfer deed should be "truly stated," the Act for that purpose is really too often rendered ineffectual by the, I regret to say, growing practice of transferring even very large amounts of Shares for a mere nominal consideration, and thus practically evading the stamp duty on the price really as between the transferor and transferee received and given. In lieu, however, of advancing any such argument, I would venture to suggest that some such course as that sanctioned by the 16 & 17 Vict., c. 59, sect. 14, "with respect to bonds of certain public Companies," and of which section here give a summary, might be usefully adopted, and would be found advantageous to the public and not detrimental to the revenue.*

It will be remembered that not long ago Parliament, on the motion of Mr. Gladstone, sanctioned the issue of certificates to bearer with respect to stock in the Public Funds; and it is submitted that somewhat similar certificates might with safety and advantage be allowed to be issued with regard to stock of Companies, and also as to fully paid-up Shares, which are but a species of stock, and may, by the Act of 1862, be at any time consolidated into actual stock.

Whether we might not also imitate our Continental neighbours, and attach Coupons (either blank, or of fixed amount, to Shares, is a further question, and forms part of the system of "Shares to bearer" advocated above.

Another reason, I think, for allowing fully paid-up Shares to pass by delivery alone is, that they would attract the attention of the large class who, almost as matter of principle, decline to have any connection with Joint Stock Companies. Many persons shrink from a nominal liability in the very safest concerns; and some, even where

* Sect. 14. The transfers of bonds and mortgages made by public Companies, under Acts of Parliament for securing moneys authorized by such Acts to be borrowed, shall be exempted from stamp duty where the bonds or mortgages have been, before any transfer thereof, stamped with quadruple *ad valorem* duties.

the Shares are fully paid-up, object to the appearance of their names on the Register; but no one would object to be the owner of a fully paid-up Share to Bearer, to which no liability whatever attached, and which required no formality of transfer or of registration. The most timid investor would feel that he could not by any possibility, under these circumstances, incur any loss beyond the sum given by him for the purchase of such fully paid-up Share, and that he held a security perfect in itself, in so far as involving no further risk, and easily negotiable.

These suggestions, however, are perhaps somewhat foreign to the original purposes of these pages. My aim was to show the expediency of allowing Companies to reduce the nominal liability on their Shares by a general and simple process, and the other points arose from the discussion of that subject.

The whole question of such reduction seems to be most fairly summed up in a few remarks kindly made on these pages by one of the leading financiers of the age.

"As the law stands, a Company started to-day may register itself with what Capital it likes, divided into what Shares it pleases. Why does the same law preclude Companies started before experience was found to be in favour of small Shares (not under £10 each) from sub-division of the nominal amount of their Shares? Either the power given by law of dividing Capital into small Shares is good and just, or the reverse. If the law which confers such power on new Companies is bad, let it be at once repealed; if it be good and just, let all Companies equally participate in the advantages it confers."

These remarks seem to me to embody the whole question at issue.

It was my intention to have here inserted a Draft Bill, formally drawn, and containing the several objects advocated above. I understand, however, while writing these observations, that the present Board of Trade intend to submit to Parliament early in the present Session a measure embodying several of these points. I therefore refrain from drawing that which now rests in abler hands, but I venture to hope that the above suggestions may not be found altogether at variance with commercial good sense and practical experience.

# VADE MECUM, OR THE NECESSARY COMPANION

[John Playford]
*Vade Mecum, Or the Necessary Companion*
(London: A.G and J.P; John Playford; and Charles Blount, 1679)

# VADE MECUM,

OR, THE

# Necessary Companion.

CONTAINING,

1. Sir S. MORLAND's Perpetual Almanack, in Copper Plates, with many useful Tables proper thereto.
2. The Computation of *Years*, comparing the Years of each King's Reign from the Conquest with the Years of Christ.
3. The Reduction of *Weights* and *Measures*.
4. The Ready Casting up any Number of *Farthings*, *Half-pence*, *Pence*, *Shillings*, *Nobles* and *Marks*; with Sir *Samuel Morland*'s New Table for GUINNEYS.
5. The Interest, and Rebate of *Money*, the Forbearance, Discompt, and Purchase of *Annuities*, at 6 *per Cent*.
6. The Rates of *Post-Letters*, both Inland and Outland, with the Times for sending or receiving them; also the *Post-Stages*, shewing the Length of each Stage, and the Distance of each Post-Town from *London*.
7. The Rates or Fares of *Coach-men*, *Carr-men*, and *Water men*.

*London*, Printed by *A.G.* and *J.P.* and are to be sold by *R. Northcot*, Bookseller, either next St. *Peter's Alley* in *Cornhill*, or at the *Anchor* and *Mariner* on *Fish-Street-Hill*; by *John Playford*, Printer, near the *Blew-Anchor* Inn in *Little-Brittain*; and by *Charles Blount*, Bookseller, at the *Black Raven* in the *Strand*, near the *Savoy*, 1679.

# THE PREFACE.

MY Profeſſion obliging me to be converſant with Mathematical Books (the Printing whereof, and Muſick, has been my chiefeſt Employment) I have obſerv'd two things many times the cauſe why Books of this nature appear abroad not ſo correct as they ſhould be; either, 1. Becauſe they are too much haſtened from the Preſs, and not time enough allowed for the ſtrict and deliberate examination of them; which in all Books ought to be done, eſpecially in theſe, for as much as one falſe Figure in a Mathematical Book, may prove a greater fault than a whole word miſtaken in Books of another kind. Or, 2. Becauſe Perſons take Tables upon truſt without trying them, and with them tranſcribe their Errors, if not increaſe them. Both theſe I have carefully avoided, ſo that I have reaſon to believe (and think I may ſay it without vanity) there never was Tables more exactly Printed than in this Book, eſpecially thoſe for *Money* and *Annuities*, for not truſting to my firſt Calculation of them, I new Calculated

every

every Table when it was in Print by the first Printed Sheet, and when I had so done, I strictly compar'd it with my first Calculation, from which care I hope there is not one false Figure in any of them.

The *Perpetual Almanack* was the ingenious Invention of that great Improver of Art, and Encourager of Artists, Sir *Samuel Morland*, by whose Rules I Calculated the *Moveable Feasts* and *Terms*, *&c.* To which I have added several useful Tables, being partly Collected, but examined, (and clear'd from the faults contracted by often Printing) before inserted.

The Table for the ready Casting up of *Money* is generally useful, especially to all manner of Tradesmen, it being applicable to any thing that concerns Buying, Selling, or Retailing of Commodities, for by it may not only be known, At a certain Price the Pound, Yard, Ell, *&c.* what any Number of Pounds, Yards, Ells, *&c.* at the same Price amounts unto; but also, Any Quantity of Pounds, Yards, *&c.* being bought by Whole-sale, what they cost by the Pound, Yard, *&c.* and at what Rate they may be Retailed to gain such profit, as the Buyer propos'd to himself in laying out his Money. As for Example, *A Person Buyes* 800 *Pounds of Sugar for* 10 l. *and desires to Retail it so as to gain* 5 l. *what does it cost him* per *Pound, and at what Rate must he sell it* per *Pound to make the aforesaid Profit.*

*of it?* Seek in the Table 'till you find 10 *l.* against 800, which you will find in Page 53, at the top whereof you have *Three-Pence*, and so much did it cost him *per* Pound. Then to find how he must sell it to gain 5 *l.* add the Profit desired to the Price paid, which together make 15 *l.* and seek for that (as before) against 800, which you will find in Page 59, at the top whereof is *Four-pence Half-peny*, and for so much must he sell each Pound to gain 5 *l.* Many more are the Uses of this Table, of which to give a particular Account would require a distinct Treatise.

The other Tables, though very true, and useful in their kind, are not so general, and therefore the Examples given of them in the Book may suffice for their Explanation.

In these Tables you may often have occasion to add together Decimal Fractions; for which take the following Directions.

Addition of Decimals is the same with Addition of Whole Numbers, always observing to place them one under another in their proper places. Decimals are cast up by Tens, be the Integer a Pound, Shilling, Peny, Farthings, or any thing else, and are distinguished from whole Numbers by a Point placed before each Fraction.

Example

## Examples.

| *Pounds.* | *Shillings.* | *Pence.* | *Farthings.* |
|---|---|---|---|
| 75.06 | 7.36 | 4.75 | 1.53 |
| 33.44 | 3.09 | 5.36 | 0.60 |
| 17.99 | 4.67 | 0.72 | 1.07 |
| 126.49 | 15.12 | 10.83 | 3.20 |

To Caſt up the firſt Example of Pounds, I begin with the Decimals, and ſay, 9 and 4 is 13 and 6 is 19, I ſet down 9 and carry 1 to the next Rank; then 1 that I carried and 9 is 10 and 4 is 14, I ſet down .4 (making a Point before it to diſtinguiſh the Fraction from the whole Number) and carry 1 to the Pounds; then 1 and 7 is 8 and 3 is 11 and 5 is 16, I ſet down 6 and carry 1; then 1 and 1 is 2 and 3 is 5 and 7 is 12, which I ſet down, and the whole Sum is 126 *l.* and 49 Hundred Parts of a Pound. And after this manner are the other Examples caſt up.

This I thought neceſſary to inſert here, it being omitted in its proper place.

To conclude, you will find nothing in this Book but what is very uſeful, according to the Truth of which; you may approve or diſlike the Endeavours of,

*Your Servant,*

JOHN PLAYFORD.

# Sir *SAMUEL MORLAND's* Perpetual Almanack.

A Table shewing the Dominical Letter from the first year of Our Lord to the year 3400 & may be continued for ever

| | | | | 1 | 2 | 3 | 4 | 5 | 6 | 7 |
|---|---|---|---|---|---|---|---|---|---|---|
| | | | | DC | ED | FE | GF | AG | BA | CB |
| | | | | 000<br>700<br>1400<br>2100<br>2800 | 100<br>800<br>1500<br>2200<br>2900 | 200<br>900<br>1600<br>2300<br>3000 | 300<br>1000<br>1700<br>2400<br>3100 | 400<br>1100<br>1800<br>2500<br>3200 | 500<br>1200<br>1900<br>2600<br>3300 | 600<br>1300<br>2000<br>2700<br>3400 |
| 0 | 28 | 56 | 84 | DC | ED | FE | GF | AG | BA | CB |
| 1 | 29 | 57 | 85 | B | C | D | E | F | G | A |
| 2 | 30 | 58 | 86 | A | B | C | D | E | F | G |
| 3 | 31 | 59 | 87 | G | A | B | C | D | E | F |
| 4 | 32 | 60 | 88 | FE | GF | AG | BA | CB | DC | ED |
| 5 | 33 | 61 | 89 | D | E | F | G | A | B | C |
| 6 | 34 | 62 | 90 | C | D | E | F | G | A | B |
| 7 | 35 | 63 | 91 | B | C | D | E | F | G | A |
| 8 | 36 | 64 | 92 | AG | BA | CB | DC | ED | FE | GF |
| 9 | 37 | 65 | 93 | F | G | A | B | C | D | E |
| 10 | 38 | 66 | 94 | E | F | G | A | B | C | D |
| 11 | 39 | 67 | 95 | D | E | F | G | A | B | C |
| 12 | 40 | 68 | 96 | CB | DC | ED | FE | GF | AG | BA |
| 13 | 41 | 69 | 97 | A | B | C | D | E | F | G |
| 14 | 42 | 70 | 98 | G | A | B | C | D | E | F |
| 15 | 43 | 71 | 99 | F | G | A | B | C | D | E |
| 16 | 44 | 72 | | ED | FE | GF | AG | BA | CB | DC |
| 17 | 45 | 73 | | C | D | E | F | G | A | B |
| 18 | 46 | 74 | | B | C | D | E | F | G | A |
| 19 | 47 | 75 | | A | B | C | D | E | F | G |
| 20 | 48 | 76 | | GF | AG | BA | CB | DC | ED | FE |
| 21 | 49 | 77 | | E | F | G | A | B | C | D |
| 22 | 50 | 78 | | D | E | F | G | A | B | C |
| 23 | 51 | 79 | | C | D | E | F | G | A | B |
| 24 | 52 | 80 | | BA | CB | DC | ED | FE | GF | AG |
| 25 | 53 | 81 | | G | A | B | C | D | E | F |
| 26 | 54 | 82 | | F | G | A | B | C | D | E |
| 27 | 55 | 83 | | E | F | G | A | B | C | D |
| | | | | 1 | 2 | 3 | 4 | 5 | 6 | 7 |

A Table
Shewing by the help of ye Dominical Letter what day of the week any Month of the year begins for ever

| | A | B | C | D | E | F | G |
|---|---|---|---|---|---|---|---|
| Ian 31 | *Sund:* | *Satur:* | *Fryd:* | *Thur:* | *Wedn:* | *Tuesd:* | *Mun:* |
| Feb 28 | *Wedn:* | *Tuesd:* | *Mund:* | *Sund:* | *Satur:* | *Fryd:* | *Thur:* |
| Mar 31 | *Wedn:* | *Tuesd:* | *Mund:* | *Sund:* | *Satur:* | *Fryd:* | *Thur:* |
| Apr 30 | *Satur:* | *Fryd:* | *Thur:* | *Wedn:* | *Tuesd:* | *Mund:* | *Sund:* |
| May 31 | *Mund:* | *Sund:* | *Satur:* | *Fryd:* | *Thur:* | *Wedn:* | *Tuesd:* |
| Iun 30 | *Thur:* | *Wedn:* | *Tuesd:* | *Mund:* | *Sund:* | *Satur:* | *Fryd:* |
| Iuly 31 | *Satur:* | *Fryd:* | *Thur:* | *Wedn:* | *Tuesd:* | *Mund:* | *Sund:* |
| Aug 31 | *Tuesd:* | *Mund:* | *Sund:* | *Satur:* | *Fryd:* | *Thur:* | *Wedn:* |
| Sep 30 | *Fryd:* | *Thur:* | *Wedn:* | *Tuesd:* | *Mund:* | *Sund:* | *Satur:* |
| Oct 31 | *Sund:* | *Satur:* | *Fryd:* | *Thur:* | *Wedn:* | *Tuesd:* | *Mund:* |
| Nou 30 | *Wedn:* | *Tuesd:* | *Mund:* | *Sund:* | *Satur:* | *Fryd:* | *Thur:* |
| Dec 31 | *Fryd:* | *Thur:* | *Wedn:* | *Tuesd:* | *Mund:* | *Sund:* | *Satur:* |

## The 7 Varieties of the Days of ye Week for finding ye day of the Month.

| Wedn: | 1 | 8 | 15 | 22 | 29 |
|---|---|---|---|---|---|
| Thurſdays | 2 | 9 | 16 | 23 | 30 |
| Frydays | 3 | 10 | 17 | 24 | 31 |
| Saturdays | 4 | 11 | 18 | 25 | |
| Sundays | 5 | 12 | 19 | 26 | |
| Mundays | 6 | 13 | 20 | 27 | |
| Tueſdays | 7 | 14 | 21 | 28 | |

| Sund: | 1 | 8 | 15 | 22 | 29 |
|---|---|---|---|---|---|
| Mundays | 2 | 9 | 16 | 23 | 30 |
| Tueſdays | 3 | 10 | 17 | 24 | 31 |
| Wedneſdays | 4 | 11 | 18 | 25 | |
| Thurſdays | 5 | 12 | 19 | 26 | |
| Frydays | 6 | 13 | 20 | 27 | |
| Saturdays | 7 | 14 | 21 | 28 | |

| Thurſd: | 1 | 8 | 15 | 22 | 29 |
|---|---|---|---|---|---|
| Frydays | 2 | 9 | 16 | 23 | 30 |
| Saturdays | 3 | 10 | 17 | 24 | 31 |
| Sundays | 4 | 11 | 18 | 25 | |
| Mundays | 5 | 12 | 19 | 26 | |
| Tueſdays | 6 | 13 | 20 | 27 | |
| Wedneſdays | 7 | 14 | 21 | 28 | |

| Mund: | 1 | 8 | 15 | 22 | 29 |
|---|---|---|---|---|---|
| Tueſdays | 2 | 9 | 16 | 23 | 30 |
| Wedneſdays | 3 | 10 | 17 | 24 | 31 |
| Thurſdays | 4 | 11 | 18 | 25 | |
| Frydays | 5 | 12 | 19 | 26 | |
| Saturdays | 6 | 13 | 20 | 27 | |
| Sundays | 7 | 14 | 21 | 28 | |

| Fryd: | 1 | 8 | 15 | 22 | 29 |
|---|---|---|---|---|---|
| Saturdays | 2 | 9 | 16 | 23 | 30 |
| Sundays | 3 | 10 | 17 | 24 | 31 |
| Mundays | 4 | 11 | 18 | 25 | |
| Tueſdays | 5 | 12 | 19 | 26 | |
| Wedneſdays | 6 | 13 | 20 | 27 | |
| Thurſdays | 7 | 14 | 21 | 28 | |

| Tueſd: | 1 | 8 | 15 | 22 | 29 |
|---|---|---|---|---|---|
| Wedneſdays | 2 | 9 | 16 | 23 | 30 |
| Thurſdays | 3 | 10 | 17 | 24 | 31 |
| Frydays | 4 | 11 | 18 | 25 | |
| Saturdays | 5 | 12 | 19 | 26 | |
| Sundays | 6 | 13 | 20 | 27 | |
| Mundays | 7 | 14 | 21 | 28 | |

| Saturd: | 1 | 8 | 15 | 22 | 29 |
|---|---|---|---|---|---|
| Sundays | 2 | 9 | 16 | 23 | 30 |
| Mundays | 3 | 10 | 17 | 24 | 31 |
| Tueſdays | 4 | 11 | 18 | 25 | |
| Wedneſdays | 5 | 12 | 19 | 26 | |
| Thurſdays | 6 | 13 | 20 | 27 | |
| Frydays | 7 | 14 | 21 | 28 | |

## The Use of the Three foregoing Tables.

1. THe first shews the *Dominical Letter*, from the first year of our Lord to the year 3400, (and may easily be continued for ever.)

*Example*. The *Dominical Letters* for any years under 100 are expressed in the first Column of Letters, against the particular Numbers in the Margin, as the *Dominical Letters* for 28, 56, and 84, are *D C*; for 1, 29, 57, and 85, the Letter is *B*; for 2, 30, 58, and 86, it is *A*, &c. But for all even Hundreds or Thousands (which are always *Leap-years*) the *Dominical Letters* are set above them at the top of their respective Columns, as for the years 700, 1400, 2100, 2800, the *Dominical Letters* are *D C*; for 100, 800, 1500, 2200, 2900, *E D*, &c. And for any other Number the Rule is for ever this, *Where* the Marginal Number (equal to the Fraction or part of an Hundred sought) meets with the Column where the Number of Hundreds or Thousands (which is the other part of the Number sought) is exprest, the Letter or Letters *there* placed is the *Dominical Letter* or *Letters* for that year; as suppose the *Dominical Letter* for the year 1679 be demanded, under 1600 and against 79 I find *E*, which is the *Dominical Letter* for that year; or if it were for the year 1680, under 1600 and against 80 I find *D C*, which are the *Dominical Letters* for that year, the first of them *D*, being used only 'till St. *Matthias* Eve, and the other *C*, to the years end. And after this manner you may readily find the *Dominical Letter* for any year past, present, or to come; always beginning the Year on the First of *January*.

*Note*, That every *Leap-year* has two *Dominical Letters*, the first being used (as aforesaid) only 'till St. *Matthias*'s Eve, and the last the remaining part of the year. Also then *February* has 29 days, otherwise but 28.

2. The

2. The ſecond ſhews, how (by the *Dominical Letter*) to find what Day of the Week any Month begins, for ever, Example. *Upon what Day of the Week does July* 1679. *begin?* By the firſt Table I find the *Dominical Letter* E. for that year, then under *E* in the ſecond Table, and againſt *July*, I find *Tueſday*, which anſwers the Queſtion. Under every Month is the Number of Days contained therein.

3. The third Table ſhews, how (by knowing what Day of the Week the Month begins) to find the Day of the Month. Example. *What Day of the Month is the ſecond* Thurſday *in* July, 1679? Having found the Month to begin on *Tueſday*, I look in the Diviſion of this Table beginning with that Day, and againſt *Thurſday*, I find 3, 10, 17, 24, 31. which are all the *Thurſdays* in that Month; the ſecond anſwering the Queſtion, being the 10*th* Day.

Theſe Tables are of excellent Uſe, for by them may be readily found not only the preſent Day of the Month for ever; but alſo,

Firſt, What Day of the Week any Day of the Month was, or will be, of any year paſt, or to come. Example. *I would know what Day of the Week the* 5*th of* November *was on in the Year* 1605? By the firſt Table I find the *Dominical Letter* for that year to be *F*; by the ſecond I find *November* began on a *Friday*; and by the third I find that the Fifth of *November* that year was on a *Tueſday*. Again, *I would know what Day of the Week the* 30th *of* January *will be on in the Year* 1685? Firſt I find the *Dominical Letter* for that year will be *D*, then that *January* will begin on a *Thurſday*; and laſtly, that the 30*th* of that Month will be on a *Friday*.

Secondly, What Day of the Month was or will be on any Day, of any Week, of any Month, of any Years paſt, or to come. Example. *I deſire to know on what Day of the Month the firſt* Tueſday *was in* November 1605? Having by the foregoing Rules found *November* for that Year to begin on a *Friday*, I preſently find that the firſt *Tueſday* was the Fifth Day of the Month. Again, *I deſire*

*desire to know on what Day of the Month the Fifth* Friday *will be in* January, 1685? Having found that *January* in that Year begins on a *Thursday*, I find that the Fifth *Friday* will be on the 30*th* Day of that Month.

---

## *Remarkable Days.*

| | D. M. |
|---|---|
| V*Alentine* ———————— | *Febr.* 14 |
| Equal Day and Night ———————— | *Mar.* 10 |
| St. *George* ———————— | *April* 23 |
| L[illegible]est Day, or *Barnaby* ———————— | *June* 11 |
| Ele[illegible]tion of Sheriffs in *London* ———————— | *June* 24 |
| *Swithin* ———————— | *July* 15 |
| Dog-days begin ———————— | *July* 19 |
| Lammas ———————— | *Aug.* 2 |
| Dog-days end ———————— | *Aug.* 27 |
| Equal Day and Night ———————— | *Sept.* 12 |
| Sheriffs of *London* Sworn ———————— | *Sept.* 28 |
| Election of the Lord Mayor of *London* ———— | *Sept.* 29 |
| Lord Mayor's Day, when he is Sworn at *Westminster* ———————— | *Octo.* 29 |
| Shortest Day ———————— | *Dec.* 11 |

---

*Fixed*

# *Fixed Feasts.*

| | D. M. |
|---|---|
| CIrcumcision, or New-years-day | Jan. 1 |
| Epiphany, or Twelfth-day | Jan. 6 |
| Conversion of St. *Paul* | Jan. 25 |
| Martyrdom of King *CHARLES* I. | Jan. 30 |
| Purification of the Virgin *Mary*, or Candlemas-day | Febr. 2 |
| St. *Matthias* | Febr. 24 |
| LADY-DAY, or Annunciation of the Virgin *Mary* | Mar. 25 |
| St. *Mark* Evangelist | April 25 |
| St. *Philip* and *Jacob*, or May-day | May 1 |
| Birth and Return of King *CHARLES* II. | May 29 |
| St. *Barnabas* Apostle | June 11 |
| MIDSUMMER, or St. *John* Baptist | June 24 |
| St. *Peter* Apostle | June 29 |
| St. *James* Apostle | July 25 |
| St. *Bartholomew* Apostle | Aug. 24 |
| St. *Matthew* Apostle | Sept. 21 |
| MICHAELMAS, or St. *Michael* the Archangel | Sept. 29 |
| St. *Luke* Evangelist | Octob. 18 |
| St. *Simon* and St. *Jude* | Octob. 28 |
| All Saints | Nov. 1 |
| Powder Treason | Nov. 5 |
| St. *Andrew* Apostle | Nov. 30 |
| St. *Thomas* Apostle | Dec. 21 |
| CHRISTMAS, or Birth of our Lord God | Dec. 25 |
| St. *Steven* Protomartyr | Dec. 26 |
| St. *John* Evangelist | Dec. 27 |
| Innocents | Dec. 28 |

*Note*, That St. *Matthias* Day is on *February* 25, in the *Leap-years*.

*Move-*

## Moveable Feasts.

| Year. | Shrove-Su. | Easter-day. | Ascen-day. | Whit-Sun. |
|---|---|---|---|---|
| 1679 | Mar. 2 | April 20 | May 29 | June 8 |
| 80 | Febr. 23 | April 11 | May 21 | May 31 |
| 81 | Febr. 13 | April 3 | May 12 | May 22 |
| 82 | Febr. 26 | April 16 | May 25 | June 4 |
| 83 | Febr. 18 | April 8 | May 17 | May 27 |
| 84 | Febr. 10 | Mar. 30 | May 8 | May 18 |
| 85 | Mar. 1 | April 19 | May 28 | June 7 |
| 86 | Febr. 14 | April 4 | May 13 | May 23 |
| 87 | Febr. 6 | Mar. 27 | May 5 | May 15 |
| 88 | Febr. 26 | April 15 | May 24 | June 3 |
| 89 | Febr. 10 | Mar. 31 | May 9 | May 19 |
| 90 | Mar. 2 | April 20 | May 29 | June 8 |
| 91 | Febr. 23 | April 12 | May 21 | May 31 |
| 92 | Febr. 7 | Mar. 27 | May 5 | May 15 |
| 93 | Febr. 26 | April 16 | May 25 | June 4 |
| 94 | Febr. 18 | April 8 | May 17 | May 27 |
| 95 | Febr. 3 | Mar. 24 | May 2 | May 12 |
| 96 | Febr. 23 | April 12 | May 21 | May 31 |
| 97 | Febr. 14 | April 4 | May 13 | May 23 |
| 98 | Mar. 6 | April 2 | June 2 | June 12 |
| 99 | Febr. 19 | April 9 | May 18 | May 28 |
| 1700 | Febr. 11 | Mar. 31 | May 9 | May 19 |
| 1 | Mar. 2 | April 20 | May 29 | June 8 |
| 2 | Febr. 15 | April 5 | May 14 | May 24 |
| 3 | Febr. 7 | Mar 28 | May 6 | May 16 |
| 4 | Febr. 27 | April 16 | May 25 | June 4 |
| 5 | Febr. 18 | April 8 | May 17 | May 27 |
| 6 | Febr. 3 | Mar. 24 | May 2 | May 12 |
| 7 | Febr. 23 | April 13 | May 22 | June 1 |
| 8 | Febr. 15 | April 4 | May 13 | May 23 |
| 9 | Mar. 6 | April 2 | June 2 | June 12 |
| 10 | Febr. 19 | April 9 | May 18 | May 28 |

Move-

## *Moveable Terms.*

| Year. | EASTER TERM | | TRINITY TERM | |
|---|---|---|---|---|
| | Begins, | Ends, | Begins, | Ends, |
| 1679 | *May* 7 | *June* 2 | *June* 20 | *July* 9 |
| 80 | *April* 28 | *May* 24 | *June* 11 | *June* 30 |
| 81 | *April* 20 | *May* 16 | *June* 3 | *June* 22 |
| 82 | *May* 3 | *May* 29 | *June* 16 | *July* 5 |
| 83 | *April* 25 | *May* 21 | *June* 8 | *June* 27 |
| 84 | *April* 16 | *May* 12 | *May* 30 | *June* 18 |
| 85 | *May* 6 | *June* 1 | *June* 19 | *July* 8 |
| 86 | *April* 21 | *May* 17 | *June* 4 | *June* 23 |
| 87 | *April* 13 | *May* 9 | *May* 27 | *June* 15 |
| 88 | *May* 2 | *May* 28 | *June* 15 | *July* 4 |
| 89 | *April* 17 | *May* 13 | *May* 31 | *June* 19 |
| 90 | *May* 7 | *June* 2 | *June* 20 | *July* 9 |
| 91 | *April* 29 | *May* 25 | *June* 12 | *July* 1 |
| 92 | *April* 13 | *May* 9 | *May* 27 | *June* 15 |
| 93 | *May* 3 | *May* 29 | *June* 16 | *July* 5 |
| 94 | *April* 25 | *May* 21 | *June* 8 | *June* 27 |
| 95 | *April* 10 | *May* 6 | *May* 24 | *June* 12 |
| 96 | *April* 29 | *May* 25 | *June* 12 | *July* 1 |
| 97 | *April* 21 | *May* 17 | *June* 4 | *June* 23 |
| 98 | *May* 11 | *June* 6 | *June* 24 | *July* 13 |
| 99 | *April* 26 | *May* 22 | *June* 9 | *June* 28 |
| 1700 | *April* 17 | *May* 13 | *May* 31 | *June* 19 |
| 1 | *May* 7 | *June* 2 | *June* 20 | *July* 9 |
| 2 | *April* 22 | *May* 18 | *June* 5 | *June* 24 |
| 3 | *April* 14 | *May* 10 | *May* 28 | *June* 16 |
| 4 | *May* 3 | *May* 29 | *June* 16 | *July* 5 |
| 5 | *April* 25 | *May* 21 | *June* 8 | *June* 27 |
| 6 | *April* 10 | *May* 6 | *May* 24 | *June* 12 |
| 7 | *April* 30 | *May* 26 | *June* 13 | *July* 2 |
| 8 | *April* 21 | *May* 17 | *June* 4 | *June* 23 |
| 9 | *May* 11 | *June* 6 | *June* 24 | *July* 13 |
| 10 | *April* 26 | *May* 22 | *June* 9 | *June* 28 |

Fixed

# *Fixed Terms, and their Returns.*

## *Fixed Terms.*

### HILLARY TERM,

| | |
|---|---|
| Begins | *Jan.* 23 |
| Ends | *Febr.* 12 |
| And hath Four Returns. | |
| 1. Octab. Hil. | *Jan.* 20 |
| 2. Quind. Hil. | *Jan.* 29 |
| 3. Craſt. Pur. | *Febr.* 3 |
| 4. Octab. Pur. | *Febr.* 10 |

### MICHAELMAS TERM,

| | |
|---|---|
| Begins | *Octo.* 23 |
| Ends | *Nov.* 28 |
| And hath Six Returns. | |
| 1. Tres Mich. | *Octo.* 21 |
| 2. Mens. Mich. | *Octo.* 29 |
| 3. Craſt. An. | *Nov.* 4 |
| 4. Craſt. Mar. | *Nov.* 11 |
| 5. Oct. Mar. | *Nov.* 18 |
| 6. Quin Mar. | *Nov.* 27 |

THe Act of Batchelors in *Cambridge* and *Oxford* the Firſt Day of Lent. The Act of Maſters, in *Cambridge*, *July* 3. in *Oxford*, *July* 8.

*Cambridge* Commencement, the Firſt Sunday in *July*.

*Oxford* Act, the Second Sunday in *July*.

A

## *A TABLE for the Latitude of* LONDON, *shewing for ever the Time of Day-break, Twilight, and the Length of the Days and Nights, throughout the Year.*

| *Month.* | | *Day-break.* | | *Twilight.* | | *Day's length.* | | *Night's length.* | |
|---|---|---|---|---|---|---|---|---|---|
| | | H. | M. | H. | M. | H. | M. | H. | M. |
| *Jan.* | 1 | 5 | 54 | 6 | 6 | 7 | 56 | 16 | 4 |
| | 11 | 5 | 45 | 6 | 18 | 8 | 22 | 15 | 38 |
| | 21 | 5 | 35 | 6 | 25 | 8 | 52 | 15 | 8 |
| *Febr.* | 1 | 5 | 17 | 6 | 43 | 9 | 26 | 14 | 34 |
| | 11 | 5 | 0 | 7 | 0 | 10 | 2 | 13 | 58 |
| | 21 | 4 | 45 | 7 | 15 | 10 | 36 | 13 | 24 |
| *Mar.* | 1 | 4 | 20 | 7 | 40 | 11 | 14 | 12 | 46 |
| | 11 | 3 | 59 | 8 | 1 | 12 | 0 | 12 | 0 |
| | 21 | 3 | 34 | 8 | 22 | 12 | 36 | 11 | 24 |
| *April* | 1 | 3 | 55 | 8 | 55 | 13 | 20 | 10 | 40 |
| | 11 | 2 | 38 | 9 | 22 | 14 | 4 | 9 | 56 |
| | 21 | 2 | 2 | 9 | 58 | 14 | 40 | 9 | 20 |
| *May* | 1 | 1 | 30 | 10 | 30 | 15 | 16 | 8 | 44 |
| | 11 | 0 | 30 | 11 | 30 | 15 | 42 | 8 | 18 |
| | 21 | | | | | 16 | 10 | 7 | 50 |
| *June* | 1 | *All Day* | | *No Night* | | 16 | 20 | 7 | 40 |
| | 11 | *and* | | *but* | | 16 | 26 | 7 | 34 |
| | 21 | *no Night.* | | *Twilight.* | | 16 | 20 | 7 | 40 |
| *July* | 1 | | | | | 16 | 6 | 7 | 54 |
| | 11 | 0 | 42 | 11 | 18 | 15 | 42 | 8 | 18 |
| | 21 | 1 | 22 | 10 | 38 | 15 | 18 | 8 | 42 |
| *Aug.* | 1 | 2 | 0 | 10 | 0 | 14 | 42 | 9 | 18 |
| | 11 | 2 | 21 | 9 | 39 | 14 | 4 | 9 | 56 |
| | 21 | 3 | 0 | 9 | 0 | 13 | 28 | 10 | 32 |
| *Sept.* | 1 | 3 | 30 | 8 | 30 | 12 | 46 | 11 | 14 |
| | 11 | 3 | 59 | 8 | 1 | 12 | 8 | 11 | 52 |
| | 21 | 4 | 19 | 7 | 41 | 11 | 28 | 12 | 32 |
| *Octob.* | 1 | 4 | 48 | 7 | 12 | 10 | 48 | 13 | 12 |
| | 11 | 5 | 0 | 7 | 0 | 10 | 8 | 13 | 52 |
| | 21 | 5 | 18 | 6 | 42 | 9 | 50 | 14 | 10 |
| *Nov.* | 1 | 5 | 37 | 6 | 27 | 8 | 52 | 15 | 8 |
| | 11 | 5 | 45 | 6 | 17 | 8 | 22 | 15 | 38 |
| | 21 | 5 | 54 | 6 | 6 | 7 | 58 | 16 | 2 |
| *Dec.* | 1 | 5 | 57 | 6 | 3 | 7 | 40 | 16 | 20 |
| | 11 | 6 | 0 | 6 | 0 | 7 | 34 | 16 | 26 |
| | 21 | 5 | 8 | 6 | 2 | 7 | 44 | 16 | 16 |

## *Sun's Riſing and Setting*

| Days of the Month. | January. Sun riſes H. M. | January. Sun ſets H. M. | February. Sun riſes H. M. | February. Sun ſets H. M. | March. Sun riſes H. M. | March. Sun ſets H. M. |
|---|---|---|---|---|---|---|
| 1 | 8 9 | 3 51 | 7 18 | 4 42 | 6 20 | 5 40 |
| 2 | 8 8 | 3 52 | 7 17 | 4 43 | 6 18 | 5 42 |
| 3 | 8 7 | 3 53 | 7 15 | 4 45 | 6 16 | 5 44 |
| 4 | 8 6 | 3 54 | 7 13 | 4 47 | 6 14 | 5 46 |
| 5 | 8 4 | 3 56 | 7 11 | 4 49 | 6 11 | 5 49 |
| 6 | 8 3 | 3 57 | 7 9 | 4 51 | 6 8 | 5 52 |
| 7 | 8 1 | 3 59 | 7 7 | 4 53 | 6 6 | 5 54 |
| 8 | 8 0 | 4 0 | 7 5 | 4 55 | 6 4 | 5 56 |
| 9 | 7 58 | 4 2 | 7 3 | 4 57 | 6 2 | 5 58 |
| 10 | 7 56 | 4 4 | 7 1 | 4 59 | 6 0 | 6 0 |
| 11 | 7 55 | 4 5 | 6 59 | 5 1 | 5 58 | 6 2 |
| 12 | 7 54 | 4 6 | 6 57 | 5 3 | 5 56 | 6 4 |
| 13 | 7 52 | 4 8 | 6 54 | 5 6 | 5 54 | 6 6 |
| 14 | 7 51 | 4 9 | 6 52 | 5 8 | 5 52 | 6 8 |
| 15 | 7 50 | 4 10 | 6 50 | 5 10 | 5 50 | 6 10 |
| 16 | 7 48 | 4 12 | 6 48 | 5 12 | 5 48 | 6 12 |
| 17 | 7 46 | 4 14 | 6 46 | 5 14 | 5 46 | 6 14 |
| 18 | 7 44 | 4 16 | 6 44 | 5 16 | 5 44 | 6 16 |
| 19 | 7 43 | 4 17 | 6 42 | 5 18 | 5 42 | 6 18 |
| 20 | 7 41 | 4 19 | 6 40 | 5 20 | 5 40 | 6 20 |
| 21 | 7 39 | 4 21 | 6 38 | 5 22 | 5 38 | 6 22 |
| 22 | 7 37 | 4 23 | 6 36 | 5 24 | 5 36 | 6 24 |
| 23 | 7 35 | 4 25 | 6 34 | 5 26 | 5 34 | 6 26 |
| 24 | 7 34 | 4 26 | 6 32 | 5 28 | 5 32 | 6 28 |
| 25 | 7 32 | 4 28 | 6 30 | 5 30 | 5 30 | 6 30 |
| 26 | 7 30 | 4 30 | 6 29 | 5 31 | 5 28 | 6 32 |
| 27 | 7 28 | 4 32 | 6 27 | 5 33 | 5 26 | 6 34 |
| 28 | 7 26 | 4 34 | 6 24 | 5 36 | 5 24 | 6 36 |
| 29 | 7 24 | 4 36 | 6 22 | 5 38 | 5 22 | 6 38 |
| 30 | 7 22 | 4 38 | | | 5 20 | 6 40 |
| 31 | 7 20 | 4 40 | | | 5 18 | 6 42 |

## *throughout the whole Year.*

| Days of the Month. | *April.* Sun rises | *April.* Sun sets | *May.* Sun rises | *May.* Sun sets | *June.* Sun rises | *June.* Sun sets |
|---|---|---|---|---|---|---|
| | *H. M* | *H. M.* | *H. M.* | *H. M.* | *H. M.* | *H. M.* |
| 1 | 5 16 | 6 44 | 4 19 | 7 41 | 3 42 | 8 18 |
| 2 | 5 14 | 6 46 | 4 17 | 7 43 | 3 42 | 8 18 |
| 3 | 5 12 | 6 48 | 4 15 | 7 45 | 3 42 | 8 18 |
| 4 | 5 10 | 6 50 | 4 14 | 7 46 | 3 41 | 8 19 |
| 5 | 5 8 | 6 52 | 4 12 | 7 48 | 3 41 | 8 19 |
| 6 | 5 6 | 6 54 | 4 11 | 7 49 | 3 41 | 8 19 |
| 7 | 5 5 | 6 55 | 4 10 | 7 50 | 3 41 | 8 19 |
| 8 | 5 3 | 6 57 | 4 8 | 7 52 | 3 41 | 8 19 |
| 9 | 5 2 | 6 58 | 4 7 | 7 53 | 3 41 | 8 19 |
| 10 | 5 0 | 7 0 | 4 6 | 7 54 | 3 41 | 8 19 |
| 11 | 4 57 | 7 3 | 4 4 | 7 56 | 3 41 | 8 19 |
| 12 | 4 55 | 7 5 | 4 3 | 7 57 | 3 41 | 8 19 |
| 13 | 4 53 | 7 7 | 4 2 | 7 58 | 3 41 | 8 19 |
| 14 | 4 51 | 7 9 | 4 0 | 8 0 | 3 41 | 8 19 |
| 15 | 4 49 | 7 11 | 3 59 | 8 1 | 3 41 | 8 19 |
| 16 | 4 47 | 7 13 | 3 58 | 8 2 | 3 41 | 8 19 |
| 17 | 4 45 | 7 15 | 3 57 | 8 3 | 3 41 | 8 19 |
| 18 | 4 43 | 7 17 | 3 56 | 8 4 | 3 41 | 8 19 |
| 19 | 4 41 | 7 19 | 3 55 | 8 5 | 3 42 | 8 18 |
| 20 | 4 39 | 7 21 | 3 53 | 8 7 | 3 42 | 8 18 |
| 21 | 4 38 | 7 22 | 3 52 | 8 8 | 3 42 | 8 18 |
| 22 | 4 36 | 7 24 | 3 51 | 8 9 | 3 43 | 8 17 |
| 23 | 4 34 | 7 26 | 3 50 | 8 10 | 3 44 | 8 16 |
| 24 | 4 32 | 7 28 | 3 49 | 8 11 | 3 44 | 8 16 |
| 25 | 4 30 | 7 30 | 3 48 | 8 12 | 3 45 | 8 15 |
| 26 | 4 28 | 7 32 | 3 47 | 8 13 | 3 46 | 8 14 |
| 27 | 4 27 | 7 33 | 3 46 | 8 14 | 3 47 | 8 13 |
| 28 | 4 25 | 7 35 | 3 45 | 8 15 | 3 48 | 8 12 |
| 29 | 4 23 | 7 37 | 3 45 | 8 15 | 3 49 | 8 11 |
| 30 | 4 21 | 7 39 | 3 44 | 8 16 | 3 50 | 8 12 |
| 31 | | | 3 43 | 8 17 | | |

## Sun's Rising and Setting

| Days of the Month | July. Sun rises H. | July. Sun rises M. | July. Sun sets H. | July. Sun sets M. | August. Sun rises H. | August. Sun rises M. | August. Sun sets H. | August. Sun sets M. | September. Sun rises H. | September. Sun rises M. | September. Sun sets H. | September. Sun sets M. |
|---|---|---|---|---|---|---|---|---|---|---|---|---|
| 1 | 3 | 51 | 8 | 9 | 4 | 35 | 7 | 25 | 5 | 35 | 6 | 25 |
| 2 | 3 | 52 | 8 | 8 | 4 | 36 | 7 | 24 | 5 | 37 | 6 | 23 |
| 3 | 3 | 52 | 8 | 8 | 4 | 38 | 7 | 22 | 5 | 39 | 6 | 21 |
| 4 | 3 | 53 | 8 | 7 | 4 | 40 | 7 | 20 | 5 | 41 | 6 | 19 |
| 5 | 3 | 54 | 8 | 6 | 4 | 41 | 7 | 19 | 5 | 43 | 6 | 17 |
| 6 | 3 | 56 | 8 | 4 | 4 | 43 | 7 | 17 | 5 | 45 | 6 | 15 |
| 7 | 3 | 57 | 8 | 3 | 4 | 45 | 7 | 15 | 5 | 47 | 6 | 13 |
| 8 | 3 | 58 | 8 | 2 | 4 | 47 | 7 | 13 | 5 | 49 | 6 | 11 |
| 9 | 3 | 59 | 8 | 1 | 4 | 48 | 7 | 12 | 5 | 51 | 6 | 9 |
| 10 | 4 | 0 | 8 | 0 | 4 | 50 | 7 | 10 | 5 | 53 | 6 | 7 |
| 11 | 4 | 2 | 7 | 58 | 4 | 52 | 7 | 8 | 5 | 56 | 6 | 4 |
| 12 | 4 | 3 | 7 | 57 | 4 | 54 | 7 | 6 | 5 | 58 | 6 | 2 |
| 13 | 4 | 4 | 7 | 56 | 4 | 56 | 7 | 4 | 6 | 0 | 6 | 0 |
| 14 | 4 | 6 | 7 | 54 | 4 | 58 | 7 | 2 | 6 | 2 | 5 | 58 |
| 15 | 4 | 7 | 7 | 53 | 5 | 0 | 7 | 0 | 6 | 4 | 5 | 56 |
| 16 | 4 | 8 | 7 | 52 | 5 | 2 | 6 | 58 | 6 | 6 | 5 | 54 |
| 17 | 4 | 10 | 7 | 50 | 5 | 4 | 6 | 56 | 6 | 9 | 5 | 51 |
| 18 | 4 | 11 | 7 | 49 | 5 | 6 | 6 | 54 | 6 | 11 | 5 | 49 |
| 19 | 4 | 12 | 7 | 48 | 5 | 8 | 6 | 52 | 6 | 13 | 5 | 47 |
| 20 | 4 | 14 | 7 | 46 | 5 | 10 | 6 | 50 | 6 | 15 | 5 | 45 |
| 21 | 4 | 15 | 7 | 45 | 5 | 12 | 6 | 48 | 6 | 17 | 5 | 43 |
| 22 | 4 | 17 | 7 | 43 | 5 | 14 | 6 | 46 | 6 | 19 | 5 | 41 |
| 23 | 4 | 18 | 7 | 42 | 5 | 16 | 6 | 44 | 6 | 21 | 5 | 39 |
| 24 | 4 | 29 | 7 | 40 | 5 | 18 | 6 | 42 | 6 | 23 | 5 | 37 |
| 25 | 4 | 22 | 7 | 38 | 5 | 20 | 6 | 40 | 6 | 25 | 5 | 35 |
| 26 | 4 | 23 | 7 | 37 | 5 | 22 | 6 | 38 | 6 | 27 | 5 | 33 |
| 27 | 4 | 25 | 7 | 35 | 5 | 24 | 6 | 36 | 6 | 29 | 5 | 31 |
| 28 | 4 | 27 | 7 | 33 | 5 | 26 | 6 | 34 | 6 | 31 | 5 | 29 |
| 29 | 4 | 28 | 7 | 32 | 5 | 28 | 6 | 32 | 6 | 33 | 5 | 27 |
| 30 | 4 | 30 | 7 | 30 | 5 | 30 | 6 | 30 | 6 | 35 | 5 | 25 |
| 31 | 4 | 32 | 7 | 28 | 5 | 32 | 6 | 28 | | | | |

**throughout the whole Year.**

| Days of the Month. | October. | | | | November. | | | | December. | | | |
|---|---|---|---|---|---|---|---|---|---|---|---|---|
| | Sun rises | | Sun sets | | Sun rises | | Sun sets | | Sun rises | | Sun sets | |
| | H. | M. | H. | M. | H. | M. | H. | M. | H. | M. | H. | M. |
| 1 | 6 | 38 | 5 | 22 | 7 | 38 | 4 | 22 | 8 | 16 | 3 | 44 |
| 2 | 6 | 40 | 5 | 20 | 7 | 39 | 4 | 21 | 8 | 16 | 3 | 44 |
| 3 | 6 | 42 | 5 | 18 | 7 | 41 | 4 | 19 | 8 | 17 | 3 | 43 |
| 4 | 6 | 44 | 5 | 16 | 7 | 42 | 4 | 18 | 8 | 17 | 3 | 43 |
| 5 | 6 | 46 | 5 | 14 | 7 | 44 | 4 | 16 | 8 | 18 | 3 | 42 |
| 6 | 6 | 48 | 5 | 12 | 7 | 46 | 4 | 14 | 8 | 18 | 3 | 42 |
| 7 | 6 | 50 | 5 | 10 | 7 | 47 | 4 | 13 | 8 | 18 | 3 | 42 |
| 8 | 6 | 52 | 5 | 8 | 7 | 49 | 4 | 11 | 8 | 19 | 3 | 41 |
| 9 | 6 | 54 | 5 | 6 | 7 | 51 | 4 | 9 | 8 | 19 | 3 | 41 |
| 10 | 6 | 56 | 5 | 4 | 7 | 52 | 4 | 8 | 8 | 19 | 3 | 41 |
| 11 | 6 | 58 | 5 | 2 | 7 | 54 | 4 | 6 | 8 | 19 | 3 | 41 |
| 12 | 7 | 0 | 5 | 0 | 7 | 55 | 4 | 5 | 8 | 19 | 3 | 41 |
| 13 | 7 | 2 | 4 | 58 | 7 | 57 | 4 | 3 | 8 | 19 | 3 | 41 |
| 14 | 7 | 4 | 4 | 56 | 7 | 58 | 4 | 2 | 8 | 19 | 3 | 41 |
| 15 | 7 | 6 | 4 | 54 | 8 | 0 | 4 | 0 | 8 | 19 | 3 | 41 |
| 16 | 7 | 8 | 4 | 52 | 8 | 1 | 3 | 59 | 8 | 18 | 3 | 42 |
| 17 | 7 | 10 | 4 | 50 | 8 | 3 | 3 | 57 | 8 | 18 | 3 | 42 |
| 18 | 7 | 12 | 4 | 48 | 8 | 4 | 3 | 56 | 8 | 18 | 3 | 42 |
| 19 | 7 | 14 | 4 | 46 | 8 | 5 | 3 | 55 | 8 | 17 | 3 | 43 |
| 20 | 7 | 16 | 4 | 44 | 8 | 7 | 3 | 53 | 8 | 17 | 3 | 43 |
| 21 | 7 | 18 | 4 | 42 | 8 | 8 | 3 | 52 | 8 | 16 | 3 | 44 |
| 22 | 7 | 20 | 4 | 40 | 8 | 9 | 3 | 51 | 8 | 16 | 3 | 44 |
| 23 | 7 | 22 | 4 | 38 | 8 | 10 | 3 | 50 | 8 | 15 | 3 | 45 |
| 24 | 7 | 23 | 4 | 37 | 8 | 11 | 3 | 49 | 8 | 14 | 3 | 46 |
| 25 | 7 | 25 | 4 | 35 | 8 | 12 | 3 | 48 | 8 | 14 | 3 | 46 |
| 26 | 7 | 27 | 4 | 33 | 8 | 12 | 3 | 48 | 8 | 13 | 3 | 47 |
| 27 | 7 | 29 | 4 | 31 | 8 | 13 | 3 | 47 | 8 | 12 | 3 | 48 |
| 28 | 7 | 31 | 4 | 29 | 8 | 14 | 3 | 46 | 8 | 12 | 3 | 48 |
| 29 | 7 | 33 | 4 | 27 | 8 | 14 | 3 | 46 | 8 | 11 | 3 | 49 |
| 30 | 7 | 34 | 4 | 26 | 8 | 15 | 3 | 45 | 8 | 10 | 3 | 50 |
| 31 | 7 | 36 | 4 | 24 | | | | | 8 | 9 | 3 | 51 |

# A TABLE

## SHEWING

*The Time of the* New Moon *and* Full Moon, *as likewise the* First *and* Second Quadrats; *and consequently her true Age, for Twelve Years.*

| 1679. | New ☽ | | | 1 Quar. | | | Full ● | | | 2 Quar. | | |
|---|---|---|---|---|---|---|---|---|---|---|---|---|
| | *D.* | *H.* | *M.* | *D.* | *H.* | *M.* | *D.* | *H.* | *M.* | *D.* | *H.* | *M.* |
| *January* | 2<br>31 | 0<br>13 | 17<br>19 | 8 | 15 | 20 | 16 | 6 | 1 | 24 | 9 | 58 |
| *February* | *No New* ☽ | | | 7 | 2 | 26 | 15 | 0 | 28 | 23 | 2 | 26 |
| *March* | 1<br>31 | 20<br>6 | 48<br>32 | 8 | 15 | 47 | 16 | 16 | 58 | 24 | 15 | 15 |
| *April* | 29 | 7 | 26 | 7 | 6 | 56 | 14 | 23 | 45 | 22 | 23 | 57 |
| *May* | 28 | 23 | 25 | 6 | 23 | 4 | 15 | 0 | 23 | 22 | 12 | 33 |
| *June* | 27 | 9 | 59 | 5 | 15 | 58 | 13 | 15 | 54 | 20 | 9 | 8 |
| *July* | 26 | 22 | 31 | 5 | 8 | 51 | 12 | 22 | 43 | 19 | 13 | 12 |
| *August* | 25 | 13 | 14 | 4 | 1 | 6 | 11 | 6 | 15 | 17 | 20 | 3 |
| *Septem.* | 24 | 5 | 55 | 2 | 16 | 52 | 9 | 14 | 35 | 16 | 6 | 17 |
| *October.* | 24 | 3 | 31 | 2<br>31 | 6<br>18 | 39<br>38 | 8 | 23 | 16 | 15 | 20 | 39 |
| *Novem.* | 22 | 15 | 43 | 30 | 4 | 13 | 7 | 9 | 10 | 14 | 14 | 20 |
| *Decemb.* | 22 | 10 | 26 | 29 | 12 | 20 | 6 | 21 | 9 | 14 | 10 | 35 |

## Change of the Moon.

| 1680. | New ☽ | | | 1 Quar. | | | Full ● | | | 2 Quar. | | |
|---|---|---|---|---|---|---|---|---|---|---|---|---|
| | D. | H. | M. | D. | H. | M. | D. | H. | M. | D. | H. | M. |
| *January* | 21 | 0 | 59 | 27 | 19 | 19 | 5 | 10 | 6 | 13 | 7 | 3 |
| *February* | 19 | 12 | 57 | 26 | 3 | 36 | 4 | 2 | 1 | 12 | 3 | 58 |
| *March* | 19 | 22 | 20 | 26 | 11 | 26 | 4 | 18 | 39 | 12 | 21 | 55 |
| *April* | 18 | 6 | 17 | 25 | 1 | 52 | 3 | 11 | 25 | 11 | 12 | 54 |
| *May* | 17 | 13 | 50 | 24 | 14 | 59 | 3 | 3 | 9 | 11 | 2 | 56 |
| *June* | 15 | 21 | 31 | 23 | 6 | 17 | 1 | 18 | 13 | 9 | 7 | 20 |
| *July* | 15 | 16 | 39 | 22 | 23 | 12 | 1<br>30 | 7<br>19 | 22<br>17 | 8 | 12 | 15 |
| *August* | 13 | 7 | 32 | 21 | 16 | 47 | 29 | 5 | 43 | 6 | 15 | 2 |
| *Septem.* | 12 | 6 | 57 | 20 | 10 | 31 | 27 | 8 | 8 | 4 | 21 | 28 |
| *October* | 13 | 2 | 58 | 20 | 1 | 30 | 27 | 1 | 19 | 4 | 5 | 23 |
| *Novem.* | 10 | 18 | 13 | 18 | 18 | 50 | 25 | 11 | 20 | 2 | 16 | 19 |
| *Decemb.* | 10 | 13 | 33 | 18 | 7 | 34 | 24 | 20 | 22 | 2 | 9 | 34 |

| 1681. | New ☽ | | | 1 Quar. | | | Full ● | | | 2 Quar. | | |
|---|---|---|---|---|---|---|---|---|---|---|---|---|
| | D. | H. | M. | D. | H. | M. | D. | H. | M. | D. | H. | M. |
| *January* | 9 | 7 | 52 | 16 | 17 | 25 | 23 | 10 | 6 | 1<br>31 | 4<br>0 | 18<br>27 |
| *February* | 7 | 23 | 48 | 15 | 0 | 37 | 21 | 23 | 6 | *No* 2. *Qu.* | | |
| *March* | 9 | 12 | 43 | 16 | 6 | 45 | 23 | 13 | 24 | 1<br>31 | 20<br>15 | 45<br>15 |
| *April* | 7 | 23 | 3 | 14 | 13 | 24 | 22 | 4 | 29 | 30 | 7 | 34 |
| *May* | 7 | 7 | 11 | 13 | 21 | 47 | 21 | 19 | 58 | 29 | 20 | 41 |
| *June* | 5 | 13 | 7 | 12 | 8 | 53 | 20 | 10 | 45 | 28 | 6 | 24 |
| *July* | 4 | 21 | 41 | 11 | 22 | 40 | 20 | 1 | 18 | 27 | 14 | 25 |
| *August* | 3 | 4 | 57 | 10 | 14 | 3 | 18 | 14 | 20 | 25 | 20 | 7 |
| *Septem.* | 1 | 14 | 43 | 9 | 8 | 9 | 17 | 4 | 5 | 24 | 1 | 3 |
| *October* | 1<br>30 | 3<br>18 | 9<br>43 | 9 | 3 | 20 | 16 | 16 | 4 | 23 | 8 | 1 |
| *Novem.* | 29 | 12 | 56 | 7 | 22 | 38 | 15 | 5 | 8 | 21 | 17 | 50 |
| *Decemb.* | 29 | 8 | 26 | 7 | 16 | 36 | 14 | 13 | 52 | 21 | 8 | 8 |

## Change of the Moon.

| 1682. | New ☽ | | | 1 Quar. | | | Full ● | | | 2 Quar. | | |
|---|---|---|---|---|---|---|---|---|---|---|---|---|
| | D. | H. | M. | D. | H. | M. | D. | H. | M. | D. | H. | M. |
| January | 28 | 3 | 32 | 6 | 8 | 21 | 13 | 0 | 12 | 19 | 23 | 20 |
| February | 26 | 20 | 48 | 4 | 20 | 58 | 11 | 11 | 25 | 18 | 17 | 37 |
| March | 28 | 10 | 56 | 6 | 5 | 11 | 12 | 21 | 45 | 20 | 12 | 33 |
| April | 26 | 22 | 9 | 4 | 10 | 51 | 11 | 9 | 34 | 19 | 6 | 45 |
| May | 26 | 7 | 2 | 3 | 15 | 29 | 10 | 22 | 17 | 18 | 23 | 49 |
| June | 24 | 14 | 52 | 1 | 20 | 49 | 9 | 11 | 57 | 17 | 14 | 50 |
| July | 23 | 21 | 31 | 1<br>30 | 5<br>14 | 4<br>13 | 9 | 2 | 32 | 17 | 3 | 57 |
| August | 22 | 4 | 44 | 26 | 6 | 31 | 7 | 17 | 6 | 15 | 14 | 30 |
| Septem. | 20 | 13 | 59 | 28 | 0 | 2 | 6 | 9 | 34 | 13 | 23 | 0 |
| October | 20 | 1 | 18 | 27 | 19 | 39 | 6 | 1 | 4 | 13 | 5 | 58 |
| Novem. | 18 | 15 | 22 | 26 | 16 | 17 | 4 | 15 | 3 | 11 | 14 | 53 |
| Decemb. | 18 | 8 | 32 | 26 | 12 | 20 | 4 | 5 | 7 | 10 | 20 | 37 |

| 1683. | New ☽ | | | 1 Quar. | | | Full ● | | | 2 Quar. | | |
|---|---|---|---|---|---|---|---|---|---|---|---|---|
| | D. | H. | M. | D. | H. | M. | D. | H. | M. | D. | H. | M. |
| January | 17 | 3 | 10 | 25 | 6 | 22 | 2 | 18 | 28 | 9 | 7 | 5 |
| February | 15 | 21 | 57 | 23 | 21 | 6 | 1 | 2 | 39 | 7 | 20 | 17 |
| March | 17 | 15 | 39 | 25 | 7 | 36 | 2<br>31 | 7<br>21 | 58<br>45 | 9 | 11 | 32 |
| April | 16 | 6 | 46 | 23 | 14 | 28 | 30 | 7 | 5 | 8 | 4 | 15 |
| May | 15 | 19 | 26 | 22 | 18 | 37 | 29 | 17 | 40 | 7 | 21 | 32 |
| June | 14 | 5 | 40 | 20 | 22 | 31 | 28 | 5 | 12 | 6 | 14 | 34 |
| July | 13 | 14 | 15 | 20 | 5 | 40 | 27 | 19 | 3 | 6 | 7 | 4 |
| August | 11 | 22 | 9 | 18 | 12 | 43 | 26 | 10 | 31 | 4 | 22 | 31 |
| Septem. | 10 | 5 | 55 | 17 | 1 | 7 | 25 | 3 | 23 | 3 | 12 | 9 |
| October | 9 | 14 | 55 | 16 | 17 | 17 | 24 | 20 | 52 | 3 | 0 | 8 |
| Novem. | 8 | 1 | 26 | 15 | 12 | 25 | 23 | 13 | 42 | 1<br>30 | 10<br>17 | 2<br>42 |
| Decemb. | 7 | 14 | 16 | 15 | 9 | 21 | 23 | 5 | 2 | 30 | 1 | 34 |

## *Change of the Moon.*

| 1684. | New ☽ | | | 1 Quar. | | | Full ● | | | 2 Quar. | | |
|---|---|---|---|---|---|---|---|---|---|---|---|---|
| | *D.* | *H.* | *M.* | *D.* | *H.* | *M.* | *D.* | *H.* | *M.* | *D.* | *H.* | *M.* |
| *January* | 6 | 5 | 34 | 14 | 6 | 25 | 21 | 20 | 3 | 28 | 9 | 42 |
| *February* | 4 | 22 | 16 | 13 | 1 | 51 | 20 | 4 | 49 | 26 | 19 | 30 |
| *March* | 5 | 15 | 25 | 13 | 18 | 13 | 20 | 14 | 0 | 27 | 7 | 29 |
| *April* | 4 | 9 | 1 | 12 | 7 | 8 | 18 | 21 | 55 | 25 | 21 | 10 |
| *May* | 4 | 0 | 51 | 11 | 16 | 3 | 18 | 5 | 34 | 25 | 12 | 32 |
| *June* | 2 | 14 | 42 | 9 | 21 | 50 | 16 | 14 | 35 | 24 | 5 | 16 |
| *July* | 2<br>31 | 2<br>14 | 26<br>7 | 9 | 1 | 37 | 16 | 0 | 31 | 23 | 21 | 52 |
| *August* | 29 | 22 | 20 | 7 | 7 | 35 | 14 | 12 | 52 | 22 | 15 | 4 |
| *Septem.* | 28 | 7 | 33 | 5 | 12 | 20 | 13 | 8 | 0 | 21 | 7 | 40 |
| *October* | 27 | 16 | 46 | 4 | 21 | 20 | 12 | 21 | 5 | 20 | 23 | 0 |
| *Novem.* | 26 | 2 | 58 | 3 | 14 | 11 | 11 | 15 | 37 | 19 | 11 | 18 |
| *Decemb.* | 25 | 14 | 32 | 3 | 6 | 27 | 11 | 10 | 18 | 18 | 23 | 0 |

| 1685. | New ☽ | | | 1 Quar. | | | Full ● | | | 2 Quar. | | |
|---|---|---|---|---|---|---|---|---|---|---|---|---|
| | *D.* | *H.* | *M.* | *D.* | *H.* | *M.* | *D.* | *H.* | *M.* | *D.* | *H.* | *M.* |
| *January* | 24 | 3 | 38 | 2<br>31 | 2<br>23 | 28<br>4 | 10 | 3 | 34 | 17 | 7 | 5 |
| *February* | 22 | 18 | 19 | *No* 1. *Qu.* | | | 8 | 17 | 52 | 15 | 13 | 59 |
| *March* | 24 | 9 | 45 | 2 | 20 | 4 | 10 | 5 | 49 | 16 | 20 | 58 |
| *April* | 23 | 1 | 35 | 1 | 9 | 44 | 8 | 14 | 58 | 15 | 5 | 25 |
| *May* | 22 | 18 | 1 | 1<br>30 | 3<br>14 | 39<br>57 | 7 | 22 | 48 | 14 | 15 | 59 |
| *June* | 21 | 7 | 49 | 28 | 23 | 10 | 6 | 5 | 0 | 13 | 4 | 49 |
| *July* | 20 | 21 | 22 | 28 | 4 | 50 | 5 | 13 | 4 | 12 | 19 | 41 |
| *August* | 19 | 10 | 10 | 26 | 9 | 19 | 3 | 21 | 41 | 11 | 12 | 37 |
| *Septem.* | 17 | 21 | 53 | 24 | 14 | 57 | 2 | 8 | 39 | 10 | 9 | 55 |
| *October* | 17 | 8 | 45 | 23 | 22 | 50 | 1<br>31 | 23<br>15 | 36<br>26 | 10 | 1 | 31 |
| *Novem.* | 15 | 20 | 16 | 22 | 10 | 52 | 30 | 10 | 24 | 8 | 19 | 42 |
| *Decemb* | 15 | 5 | 27 | 22 | 2 | 20 | 30 | 5 | 56 | 8 | 8 | 5 |

## *Change of the Moon.*

| 1686. | New ☽ | | | 1 Quar. | | | Full ● | | | 2 Quar. | | |
|---|---|---|---|---|---|---|---|---|---|---|---|---|
| | *D.* | *H.* | *M.* | *D.* | *H.* | *M.* | *D.* | *H.* | *M.* | *D.* | *H.* | *M.* |
| *January* | 13 | 11 | 59 | 20 | 20 | 50 | 28 | 22 | 12 | 7 | 1 | 12 |
| *February* | 12 | 1 | 26 | 20 | 15 | 37 | 27 | 16 | 20 | 5 | 7 | 57 |
| *March* | 13 | 14 | 2 | 21 | 11 | 1 | 29 | 6 | 56 | 6 | 18 | 39 |
| *April* | 12 | 4 | 32 | 20 | 5 | 13 | 27 | 15 | 1 | 5 | 0 | 7 |
| *May* | 11 | 16 | 9 | 19 | 21 | 18 | 26 | 23 | 0 | 4 | 5 | 41 |
| *June* | 10 | 9 | 16 | 18 | 11 | 42 | 25 | 5 | 55 | 2 | 12 | 50 |
| *July* | 9 | 23 | 59 | 17 | 21 | 57 | 24 | 12 | 40 | 1<br>31 | 23<br>14 | 5<br>12 |
| *August* | 8 | 15 | 7 | 16 | 4 | 15 | 22 | 20 | 50 | 30 | 4 | 2 |
| *Septem.* | 7 | 5 | 58 | 14 | 13 | 15 | 21 | 6 | 46 | 28 | 2 | 32 |
| *October* | 6 | 20 | 1 | 13 | 19 | 18 | 20 | 19 | 22 | 28 | 18 | 17 |
| *Novem.* | 5 | 9 | 16 | 12 | 2 | 13 | 19 | 11 | 24 | 27 | 14 | 30 |
| *Decemb.* | 4 | 21 | 4 | 11 | 13 | 5 | 19 | 5 | 15 | 27 | 9 | 21 |

| 1687. | New ☽ | | | 1 Quar. | | | Full ● | | | 2 Quar. | | |
|---|---|---|---|---|---|---|---|---|---|---|---|---|
| | *D.* | *H.* | *M.* | *D.* | *H.* | *M.* | *D.* | *H.* | *M.* | *D.* | *H.* | *M.* |
| *January* | 3 | 7 | 55 | 10 | 0 | 24 | 18 | 0 | 27 | 26 | 1 | 28 |
| *February* | 1 | 18 | 13 | 8 | 12 | 38 | 16 | 19 | 26 | 22 | 22 | 47 |
| *March* | 3 | 4 | 3 | 10 | 8 | 49 | 18 | 12 | 17 | 25 | 22 | 47 |
| *April* | 1 | 14 | 8 | 9 | 2 | 25 | 17 | 2 | 18 | 24 | 4 | 2 |
| *May* | 1<br>30 | 0<br>12 | 40<br>24 | 8 | 19 | 55 | 16 | 14 | 4 | 23 | 8 | 12 |
| *June* | 29 | 1 | 29 | 7 | 12 | 56 | 14 | 22 | 30 | 21 | 12 | 52 |
| *July* | 28 | 16 | 4 | 7 | 4 | 51 | 14 | 6 | 24 | 20 | 20 | 12 |
| *August* | 27 | 7 | 59 | 5 | 18 | 38 | 12 | 15 | 11 | 19 | 2 | 56 |
| *Septem.* | 26 | 0 | 29 | 4 | 6 | 2 | 10 | 21 | 30 | 17 | 21 | 16 |
| *October* | 25 | 10 | 50 | 3 | 14 | 10 | 10 | 6 | 49 | 17 | 14 | 53 |
| *Novem.* | 24 | 8 | 38 | 2 | 0 | 22 | 8 | 18 | 26 | 16 | 10 | 56 |
| *Decemb.* | 23 | 22 | 30 | 1<br>30 | 7<br>15 | 16<br>16 | 8 | 8 | 31 | 16 | 8 | 5 |

## *Change of the Moon.*

| 1688. | New ☽ | | | 1 Quar. | | | Full ● | | | 2 Quar. | | |
|---|---|---|---|---|---|---|---|---|---|---|---|---|
| | *D.* | *H.* | *M.* | *D.* | *H.* | *M.* | *D.* | *H.* | *M.* | *D.* | *H.* | *M.* |
| *January* | 22 | 10 | 12 | 29 | 0 | 57 | 7 | 1 | 12 | 15 | 4 | 50 |
| *February* | 20 | 20 | 24 | 27 | 12 | 39 | 5 | 19 | 4 | 13 | 22 | 30 |
| *March* | 21 | 5 | 15 | 28 | 2 | 29 | 6 | 13 | 58 | 14 | 13 | 14 |
| *April* | 19 | 15 | 27 | 26 | 18 | 14 | 5 | 6 | 4 | 13 | 0 | 4 |
| *May* | 18 | 16 | 10 | 26 | 10 | 41 | 4 | 21 | 36 | 12 | 6 | 56 |
| *June* | 17 | 3 | 5 | 25 | 3 | 34 | 3 | 9 | 56 | 10 | 5 | 46 |
| *July* | 16 | 19 | 47 | 24 | 20 | 34 | 2 | 20 | 38 | 9 | 15 | 10 |
| *August* | 15 | 9 | 10 | 23 | 12 | 34 | 1<br>30 | 5<br>14 | 49<br>26 | 7 | 20 | 45 |
| *Septem.* | 14 | 0 | 49 | 22 | 3 | 42 | 28 | 23 | 0 | 6 | 4 | [illegible] |
| *October* | 13 | 18 | 40 | 21 | 16 | 59 | 28 | 8 | 12 | 5 | 16 | [illegible] |
| *Novem.* | 12 | 12 | 54 | 20 | 4 | 8 | 26 | 19 | 5 | 4 | 2 | 51 |
| *Decemb.* | 12 | 6 | 68 | 19 | 13 | 2 | 26 | 7 | 42 | 4 | 6 | 15 |

| 1689. | New ☽ | | | 1 Quar. | | | Full ● | | | 2 Quar. | | |
|---|---|---|---|---|---|---|---|---|---|---|---|---|
| | *D.* | *H.* | *M.* | *D.* | *H.* | *M.* | *D.* | *H.* | *M.* | *D.* | *H.* | *M.* |
| *January* | 10 | 22 | 10 | 17 | 20 | 26 | 24 | 22 | 12 | 3 | 1 | 2 |
| *February* | 9 | 11 | 21 | 26 | 3 | 41 | 23 | 14 | 12 | 1 | 11 | 56 |
| *March* | 10 | 21 | 57 | 17 | 12 | 17 | 25 | 16 | 4 | 3 | 17 | 8 |
| *April* | 9 | 6 | 32 | 15 | 22 | 42 | 23 | 23 | 0 | 2 | 9 | 31 |
| *May* | 8 | 13 | 34 | 15 | 11 | 21 | 23 | 14 | 19 | 1<br>31 | 22<br>7 | 26<br>40 |
| *June* | 6 | 22 | 8 | 14 | 1 | 51 | 22 | 4 | 18 | 29 | 13 | 56 |
| *July* | 6 | 5 | 28 | 17 | 13 | 54 | 21 | 16 | 58 | 28 | 18 | 7 |
| *August* | 4 | 15 | 21 | 12 | 11 | 13 | 20 | 4 | 17 | 26 | 22 | 38 |
| *Septem.* | 3 | 3 | 39 | 11 | 5 | 17 | 18 | 17 | 46 | 35 | 8 | 13 |
| *October* | 2 | 18 | 55 | 10 | 23 | 0 | 18 | 0 | 40 | 24 | 14 | 21 |
| *Novem.* | 1 | 12 | 35 | 9 | 15 | 35 | 16 | 10 | 30 | 23 | 5 | 22 |
| *Decemb.* | 1<br>31 | 1<br>3 | 4<br>2 | 9 | 6 | 0 | 15 | 22 | 2 | 22 | 22 | 42 |

## Change of the Moon, and Eclipses.

| 1690. | New ☽ | | | 1 Quar. | | | Full ● | | | 2 Quar. | | |
|---|---|---|---|---|---|---|---|---|---|---|---|---|
| | D. | H. | M. | D. | H. | M. | D. | H. | M. | D. | H. | M. |
| January | 29 | 20 | 17 | 7 | 16 | 53 | 14 | 15 | 38 | 21 | 18 | 8 |
| February | 28 | 11 | 4 | 6 | 1 | 49 | 12 | 20 | 39 | 20 | 14 | 24 |
| March | 29 | 22 | 8 | 7 | 8 | 6 | 14 | 10 | 14 | 22 | 9 | 46 |
| April | 28 | 6 | 59 | 5 | 14 | 2 | 13 | 21 | 34 | 21 | 3 | 7 |
| May | 27 | 14 | 31 | 4 | 21 | 0 | 12 | 15 | 19 | 20 | 17 | 53 |
| June | 25 | 21 | 21 | 3 | 6 | 30 | 11 | 4 | 13 | 19 | 5 | 43 |
| July | 25 | 4 | 42 | 2 | 18 | 27 | 10 | 21 | 28 | 18 | 14 | 45 |
| August | 23 | 13 | 21 | 1<br>31 | 9<br>2 | 18<br>23 | 9 | 11 | 45 | 16 | 21 | 32 |
| Septem. | 22 | 0 | 32 | 29 | 21 | 12 | 8 | 1 | 42 | 15 | 3 | 8 |
| October | 21 | 13 | 10 | 29 | 15 | 19 | 7 | 14 | 26 | 14 | 10 | 35 |
| Novem. | 20 | 7 | 34 | 28 | 9 | 51 | 6 | 0 | 25 | 12 | 16 | 52 |
| Decemb. | 20 | 2 | 42 | 28 | 5 | 5 | 5 | 13 | 11 | 12 | 4 | 25 |

### A Catalogue of the Eclipses visible in England, from 1678, to the Year 1690.

| Year. | Month. | D. | H. | M. | Lun. | Dig. | Min. |
|---|---|---|---|---|---|---|---|
| 1681 | August | 18 | 14 | 22 | ☽ | 10 | 35 |
| 1682 | August | 7 | 17 | 56 | ☽ | 18 | 50 |
| 1682 | February | 11 | 11 | 28 | ☽ | 19 | 48 |
| 1683 | January | 17 | 4 | 27 | ☉ | 10 | 30 |
| 1684 | June | 16 | 14 | 17 | ☽ | 1 | 35 |
| 1684 | July | 2 | 3 | 10 | ☉ | 8 | 0 |
| 1685 | November | 30 | 10 | 20 | ☽ | 21 | 45 |
| 1686 | November | 19 | 11 | 22 | ☽ | 7 | 35 |
| 1687 | May | 1 | 1 | 25 | ☉ | 1 | 40 |
| 1688 | April | 5 | 6 | 4 | ☽ | 6 | 49 |
| 1689 | March | 25 | 6 | 41 | ☽ | 21 | 19 |
| 1689 | September | 18 | 14 | 46 | ☽ | 20 | 39 |
| 1690 | March | 14 | 10 | 14 | ☽ | 5 | 53 |

## *A Tide-Table.*

*By the Moon's Age, to find the time of High-Water at the Places following.*

| *The Moon's Age.* | | *LONDON, Tinmouth, Whitebay.* | | *Berwick, Bridlington-bay.* | | *Scarbrow* 4ter Tide, *Severn.* | | *Newcastle, Falmouth, Dartmouth.* | |
|---|---|---|---|---|---|---|---|---|---|
| *Days.* | | H. | M. | H. | M. | H. | M. | H. | M. |
| 1 | 16 | 3 | 48 | 4 | 33 | 5 | 18 | 6 | 3 |
| 2 | 17 | 4 | 30 | 5 | 21 | 6 | 6 | 6 | 51 |
| 3 | 18 | 5 | 24 | 6 | 9 | 6 | 54 | 7 | 39 |
| 4 | 19 | 6 | 12 | 6 | 57 | 7 | 42 | 8 | 27 |
| 5 | 20 | 7 | 0 | 7 | 45 | 8 | 30 | 9 | 15 |
| 6 | 21 | 7 | 48 | 8 | 33 | 9 | 18 | 10 | 3 |
| 7 | 22 | 8 | 36 | 9 | 21 | 10 | 6 | 10 | 51 |
| 8 | 23 | 9 | 24 | 10 | 9 | 10 | 54 | 11 | 39 |
| 9 | 24 | 10 | 12 | 10 | 57 | 11 | 42 | 12 | 27 |
| 10 | 25 | 11 | 0 | 11 | 45 | 12 | 30 | 1 | 15 |
| 11 | 26 | 11 | 48 | 12 | 33 | 1 | 10 | 2 | 3 |
| 12 | 27 | 12 | 36 | 1 | 21 | 2 | 6 | 2 | 51 |
| 13 | 28 | 1 | 24 | 2 | 9 | 2 | 54 | 3 | 39 |
| 14 | 29 | 2 | 12 | 2 | 57 | 3 | 42 | 4 | 27 |
| 15 | 30 | 3 | 0 | 3 | 45 | 4 | 30 | 5 | 15 |

| *The Moon's Age.* | | *Queenbor. Southampt. Portsmouth.* | | *Rochester,* West end of *Nowr.* | | *Gravesend, Downs, Blackness.* | | *Dundee,* S. *Andrews, Bell Isle.* | |
|---|---|---|---|---|---|---|---|---|---|
| *Days.* | | H. | M. | H. | M. | H. | M. | H. | M. |
| 1 | 16 | 12 | 48 | 1 | 33 | 2 | 18 | 3 | 3 |
| 2 | 17 | 1 | 36 | 2 | 21 | 3 | 6 | 3 | 51 |
| 3 | 18 | 2 | 24 | 3 | 9 | 3 | 54 | 4 | 39 |
| 4 | 19 | 3 | 12 | 3 | 57 | 4 | 42 | 5 | 27 |
| 5 | 20 | 4 | 0 | 4 | 45 | 5 | 30 | 6 | 15 |
| 6 | 21 | 4 | 48 | 5 | 33 | 6 | 18 | 7 | 3 |
| 7 | 22 | 5 | 36 | 6 | 21 | 7 | 6 | 7 | 51 |
| 8 | 23 | 6 | 24 | 7 | 9 | 7 | 54 | 8 | 39 |
| 9 | 24 | 7 | 12 | 7 | 57 | 8 | 42 | 9 | 27 |
| 10 | 25 | 8 | 0 | 8 | 45 | 9 | 30 | 10 | 15 |
| 11 | 26 | 8 | 48 | 9 | 33 | 10 | 18 | 11 | 3 |
| 12 | 27 | 9 | 36 | 10 | 21 | 11 | 6 | 11 | 51 |
| 13 | 28 | 10 | 24 | 11 | 9 | 11 | 54 | 12 | 39 |
| 14 | 29 | 11 | 12 | 11 | 57 | 12 | 42 | 1 | 27 |
| 15 | 30 | 12 | 0 | 12 | 45 | 1 | 30 | 2 | 15 |

## *The Use of the Table of the* Changes *of the* Moon.

BEfore I ſet down any Example, I think it requiſite to advertize you, That in the Computation of Hours in this Table, the firſt is to be reckoned from Noon, ſo that the ſixth day 23 hours, is 11 of the Clock the ſeventh day; this being premiſed, I ſhall give you only two Examples to illuſtrate this Table.

*Example* 1.

*On what Day is the Moon at Full in* May, 1679?

Having found the Table for 1679, I ſeek for *May* in the firſt Column, and having found it, I find right againſt it in the fourth Column (under the Title *Full Moon*) 15:0:23, which is the fifteenth day near half an hour paſt 12, and then is the Moon at Full; and after this manner is the time of New Moon, *&c.* found.

*Example* 2.

*What is the Moon's Age* March 25, 1680?

By the Table for 1680, I find the New Moon to be on the 20*th* day; wherefore it neceſſarily follows, that on the 25*th* day the Moon muſt be 5 days old.

## *The Use of the* TIDE-TABLE.

Example.

*What Hour is it High-Water at* London-Bridge *on* March 25, 1680?

Having by the foregoing Rules found the Moon to be then 5 days old, I ſeek that Number in the firſt Column under the Moon's Age, and right againſt it under *London* in the ſecond Column I find 7:0, from whence I conclude, that it will be High-Water there at 7 of the Clock that day. And having the Moon's Age, you may readily find the time of High-Water at any of the Places mentioned in the Table, in their reſpective Columns.

*A Cata-*

# *A Catalogue of the Counties, Cities, Market-Towns, and Pariſhes, in* England *and* Wales.

| Counties in *England.* | Cities. | Mark. T. | Pariſhes. |
|---|---|---|---|
| Bedford | | 10 | 116 |
| Berks | | 11 | 140 |
| Buckingham | | 11 | 185 |
| Cambridge | | 8 | 163 |
| Cheſter | 1 | 13 | 68 |
| Cornwall | | 23 | 161 |
| Cumberland | 1 | 9 | 58 |
| Darby | | 8 | 106 |
| Devon | 1 | 40 | 324 |
| Dorſet | | 18 | 248 |
| Durham | 1 | 6 | 118 |
| Eſſex | 1 | 21 | 415 |
| Gloceſter | 1 | 25 | 280 |
| Hantſhire | 1 | 18 | 253 |
| Hertford | | 18 | 120 |
| Hereford | 1 | 8 | 176 |
| Huntington | | 6 | 78 |
| Kent | 2 | 17 | 398 |
| Lancaſter | | 15 | 36 |
| Leiceſter | 1 | 12 | 200 |
| Lincoln | 1 | 30 | 630 |
| Middleſex | 2 | 18 | 73 |
| Norfolk | 1 | 27 | 660 |
| Northampton | 1 | 11 | 326 |
| Northumberl. | | 5 | 47 |
| Nottingham | | 8 | 168 |
| Oxford | 1 | 10 | 280 |
| Rutland | | 2 | 47 |

| Counties in *England.* | Cities. | Mark. T. | Pariſhes. |
|---|---|---|---|
| Salop | | 13 | 170 |
| Somerſet | 3 | 29 | 385 |
| Stafford | 1 | 12 | 130 |
| Suffolk | | 18 | 575 |
| Surrey | | 7 | 140 |
| Suſſex | 1 | 18 | 312 |
| Warwick | | 15 | 158 |
| Weſtmorland | | 4 | 26 |
| Wilts | 1 | 21 | 304 |
| Worceſter | 1 | 7 | 132 |
| York | 1 | 46 | 563 |

| Counties in *Wales.* | Cities. | Mark. T. | Pariſhes. |
|---|---|---|---|
| Angleſey | | 2 | 74 |
| Brecknock | | 3 | 61 |
| Cardigan | | 4 | 64 |
| Carmarthen | | 6 | 87 |
| Carnarvan | | 5 | 68 |
| Denbigh | | 3 | 57 |
| Flint | | 3 | 28 |
| Glamorgan | | 6 | 118 |
| Merioneth | | 3 | 37 |
| Monmouth | | 6 | 127 |
| Montgomery | | 6 | 47 |
| Pembrook | | 5 | 145 |
| Radnor | | 5 | 52 |

A Table

## *A Table of Expence.*

| By the Day. | | By the Week. | | | By the Month. | | | By the Year. | | |
|---|---|---|---|---|---|---|---|---|---|---|
| *s.* | *d.* | *l.* | *s.* | *d.* | *l.* | *s.* | *d.* | *l.* | *s.* | *d.* |
| 0 | 1 | 0 | 0 | 7 | 0 | 2 | 4 | 1 | 10 | 5 |
| 0 | 2 | 0 | 1 | 2 | 0 | 4 | 8 | 3 | 0 | 10 |
| 0 | 3 | 0 | 1 | 9 | 0 | 7 | 0 | 4 | 11 | 3 |
| 0 | 4 | 0 | 2 | 4 | 0 | 9 | 4 | 6 | 1 | 8 |
| 0 | 5 | 0 | 2 | 11 | 0 | 11 | 8 | 7 | 12 | 1 |
| 0 | 6 | 0 | 3 | 6 | 0 | 14 | 0 | 9 | 2 | 6 |
| 0 | 7 | 0 | 4 | 1 | 0 | 16 | 4 | 10 | 12 | 11 |
| 0 | 8 | 0 | 4 | 8 | 0 | 18 | 8 | 12 | 3 | 4 |
| 0 | 9 | 0 | 5 | 3 | 1 | 1 | 0 | 13 | 13 | 9 |
| 0 | 10 | 0 | 5 | 10 | 1 | 3 | 4 | 15 | 4 | 2 |
| 0 | 11 | 0 | 6 | 5 | 1 | 5 | 8 | 16 | 14 | 7 |
| 1 | 0 | 0 | 7 | 0 | 1 | 8 | 0 | 18 | 5 | 0 |
| 2 | 0 | 0 | 14 | 0 | 2 | 16 | 0 | 36 | 10 | 0 |
| 3 | 0 | 1 | 1 | 0 | 4 | 4 | 0 | 54 | 15 | 0 |
| 4 | 0 | 1 | 8 | 0 | 5 | 12 | 0 | 73 | 0 | 0 |
| 5 | 0 | 1 | 15 | 0 | 7 | 0 | 0 | 91 | 5 | 0 |
| 6 | 0 | 2 | 2 | 0 | 8 | 8 | 0 | 109 | 10 | 0 |
| 7 | 0 | 2 | 9 | 0 | 9 | 16 | 0 | 127 | 15 | 0 |
| 8 | 0 | 2 | 16 | 0 | 11 | 4 | 0 | 146 | 0 | 0 |
| 9 | 0 | 3 | 3 | 0 | 12 | 12 | 0 | 164 | 5 | 0 |
| 10 | 0 | 3 | 10 | 0 | 14 | 0 | 0 | 182 | 10 | 0 |
| 11 | 0 | 3 | 17 | 0 | 15 | 8 | 0 | 200 | 15 | 0 |
| 12 | 0 | 4 | 4 | 0 | 16 | 16 | 0 | 219 | 0 | 0 |
| 13 | 0 | 4 | 11 | 0 | 18 | 4 | 0 | 237 | 5 | 0 |
| 14 | 0 | 4 | 18 | 0 | 19 | 12 | 0 | 255 | 10 | 0 |
| 15 | 0 | 5 | 5 | 0 | 21 | 0 | 0 | 273 | 15 | 0 |
| 16 | 0 | 5 | 12 | 0 | 22 | 8 | 0 | 292 | 0 | 0 |
| 17 | 0 | 5 | 19 | 0 | 23 | 16 | 0 | 310 | 5 | 0 |
| 18 | 0 | 6 | 6 | 0 | 25 | 4 | 0 | 328 | 10 | 0 |
| 19 | 0 | 6 | 13 | 0 | 26 | 12 | 0 | 346 | 15 | 0 |
| 20 | 0 | 7 | 0 | 0 | 28 | 0 | 0 | 365 | 0 | 0 |

*Note*. That in these Tables of Expence a Month consists but of 28 Days.

## *A Table of Expence.*

| By the Year. | By the Month. | | | By the Week. | | | By the Day. | | |
|---|---|---|---|---|---|---|---|---|---|
| *l.* | *l.* | *s.* | *d.* | *l.* | *s.* | *d.* | *l.* | *s.* | *d.* |
| 1 | 0 | 1 | 6.46 | 0 | 0 | 4.62 | 0 | 0 | 0.66 |
| 2 | 0 | 3 | 0.92 | 0 | 0 | 9.23 | 0 | 0 | 1.32 |
| 3 | 0 | 4 | 7.38 | 0 | 1 | 1.85 | 0 | 0 | 1.97 |
| 4 | 0 | 6 | 1.84 | 0 | 1 | 6.46 | 0 | 0 | 2.63 |
| 5 | 0 | 7 | 8.30 | 0 | 1 | 11.08 | 0 | 0 | 3.29 |
| 6 | 0 | 9 | 2.77 | 0 | 2 | 3.69 | 0 | 0 | 3.95 |
| 7 | 0 | 10 | 9.23 | 0 | 2 | 8.31 | 0 | 0 | 4.60 |
| 8 | 0 | 12 | 3.69 | 0 | 3 | 0.93 | 0 | 0 | 5.26 |
| 9 | 0 | 13 | 10.15 | 0 | 3 | 5.54 | 0 | 0 | 5.92 |
| 10 | 0 | 15 | 4.61 | 0 | 3 | 10.16 | 0 | 0 | 6.58 |
| 11 | 0 | 16 | 11.07 | 0 | 4 | 2.77 | 0 | 0 | 7.23 |
| 12 | 0 | 18 | 5.54 | 0 | 4 | 7.39 | 0 | 0 | 7.89 |
| 13 | 1 | 0 | 0.00 | 0 | 5 | 0.00 | 0 | 0 | 8.55 |
| 14 | 1 | 1 | 6.46 | 0 | 5 | 4.62 | 0 | 0 | 9.21 |
| 15 | 1 | 3 | 0.92 | 0 | 5 | 9.24 | 0 | 0 | 9.86 |
| 16 | 1 | 4 | 7.38 | 0 | 6 | 1.85 | 0 | 0 | 10.52 |
| 17 | 1 | 6 | 1.84 | 0 | 6 | 6.47 | 0 | 0 | 11.18 |
| 18 | 1 | 7 | 8.30 | 0 | 6 | 11.08 | 0 | 0 | 11.84 |
| 19 | 1 | 9 | 2.76 | 0 | 7 | 3.70 | 0 | 1 | 0.49 |
| 20 | 1 | 10 | 9.23 | 0 | 7 | 8.31 | 0 | 1 | 1.15 |
| 30 | 2 | 6 | 1.84 | 0 | 11 | 6.47 | 0 | 1 | 7.73 |
| 40 | 3 | 1 | 6.45 | 0 | 15 | 4.63 | 0 | 2 | 2.30 |
| 50 | 3 | 16 | 11.06 | 0 | 19 | 2.78 | 0 | 2 | 8.88 |
| 60 | 4 | 12 | 3.68 | 1 | 3 | 0.94 | 0 | 3 | 3.45 |
| 70 | 5 | 7 | 8.29 | 1 | 6 | 11.10 | 0 | 3 | 10.03 |
| 80 | 6 | 3 | 0.90 | 1 | 10 | 9.25 | 0 | 4 | 4.60 |
| 90 | 6 | 18 | 5.52 | 1 | 14 | 7.41 | 0 | 4 | 11.18 |
| 100 | 7 | 13 | 10.13 | 1 | 18 | 5.57 | 0 | 5 | 5.75 |
| 200 | 15 | 7 | 8.26 | 3 | 16 | 11.14 | 0 | 10 | 11.51 |
| 300 | 23 | 1 | 6.38 | 5 | 15 | 4.70 | 0 | 16 | 5.26 |
| 400 | 30 | 15 | 4.51 | 7 | 13 | 10.27 | 1 | 1 | 11.01 |
| 500 | 38 | 9 | 2.64 | 9 | 12 | 3.84 | 1 | 7 | 4.77 |
| 1000 | 76 | 18 | 5.28 | 19 | 4 | 7.68 | 2 | 14 | 9.53 |

## A Table of KINGS since the Conquest.

| Kings Names. | Born | Began to Reign | | Reign. Y. | M. | Buried at |
|---|---|---|---|---|---|---|
| *W. Conq.* | 1023 | 1066 | *Octo.* 14 | 20 | 11 | *Caen. Nor.* |
| *W. Rufus* | 1057 | 1087 | *Sep.* 9 | 12 | 11 | *Winchester.* |
| *Henry* 1 | 1068 | 1100 | *Aug.* 1 | 35 | 4 | *Reading.* |
| *Stephen* | 1105 | 1135 | *Dec.* 2 | 18 | 11 | *Feversham.* |
| The *Saxon* Line Restored. | | | | | | |
| *Henry* 2 | 1132 | 1154 | *Octo.* 25 | 34 | 9 | *Fountev.* |
| *Richard* 1 | 1155 | 1189 | *July* 6 | 9 | 9 | *Fountev.* |
| *John* | 1165 | 1199 | *April* 6 | 17 | 7 | *Worcester.* |
| *Henry* 3 | 1207 | 1216 | *Octo.* 19 | 56 | 1 | *Westminster.* |
| *Edward* 1 | 1239 | 1272 | *Nov.* 16 | 34 | 8 | *Westminster.* |
| *Edward* 2 | 1283 | 1307 | *July* 7 | 19 | 7 | *Glocester.* |
| *Edward* 3 | 1312 | 1326 | *Jan.* 25 | 50 | 5 | *Westminster.* |
| *Richard* 2 | 1366 | 1377 | *June* 21 | 22 | 3 | *Westminster.* |
| The Line of *Lancaster.* | | | | | | |
| *Henry* 4 | 1367 | 1399 | *Sept.* 29 | 13 | 6 | *Canterbury.* |
| *Henry* 5 | 1384 | 1412 | *Mar.* 20 | 9 | 5 | *Westminster.* |
| *Henry* 6 | 1421 | 1422 | *Aug.* 31 | 38 | 6 | *Windsor.* |
| The Line of *York.* | | | | | | |
| *Edward* 4 | 1442 | 1460 | *Mar.* 4 | 22 | 1 | *Winchester.* |
| *Edward* 5 | 1471 | 1483 | *April* 9 | 0 | 2 | not known |
| *Richard* 3 | 1448 | 1483 | *June* 22 | 2 | 2 | *Leicester.* |
| The Families United. | | | | | | |
| *Henry* 7 | 1455 | 1485 | *Aug.* 22 | 23 | 8 | *Westminster.* |
| *Henry* 8 | 1491 | 1509 | *April* 22 | 37 | 10 | *Windsor.* |
| *Edward* 6 | 1537 | 1546 | *Jan.* 28 | 6 | 5 | *Westminster.* |
| Q. *Mary.* | 1518 | 1553 | *July* 6 | 5 | 4 | *Westminster.* |
| Q. *Eliz.* | 1533 | 1558 | *Nov.* 17 | 44 | 4 | *Westminster.* |
| The Union of the two Kingdoms. | | | | | | |
| *James* | 1566 | 1602 | *Mar.* 24 | 22 | 0 | *Westminster.* |
| *Charles* 1 | 1600 | 1625 | *Mar.* 27 | 23 | 11 | *Windsor.* |
| *Charles* 2 | 1630 | 1648 | *Jan* 30 | *God grant long to Reig[n]* | | |

*Compu-*

## *Computation of Years.*

| W. Conq. | |
|---|---|
| *A.R.* | *A.Ch.* |
| 1 | 1066 |
| 2 | 1067 |
| 3 | 1068 |
| 4 | 1069 |
| 5 | 1070 |
| 6 | 1071 |
| 7 | 1072 |
| 8 | 1073 |
| 9 | 1074 |
| 10 | 1075 |
| 11 | 1076 |
| 12 | 1077 |
| 13 | 1078 |
| 14 | 1079 |
| 15 | 1080 |
| 16 | 1081 |
| 17 | 1082 |
| 18 | 1083 |
| 19 | 1084 |
| 20 | 1085 |
| 21 | 1086 |
| 22 | 1087 |

| W. Rufus. | |
|---|---|
| 1 | 1087 |
| 2 | 1088 |
| 3 | 1089 |
| 4 | 1090 |
| 5 | 1091 |
| 6 | 1092 |
| 7 | 1093 |
| 8 | 1094 |
| 9 | 1095 |

| Will. Rufus. | |
|---|---|
| *A.R.* | *A.Ch.* |
| 10 | 1096 |
| 11 | 1097 |
| 12 | 1098 |
| 13 | 1099 |
| 14 | 1100 |

| Henry I. | |
|---|---|
| 1 | 1100 |
| 2 | 1101 |
| 3 | 1102 |
| 4 | 1103 |
| 5 | 1104 |
| 6 | 1105 |
| 7 | 1106 |
| 8 | 1107 |
| 9 | 1108 |
| 10 | 1109 |
| 11 | 1110 |
| 12 | 1111 |
| 13 | 1112 |
| 14 | 1113 |
| 15 | 1114 |
| 16 | 1115 |
| 17 | 1116 |
| 18 | 1117 |
| 19 | 1118 |
| 20 | 1119 |
| 21 | 1120 |
| 22 | 1121 |
| 23 | 1122 |
| 24 | 1123 |
| 25 | 1124 |
| 26 | 1125 |

| Henry I. | |
|---|---|
| *A.R.* | *A.Ch.* |
| 27 | 1126 |
| 28 | 1127 |
| 29 | 1128 |
| 30 | 1129 |
| 31 | 1130 |
| 32 | 1131 |
| 33 | 1132 |
| 34 | 1133 |
| 35 | 1134 |
| 36 | 1135 |

| Stephen. | |
|---|---|
| 1 | 1135 |
| 2 | 1136 |
| 3 | 1137 |
| 4 | 1138 |
| 5 | 1139 |
| 6 | 1140 |
| 7 | 1141 |
| 8 | 1142 |
| 9 | 1143 |
| 10 | 1144 |
| 11 | 1145 |
| 12 | 1146 |
| 13 | 1147 |
| 14 | 1148 |
| 15 | 1149 |
| 16 | 1150 |
| 17 | 1151 |
| 18 | 1152 |
| 19 | 1153 |
| 20 | 1154 |

| Henry II. | |
|---|---|
| *A.R.* | *A.Ch.* |
| 1 | 1154 |
| 2 | 1155 |
| 3 | 1156 |
| 4 | 1157 |
| 5 | 1158 |
| 6 | 1159 |
| 7 | 1160 |
| 8 | 1161 |
| 9 | 1162 |
| 10 | 1163 |
| 11 | 1164 |
| 12 | 1165 |
| 13 | 1166 |
| 14 | 1167 |
| 15 | 1168 |
| 16 | 1169 |
| 17 | 1170 |
| 18 | 1171 |
| 19 | 1172 |
| 20 | 1173 |
| 21 | 1174 |
| 22 | 1175 |
| 23 | 1176 |
| 24 | 1177 |
| 25 | 1178 |
| 26 | 1179 |
| 27 | 1180 |
| 28 | 1181 |
| 29 | 1182 |
| 30 | 1183 |
| 31 | 1184 |
| 32 | 1185 |
| 33 | 1186 |
| 34 | 1187 |

# Computation of Years.

### Henry II.

| A.R. | A.Ch. |
|---|---|
| 35 | 1188 |
| 36 | 1189 |

### Richar. I.

| A.R. | A.Ch. |
|---|---|
| 1 | 1189 |
| 2 | 1190 |
| 3 | 1191 |
| 4 | 1192 |
| 5 | 1193 |
| 6 | 1194 |
| 7 | 1195 |
| 8 | 1196 |
| 9 | 1197 |
| 10 | 1198 |
| 11 | 1199 |

### John.

| A.R. | A.Ch. |
|---|---|
| 1 | 1199 |
| 2 | 1200 |
| 3 | 1201 |
| 4 | 1202 |
| 5 | 1203 |
| 6 | 1204 |
| 7 | 1205 |
| 8 | 1206 |
| 9 | 1207 |
| 10 | 1208 |
| 11 | 1209 |
| 12 | 1210 |
| 13 | 1211 |
| 14 | 1212 |
| 15 | 1213 |
| 16 | 1214 |
| 17 | 1215 |
| 18 | 1216 |

### Henr. III

| A.R. | A.Ch. |
|---|---|
| 1 | 1216 |
| 2 | 1217 |
| 3 | 1218 |
| 4 | 1219 |
| 5 | 1220 |
| 6 | 1221 |
| 7 | 1222 |
| 8 | 1223 |
| 9 | 1224 |
| 10 | 1225 |
| 11 | 1226 |
| 12 | 1227 |
| 13 | 1228 |
| 14 | 1229 |
| 15 | 1230 |
| 16 | 1231 |
| 17 | 1232 |
| 18 | 1233 |
| 19 | 1234 |
| 20 | 1235 |
| 21 | 1236 |
| 22 | 1237 |
| 23 | 1238 |
| 24 | 1239 |
| 25 | 1240 |
| 26 | 1241 |
| 27 | 1242 |
| 28 | 1243 |
| 29 | 1244 |
| 30 | 1245 |
| 31 | 1246 |
| 32 | 1247 |
| 33 | 1248 |
| 34 | 1249 |
| 35 | 1250 |
| 36 | 1251 |
| 37 | 1252 |
| 38 | 1253 |
| 39 | 1254 |
| 40 | 1255 |
| 41 | 1256 |
| 42 | 1257 |
| 43 | 1258 |
| 44 | 1259 |
| 45 | 1260 |
| 46 | 1261 |
| 47 | 1262 |
| 48 | 1263 |
| 49 | 1264 |
| 50 | 1265 |
| 51 | 1266 |
| 52 | 1267 |
| 53 | 1268 |
| 54 | 1269 |
| 55 | 1270 |
| 56 | 1271 |
| 57 | 1272 |

### Edwar. I.

| A.R. | A.Ch. |
|---|---|
| 1 | 1272 |
| 2 | 1273 |
| 3 | 1274 |
| 4 | 1275 |
| 5 | 1276 |
| 6 | 1277 |
| 7 | 1278 |
| 8 | 1279 |
| 9 | 1280 |
| 10 | 1281 |
| 11 | 1282 |
| 12 | 1283 |
| 13 | 1284 |
| 14 | 1285 |
| 15 | 1286 |
| 16 | 1287 |
| 17 | 1288 |
| 18 | 1289 |
| 19 | 1290 |
| 20 | 1291 |
| 21 | 1292 |
| 22 | 1293 |
| 23 | 1294 |
| 24 | 1295 |
| 25 | 1296 |
| 26 | 1297 |
| 27 | 1298 |
| 28 | 1299 |
| 29 | 1300 |
| 30 | 1301 |
| 31 | 1302 |
| 32 | 1303 |
| 33 | 1304 |
| 34 | 1305 |
| 35 | 1306 |
| 36 | 1307 |

## Computation of Years.

| Edw. II. A.R. | A.Ch. |
|---|---|
| 1 | 1307 |
| 2 | 1308 |
| 3 | 1309 |
| 4 | 1310 |
| 5 | 1311 |
| 6 | 1312 |
| 7 | 1313 |
| 8 | 1314 |
| 9 | 1315 |
| 10 | 1316 |
| 11 | 1317 |
| 12 | 1318 |
| 13 | 1319 |
| 14 | 1320 |
| 15 | 1321 |
| 16 | 1322 |
| 17 | 1323 |
| 18 | 1324 |
| 19 | 1325 |
| 20 | 1326 |

| Edw. III. A.R. | A.Ch. |
|---|---|
| 1 | 1326 |
| 2 | 1327 |
| 3 | 1328 |
| 4 | 1329 |
| 5 | 1330 |
| 6 | 1331 |
| 7 | 1332 |
| 8 | 1333 |
| 9 | 1334 |
| 10 | 1335 |
| 11 | 1336 |
| 12 | 1337 |
| 13 | 1338 |
| 14 | 1339 |
| 15 | 1340 |
| 16 | 1341 |
| 17 | 1342 |
| 18 | 1343 |
| 19 | 1344 |
| 20 | 1345 |
| 21 | 1346 |
| 22 | 1347 |
| 23 | 1348 |
| 24 | 1349 |
| 25 | 1350 |
| 26 | 1351 |
| 27 | 1352 |
| 28 | 1353 |
| 29 | 1354 |
| 30 | 1355 |
| 31 | 1356 |
| 32 | 1357 |
| 33 | 1358 |
| 34 | 1359 |
| 35 | 1360 |
| 36 | 1361 |
| 37 | 1362 |
| 38 | 1363 |
| 39 | 1364 |
| 40 | 1365 |
| 41 | 1366 |
| 42 | 1367 |
| 43 | 1368 |
| 44 | 1369 |
| 45 | 1370 |
| 46 | 1371 |
| 47 | 1372 |
| 48 | 1373 |
| 49 | 1374 |
| 50 | 1375 |
| 51 | 1376 |
| 52 | 1377 |

| Rich. II. A.R. | A.Ch. |
|---|---|
| 1 | 1377 |
| 2 | 1378 |
| 3 | 1379 |
| 4 | 1380 |
| 5 | 1381 |
| 6 | 1382 |
| 7 | 1383 |
| 8 | 1384 |
| 9 | 1385 |
| 10 | 1386 |
| 11 | 1387 |
| 12 | 1388 |
| 13 | 1389 |
| 14 | 1390 |
| 15 | 1391 |
| 16 | 1392 |
| 17 | 1393 |
| 18 | 1394 |
| 19 | 1395 |
| 20 | 1396 |
| 21 | 1397 |
| 22 | 1398 |
| 23 | 1399 |

| Henr. IV. A.R. | A.Ch. |
|---|---|
| 1 | 1399 |
| 2 | 1400 |
| 3 | 1401 |
| 4 | 1402 |
| 5 | 1403 |
| 6 | 1404 |
| 7 | 1405 |
| 8 | 1406 |
| 9 | 1407 |
| 10 | 1408 |
| 11 | 1409 |
| 12 | 1410 |
| 13 | 1411 |
| 14 | 1412 |

| Henry V. A.R. | A.Ch. |
|---|---|
| 1 | 1412 |
| 2 | 1413 |
| 3 | 1414 |
| 4 | 1415 |
| 5 | 1416 |
| 6 | 1417 |
| 7 | 1418 |
| 8 | 1419 |
| 9 | 1420 |
| 10 | 1421 |
| 11 | 1422 |

| Henr. VI. A.R. | A.Ch. |
|---|---|
| 1 | 1422 |
| 2 | 1423 |
| 3 | 1424 |
| 4 | 1425 |
| 5 | 1426 |

## Computation of Years.

| Henry VI. | |
|---|---|
| A.R. | A.Ch. |
| 6 | 1427 |
| 7 | 1428 |
| 8 | 1429 |
| 9 | 1430 |
| 10 | 1431 |
| 11 | 1432 |
| 12 | 1433 |
| 13 | 1434 |
| 14 | 1435 |
| 15 | 1436 |
| 16 | 1437 |
| 17 | 1438 |
| 18 | 1439 |
| 19 | 1440 |
| 20 | 1441 |
| 21 | 1442 |
| 22 | 1443 |
| 23 | 1444 |
| 24 | 1445 |
| 25 | 1446 |
| 26 | 1447 |
| 27 | 1448 |
| 28 | 1449 |
| 29 | 1450 |
| 30 | 1451 |
| 31 | 1452 |
| 32 | 1453 |
| 33 | 1454 |
| 34 | 1455 |
| 35 | 1456 |
| 36 | 1457 |
| 37 | 1458 |
| 38 | 1459 |
| 39 | 1460 |

| Edw. IV. | |
|---|---|
| A.R. | A.Ch. |
| 1 | 1460 |
| 2 | 1461 |
| 3 | 1462 |
| 4 | 1463 |
| 5 | 1464 |
| 6 | 1465 |
| 7 | 1466 |
| 8 | 1467 |
| 9 | 1468 |
| 10 | 1469 |
| 11 | 1470 |
| 12 | 1471 |
| 13 | 1472 |
| 14 | 1473 |
| 15 | 1474 |
| 16 | 1475 |
| 17 | 1476 |
| 18 | 1477 |
| 19 | 1478 |
| 20 | 1479 |
| 21 | 1480 |
| 22 | 1481 |
| 23 | 1482 |
| 24 | 1483 |

| Edw. V. | |
|---|---|
| 1 | 1483 |

| Rich. III. | |
|---|---|
| 1 | 1483 |
| 2 | 1484 |
| 3 | 1485 |

| Hen. VII | |
|---|---|
| A.R. | A.Ch. |
| 1 | 1485 |
| 2 | 1486 |
| 3 | 1487 |
| 4 | 1488 |
| 5 | 1489 |
| 6 | 1490 |
| 7 | 1491 |
| 8 | 1492 |
| 9 | 1493 |
| 10 | 1494 |
| 11 | 1495 |
| 12 | 1496 |
| 13 | 1497 |
| 14 | 1498 |
| 15 | 1499 |
| 16 | 1500 |
| 17 | 1501 |
| 18 | 1502 |
| 19 | 1503 |
| 20 | 1504 |
| 21 | 1505 |
| 22 | 1506 |
| 23 | 1507 |
| 24 | 1508 |
| 25 | 1509 |

| Hen. VIII. | |
|---|---|
| 1 | 1509 |
| 2 | 1510 |
| 3 | 1511 |
| 4 | 1512 |
| 5 | 1513 |
| 6 | 1514 |

| Henry VIII. | |
|---|---|
| A.R. | A.Ch. |
| 7 | 1515 |
| 8 | 1516 |
| 9 | 1517 |
| 10 | 1518 |
| 11 | 1519 |
| 12 | 1520 |
| 13 | 1521 |
| 14 | 1522 |
| 15 | 1523 |
| 16 | 1524 |
| 17 | 1525 |
| 18 | 1526 |
| 19 | 1527 |
| 20 | 1528 |
| 21 | 1529 |
| 22 | 1530 |
| 23 | 1531 |
| 24 | 1532 |
| 25 | 1533 |
| 26 | 1534 |
| 27 | 1535 |
| 28 | 1536 |
| 29 | 1537 |
| 30 | 1538 |
| 31 | 1539 |
| 32 | 1540 |
| 33 | 1541 |
| 34 | 1542 |
| 35 | 1543 |
| 36 | 1544 |
| 37 | 1545 |
| 38 | 1546 |

## *Computation of Years.*

| Edw. VI. | | Q.Elizabeth. | | James. | | Charles I. | |
|---|---|---|---|---|---|---|---|
| *A.R.* | *A.Ch.* | *A.R.* | *A.Ch.* | *A.R.* | *A.Ch.* | *A.R.* | *A.Ch.* |
| 1 | 1546 | 13 | 1570 | 1 | 1602 | 8 | 1632 |
| 2 | 1547 | 14 | 1571 | 2 | 1603 | 9 | 1633 |
| 3 | 1548 | 15 | 1572 | 3 | 1604 | 10 | 1634 |
| 4 | 1549 | 16 | 1573 | 4 | 1605 | 11 | 1635 |
| 5 | 1550 | 17 | 1574 | 5 | 1606 | 12 | 1636 |
| 6 | 1551 | 18 | 1575 | 6 | 1607 | 13 | 1637 |
| 7 | 1552 | 19 | 1576 | 7 | 1608 | 14 | 1638 |
| 8 | 1553 | 20 | 1577 | 8 | 1609 | 15 | 1639 |
| | | 21 | 1578 | 9 | 1610 | 16 | 1640 |
| Q. Mary. | | 22 | 1579 | 10 | 1611 | 17 | 1641 |
| 1 | 1553 | 23 | 1580 | 11 | 1612 | 18 | 1642 |
| 2 | 1554 | 24 | 1581 | 12 | 1613 | 19 | 1643 |
| 3 | 1555 | 25 | 1582 | 13 | 1614 | 20 | 1644 |
| 4 | 1556 | 26 | 1583 | 14 | 1615 | 21 | 1645 |
| 5 | 1557 | 27 | 1584 | 15 | 1616 | 22 | 1646 |
| 6 | 1558 | 28 | 1585 | 16 | 1617 | 23 | 1647 |
| | | 29 | 1586 | 17 | 1618 | 24 | 1648 |
| Q.Elizab. | | 30 | 1587 | 18 | 1619 | | |
| 1 | 1558 | 31 | 1588 | 19 | 1620 | Charl. II. | |
| 2 | 1559 | 32 | 1589 | 20 | 1621 | 1 | 1648 |
| 3 | 1560 | 33 | 1590 | 21 | 1622 | 2 | 1649 |
| 4 | 1561 | 34 | 1591 | 22 | 1623 | 3 | 1650 |
| 5 | 1562 | 35 | 1592 | 23 | 1624 | 4 | 1651 |
| 6 | 1563 | 36 | 1593 | 24 | 1625 | 5 | 1652 |
| 7 | 1564 | 37 | 1594 | | | 6 | 1653 |
| 8 | 1565 | 38 | 1595 | Charl. I. | | 7 | 1654 |
| 9 | 1566 | 39 | 1596 | 1 | 1625 | 8 | 1655 |
| 10 | 1567 | 40 | 1597 | 2 | 1626 | 9 | 1656 |
| 11 | 1568 | 41 | 1598 | 3 | 1627 | 10 | 1657 |
| 12 | 1569 | 42 | 1599 | 4 | 1628 | 11 | 1658 |
| | | 43 | 1600 | 5 | 1629 | 12 | 1659 |
| | | 44 | 1601 | 6 | 1630 | 13 | 1660 |
| | | 45 | 1602 | 7 | 1631 | 14 | 1661 |

## *Computation of Years.*

| Charles II. | | Charles II. | | Charles II. | | Charles II. | |
|---|---|---|---|---|---|---|---|
| *A.R.* | *A.Ch.* | *A.R.* | *A.Ch.* | *A.R.* | *A.Ch.* | *A.R.* | *A.Ch.* |
| 15 | 1662 | 27 | 1674 | 39 | 1686 | 51 | 1698 |
| 16 | 1663 | 28 | 1675 | 40 | 1687 | 52 | 1699 |
| 17 | 1664 | 29 | 1676 | 41 | 1688 | 53 | 1700 |
| 18 | 1665 | 30 | 1677 | 42 | 1689 | 54 | 1701 |
| 19 | 1666 | 31 | 1678 | 43 | 1690 | 55 | 1702 |
| 20 | 1667 | 32 | 1679 | 44 | 1691 | 56 | 1703 |
| 21 | 1668 | 33 | 1680 | 45 | 1692 | 57 | 1704 |
| 22 | 1669 | 34 | 1681 | 46 | 1693 | 58 | 1705 |
| 23 | 1670 | 35 | 1682 | 47 | 1694 | 59 | 1706 |
| 24 | 1671 | 36 | 1683 | 48 | 1695 | 60 | 1707 |
| 25 | 1672 | 37 | 1684 | 49 | 1696 | 61 | 1708 |
| 26 | 1673 | 38 | 1685 | 50 | 1697 | 62 | 1709 |

By this and the former *Regal Table*, may eaſily be found the year of each King's Reign correſponding to the year of our Lord, always remembring to begin the year of our Lord, from *March* 25.

*Example.*

I have a Deed bearing Date the 17*th* of *May*, in the Two and Twentieth Year of the Reign of King *Charles* the Second, but the Year of our Lord is omitted; I deſire to know in what Year of our Lord this Deed was made?

I find by this Table that the beginning of the Two and Twentieth Year of the King's Reign is in 1669, but I cannot find here what Month his Reign began in; wherefore I turn to the firſt *Regal Table*, and find there that he began his Reign the 30*th* of *January*, 1648. from whence I conclude, that the 17*th* of *May* in the firſt Year of his Reign muſt be in the Year of our Lord 1649, which proves by conſequence that the 17*th* of *May*, in the Two and Twentieth Year of his Reign muſt be in the Year of our Lord 1670.

REDUC-

# *REDUCTION OF*
# VVEIGHTS
# *AND*
# MEASURES.

| *Troy Weight.* | | | *Grains.* |
|---|---|---|---|
| *Peny-weight.* | | | 24 |
| *Ounces.* | | 20 | 480 |
| *Pound.* | 12 | 240 | 5760 |

BY *Troy Weight* is weighed Gold, Silver, Jewels, Amber, Electuaries, Bread Corn, and Liquors; and from this Weight all Measures for wet and dry Commodities are taken.

The Pound *Troy* is in proportion to the Pound *Averdupois* as 17 to 14, and the Ounce as 51 to 56.

Gold to Silver is in proportion as 12 to 1, and the Value of both in *England* is as follows: One Peny-weight of Angel Gold is worth 4 *s* 2 *d.* 2 *q.* of Crown Gold 3 *s.* 10 *d.* 2 *q.* and of Soveraign 3 *s.* 6 *d.* 2 *q.* The Standard of Sterling Silver is 11 Ounces, and 2 Peny-weight of fine Silver, and 18 Peny-weight of Alloy of Copper; so that 12 Ounces of pure Silver without any Alloy is worth 3 *l.* 4 *s.* 6 *d.* and an Ounce 5 *s.* 4 *d.* 2 *q.* but with Alloy the Pound is worth no more than 3 *l.* and the Ounce 5 *s.*

The

## *Apothecaries Weight,* &c.

The Standard for Gold is in the Pound Troy 11 Ounces of fine Gold, and 1 Ounce of Alloy.

Our Gold is of equal fineneſs with the *Spaniſh*, *French*, and *Flemiſh*; but our Silver Coin has leſs of Alloy in it than either *French* or *Dutch*.

When Wheat is at 5 Shillings *per* Buſhel, then a Peny Wheaten Loaf is to weigh 11 Ounces *Troy*, and Three Half-peny White Loaves the like weight; and the Houſhold Peny Loaf is to weigh 14 $\frac{2}{3}$ Ounces; and so for a greater or leſſer weight proportionably: And if a Baker want but one Ounce in 36, for the firſt, ſecond, and third fault he may be amerced, but for the fourth he is to ſtand in the Pillory without redemption.

| *Apothecaries Weight.* | | | | *Grains.* |
|---|---|---|---|---|
| | | | *Scruples.* | 20 |
| | | *Drams.* | 3 | 60 |
| | *Ounces.* | 8 | 24 | 480 |
| *Pound.* | 12 | 96 | 288 | 5760 |

*Apothecaries* in making up their Medicines uſe this Weight, but they buy and ſell their Drugs by the *Averdupois*.

| *Averdupois Weight.* | | | | | *Drams.* |
|---|---|---|---|---|---|
| | | | | *Ounces.* | 16 |
| | | | *Pounds.* | 16 | 256 |
| | | *Quarters.* | 28 | 448 | 7168 |
| | *Hundreds.* | 4 | 112 | 1792 | 28672 |
| *Tun.* | 20 | 80 | 2240 | 35840 | 573440 |

By *Averdupois* Weight is weighed all manner of things that have waſte, as all Phyſical Drugs and Grocery, Roſin, Wax,

## *Liquid Meaſures.*

Wax, Pitch, Tar, Tallow, Soap, Hemp, Flax, *&c.* all baſe Metals and Minerals, as Iron, Steel, Lead, Tin, Copper, Alum, Copperas, *&c.* The Tun *Averdupois* is 20 Hundred of all things, except Lead, which has but 19 Hundred and a half to the Tun or Fodder. The Hundred Weight *Averdupois* contains 112 Pound, the Half Hundred 56 Pound, the Quarter 28 Pound, the Stone (or half Quarter of the Hundred) 14 Pound; and thus is Iron and Shot weighed; but Alom, Cinnamon, Nutmegs, Pepper, and Sugar, have but 13 Pound and a half to the Stone, or half Quarter of the Hundred, 27 Pound to the Quarter, 54 Pound to the half, and 108 Pound to the whole Hundred. *Eſſex* Cheeſe and Butter are weighed by the Clove, or half Stone, allowing 8 Pound to each Clove, and 32 Cloves, or 256 Pound to the Wey; and in *Suffolk* they allow 42 Cloves, or 336 Pound to the Wey. Wool is ſold by the Clove, allowing but 7 Pound to the Clove, 14 Pound to the Stone, 28 Pound to the Tod, 182 Pound to the Wey, 364 Pound to the Sack, and 4368 Pound to the Laſt. A Fagot of Steel is 120 Pound. A burden of Gad Steel is 9 Score, or 180 Pound. 56 Pound of Butter, or 60 Pound of Soap make a Firkin, and 2 Firkins of either make a Barrel. *Butchers* allow but 8 Pound to the Stone.

*Ale Meaſure.*

| | | | | | | *Pints.* |
|---|---|---|---|---|---|---|
| | | | | | *Quarts.* | 2 |
| | | | | *Pottles.* | 2 | 4 |
| | | | *Gallons.* | 2 | 4 | 8 |
| | | *Firkins.* | 8 | 16 | 32 | 64 |
| | *Kilderkins.* | 2 | 16 | 32 | 64 | 128 |
| *Barrel.* | 2 | 4 | 32 | 64 | 128 | 256 |

Veſſels for Butter, Fiſh, and Soap, are made after the Ale Meaſure, 12 Ale Barrels making a Laſt.

Beer

# Liquid and Dry Measures.

## Beer Measure.

| | Kilderkins | Firkins | Gallons | Pottles | Quarts | Pints. |
|---|---|---|---|---|---|---|
| Quarts. | | | | | | 2 |
| Pottles. | | | | | 2 | 4 |
| Gallons. | | | | 2 | 4 | 8 |
| Firkins. | | | 9 | 18 | 36 | 72 |
| Kilderkins. | | 2 | 18 | 36 | 72 | 144 |
| Barrel. | 2 | 4 | 36 | 72 | 144 | 288 |

## Wine Measure.

| | | | Gallons. |
|---|---|---|---|
| Hogsheads. | | | 63 |
| Pipe or Butt. | | 2 | 126 |
| Tun. | 2 | 4 | 252 |

| | | Gallons |
|---|---|---|
| Tierce. | | 42 |
| | 2 | 84 |
| | 3 | 126 |

## Dry Measures.

| | Wey | Quarters | Bushels | Pecks | Gallons | Pottles | Quarts | Pints. |
|---|---|---|---|---|---|---|---|---|
| Quarts. | | | | | | | | 2 |
| Pottles. | | | | | | | 2 | 4 |
| Gallons. | | | | | | 2 | 4 | 8 |
| Pecks | | | | | 2 | 4 | 8 | 16 |
| Bushels. | | | | 4 | 8 | 16 | 32 | 64 |
| Quarters. | | | 8 | 32 | 64 | 128 | 256 | 512 |
| Wey. | | 5 | 40 | 160 | 320 | 640 | 1280 | 2560 |
| Last. | 2 | 10 | 80 | 320 | 640 | 1280 | 2560 | 5120 |

A Bushel Water-Measure contains 5 Pecks. Some make 6 Quarters of Meal a Wey, and 1 Wey 3 Quarters a Last.

Long

## *Long and Square Meaſures.*

| *Long Meaſure.* | | | | | *Inches.* |
|---|---|---|---|---|---|
| | | | | *Feet.* | 12 |
| | | | *Yards.* | 3 | 36 |
| | | *Poles.* | $5\frac{1}{2}$ | $16\frac{1}{2}$ | 198 |
| | *Furlongs.* | 40 | 220 | 660 | 7920 |
| *Mile.* | 8 | 320 | 1760 | 5280 | 63360 |

| *Superficial or Square Meaſure.* | | | | | *Feet.* |
|---|---|---|---|---|---|
| | | | | *Yards.* | 9 |
| | | | *Poles.* | $30\frac{1}{4}$ | $272\frac{1}{4}$ |
| | | *Roods.* | 40 | 1210 | 10890 |
| | *Acres.* | 4 | 160 | 4840 | 43560 |
| *Mile.* | 640 | 2560 | 102400 | 3097600 | 27878400 |

In this laſt Table you have in a ſquare Mile 640 ſquare Acres, 2560 ſquare Roods, &c. in a ſquare Acre 4 ſquare Roods, 160 ſquare Poles, &c. in a ſquare Pole $30\frac{1}{4}$ ſquare Yards, and $272\frac{1}{4}$ ſquare Inches; and in a ſquare Yard 9 ſquare Feet. Which being rightly underſtood, all theſe Tables of Reduction are ſufficiently explained.

*A Table*

*A Table for the Reduction of Pounds into Shillings, Pence, and Farthings.*

| | Pence. | Farthin. | Shillin. | Pence. | Farthin. |
|---|---|---|---|---|---|
| | 1 | 4 | 5 | 60 | 240 |
| | 2 | 8 | 6 | 72 | 288 |
| | 3 | 12 | 7 | 84 | 336 |
| | 4 | 16 | 8 | 96 | 384 |
| | 5 | 20 | 9 | 108 | 432 |
| | 6 | 24 | 10 | 120 | 480 |
| | 7 | 28 | 11 | 132 | 528 |
| | 8 | 32 | 12 | 144 | 576 |
| | 9 | 36 | 13 | 156 | 624 |
| | 10 | 40 | 14 | 168 | 672 |
| Shill. | 11 | 44 | 15 | 180 | 720 |
| 1 | 12 | 48 | 16 | 192 | 768 |
| 2 | 24 | 96 | 17 | 204 | 816 |
| 3 | 36 | 144 | 18 | 216 | 864 |
| 4 | 48 | 192 | 19 | 228 | 912 |

| Pounds. | Shillings. | Pence. | Farthings. |
|---|---|---|---|
| 1 | 20 | 240 | 960 |
| 2 | 40 | 480 | 1920 |
| 3 | 60 | 720 | 2880 |
| 4 | 80 | 960 | 3840 |
| 5 | 100 | 1200 | 4800 |
| 6 | 120 | 1440 | 5760 |
| 7 | 140 | 1680 | 6720 |
| 8 | 160 | 1920 | 7680 |
| 9 | 180 | 2160 | 8640 |
| 10 | 200 | 2400 | 9600 |

*A Tabl*

# A TABLE

*FOR*

The ready Caſting up any Number of Farthings, Half-pence, Pence, or Shillings; where may be found by Inſpection what the Great Hundred comes to, at any Rate the Pound, from One Farthing to Ten Shillings.

## *Multiplication of a Farthing.*

| | *l.* | *s.* | *d.* | *q.* | | *l.* | *s.* | *d.* | *q.* |
|---|---|---|---|---|---|---|---|---|---|
| 1 | 0 | 0 | 0 | 1 | 36 | 0 | 0 | 9 | 0 |
| 2 | 0 | 0 | 0 | 2 | 37 | 0 | 0 | 9 | 1 |
| 3 | 0 | 0 | 0 | 3 | 38 | 0 | 0 | 9 | 2 |
| 4 | 0 | 0 | 1 | 0 | 39 | 0 | 0 | 9 | 3 |
| 5 | 0 | 0 | 1 | 1 | 40 | 0 | 0 | 10 | 0 |
| 6 | 0 | 0 | 1 | 2 | 50 | 0 | 1 | 0 | 2 |
| 7 | 0 | 0 | 1 | 3 | (56) | 0 | 1 | 2 | 0 |
| 8 | 0 | 0 | 2 | 0 | 60 | 0 | 1 | 3 | 0 |
| 9 | 0 | 0 | 2 | 1 | 70 | 0 | 1 | 5 | 2 |
| 10 | 0 | 0 | 2 | 2 | 80 | 0 | 1 | 8 | 0 |
| 11 | 0 | 0 | 2 | 3 | (84) | 0 | 1 | 9 | 0 |
| 12 | 0 | 0 | 3 | 0 | 90 | 0 | 1 | 10 | 2 |
| 13 | 0 | 0 | 3 | 1 | 100 | 0 | 2 | 1 | 0 |
| 14 | 0 | 0 | 3 | 2 | (112) | 0 | 2 | 4 | 0 |
| 15 | 0 | 0 | 3 | 3 | 200 | 0 | 4 | 2 | 0 |
| 16 | 0 | 0 | 4 | 0 | (224) | 0 | 4 | 8 | 0 |
| 17 | 0 | 0 | 4 | 1 | 300 | 0 | 6 | 3 | 0 |
| 18 | 0 | 0 | 4 | 2 | (336) | 0 | 7 | 0 | 0 |
| 19 | 0 | 0 | 4 | 3 | 400 | 0 | 8 | 4 | 0 |
| 20 | 0 | 0 | 5 | 0 | (448) | 0 | 9 | 4 | 0 |
| 21 | 0 | 0 | 5 | 1 | 500 | 0 | 10 | 5 | 0 |
| 22 | 0 | 0 | 5 | 2 | (560) | 0 | 11 | 8 | 0 |
| 23 | 0 | 0 | 5 | 3 | 600 | 0 | 12 | 6 | 0 |
| 24 | 0 | 0 | 6 | 0 | (672) | 0 | 14 | 0 | 0 |
| 25 | 0 | 0 | 6 | 1 | 700 | 0 | 14 | 7 | 0 |
| 26 | 0 | 0 | 6 | 2 | (784) | 0 | 16 | 4 | 0 |
| 27 | 0 | 0 | 6 | 3 | 800 | 0 | 16 | 8 | 0 |
| (28) | 0 | 0 | 7 | 0 | (896) | 0 | 18 | 8 | 0 |
| 29 | 0 | 0 | 7 | 1 | 900 | 0 | 18 | 9 | 0 |
| 30 | 0 | 0 | 7 | 2 | 1000 | 1 | 0 | 10 | 0 |
| 31 | 0 | 0 | 7 | 3 | 2000 | 2 | 1 | 8 | 0 |
| 32 | 0 | 0 | 8 | 0 | 3000 | 3 | 2 | 6 | 0 |
| 33 | 0 | 0 | 8 | 1 | 4000 | 4 | 3 | 4 | 0 |
| 34 | 0 | 0 | 8 | 2 | 5000 | 5 | 4 | 2 | 0 |
| 35 | 0 | 0 | 8 | 3 | 10000 | 10 | 8 | 4 | 0 |

## *A Half-peny, or Two Farthings.*

| | l. | s. | d. | q. | | l. | s. | d. | q. |
|---|---|---|---|---|---|---|---|---|---|
| 1 | 0 | 0 | 0 | 2 | 36 | 0 | 1 | 6 | 0 |
| 2 | 0 | 0 | 1 | 0 | 37 | 0 | 1 | 6 | 2 |
| 3 | 0 | 0 | 1 | 2 | 38 | 0 | 1 | 7 | 0 |
| 4 | 0 | 0 | 2 | 0 | 39 | 0 | 1 | 7 | 2 |
| 5 | 0 | 0 | 2 | 2 | 40 | 0 | 1 | 8 | 0 |
| 6 | 0 | 0 | 3 | 0 | 50 | 0 | 2 | 1 | 0 |
| 7 | 0 | 0 | 3 | 2 | (56) | 0 | 2 | 4 | 0 |
| 8 | 0 | 0 | 4 | 0 | 60 | 0 | 2 | 6 | 0 |
| 9 | 0 | 0 | 4 | 2 | 70 | 0 | 2 | 11 | 0 |
| 10 | 0 | 0 | 5 | 0 | 80 | 0 | 3 | 4 | 0 |
| 11 | 0 | 0 | 5 | 2 | (84) | 0 | 3 | 6 | 0 |
| 12 | 0 | 0 | 6 | 0 | 90 | 0 | 3 | 9 | 0 |
| 13 | 0 | 0 | 6 | 2 | 100 | 0 | 4 | 2 | 0 |
| 14 | 0 | 0 | 7 | 0 | (112) | 0 | 4 | 8 | 0 |
| 15 | 0 | 0 | 7 | 2 | 200 | 0 | 8 | 4 | 0 |
| 16 | 0 | 0 | 8 | 0 | (224) | 0 | 9 | 4 | 0 |
| 17 | 0 | 0 | 8 | 2 | 300 | 0 | 12 | 6 | 0 |
| 18 | 0 | 0 | 9 | 0 | (336) | 0 | 14 | 0 | 0 |
| 19 | 0 | 0 | 9 | 2 | 400 | 0 | 16 | 8 | 0 |
| 20 | 0 | 0 | 10 | 0 | (448) | 0 | 18 | 8 | 0 |
| 21 | 0 | 0 | 10 | 2 | 500 | 1 | 0 | 10 | 0 |
| 22 | 0 | 0 | 11 | 0 | (560) | 1 | 3 | 4 | 0 |
| 23 | 0 | 0 | 11 | 2 | 600 | 1 | 5 | 0 | 0 |
| 24 | 0 | 1 | 0 | 0 | (672) | 1 | 8 | 0 | 0 |
| 25 | 0 | 1 | 0 | 2 | 700 | 1 | 9 | 2 | 0 |
| 26 | 0 | 1 | 1 | 0 | (784) | 1 | 12 | 8 | 0 |
| 27 | 0 | 1 | 1 | 2 | 800 | 1 | 13 | 4 | 0 |
| (28) | 0 | 1 | 2 | 0 | (896) | 1 | 17 | 4 | 0 |
| 29 | 0 | 1 | 2 | 2 | 900 | 1 | 17 | 6 | 0 |
| 30 | 0 | 1 | 3 | 0 | 1000 | 2 | 1 | 8 | 0 |
| 31 | 0 | 1 | 3 | 2 | 2000 | 4 | 3 | 4 | 0 |
| 32 | 0 | 1 | 4 | 0 | 3000 | 6 | 5 | 0 | 0 |
| 33 | 0 | 1 | 4 | 2 | 4000 | 8 | 6 | 8 | 0 |
| 34 | 0 | 1 | 5 | 0 | 5000 | 10 | 8 | 4 | 0 |
| 35 | 0 | 1 | 5 | 2 | 10000 | 20 | 16 | 8 | 0 |

## Three Farthings.

| | l. | s. | d. | q. | | l. | s. | d. | q. |
|---|---|---|---|---|---|---|---|---|---|
| 1 | 0 | 0 | 0 | 3 | 36 | 0 | 2 | 3 | 0 |
| 2 | 0 | 0 | 1 | 2 | 37 | 0 | 2 | 3 | 3 |
| 3 | 0 | 0 | 2 | 1 | 38 | 0 | 2 | 4 | 2 |
| 4 | 0 | 0 | 3 | 0 | 39 | 0 | 2 | 5 | 1 |
| 5 | 0 | 0 | 3 | 3 | 40 | 0 | 2 | 6 | 0 |
| 6 | 0 | 0 | 4 | 2 | 50 | 0 | 3 | 1 | 2 |
| 7 | 0 | 0 | 5 | 1 | (56) | 0 | 3 | 6 | 0 |
| 8 | 0 | 0 | 6 | 0 | 60 | 0 | 3 | 9 | 0 |
| 9 | 0 | 0 | 6 | 3 | 70 | 0 | 4 | 4 | 2 |
| 10 | 0 | 0 | 7 | 2 | 80 | 0 | 5 | 0 | 0 |
| 11 | 0 | 0 | 8 | 1 | (84) | 0 | 5 | 3 | 0 |
| 12 | 0 | 0 | 9 | 0 | 90 | 0 | 5 | 7 | 2 |
| 13 | 0 | 0 | 9 | 3 | 100 | 0 | 6 | 3 | 0 |
| 14 | 0 | 0 | 10 | 2 | (112) | 0 | 7 | 0 | 0 |
| 15 | 0 | 0 | 11 | 1 | 200 | 0 | 12 | 6 | 0 |
| 16 | 0 | 1 | 0 | 0 | (224) | 0 | 14 | 0 | 0 |
| 17 | 0 | 1 | 0 | 3 | 300 | 0 | 18 | 9 | 0 |
| 18 | 0 | 1 | 1 | 2 | (336) | 1 | 1 | 0 | 0 |
| 19 | 0 | 1 | 2 | 1 | 400 | 1 | 5 | 0 | 0 |
| 20 | 0 | 1 | 3 | 0 | (448) | 1 | 8 | 0 | 0 |
| 21 | 0 | 1 | 3 | 3 | 500 | 1 | 11 | 3 | 0 |
| 22 | 0 | 1 | 4 | 2 | (560) | 1 | 15 | 0 | 0 |
| 23 | 0 | 1 | 5 | 1 | 600 | 1 | 17 | 6 | 0 |
| 24 | 0 | 1 | 6 | 0 | (672) | 2 | 2 | 0 | 0 |
| 25 | 0 | 1 | 6 | 3 | 700 | 2 | 3 | 9 | 0 |
| 26 | 0 | 1 | 7 | 2 | (784) | 2 | 9 | 0 | 0 |
| 27 | 0 | 1 | 8 | 1 | 800 | 2 | 10 | 0 | 0 |
| (28) | 0 | 1 | 9 | 0 | (896) | 2 | 16 | 0 | 0 |
| 29 | 0 | 1 | 9 | 3 | 900 | 2 | 16 | 3 | 0 |
| 30 | 0 | 1 | 10 | 2 | 1000 | 3 | 2 | 6 | 0 |
| 31 | 0 | 1 | 11 | 1 | 2000 | 6 | 5 | 0 | 0 |
| 32 | 0 | 2 | 0 | 0 | 3000 | 9 | 7 | 6 | 0 |
| 33 | 0 | 2 | 0 | 3 | 4000 | 12 | 10 | 0 | 0 |
| 34 | 0 | 2 | 1 | 2 | 5000 | 15 | 12 | 6 | 0 |
| 35 | 0 | 2 | 2 | 1 | 10000 | 31 | 5 | 0 | 0 |

## A Peny.

| | l. | s. | d. | | l. | s. | d. |
|---|---|---|---|---|---|---|---|
| 1 | 0 | 0 | 1 | 36 | 0 | 3 | 0 |
| 2 | 0 | 0 | 2 | 37 | 0 | 3 | 1 |
| 3 | 0 | 0 | 3 | 38 | 0 | 3 | 2 |
| 4 | 0 | 0 | 4 | 39 | 0 | 3 | 3 |
| 5 | 0 | 0 | 5 | 40 | 0 | 3 | 4 |
| 6 | 0 | 0 | 6 | 50 | 0 | 4 | 2 |
| 7 | 0 | 0 | 7 | (56) | 0 | 4 | 8 |
| 8 | 0 | 0 | 8 | 60 | 0 | 5 | 0 |
| 9 | 0 | 0 | 9 | 70 | 0 | 5 | 10 |
| 10 | 0 | 0 | 10 | 80 | 0 | 6 | 8 |
| 11 | 0 | 0 | 11 | (84) | 0 | 7 | 0 |
| 12 | 0 | 1 | 0 | 90 | 0 | 7 | 6 |
| 13 | 0 | 1 | 1 | 100 | 0 | 8 | 4 |
| 14 | 0 | 1 | 2 | (112) | 0 | 9 | 4 |
| 15 | 0 | 1 | 3 | 200 | 0 | 16 | 8 |
| 16 | 0 | 1 | 4 | (224) | 0 | 18 | 8 |
| 17 | 0 | 1 | 5 | 300 | 1 | 5 | 0 |
| 18 | 0 | 1 | 6 | (336) | 1 | 8 | 0 |
| 19 | 0 | 1 | 7 | 400 | 1 | 13 | 4 |
| 20 | 0 | 1 | 8 | (448) | 1 | 17 | 4 |
| 21 | 0 | 1 | 9 | 500 | 2 | 1 | 8 |
| 22 | 0 | 1 | 10 | (560) | 2 | 6 | 8 |
| 23 | 0 | 1 | 11 | 600 | 2 | 10 | 0 |
| 24 | 0 | 2 | 0 | (672) | 2 | 16 | 0 |
| 25 | 0 | 2 | 1 | 700 | 2 | 18 | 4 |
| 26 | 0 | 2 | 2 | (784) | 3 | 5 | 4 |
| 27 | 0 | 2 | 3 | 800 | 3 | 6 | 8 |
| (28) | 0 | 2 | 4 | (896) | 3 | 14 | 8 |
| 29 | 0 | 2 | 5 | 900 | 3 | 15 | 0 |
| 30 | 0 | 2 | 6 | 1000 | 4 | 3 | 4 |
| 31 | 0 | 2 | 7 | 2000 | 8 | 6 | 8 |
| 32 | 0 | 2 | 8 | 3000 | 12 | 10 | 0 |
| 33 | 0 | 2 | 9 | 4000 | 16 | 13 | 4 |
| 34 | 0 | 2 | 10 | 5000 | 20 | 16 | 8 |
| 35 | 0 | 2 | 11 | 10000 | 41 | 13 | 4 |

## *A Peny-farthing, or Five Farthings.*

| | l. | s. | d. | q. | | l. | s. | d. | q. |
|---|---|---|---|---|---|---|---|---|---|
| 1 | 0 | 0 | 1 | 1 | 36 | 0 | 3 | 9 | 0 |
| 2 | 0 | 0 | 2 | 2 | 37 | 0 | 3 | 10 | 1 |
| 3 | 0 | 0 | 3 | 3 | 38 | 0 | 3 | 11 | 2 |
| 4 | 0 | 0 | 5 | 0 | 39 | 0 | 4 | 0 | 3 |
| 5 | 0 | 0 | 6 | 1 | 40 | 0 | 4 | 2 | 0 |
| 6 | 0 | 0 | 7 | 2 | 50 | 0 | 5 | 2 | 2 |
| 7 | 0 | 0 | 8 | 3 | (56) | 0 | 5 | 10 | 0 |
| 8 | 0 | 0 | 10 | 0 | 60 | 0 | 6 | 3 | 0 |
| 9 | 0 | 0 | 11 | 1 | 70 | 0 | 7 | 3 | 2 |
| 10 | 0 | 1 | 0 | 2 | 80 | 0 | 8 | 4 | 0 |
| 11 | 0 | 1 | 1 | 3 | (84) | 0 | 8 | 9 | 0 |
| 12 | 0 | 1 | 3 | 0 | 90 | 0 | 9 | 4 | 2 |
| 13 | 0 | 1 | 4 | 1 | 100 | 0 | 10 | 5 | 0 |
| 14 | 0 | 1 | 5 | 2 | (112) | 0 | 11 | 8 | 0 |
| 15 | 0 | 1 | 6 | 3 | 200 | 1 | 0 | 10 | 0 |
| 16 | 0 | 1 | 8 | 0 | (224) | 1 | 3 | 4 | 0 |
| 17 | 0 | 1 | 9 | 1 | 300 | 1 | 11 | 3 | 0 |
| 18 | 0 | 1 | 10 | 2 | (336) | 1 | 15 | 0 | 0 |
| 19 | 0 | 1 | 11 | 3 | 400 | 2 | 1 | 8 | 0 |
| 20 | 0 | 2 | 1 | 0 | (448) | 2 | 6 | 8 | 0 |
| 21 | 0 | 2 | 2 | 1 | 500 | 2 | 12 | 1 | 0 |
| 22 | 0 | 2 | 3 | 2 | (560) | 2 | 18 | 4 | 0 |
| 23 | 0 | 2 | 4 | 3 | 600 | 3 | 2 | 6 | 0 |
| 24 | 0 | 2 | 6 | 0 | (672) | 3 | 10 | 0 | 0 |
| 25 | 0 | 2 | 7 | 1 | 700 | 3 | 12 | 11 | 0 |
| 26 | 0 | 2 | 8 | 2 | (784) | 4 | 1 | 8 | 0 |
| 27 | 0 | 2 | 9 | 3 | 800 | 4 | 3 | 4 | 0 |
| (28) | 0 | 2 | 11 | 0 | (896) | 4 | 13 | 4 | 0 |
| 29 | 0 | 3 | 0 | 1 | 900 | 4 | 13 | 9 | 0 |
| 30 | 0 | 3 | 1 | 2 | 1000 | 5 | 4 | 2 | 0 |
| 31 | 0 | 3 | 2 | 3 | 2000 | 10 | 8 | 4 | 0 |
| 32 | 0 | 3 | 4 | 0 | 3000 | 15 | 12 | 6 | 0 |
| 33 | 0 | 3 | 5 | 1 | 4000 | 20 | 16 | 8 | 0 |
| 34 | 0 | 3 | 6 | 2 | 5000 | 26 | 0 | 10 | 0 |
| 35 | 0 | 3 | 7 | 3 | 10000 | 52 | 1 | 8 | 0 |

## Three-half-pence, or Six Farthings.

| | l. | s. | d. | q. | | l. | s. | d. | q. |
|---|---|---|---|---|---|---|---|---|---|
| 1 | 0 | 0 | 1 | 2 | 36 | 0 | 4 | 6 | 0 |
| 2 | 0 | 0 | 3 | 0 | 37 | 0 | 4 | 7 | 2 |
| 3 | 0 | 0 | 4 | 2 | 38 | 0 | 4 | 9 | 0 |
| 4 | 0 | 0 | 6 | 0 | 39 | 0 | 4 | 10 | 2 |
| 5 | 0 | 0 | 7 | 2 | 40 | 0 | 5 | 0 | 0 |
| 6 | 0 | 0 | 9 | 0 | 50 | 0 | 6 | 3 | 0 |
| 7 | 0 | 0 | 10 | 2 | (56) | 0 | 7 | 0 | 0 |
| 8 | 0 | 1 | 0 | 0 | 60 | 0 | 7 | 6 | 0 |
| 9 | 0 | 1 | 1 | 2 | 70 | 0 | 8 | 9 | 0 |
| 10 | 0 | 1 | 3 | 0 | 80 | 0 | 10 | 0 | 0 |
| 11 | 0 | 1 | 4 | 2 | (84) | 0 | 10 | 6 | 0 |
| 12 | 0 | 1 | 6 | 0 | 90 | 0 | 11 | 3 | 0 |
| 13 | 0 | 1 | 7 | 2 | 100 | 0 | 12 | 6 | 0 |
| 14 | 0 | 1 | 9 | 0 | (112) | 0 | 14 | 0 | 0 |
| 15 | 0 | 1 | 10 | 2 | 200 | 1 | 5 | 0 | 0 |
| 16 | 0 | 2 | 0 | 0 | (224) | 1 | 8 | 0 | 0 |
| 17 | 0 | 2 | 1 | 2 | 300 | 1 | 17 | 6 | 0 |
| 18 | 0 | 2 | 3 | 0 | (336) | 2 | 2 | 0 | 0 |
| 19 | 0 | 2 | 4 | 2 | 400 | 2 | 10 | 0 | 0 |
| 20 | 0 | 2 | 6 | 0 | (448) | 2 | 16 | 0 | 0 |
| 21 | 0 | 2 | 7 | 2 | 500 | 3 | 2 | 6 | 0 |
| 22 | 0 | 2 | 9 | 0 | (560) | 3 | 10 | 0 | 0 |
| 23 | 0 | 2 | 10 | 2 | 600 | 3 | 15 | 0 | 0 |
| 24 | 0 | 3 | 0 | 0 | (672) | 4 | 4 | 0 | 0 |
| 25 | 0 | 3 | 1 | 2 | 700 | 4 | 7 | 6 | 0 |
| 26 | 0 | 3 | 3 | 0 | (784) | 4 | 18 | 0 | 0 |
| 27 | 0 | 3 | 4 | 2 | 800 | 5 | 0 | 0 | 0 |
| (28) | 0 | 3 | 6 | 0 | (896) | 5 | 12 | 0 | 0 |
| 29 | 0 | 3 | 7 | 2 | 900 | 5 | 12 | 6 | 0 |
| 30 | 0 | 3 | 9 | 0 | 1000 | 6 | 5 | 0 | 0 |
| 31 | 0 | 3 | 10 | 2 | 2000 | 12 | 10 | 0 | 0 |
| 32 | 0 | 4 | 0 | 0 | 3000 | 18 | 15 | 0 | 0 |
| 33 | 0 | 4 | 1 | 2 | 4000 | 25 | 0 | 0 | 0 |
| 34 | 0 | 4 | 3 | 0 | 5000 | 31 | 5 | 0 | 0 |
| 35 | 0 | 4 | 4 | 2 | 10000 | 62 | 10 | 0 | 0 |

## Seven Farthings.

| | l. | s. | d. | q. | | l. | s. | d. | q. |
|---|---|---|---|---|---|---|---|---|---|
| 1 | 0 | 0 | 1 | 3 | 36 | 0 | 5 | 3 | 0 |
| 2 | 0 | 0 | 3 | 2 | 37 | 0 | 5 | 4 | 3 |
| 3 | 0 | 0 | 5 | 1 | 38 | 0 | 5 | 6 | 2 |
| 4 | 0 | 0 | 7 | 0 | 39 | 0 | 5 | 8 | 1 |
| 5 | 0 | 0 | 8 | 3 | 40 | 0 | 5 | 10 | 0 |
| 6 | 0 | 0 | 10 | 2 | 50 | 0 | 7 | 3 | 2 |
| 7 | 0 | 1 | 0 | 1 | (56) | 0 | 8 | 2 | 0 |
| 8 | 0 | 1 | 2 | 0 | 60 | 0 | 8 | 9 | 0 |
| 9 | 0 | 1 | 3 | 3 | 70 | 0 | 10 | 2 | 2 |
| 10 | 0 | 1 | 5 | 2 | 80 | 0 | 11 | 8 | 0 |
| 11 | 0 | 1 | 7 | 1 | (84) | 0 | 12 | 3 | 0 |
| 12 | 0 | 1 | 9 | 0 | 90 | 0 | 13 | 1 | 2 |
| 13 | 0 | 1 | 10 | 3 | 100 | 0 | 14 | 7 | 0 |
| 14 | 0 | 2 | 0 | 2 | (112) | 0 | 16 | 4 | 0 |
| 15 | 0 | 2 | 2 | 1 | 200 | 1 | 9 | 2 | 0 |
| 16 | 0 | 2 | 4 | 0 | (224) | 1 | 12 | 8 | 0 |
| 17 | 0 | 2 | 5 | 3 | 300 | 2 | 3 | 9 | 0 |
| 18 | 0 | 2 | 7 | 2 | (336) | 2 | 9 | 0 | 0 |
| 19 | 0 | 2 | 9 | 1 | 400 | 2 | 18 | 4 | 0 |
| 20 | 0 | 2 | 11 | 0 | (448) | 3 | 5 | 4 | 0 |
| 21 | 0 | 3 | 0 | 3 | 500 | 3 | 12 | 11 | 0 |
| 22 | 0 | 3 | 2 | 2 | (560) | 4 | 1 | 8 | 0 |
| 23 | 0 | 3 | 4 | 1 | 600 | 4 | 7 | 6 | 0 |
| 24 | 0 | 3 | 6 | 0 | (672) | 4 | 18 | 0 | 0 |
| 25 | 0 | 3 | 7 | 3 | 700 | 5 | 2 | 1 | 0 |
| 26 | 0 | 3 | 9 | 2 | (784) | 5 | 14 | 4 | 0 |
| 27 | 0 | 3 | 11 | 1 | 800 | 5 | 16 | 8 | 0 |
| (28) | 0 | 4 | 1 | 0 | (896) | 6 | 10 | 8 | 0 |
| 29 | 0 | 4 | 2 | 3 | 900 | 6 | 11 | 3 | 0 |
| 30 | 0 | 4 | 4 | 2 | 1000 | 7 | 5 | 10 | 0 |
| 31 | 0 | 4 | 6 | 1 | 2000 | 14 | 11 | 8 | 0 |
| 32 | 0 | 4 | 8 | 0 | 3000 | 21 | 17 | 6 | 0 |
| 33 | 0 | 4 | 9 | 3 | 4000 | 29 | 3 | 4 | 0 |
| 34 | 0 | 4 | 11 | 2 | 5000 | 36 | 9 | 2 | 0 |
| 35 | 0 | 5 | 1 | 1 | 10000 | 72 | 18 | 4 | 0 |

## Two-Pence.

| | l. | s. | d. | | l. | s. | d. |
|---|---|---|---|---|---|---|---|
| 1 | 0 | 0 | 2 | 36 | 0 | 6 | 0 |
| 2 | 0 | 0 | 4 | 37 | 0 | 6 | 2 |
| 3 | 0 | 0 | 6 | 38 | 0 | 6 | 4 |
| 4 | 0 | 0 | 8 | 39 | 0 | 6 | 6 |
| 5 | 0 | 0 | 10 | 40 | 0 | 6 | 8 |
| 6 | 0 | 1 | 0 | 50 | 0 | 8 | 4 |
| 7 | 0 | 1 | 2 | (56) | 0 | 9 | 4 |
| 8 | 0 | 1 | 4 | 60 | 0 | 10 | 0 |
| 9 | 0 | 1 | 6 | 70 | 0 | 11 | 8 |
| 10 | 0 | 1 | 8 | 80 | 0 | 13 | 4 |
| 11 | 0 | 1 | 10 | (84) | 0 | 14 | 0 |
| 12 | 0 | 2 | 0 | 90 | 0 | 15 | 0 |
| 13 | 0 | 2 | 2 | 100 | 0 | 16 | 8 |
| 14 | 0 | 2 | 4 | (112) | 0 | 18 | 8 |
| 15 | 0 | 2 | 6 | 200 | 1 | 13 | 4 |
| 16 | 0 | 2 | 8 | (224) | 1 | 17 | 4 |
| 17 | 0 | 2 | 10 | 300 | 2 | 10 | 0 |
| 18 | 0 | 3 | 0 | (336) | 2 | 16 | 0 |
| 19 | 0 | 3 | 2 | 400 | 3 | 6 | 8 |
| 20 | 0 | 3 | 4 | (448) | 3 | 14 | 8 |
| 21 | 0 | 3 | 6 | 500 | 4 | 3 | 4 |
| 22 | 0 | 3 | 8 | (560) | 4 | 13 | 4 |
| 23 | 0 | 3 | 10 | 600 | 5 | 0 | 0 |
| 24 | 0 | 4 | 0 | (672) | 5 | 12 | 0 |
| 25 | 0 | 4 | 2 | 700 | 5 | 16 | 8 |
| 26 | 0 | 4 | 4 | (784) | 6 | 10 | 8 |
| 27 | 0 | 4 | 6 | 800 | 6 | 13 | 4 |
| (28) | 0 | 4 | 8 | (896) | 7 | 9 | 4 |
| 29 | 0 | 4 | 10 | 900 | 7 | 10 | 0 |
| 30 | 0 | 5 | 0 | 1000 | 8 | 6 | 8 |
| 31 | 0 | 5 | 2 | 2000 | 16 | 13 | 4 |
| 32 | 0 | 5 | 4 | 3000 | 25 | 0 | 0 |
| 33 | 0 | 5 | 6 | 4000 | 33 | 6 | 8 |
| 34 | 0 | 5 | 8 | 5000 | 41 | 13 | 4 |
| 35 | 0 | 5 | 10 | 10000 | 83 | 6 | 8 |

## Two-pence Farthing, or Nine Farthings.

| | l. | s. | d. | q. | | l. | s. | d. | q. |
|---|---|---|---|---|---|---|---|---|---|
| 1 | 0 | 0 | 2 | 1 | 36 | 0 | 6 | 9 | 0 |
| 2 | 0 | 0 | 4 | 2 | 37 | 0 | 6 | 11 | 1 |
| 3 | 0 | 0 | 6 | 3 | 38 | 0 | 7 | 1 | 2 |
| 4 | 0 | 0 | 9 | 0 | 39 | 0 | 7 | 3 | 3 |
| 5 | 0 | 0 | 11 | 1 | 40 | 0 | 7 | 6 | 0 |
| 6 | 0 | 1 | 1 | 2 | 50 | 0 | 9 | 4 | 2 |
| 7 | 0 | 1 | 3 | 3 | (56) | 0 | 10 | 6 | 0 |
| 8 | 0 | 1 | 6 | 0 | 60 | 0 | 11 | 3 | 0 |
| 9 | 0 | 1 | 8 | 1 | 70 | 0 | 13 | 1 | 2 |
| 10 | 0 | 1 | 10 | 2 | 80 | 0 | 15 | 0 | 0 |
| 11 | 0 | 2 | 0 | 3 | (84) | 0 | 15 | 9 | 0 |
| 12 | 0 | 2 | 3 | 0 | 90 | 0 | 16 | 10 | 2 |
| 13 | 0 | 2 | 5 | 1 | 100 | 0 | 18 | 9 | 0 |
| 14 | 0 | 2 | 7 | 2 | (112) | 1 | 1 | 0 | 0 |
| 15 | 0 | 2 | 9 | 3 | 200 | 1 | 17 | 6 | 0 |
| 16 | 0 | 3 | 0 | 0 | (224) | 2 | 2 | 0 | 0 |
| 17 | 0 | 3 | 2 | 1 | 300 | 2 | 16 | 3 | 0 |
| 18 | 0 | 3 | 4 | 2 | (336) | 3 | 3 | 0 | 0 |
| 19 | 0 | 3 | 6 | 3 | 400 | 3 | 15 | 0 | 0 |
| 20 | 0 | 3 | 9 | 0 | (448) | 4 | 4 | 0 | 0 |
| 21 | 0 | 3 | 11 | 1 | 500 | 4 | 13 | 9 | 0 |
| 22 | 0 | 4 | 1 | 2 | (560) | 5 | 5 | 0 | 0 |
| 23 | 0 | 4 | 3 | 3 | 600 | 5 | 12 | 6 | 0 |
| 24 | 0 | 4 | 6 | 0 | (672) | 6 | 6 | 0 | 0 |
| 25 | 0 | 4 | 8 | 1 | 700 | 6 | 11 | 3 | 0 |
| 26 | 0 | 4 | 10 | 2 | (784) | 7 | 7 | 0 | 0 |
| 27 | 0 | 5 | 0 | 3 | 800 | 7 | 10 | 0 | 0 |
| (28) | 0 | 5 | 3 | 0 | (896) | 8 | 8 | 0 | 0 |
| 29 | 0 | 5 | 5 | 1 | 900 | 8 | 8 | 9 | 0 |
| 30 | 0 | 5 | 7 | 2 | 1000 | 9 | 7 | 6 | 0 |
| 31 | 0 | 5 | 9 | 3 | 2000 | 18 | 15 | 0 | 0 |
| 32 | 0 | 6 | 0 | 0 | 3000 | 28 | 2 | 6 | 0 |
| 33 | 0 | 6 | 2 | 1 | 4000 | 37 | 10 | 9 | 0 |
| 34 | 0 | 6 | 4 | 2 | 5000 | 46 | 17 | 6 | 0 |
| 35 | 0 | 6 | 6 | 3 | 10000 | 93 | 15 | 9 | 0 |

## *Two-pence Half-peny, or Ten Farthings.*

| | l. | s. | d | q. | | l. | s. | d. | q. |
|---|---|---|---|---|---|---|---|---|---|
| 1 | 0 | 0 | 2 | 2 | 36 | 0 | 7 | 6 | 0 |
| 2 | 0 | 0 | 5 | 0 | 37 | 0 | 7 | 8 | 2 |
| 3 | 0 | 0 | 7 | 2 | 38 | 0 | 7 | 11 | 0 |
| 4 | 0 | 0 | 10 | 0 | 39 | 0 | 8 | 1 | 2 |
| 5 | 0 | 1 | 0 | 2 | 40 | 0 | 8 | 4 | 0 |
| 6 | 0 | 1 | 3 | 0 | 50 | 0 | 10 | 5 | 0 |
| 7 | 0 | 1 | 5 | 2 | (56) | 0 | 11 | 8 | 0 |
| 8 | 0 | 1 | 8 | 0 | 60 | 0 | 12 | 6 | 0 |
| 9 | 0 | 1 | 10 | 2 | 70 | 0 | 14 | 7 | 0 |
| 10 | 0 | 2 | 1 | 0 | 80 | 0 | 16 | 8 | 0 |
| 11 | 0 | 2 | 3 | 2 | (84) | 0 | 17 | 6 | 0 |
| 12 | 0 | 2 | 6 | 0 | 90 | 0 | 18 | 9 | 0 |
| 13 | 0 | 2 | 8 | 2 | 100 | 1 | 0 | 10 | 0 |
| 14 | 0 | 2 | 11 | 0 | (112) | 1 | 3 | 4 | 0 |
| 15 | 0 | 3 | 1 | 2 | 200 | 2 | 1 | 8 | 0 |
| 16 | 0 | 3 | 4 | 0 | (224) | 2 | 6 | 8 | 0 |
| 17 | 0 | 3 | 6 | 2 | 300 | 3 | 2 | 6 | 0 |
| 18 | 0 | 3 | 9 | 0 | (336) | 3 | 10 | 0 | 0 |
| 19 | 0 | 3 | 11 | 2 | 400 | 4 | 3 | 4 | 0 |
| 20 | 0 | 4 | 2 | 0 | (448) | 4 | 13 | 4 | 0 |
| 21 | 0 | 4 | 4 | 2 | 500 | 5 | 4 | 2 | 0 |
| 22 | 0 | 4 | 7 | 0 | (560) | 5 | 16 | 8 | 0 |
| 23 | 0 | 4 | 9 | 2 | 600 | 6 | 5 | 0 | 0 |
| 24 | 0 | 5 | 0 | 0 | (672) | 7 | 0 | 0 | 0 |
| 25 | 0 | 5 | 2 | 2 | 700 | 7 | 5 | 10 | 0 |
| 26 | 0 | 5 | 5 | 0 | (784) | 8 | 3 | 4 | 0 |
| 27 | 0 | 5 | 7 | 2 | 800 | 8 | 6 | 8 | 0 |
| (28) | 0 | 5 | 10 | 0 | (896) | 9 | 6 | 8 | 0 |
| 29 | 0 | 6 | 0 | 2 | 900 | 9 | 7 | 6 | 0 |
| 30 | 0 | 6 | 3 | 0 | 1000 | 10 | 8 | 4 | 0 |
| 31 | 0 | 6 | 5 | 2 | 2000 | 20 | 16 | 8 | 0 |
| 32 | 0 | 6 | 8 | 0 | 3000 | 31 | 5 | 0 | 0 |
| 33 | 0 | 6 | 10 | 2 | 4000 | 41 | 13 | 4 | 0 |
| 34 | 0 | 7 | 1 | 0 | 5000 | 52 | 1 | 8 | 0 |
| 35 | 0 | 7 | 3 | 2 | 10000 | 104 | 3 | 4 | 0 |

## Two-pence Three Farthings.

| | l. | s. | d. | q. | | l. | s. | d. | q. |
|---|---|---|---|---|---|---|---|---|---|
| 1 | 0 | 0 | 2 | 3 | 36 | 0 | 8 | 3 | 0 |
| 2 | 0 | 0 | 5 | 2 | 37 | 0 | 8 | 5 | 3 |
| 3 | 0 | 0 | 8 | 1 | 38 | 0 | 8 | 8 | 2 |
| 4 | 0 | 0 | 11 | 0 | 39 | 0 | 8 | 11 | 1 |
| 5 | 0 | 1 | 1 | 3 | 40 | 0 | 9 | 2 | 0 |
| 6 | 0 | 1 | 4 | 2 | 50 | 0 | 11 | 5 | 2 |
| 7 | 0 | 1 | 7 | 1 | (56) | 0 | 12 | 10 | 0 |
| 8 | 0 | 1 | 10 | 0 | 60 | 0 | 13 | 9 | 0 |
| 9 | 0 | 2 | 0 | 3 | 70 | 0 | 16 | 0 | 2 |
| 10 | 0 | 2 | 3 | 2 | 80 | 0 | 18 | 4 | 0 |
| 11 | 0 | 2 | 6 | 1 | (84) | 0 | 19 | 3 | 0 |
| 12 | 0 | 2 | 9 | 0 | 90 | 1 | 0 | 7 | 2 |
| 13 | 0 | 2 | 11 | 3 | 100 | 1 | 2 | 11 | 0 |
| 14 | 0 | 3 | 2 | 2 | (112) | 1 | 5 | 8 | 0 |
| 15 | 0 | 3 | 5 | 1 | 200 | 2 | 5 | 10 | 0 |
| 16 | 0 | 3 | 8 | 0 | (224) | 2 | 11 | 4 | 0 |
| 17 | 0 | 3 | 10 | 3 | 300 | 3 | 8 | 9 | 0 |
| 18 | 0 | 4 | 1 | 2 | (336) | 3 | 17 | 0 | 0 |
| 19 | 0 | 4 | 4 | 1 | 400 | 4 | 11 | 8 | 0 |
| 20 | 0 | 4 | 7 | 0 | (448) | 5 | 2 | 8 | 0 |
| 21 | 0 | 4 | 9 | 3 | 500 | 5 | 14 | 7 | 0 |
| 22 | 0 | 5 | 0 | 2 | (560) | 6 | 8 | 4 | 0 |
| 23 | 0 | 5 | 3 | 1 | 600 | 6 | 17 | 6 | 0 |
| 24 | 0 | 5 | 6 | 0 | (672) | 7 | 14 | 0 | 0 |
| 25 | 0 | 5 | 8 | 3 | 700 | 8 | 0 | 5 | 0 |
| 26 | 0 | 5 | 11 | 2 | (784) | 8 | 19 | 8 | 0 |
| 27 | 0 | 6 | 2 | 1 | 800 | 9 | 3 | 4 | 0 |
| (28) | 0 | 6 | 5 | 0 | (896) | 10 | 5 | 4 | 0 |
| 29 | 0 | 6 | 7 | 3 | 900 | 10 | 6 | 3 | 0 |
| 30 | 0 | 6 | 10 | 2 | 1000 | 11 | 9 | 2 | 0 |
| 31 | 0 | 7 | 1 | 1 | 2000 | 22 | 18 | 4 | 0 |
| 32 | 0 | 7 | 4 | 0 | 3000 | 34 | 7 | 6 | 0 |
| 33 | 0 | 7 | 6 | 3 | 4000 | 45 | 16 | 8 | 0 |
| 34 | 0 | 7 | 9 | 2 | 5000 | 57 | 5 | 10 | 0 |
| 35 | 0 | 8 | 0 | 1 | 10000 | 114 | 11 | 8 | 0 |

## Three-Pence.

| | l. | s. | d. | | l. | s. | d. |
|---|---|---|---|---|---|---|---|
| 1 | 0 | 0 | 3 | 36 | 0 | 9 | 0 |
| 2 | 0 | 0 | 6 | 37 | 0 | 9 | 3 |
| 3 | 0 | 0 | 9 | 38 | 0 | 9 | 6 |
| 4 | 0 | 1 | 0 | 39 | 0 | 9 | 9 |
| 5 | 0 | 1 | 3 | 40 | 0 | 10 | 0 |
| 6 | 0 | 1 | 6 | 50 | 0 | 12 | 6 |
| 7 | 0 | 1 | 9 | (56) | 0 | 14 | 0 |
| 8 | 0 | 2 | 0 | 60 | 0 | 15 | 0 |
| 9 | 0 | 2 | 3 | 70 | 0 | 17 | 6 |
| 10 | 0 | 2 | 6 | 80 | 1 | 0 | 0 |
| 11 | 0 | 2 | 9 | (84) | 1 | 1 | 0 |
| 12 | 0 | 3 | 0 | 90 | 1 | 2 | 6 |
| 13 | 0 | 3 | 3 | 100 | 1 | 5 | 0 |
| 14 | 0 | 3 | 6 | (112) | 1 | 8 | 0 |
| 15 | 0 | 3 | 9 | 200 | 2 | 10 | 0 |
| 16 | 0 | 4 | 0 | (224) | 2 | 16 | 0 |
| 17 | 0 | 4 | 3 | 300 | 3 | 15 | 0 |
| 18 | 0 | 4 | 6 | (336) | 4 | 4 | 0 |
| 19 | 0 | 4 | 9 | 400 | 5 | 0 | 0 |
| 20 | 0 | 5 | 0 | (448) | 5 | 12 | 0 |
| 21 | 0 | 5 | 3 | 500 | 6 | 5 | 0 |
| 22 | 0 | 5 | 6 | (560) | 7 | 0 | 0 |
| 23 | 0 | 5 | 9 | 600 | 7 | 10 | 0 |
| 24 | 0 | 6 | 0 | (672) | 8 | 8 | 0 |
| 25 | 0 | 6 | 3 | 700 | 8 | 15 | 0 |
| 26 | 0 | 6 | 6 | (784) | 9 | 16 | 0 |
| 27 | 0 | 6 | 9 | 800 | 10 | 0 | 0 |
| (28) | 0 | 7 | 0 | (896) | 11 | 4 | 0 |
| 29 | 0 | 7 | 3 | 900 | 11 | 5 | 0 |
| 30 | 0 | 7 | 6 | 1000 | 12 | 10 | 0 |
| 31 | 0 | 7 | 9 | 2000 | 25 | 0 | 0 |
| 32 | 0 | 8 | 0 | 3000 | 37 | 10 | 0 |
| 33 | 0 | 8 | 3 | 4000 | 50 | 0 | 0 |
| 34 | 0 | 8 | 6 | 5000 | 62 | 10 | 0 |
| 35 | 0 | 8 | 9 | 10000 | 125 | 0 | 0 |

## *Three-pence Farthing.*

| | l. | s. | d. | q. | | l. | s. | d. | q. |
|---|---|---|---|---|---|---|---|---|---|
| 1 | 0 | 0 | 3 | 1 | 36 | 0 | 9 | 9 | 0 |
| 2 | 0 | 0 | 6 | 2 | 37 | 0 | 10 | 0 | 1 |
| 3 | 0 | 0 | 9 | 3 | 38 | 0 | 10 | 3 | 2 |
| 4 | 0 | 1 | 1 | 0 | 39 | 0 | 10 | 6 | 3 |
| 5 | 0 | 1 | 4 | 1 | 40 | 0 | 10 | 10 | 0 |
| 6 | 0 | 1 | 7 | 2 | 50 | 0 | 13 | 6 | 2 |
| 7 | 0 | 1 | 10 | 3 | (56) | 0 | 15 | 2 | 0 |
| 8 | 0 | 2 | 2 | 0 | 60 | 0 | 16 | 3 | 0 |
| 9 | 0 | 2 | 5 | 1 | 70 | 0 | 18 | 11 | 2 |
| 10 | 0 | 2 | 8 | 2 | 80 | 1 | 1 | 8 | 0 |
| 11 | 0 | 2 | 11 | 3 | (84) | 1 | 2 | 9 | 0 |
| 12 | 0 | 3 | 3 | 0 | 90 | 1 | 4 | 4 | 2 |
| 13 | 0 | 3 | 6 | 1 | 100 | 1 | 7 | 1 | 0 |
| 14 | 0 | 3 | 9 | 2 | (112) | 1 | 10 | 4 | 0 |
| 15 | 0 | 4 | 0 | 3 | 200 | 2 | 14 | 2 | 0 |
| 16 | 0 | 4 | 4 | 0 | (224) | 3 | 0 | 8 | 0 |
| 17 | 0 | 4 | 7 | 1 | 300 | 4 | 1 | 3 | 0 |
| 18 | 0 | 4 | 10 | 2 | (336) | 4 | 11 | 0 | 0 |
| 19 | 0 | 5 | 1 | 3 | 400 | 5 | 8 | 4 | 0 |
| 20 | 0 | 5 | 5 | 0 | (448) | 6 | 1 | 4 | 0 |
| 21 | 0 | 5 | 8 | 1 | 500 | 6 | 15 | 5 | 0 |
| 22 | 0 | 5 | 11 | 2 | (560) | 7 | 11 | 8 | 0 |
| 23 | 0 | 6 | 2 | 3 | 600 | 8 | 2 | 6 | 0 |
| 24 | 0 | 6 | 6 | 0 | (672) | 9 | 2 | 0 | 0 |
| 25 | 0 | 6 | 9 | 1 | 700 | 9 | 9 | 7 | 0 |
| 26 | 0 | 7 | 0 | 2 | (784) | 10 | 12 | 4 | 0 |
| 27 | 0 | 7 | 3 | 3 | 800 | 10 | 16 | 8 | 0 |
| (28) | 0 | 7 | 7 | 0 | (896) | 12 | 2 | 8 | 0 |
| 29 | 0 | 7 | 10 | 1 | 900 | 12 | 3 | 9 | 0 |
| 30 | 0 | 8 | 1 | 2 | 1000 | 13 | 10 | 10 | 0 |
| 31 | 0 | 8 | 4 | 3 | 2000 | 27 | 1 | 8 | 0 |
| 32 | 0 | 8 | 8 | 0 | 3000 | 40 | 12 | 6 | 0 |
| 33 | 0 | 8 | 11 | 1 | 4000 | 54 | 3 | 4 | 0 |
| 34 | 0 | 9 | 2 | 2 | 5000 | 67 | 14 | 2 | 0 |
| 35 | 0 | 9 | 5 | 3 | 10000 | 135 | 8 | 4 | 0 |

## Three-pence Half-peny.

| | l. | s. | d. | q. | | l. | s. | d. | q. |
|---|---|---|---|---|---|---|---|---|---|
| 1 | 0 | 0 | 3 | 2 | 36 | 0 | 10 | 6 | 0 |
| 2 | 0 | 0 | 7 | 0 | 37 | 0 | 10 | 9 | 2 |
| 3 | 0 | 0 | 10 | 2 | 38 | 0 | 11 | 1 | 0 |
| 4 | 0 | 1 | 2 | 0 | 39 | 0 | 11 | 4 | 2 |
| 5 | 0 | 1 | 5 | 2 | 40 | 0 | 11 | 8 | 0 |
| 6 | 0 | 1 | 9 | 0 | 50 | 0 | 14 | 7 | 0 |
| 7 | 0 | 2 | 0 | 2 | (56) | 0 | 16 | 4 | 0 |
| 8 | 0 | 2 | 4 | 0 | 60 | 0 | 17 | 6 | 0 |
| 9 | 0 | 2 | 7 | 2 | 70 | 1 | 0 | 5 | 0 |
| 10 | 0 | 2 | 11 | 0 | 80 | 1 | 3 | 4 | 0 |
| 11 | 0 | 3 | 2 | 2 | (84) | 1 | 4 | 6 | 0 |
| 12 | 0 | 3 | 6 | 0 | 90 | 1 | 6 | 3 | 0 |
| 13 | 0 | 3 | 9 | 2 | 100 | 1 | 9 | 2 | 0 |
| 14 | 0 | 4 | 1 | 0 | (112) | 1 | 12 | 8 | 0 |
| 15 | 0 | 4 | 4 | 2 | 200 | 2 | 18 | 4 | 0 |
| 16 | 0 | 4 | 8 | 0 | (224) | 3 | 5 | 4 | 0 |
| 17 | 0 | 4 | 11 | 2 | 300 | 4 | 7 | 6 | 0 |
| 18 | 0 | 5 | 3 | 0 | (336) | 4 | 18 | 0 | 0 |
| 19 | 0 | 5 | 6 | 2 | 400 | 5 | 16 | 8 | 0 |
| 20 | 0 | 5 | 10 | 0 | (448) | 6 | 10 | 8 | 0 |
| 21 | 0 | 6 | 1 | 2 | 500 | 7 | 5 | 10 | 0 |
| 22 | 0 | 6 | 5 | 0 | (560) | 8 | 3 | 4 | 0 |
| 23 | 0 | 6 | 8 | 2 | 600 | 8 | 15 | 0 | 0 |
| 24 | 0 | 7 | 0 | 0 | (672) | 9 | 16 | 0 | 0 |
| 25 | 0 | 7 | 3 | 2 | 700 | 10 | 4 | 2 | 0 |
| 26 | 0 | 7 | 7 | 0 | (784) | 11 | 8 | 8 | 0 |
| 27 | 0 | 7 | 10 | 2 | 800 | 11 | 13 | 4 | 0 |
| (28) | 0 | 8 | 2 | 0 | (896) | 13 | 1 | 4 | 0 |
| 29 | 0 | 8 | 5 | 2 | 900 | 13 | 2 | 6 | 0 |
| 30 | 0 | 8 | 9 | 0 | 1000 | 14 | 11 | 8 | 0 |
| 31 | 0 | 9 | 0 | 2 | 2000 | 29 | 3 | 4 | 0 |
| 32 | 0 | 9 | 4 | 0 | 3000 | 43 | 15 | 0 | 0 |
| 33 | 0 | 9 | 7 | 2 | 4000 | 58 | 6 | 8 | 0 |
| 34 | 0 | 9 | 11 | 0 | 5000 | 72 | 18 | 4 | 0 |
| 35 | 0 | 10 | 2 | 2 | 10000 | 145 | 16 | 8 | 0 |

## Three-pence Three Farthings.

| | l. | s. | d. | q. | | l. | s. | d. | q. |
|---|---|---|---|---|---|---|---|---|---|
| 1 | 0 | 0 | 3 | 3 | 36 | 0 | 11 | 3 | 0 |
| 2 | 0 | 0 | 7 | 2 | 37 | 0 | 11 | 6 | 3 |
| 3 | 0 | 0 | 11 | 1 | 38 | 0 | 11 | 10 | 2 |
| 4 | 0 | 1 | 3 | 0 | 39 | 0 | 12 | 2 | 1 |
| 5 | 0 | 1 | 6 | 3 | 40 | 0 | 12 | 6 | 0 |
| 6 | 0 | 1 | 10 | 2 | 50 | 0 | 15 | 7 | 2 |
| 7 | 0 | 2 | 2 | 1 | (56) | 0 | 17 | 6 | 0 |
| 8 | 0 | 2 | 6 | 0 | 60 | 0 | 18 | 9 | 0 |
| 9 | 0 | 2 | 9 | 3 | 70 | 1 | 1 | 10 | 2 |
| 10 | 0 | 3 | 1 | 2 | 80 | 1 | 5 | 0 | 0 |
| 11 | 0 | 3 | 5 | 1 | (84) | 1 | 6 | 3 | 0 |
| 12 | 0 | 3 | 9 | 0 | 90 | 1 | 8 | 1 | 2 |
| 13 | 0 | 4 | 0 | 3 | 100 | 1 | 11 | 3 | 0 |
| 14 | 0 | 4 | 4 | 2 | (112) | 1 | 15 | 0 | 0 |
| 15 | 0 | 4 | 8 | 1 | 200 | 3 | 2 | 6 | 0 |
| 16 | 0 | 5 | 0 | 0 | (224) | 3 | 10 | 0 | 0 |
| 17 | 0 | 5 | 3 | 3 | 300 | 4 | 13 | 9 | 0 |
| 18 | 0 | 5 | 7 | 2 | (336) | 5 | 5 | 0 | 0 |
| 19 | 0 | 5 | 11 | 1 | 400 | 6 | 5 | 0 | 0 |
| 20 | 0 | 6 | 3 | 0 | (448) | 7 | 0 | 0 | 0 |
| 21 | 0 | 6 | 6 | 3 | 500 | 7 | 16 | 3 | 0 |
| 22 | 0 | 6 | 10 | 2 | (560) | 8 | 15 | 0 | 0 |
| 23 | 0 | 7 | 2 | 1 | 600 | 9 | 7 | 6 | 0 |
| 24 | 0 | 7 | 6 | 0 | (672) | 10 | 10 | 0 | 0 |
| 25 | 0 | 7 | 9 | 3 | 700 | 10 | 18 | 9 | 0 |
| 26 | 0 | 8 | 1 | 2 | (784) | 12 | 5 | 0 | 0 |
| 27 | 0 | 8 | 5 | 1 | 800 | 12 | 10 | 0 | 0 |
| (28) | 0 | 8 | 9 | 0 | (896) | 14 | 0 | 0 | 0 |
| 29 | 0 | 9 | 0 | 3 | 900 | 14 | 1 | 3 | 0 |
| 30 | 0 | 9 | 4 | 2 | 1000 | 15 | 12 | 6 | 0 |
| 31 | 0 | 9 | 8 | 1 | 2000 | 31 | 5 | 0 | 0 |
| 32 | 0 | 10 | 0 | 0 | 3000 | 46 | 17 | 6 | 0 |
| 33 | 0 | 10 | 3 | 3 | 4000 | 62 | 10 | 0 | 0 |
| 34 | 0 | 10 | 7 | 2 | 5000 | 78 | 2 | 6 | 0 |
| 35 | 0 | 10 | 11 | 1 | 10000 | 156 | 5 | 0 | 0 |

## Four-pence, or a Groat.

| | l. | s. | d. | | l. | s. | d. |
|---|---|---|---|---|---|---|---|
| 1 | 0 | 0 | 4 | 36 | 0 | 12 | 0 |
| 2 | 0 | 0 | 8 | 37 | 0 | 12 | 4 |
| 3 | 0 | 1 | 0 | 38 | 0 | 12 | 8 |
| 4 | 0 | 1 | 4 | 39 | 0 | 13 | 0 |
| 5 | 0 | 1 | 8 | 40 | 0 | 13 | 4 |
| 6 | 0 | 2 | 0 | 50 | 0 | 16 | 8 |
| 7 | 0 | 2 | 4 | (56) | 0 | 18 | 8 |
| 8 | 0 | 2 | 8 | 60 | 1 | 0 | 0 |
| 9 | 0 | 3 | 0 | 70 | 1 | 3 | 4 |
| 10 | 0 | 3 | 4 | 80 | 1 | 6 | 8 |
| 11 | 0 | 3 | 8 | (84) | 1 | 8 | 0 |
| 12 | 0 | 4 | 0 | 90 | 1 | 10 | 0 |
| 13 | 0 | 4 | 4 | 100 | 1 | 13 | 4 |
| 14 | 0 | 4 | 8 | (112) | 1 | 17 | 4 |
| 15 | 0 | 5 | 0 | 200 | 3 | 6 | 8 |
| 16 | 0 | 5 | 4 | (224) | 3 | 14 | 8 |
| 17 | 0 | 5 | 8 | 300 | 5 | 0 | 0 |
| 18 | 0 | 6 | 0 | (336) | 5 | 12 | 0 |
| 19 | 0 | 6 | 4 | 400 | 6 | 13 | 4 |
| 20 | 0 | 6 | 8 | (448) | 7 | 9 | 4 |
| 21 | 0 | 7 | 0 | 500 | 8 | 6 | 8 |
| 22 | 0 | 7 | 4 | (560) | 9 | 6 | 8 |
| 23 | 0 | 7 | 8 | 600 | 10 | 0 | 0 |
| 24 | 0 | 8 | 0 | (672) | 11 | 4 | 0 |
| 25 | 0 | 8 | 4 | 700 | 11 | 13 | 4 |
| 26 | 0 | 8 | 8 | (784) | 13 | 1 | 4 |
| 27 | 0 | 9 | 0 | 800 | 13 | 6 | 8 |
| (28) | 0 | 9 | 4 | (896) | 14 | 18 | 8 |
| 29 | 0 | 9 | 8 | 900 | 15 | 0 | 0 |
| 30 | 0 | 10 | 0 | 1000 | 16 | 13 | 4 |
| 31 | 0 | 10 | 4 | 2000 | 33 | 6 | 8 |
| 32 | 0 | 10 | 8 | 3000 | 50 | 0 | 0 |
| 33 | 0 | 11 | 0 | 4000 | 66 | 13 | 4 |
| 34 | 0 | 11 | 4 | 5000 | 83 | 6 | 8 |
| 35 | 0 | 11 | 8 | 10000 | 166 | 13 | 4 |

## *Four-pence Farthing.*

| | l. | s. | d. | q. | | l. | s. | d. | q. |
|---|---|---|---|---|---|---|---|---|---|
| 1 | 0 | 0 | 4 | 1 | 36 | 0 | 12 | 9 | 0 |
| 2 | 0 | 0 | 8 | 2 | 37 | 0 | 13 | 1 | 1 |
| 3 | 0 | 1 | 0 | 3 | 38 | 0 | 13 | 5 | 2 |
| 4 | 0 | 1 | 5 | 0 | 39 | 0 | 13 | 9 | 3 |
| 5 | 0 | 1 | 9 | 1 | 40 | 0 | 14 | 2 | 0 |
| 6 | 0 | 2 | 1 | 2 | 50 | 0 | 17 | 8 | 2 |
| 7 | 0 | 2 | 5 | 3 | (56) | 0 | 19 | 10 | 0 |
| 8 | 0 | 2 | 10 | 0 | 60 | 1 | 1 | 3 | 0 |
| 9 | 0 | 3 | 2 | 1 | 70 | 1 | 4 | 9 | 2 |
| 10 | 0 | 3 | 6 | 2 | 80 | 1 | 8 | 4 | 0 |
| 11 | 0 | 3 | 10 | 3 | (84) | 1 | 9 | 9 | 0 |
| 12 | 0 | 4 | 3 | 0 | 90 | 1 | 11 | 10 | 2 |
| 13 | 0 | 4 | 7 | 1 | 100 | 1 | 15 | 5 | 0 |
| 14 | 0 | 4 | 11 | 2 | (112) | 1 | 19 | 8 | 0 |
| 15 | 0 | 5 | 3 | 3 | 200 | 3 | 10 | 10 | 0 |
| 16 | 0 | 5 | 8 | 0 | (224) | 3 | 19 | 4 | 0 |
| 17 | 0 | 6 | 0 | 1 | 300 | 5 | 6 | 3 | 0 |
| 18 | 0 | 6 | 4 | 2 | (336) | 5 | 19 | 0 | 0 |
| 19 | 0 | 6 | 8 | 3 | 400 | 7 | 1 | 8 | 0 |
| 20 | 0 | 7 | 1 | 0 | (448) | 7 | 18 | 8 | 0 |
| 21 | 0 | 7 | 5 | 1 | 500 | 8 | 17 | 1 | 0 |
| 22 | 0 | 7 | 9 | 2 | (560) | 9 | 18 | 4 | 0 |
| 23 | 0 | 8 | 1 | 3 | 600 | 10 | 12 | 6 | 0 |
| 24 | 0 | 8 | 6 | 0 | (672) | 11 | 18 | 0 | 0 |
| 25 | 0 | 8 | 10 | 1 | 700 | 12 | 7 | 11 | 0 |
| 26 | 0 | 9 | 2 | 2 | (784) | 13 | 17 | 8 | 0 |
| 27 | 0 | 9 | 6 | 3 | 800 | 14 | 3 | 4 | 0 |
| (28) | 0 | 9 | 11 | 0 | (896) | 15 | 17 | 4 | 0 |
| 29 | 0 | 10 | 3 | 1 | 900 | 15 | 18 | 9 | 0 |
| 30 | 0 | 10 | 7 | 2 | 1000 | 17 | 14 | 2 | 0 |
| 31 | 0 | 10 | 11 | 3 | 2000 | 35 | 8 | 4 | 0 |
| 32 | 0 | 11 | 4 | 0 | 3000 | 53 | 2 | 6 | 0 |
| 33 | 0 | 11 | 8 | 1 | 4000 | 70 | 16 | 8 | 0 |
| 34 | 0 | 12 | 0 | 2 | 5000 | 88 | 10 | 10 | 0 |
| 35 | 0 | 12 | 4 | 3 | 10000 | 177 | 1 | 8 | 0 |

## *Four-pence Half-peny.*

| | l. | s. | d. | q. | | l. | s. | d. | q. |
|---|---|---|---|---|---|---|---|---|---|
| 1 | 0 | 0 | 4 | 2 | 36 | 0 | 13 | 6 | 0 |
| 2 | 0 | 0 | 9 | 0 | 37 | 0 | 13 | 10 | 2 |
| 3 | 0 | 1 | 1 | 2 | 38 | 0 | 14 | 3 | 0 |
| 4 | 0 | 1 | 6 | 0 | 39 | 0 | 14 | 7 | 2 |
| 5 | 0 | 1 | 10 | 2 | 40 | 0 | 15 | 0 | 0 |
| 6 | 0 | 2 | 3 | 0 | 50 | 0 | 18 | 9 | 0 |
| 7 | 0 | 2 | 7 | 2 | (56) | 1 | 1 | 0 | 0 |
| 8 | 0 | 3 | 0 | 0 | 60 | 1 | 2 | 6 | 0 |
| 9 | 0 | 3 | 4 | 2 | 70 | 1 | 6 | 3 | 0 |
| 10 | 0 | 3 | 9 | 0 | 80 | 1 | 10 | 0 | 0 |
| 11 | 0 | 4 | 1 | 2 | (84) | 1 | 11 | 6 | 0 |
| 12 | 0 | 4 | 6 | 0 | 90 | 1 | 13 | 9 | 0 |
| 13 | 0 | 4 | 10 | 2 | 100 | 1 | 17 | 6 | 0 |
| 14 | 0 | 5 | 3 | 0 | (112) | 2 | 2 | 0 | 0 |
| 15 | 0 | 5 | 7 | 2 | 200 | 3 | 15 | 0 | 0 |
| 16 | 0 | 6 | 0 | 0 | (224) | 4 | 4 | 0 | 0 |
| 17 | 0 | 6 | 4 | 2 | 300 | 5 | 12 | 6 | 0 |
| 18 | 0 | 6 | 9 | 0 | (336) | 6 | 6 | 0 | 0 |
| 19 | 0 | 7 | 1 | 2 | 400 | 7 | 10 | 0 | 0 |
| 20 | 0 | 7 | 6 | 0 | (448) | 8 | 8 | 0 | 0 |
| 21 | 0 | 7 | 10 | 2 | 500 | 9 | 7 | 6 | 0 |
| 22 | 0 | 8 | 3 | 0 | (560) | 10 | 10 | 0 | 0 |
| 23 | 0 | 8 | 7 | 2 | 600 | 11 | 5 | 0 | 0 |
| 24 | 0 | 9 | 0 | 0 | (672) | 12 | 12 | 0 | 0 |
| 25 | 0 | 9 | 4 | 2 | 700 | 13 | 2 | 6 | 0 |
| 26 | 0 | 9 | 9 | 0 | (784) | 14 | 14 | 0 | 0 |
| 27 | 0 | 10 | 1 | 2 | 800 | 15 | 0 | 0 | 0 |
| (28) | 0 | 10 | 6 | 0 | (896) | 16 | 16 | 0 | 0 |
| 29 | 0 | 10 | 10 | 2 | 900 | 16 | 17 | 6 | 0 |
| 30 | 0 | 11 | 3 | 0 | 1000 | 18 | 15 | 0 | 0 |
| 31 | 0 | 11 | 7 | 2 | 2000 | 37 | 10 | 0 | 0 |
| 32 | 0 | 12 | 0 | 0 | 3000 | 56 | 5 | 0 | 0 |
| 33 | 0 | 12 | 4 | 2 | 4000 | 75 | 0 | 0 | 0 |
| 34 | 0 | 12 | 9 | 0 | 5000 | 93 | 15 | 0 | 0 |
| 35 | 0 | 13 | 1 | 2 | 10000 | 187 | 10 | 0 | 0 |

## Four-pence Three Farthings.

| | l. | s. | d. | q. | | l. | s. | d. | q. |
|---|---|---|---|---|---|---|---|---|---|
| 1 | 0 | 0 | 4 | 3 | 36 | 0 | 14 | 3 | 0 |
| 2 | 0 | 0 | 9 | 2 | 37 | 0 | 14 | 7 | 3 |
| 3 | 0 | 1 | 2 | 1 | 38 | 0 | 15 | 0 | 2 |
| 4 | 0 | 1 | 7 | 0 | 39 | 0 | 15 | 5 | 1 |
| 5 | 0 | 1 | 11 | 3 | 40 | 0 | 15 | 10 | 0 |
| 6 | 0 | 2 | 4 | 2 | 50 | 0 | 19 | 9 | 2 |
| 7 | 0 | 2 | 9 | 1 | (56) | 1 | 2 | 2 | 0 |
| 8 | 0 | 3 | 2 | 0 | 60 | 1 | 3 | 9 | 0 |
| 9 | 0 | 3 | 6 | 3 | 70 | 1 | 7 | 8 | 2 |
| 10 | 0 | 3 | 11 | 2 | 80 | 1 | 11 | 8 | 0 |
| 11 | 0 | 4 | 4 | 1 | (84) | 1 | 13 | 3 | 0 |
| 12 | 0 | 4 | 9 | 0 | 90 | 1 | 15 | 7 | 2 |
| 13 | 0 | 5 | 1 | 3 | 100 | 1 | 19 | 7 | 0 |
| 14 | 0 | 5 | 6 | 2 | (112) | 2 | 4 | 4 | 0 |
| 15 | 0 | 5 | 11 | 1 | 200 | 3 | 19 | 2 | 0 |
| 16 | 0 | 6 | 4 | 0 | (224) | 4 | 8 | 8 | 0 |
| 17 | 0 | 6 | 8 | 3 | 300 | 5 | 18 | 9 | 0 |
| 18 | 0 | 7 | 1 | 2 | (336) | 6 | 13 | 0 | 0 |
| 19 | 0 | 7 | 6 | 1 | 400 | 7 | 18 | 4 | 0 |
| 20 | 0 | 7 | 11 | 0 | (448) | 8 | 17 | 4 | 0 |
| 21 | 0 | 8 | 3 | 3 | 500 | 9 | 17 | 11 | 0 |
| 22 | 0 | 8 | 8 | 2 | (560) | 11 | 1 | 8 | 0 |
| 23 | 0 | 9 | 1 | 1 | 600 | 11 | 17 | 6 | 0 |
| 24 | 0 | 9 | 6 | 0 | (672) | 13 | 6 | 0 | 0 |
| 25 | 0 | 9 | 10 | 3 | 700 | 13 | 17 | 1 | 0 |
| 26 | 0 | 10 | 3 | 2 | (784) | 15 | 10 | 4 | 0 |
| 27 | 0 | 10 | 8 | 1 | 800 | 15 | 16 | 8 | 0 |
| (28) | 0 | 11 | 1 | 0 | (896) | 17 | 14 | 8 | 0 |
| 29 | 0 | 11 | 5 | 3 | 900 | 17 | 16 | 3 | 0 |
| 30 | 0 | 11 | 10 | 2 | 1000 | 19 | 15 | 10 | 0 |
| 31 | 0 | 12 | 3 | 1 | 2000 | 39 | 11 | 8 | 0 |
| 32 | 0 | 12 | 8 | 0 | 3000 | 59 | 7 | 6 | 0 |
| 33 | 0 | 13 | 0 | 3 | 4000 | 79 | 3 | 4 | 0 |
| 34 | 0 | 13 | 5 | 2 | 5000 | 98 | 19 | 2 | 0 |
| 35 | 0 | 13 | 10 | 1 | 10000 | 197 | 18 | 4 | 0 |

## *Five-Pence.*

| | l. | s. | d. | | l. | s. | d. |
|---|---|---|---|---|---|---|---|
| 1 | 0 | 0 | 5 | 36 | 0 | 15 | 0 |
| 2 | 0 | 0 | 10 | 37 | 0 | 15 | 5 |
| 3 | 0 | 1 | 3 | 38 | 0 | 15 | 10 |
| 4 | 0 | 1 | 8 | 39 | 0 | 16 | 3 |
| 5 | 0 | 2 | 1 | 40 | 0 | 16 | 8 |
| 6 | 0 | 2 | 6 | 50 | 1 | 0 | 10 |
| 7 | 0 | 2 | 11 | (56) | 1 | 3 | 4 |
| 8 | 0 | 3 | 4 | 60 | 1 | 5 | 0 |
| 9 | 0 | 3 | 9 | 70 | 1 | 9 | 2 |
| 10 | 0 | 4 | 2 | 80 | 1 | 13 | 4 |
| 11 | 0 | 4 | 7 | (84) | 1 | 15 | 0 |
| 12 | 0 | 5 | 0 | 90 | 1 | 17 | 6 |
| 13 | 0 | 5 | 5 | 100 | 2 | 1 | 8 |
| 14 | 0 | 5 | 10 | (112) | 2 | 6 | 8 |
| 15 | 0 | 6 | 3 | 200 | 4 | 3 | 4 |
| 16 | 0 | 6 | 8 | (224) | 4 | 13 | 4 |
| 17 | 0 | 7 | 1 | 300 | 6 | 5 | 0 |
| 18 | 0 | 7 | 6 | (336) | 7 | 0 | 0 |
| 19 | 0 | 7 | 11 | 400 | 8 | 6 | 8 |
| 20 | 0 | 8 | 4 | (448) | 9 | 6 | 8 |
| 21 | 0 | 8 | 9 | 500 | 10 | 8 | 4 |
| 22 | 0 | 9 | 2 | (560) | 11 | 13 | 4 |
| 23 | 0 | 9 | 7 | 600 | 12 | 10 | 0 |
| 24 | 0 | 10 | 0 | (672) | 14 | 0 | 0 |
| 25 | 0 | 10 | 5 | 700 | 14 | 11 | 8 |
| 26 | 0 | 10 | 10 | (784) | 16 | 6 | 8 |
| 27 | 0 | 11 | 3 | 800 | 16 | 13 | 4 |
| (28) | 0 | 11 | 8 | (896) | 18 | 13 | 4 |
| 29 | 0 | 12 | 1 | 900 | 18 | 15 | 0 |
| 30 | 0 | 12 | 6 | 1000 | 20 | 16 | 8 |
| 31 | 0 | 12 | 11 | 2000 | 41 | 13 | 4 |
| 32 | 0 | 13 | 4 | 3000 | 62 | 10 | 0 |
| 33 | 0 | 13 | 9 | 4000 | 83 | 6 | 8 |
| 34 | 0 | 14 | 2 | 5000 | 104 | 3 | 4 |
| 35 | 0 | 14 | 7 | 10000 | 208 | 6 | 8 |

## *Five-pence Farthing.*

| | l. | s. | d. | q. | | l. | s. | d. | q. |
|---|---|---|---|---|---|---|---|---|---|
| 1 | 0 | 0 | 5 | 1 | 36 | 0 | 15 | 9 | 0 |
| 2 | 0 | 0 | 10 | 2 | 37 | 0 | 16 | 2 | 1 |
| 3 | 0 | 1 | 3 | 3 | 38 | 0 | 16 | 7 | 2 |
| 4 | 0 | 1 | 9 | 0 | 39 | 0 | 17 | 0 | 3 |
| 5 | 0 | 2 | 2 | 1 | 40 | 0 | 17 | 6 | 0 |
| 6 | 0 | 2 | 7 | 2 | 50 | 1 | 1 | 10 | 2 |
| 7 | 0 | 3 | 0 | 3 | (56) | 1 | 4 | 6 | 0 |
| 8 | 0 | 3 | 6 | 0 | 60 | 1 | 6 | 3 | 0 |
| 9 | 0 | 3 | 11 | 1 | 70 | 1 | 10 | 7 | 2 |
| 10 | 0 | 4 | 4 | 2 | 80 | 1 | 15 | 0 | 0 |
| 11 | 0 | 4 | 9 | 3 | (84) | 1 | 16 | 9 | 0 |
| 12 | 0 | 5 | 3 | 0 | 90 | 1 | 19 | 4 | 2 |
| 13 | 0 | 5 | 8 | 1 | 100 | 2 | 3 | 9 | 0 |
| 14 | 0 | 6 | 1 | 2 | (112) | 2 | 9 | 0 | 0 |
| 15 | 0 | 6 | 6 | 3 | 200 | 4 | 7 | 6 | 0 |
| 16 | 0 | 7 | 0 | 0 | (224) | 4 | 18 | 0 | 0 |
| 17 | 0 | 7 | 5 | 1 | 300 | 6 | 11 | 3 | 0 |
| 18 | 0 | 7 | 10 | 2 | (336) | 7 | 7 | 0 | 0 |
| 19 | 0 | 8 | 3 | 3 | 400 | 8 | 15 | 0 | 0 |
| 20 | 0 | 8 | 9 | 0 | (448) | 9 | 16 | 0 | 0 |
| 21 | 0 | 9 | 2 | 1 | 500 | 10 | 18 | 9 | 0 |
| 22 | 0 | 9 | 7 | 2 | (560) | 12 | 5 | 0 | 0 |
| 23 | 0 | 10 | 0 | 3 | 600 | 13 | 2 | 6 | 0 |
| 24 | 0 | 10 | 6 | 0 | (672) | 14 | 14 | 0 | 0 |
| 25 | 0 | 10 | 11 | 1 | 700 | 15 | 6 | 3 | 0 |
| 26 | 0 | 11 | 4 | 2 | (784) | 17 | 3 | 0 | 0 |
| 27 | 0 | 11 | 9 | 3 | 800 | 17 | 10 | 0 | 0 |
| (28) | 0 | 12 | 3 | 0 | (896) | 19 | 12 | 0 | 0 |
| 29 | 0 | 12 | 8 | 1 | 900 | 19 | 13 | 9 | 0 |
| 30 | 0 | 13 | 1 | 2 | 1000 | 21 | 17 | 6 | 0 |
| 31 | 0 | 13 | 6 | 3 | 2000 | 43 | 15 | 0 | 0 |
| 32 | 0 | 14 | 0 | 0 | 3000 | 65 | 12 | 6 | 0 |
| 33 | 0 | 14 | 5 | 1 | 4000 | 87 | 10 | 9 | 0 |
| 34 | 0 | 14 | 10 | 2 | 5000 | 109 | 7 | 6 | 0 |
| 35 | 0 | 15 | 3 | 3 | 10000 | 218 | 15 | 0 | 0 |

## *Five-pence Half-peny.*

| | l. | s. | d. | q. | | l. | s. | d. | q. |
|---|---|---|---|---|---|---|---|---|---|
| 1 | 0 | 0 | 5 | 2 | 36 | 0 | 16 | 6 | 0 |
| 2 | 0 | 0 | 11 | 0 | 37 | 0 | 16 | 11 | 2 |
| 3 | 0 | 1 | 4 | 2 | 38 | 0 | 17 | 5 | 0 |
| 4 | 0 | 1 | 10 | 0 | 39 | 0 | 17 | 10 | 2 |
| 5 | 0 | 2 | 3 | 2 | 40 | 0 | 18 | 4 | 0 |
| 6 | 0 | 2 | 9 | 0 | 50 | 1 | 2 | 11 | 0 |
| 7 | 0 | 3 | 2 | 2 | (56) | 1 | 5 | 8 | 0 |
| 8 | 0 | 3 | 8 | 0 | 60 | 1 | 7 | 6 | 0 |
| 9 | 0 | 4 | 1 | 2 | 70 | 1 | 12 | 1 | 0 |
| 10 | 0 | 4 | 7 | 0 | 80 | 1 | 16 | 8 | 0 |
| 11 | 0 | 5 | 0 | 2 | (84) | 1 | 18 | 6 | 0 |
| 12 | 0 | 5 | 6 | 0 | 90 | 2 | 1 | 3 | 0 |
| 13 | 0 | 5 | 11 | 2 | 100 | 2 | 5 | 10 | 0 |
| 14 | 0 | 6 | 5 | 0 | (112) | 2 | 11 | 4 | 0 |
| 15 | 0 | 6 | 10 | 2 | 200 | 4 | 11 | 8 | 0 |
| 16 | 0 | 7 | 4 | 0 | (224) | 5 | 2 | 8 | 0 |
| 17 | 0 | 7 | 9 | 2 | 300 | 6 | 17 | 6 | 0 |
| 18 | 0 | 8 | 3 | 0 | (336) | 7 | 14 | 0 | 0 |
| 19 | 0 | 8 | 8 | 2 | 400 | 9 | 3 | 4 | 0 |
| 20 | 0 | 9 | 2 | 0 | (448) | 10 | 5 | 4 | 0 |
| 21 | 0 | 9 | 7 | 2 | 500 | 11 | 9 | 2 | 0 |
| 22 | 0 | 10 | 1 | 0 | (560) | 12 | 16 | 8 | 0 |
| 23 | 0 | 10 | 6 | 2 | 600 | 13 | 15 | 0 | 0 |
| 24 | 0 | 11 | 0 | 0 | (672) | 15 | 8 | 0 | 0 |
| 25 | 0 | 11 | 5 | 2 | 700 | 16 | 0 | 10 | 0 |
| 26 | 0 | 11 | 11 | 0 | (784) | 17 | 19 | 4 | 0 |
| 27 | 0 | 12 | 4 | 2 | 800 | 18 | 6 | 8 | 0 |
| (28) | 0 | 12 | 10 | 0 | (896) | 20 | 10 | 8 | 0 |
| 29 | 0 | 13 | 3 | 2 | 900 | 20 | 12 | 6 | 0 |
| 30 | 0 | 13 | 9 | 0 | 1000 | 22 | 18 | 4 | 0 |
| 31 | 0 | 14 | 2 | 2 | 2000 | 45 | 16 | 8 | 0 |
| 32 | 0 | 14 | 8 | 0 | 3000 | 68 | 15 | 0 | 0 |
| 33 | 0 | 15 | 1 | 2 | 4000 | 91 | 13 | 4 | 0 |
| 34 | 0 | 15 | 7 | 0 | 5000 | 114 | 11 | 8 | 0 |
| 35 | 0 | 16 | 0 | 2 | 10000 | 229 | 3 | 4 | 0 |

## Five-pence Three Farthings.

| | l. | s. | d. | q. | | l. | s. | d. | q. |
|---|---|---|---|---|---|---|---|---|---|
| 1 | 0 | 0 | 5 | 3 | 36 | 0 | 17 | 3 | 0 |
| 2 | 0 | 0 | 11 | 2 | 37 | 0 | 17 | 8 | 3 |
| 3 | 0 | 1 | 5 | 1 | 38 | 0 | 18 | 2 | 2 |
| 4 | 0 | 1 | 11 | 0 | 39 | 0 | 18 | 8 | 1 |
| 5 | 0 | 2 | 4 | 3 | 40 | 0 | 19 | 2 | 0 |
| 6 | 0 | 2 | 10 | 2 | 50 | 1 | 3 | 11 | 2 |
| 7 | 0 | 3 | 4 | 1 | (56) | 1 | 6 | 10 | 0 |
| 8 | 0 | 3 | 10 | 0 | 60 | 1 | 8 | 9 | 0 |
| 9 | 0 | 4 | 3 | 3 | 70 | 1 | 13 | 6 | 2 |
| 10 | 0 | 4 | 9 | 2 | 80 | 1 | 18 | 4 | 0 |
| 11 | 0 | 5 | 3 | 1 | (84) | 2 | 0 | 3 | 0 |
| 12 | 0 | 5 | 9 | 0 | 90 | 2 | 3 | 1 | 2 |
| 13 | 0 | 6 | 2 | 3 | 100 | 2 | 7 | 11 | 0 |
| 14 | 0 | 6 | 8 | 2 | (112) | 2 | 13 | 8 | 0 |
| 15 | 0 | 7 | 2 | 1 | 200 | 4 | 15 | 10 | 0 |
| 16 | 0 | 7 | 8 | 0 | (224) | 5 | 7 | 4 | 0 |
| 17 | 0 | 8 | 1 | 3 | 300 | 7 | 3 | 9 | 0 |
| 18 | 0 | 8 | 7 | 2 | (336) | 8 | 1 | 0 | 0 |
| 19 | 0 | 9 | 1 | 1 | 400 | 9 | 11 | 8 | 0 |
| 20 | 0 | 9 | 7 | 0 | (448) | 10 | 14 | 8 | 0 |
| 21 | 0 | 10 | 0 | 3 | 500 | 11 | 19 | 7 | 0 |
| 22 | 0 | 10 | 6 | 2 | (560) | 13 | 8 | 4 | 0 |
| 23 | 0 | 11 | 0 | 1 | 600 | 14 | 7 | 6 | 0 |
| 24 | 0 | 11 | 6 | 0 | (672) | 16 | 2 | 0 | 0 |
| 25 | 0 | 11 | 11 | 3 | 700 | 16 | 15 | 5 | 0 |
| 26 | 0 | 12 | 5 | 2 | (784) | 18 | 15 | 8 | 0 |
| 27 | 0 | 12 | 11 | 1 | 800 | 19 | 3 | 4 | 0 |
| (28) | 0 | 13 | 5 | 0 | (896) | 21 | 9 | 4 | 0 |
| 29 | 0 | 13 | 10 | 3 | 900 | 21 | 11 | 3 | 0 |
| 30 | 0 | 14 | 4 | 2 | 1000 | 23 | 19 | 2 | 0 |
| 31 | 0 | 14 | 10 | 1 | 2000 | 47 | 18 | 4 | 0 |
| 32 | 0 | 15 | 4 | 0 | 3000 | 71 | 17 | 6 | 0 |
| 33 | 0 | 15 | 9 | 3 | 4000 | 95 | 16 | 8 | 0 |
| 34 | 0 | 16 | 3 | 2 | 5000 | 119 | 15 | 10 | 0 |
| 35 | 0 | 16 | 9 | 1 | 10000 | 239 | 11 | 8 | 0 |

## Six-Pence.

| | l. | s. | d. | | l. | s. | d. |
|---|---|---|---|---|---|---|---|
| 1 | 0 | 0 | 6 | 36 | 0 | 18 | 0 |
| 2 | 0 | 1 | 0 | 37 | 0 | 18 | 6 |
| 3 | 0 | 1 | 6 | 38 | 0 | 19 | 0 |
| 4 | 0 | 2 | 0 | 39 | 0 | 19 | 6 |
| 5 | 0 | 2 | 6 | 40 | 1 | 0 | 0 |
| 6 | 0 | 3 | 0 | 50 | 1 | 5 | 0 |
| 7 | 0 | 3 | 6 | (56) | 1 | 8 | 0 |
| 8 | 0 | 4 | 0 | 60 | 1 | 10 | 0 |
| 9 | 0 | 4 | 6 | 70 | 1 | 15 | 0 |
| 10 | 0 | 5 | 0 | 80 | 2 | 0 | 0 |
| 11 | 0 | 5 | 6 | (84) | 2 | 2 | 0 |
| 12 | 0 | 6 | 0 | 90 | 2 | 5 | 0 |
| 13 | 0 | 6 | 6 | 100 | 2 | 10 | 0 |
| 14 | 0 | 7 | 0 | (112) | 2 | 16 | 0 |
| 15 | 0 | 7 | 6 | 200 | 5 | 0 | 0 |
| 16 | 0 | 8 | 0 | (224) | 5 | 12 | 0 |
| 17 | 0 | 8 | 6 | 300 | 7 | 10 | 0 |
| 18 | 0 | 9 | 0 | (336) | 8 | 8 | 0 |
| 19 | 0 | 9 | 6 | 400 | 10 | 0 | 0 |
| 20 | 0 | 10 | 0 | (448) | 11 | 4 | 0 |
| 21 | 0 | 10 | 6 | 500 | 12 | 10 | 0 |
| 22 | 0 | 11 | 0 | (560) | 14 | 0 | 0 |
| 23 | 0 | 11 | 6 | 600 | 15 | 0 | 0 |
| 24 | 0 | 12 | 0 | (672) | 16 | 16 | 0 |
| 25 | 0 | 12 | 6 | 700 | 17 | 10 | 0 |
| 26 | 0 | 13 | 0 | (784) | 19 | 12 | 0 |
| 27 | 0 | 13 | 6 | 800 | 20 | 0 | 0 |
| (28) | 0 | 14 | 0 | (896) | 22 | 8 | 0 |
| 29 | 0 | 14 | 6 | 900 | 22 | 10 | 0 |
| 30 | 0 | 15 | 0 | 1000 | 25 | 0 | 0 |
| 31 | 0 | 15 | 6 | 2000 | 50 | 0 | 0 |
| 32 | 0 | 16 | 0 | 3000 | 75 | 0 | 0 |
| 33 | 0 | 16 | 6 | 4000 | 100 | 0 | 0 |
| 34 | 0 | 17 | 0 | 5000 | 125 | 0 | 0 |
| 35 | 0 | 17 | 6 | 10000 | 250 | 0 | 0 |

## *Six-pence Farthing.*

| | l. | s. | d. | q. | | l. | s. | d. | q. |
|---|---|---|---|---|---|---|---|---|---|
| 1 | 0 | 0 | 6 | 1 | 36 | 0 | 18 | 9 | 0 |
| 2 | 0 | 1 | 0 | 2 | 37 | 0 | 19 | 3 | 1 |
| 3 | 0 | 1 | 6 | 3 | 38 | 0 | 19 | 9 | 2 |
| 4 | 0 | 2 | 1 | 0 | 39 | 1 | 0 | 3 | 3 |
| 5 | 0 | 2 | 7 | 1 | 40 | 1 | 0 | 10 | 0 |
| 6 | 0 | 3 | 1 | 2 | 50 | 1 | 6 | 0 | 2 |
| 7 | 0 | 3 | 7 | 3 | (56) | 1 | 9 | 2 | 0 |
| 8 | 0 | 4 | 2 | 0 | 60 | 1 | 11 | 3 | 0 |
| 9 | 0 | 4 | 8 | 1 | 70 | 1 | 16 | 5 | 2 |
| 10 | 0 | 5 | 2 | 2 | 80 | 2 | 1 | 8 | 0 |
| 11 | 0 | 5 | 8 | 3 | (84) | 2 | 3 | 9 | 0 |
| 12 | 0 | 6 | 3 | 0 | 90 | 2 | 6 | 10 | 2 |
| 13 | 0 | 6 | 9 | 1 | 100 | 2 | 12 | 1 | 0 |
| 14 | 0 | 7 | 3 | 2 | (112) | 2 | 18 | 4 | 0 |
| 15 | 0 | 7 | 9 | 3 | 200 | 5 | 4 | 2 | 0 |
| 16 | 0 | 8 | 4 | 0 | (224) | 5 | 16 | 8 | 0 |
| 17 | 0 | 8 | 10 | 1 | 300 | 7 | 16 | 3 | 0 |
| 18 | 0 | 9 | 4 | 2 | (336) | 8 | 15 | 0 | 0 |
| 19 | 0 | 9 | 10 | 3 | 400 | 10 | 8 | 4 | 0 |
| 20 | 0 | 10 | 5 | 0 | (448) | 11 | 13 | 4 | 0 |
| 21 | 0 | 10 | 11 | 1 | 500 | 13 | 0 | 5 | 0 |
| 22 | 0 | 11 | 5 | 2 | (560) | 14 | 11 | 8 | 0 |
| 23 | 0 | 11 | 11 | 3 | 600 | 15 | 12 | 6 | 0 |
| 24 | 0 | 12 | 6 | 0 | (672) | 17 | 10 | 0 | 0 |
| 25 | 0 | 13 | 0 | 1 | 700 | 18 | 4 | 7 | 0 |
| 26 | 0 | 13 | 6 | 2 | (784) | 20 | 8 | 4 | 0 |
| 27 | 0 | 14 | 0 | 3 | 800 | 20 | 16 | 8 | 0 |
| (28) | 0 | 14 | 7 | 0 | (896) | 23 | 6 | 8 | 0 |
| 29 | 0 | 15 | 1 | 1 | 900 | 23 | 8 | 9 | 0 |
| 30 | 0 | 15 | 7 | 2 | 1000 | 26 | 0 | 10 | 0 |
| 31 | 0 | 16 | 1 | 3 | 2000 | 52 | 1 | 8 | 0 |
| 32 | 0 | 16 | 8 | 0 | 3000 | 78 | 2 | 6 | 0 |
| 33 | 0 | 17 | 2 | 1 | 4000 | 104 | 3 | 4 | 0 |
| 34 | 0 | 17 | 8 | 2 | 5000 | 130 | 4 | 2 | 0 |
| 35 | 0 | 18 | 2 | 3 | 10000 | 260 | 8 | 4 | 0 |

## *Six-pence-Half-peny.*

| | l. | s. | d. | q. | | l. | s. | d. | q. |
|---|---|---|---|---|---|---|---|---|---|
| 1 | 0 | 0 | 6 | 2 | 36 | 0 | 19 | 6 | 0 |
| 2 | 0 | 1 | 1 | 0 | 37 | 1 | 0 | 0 | 2 |
| 3 | 0 | 1 | 7 | 2 | 38 | 1 | 0 | 7 | 0 |
| 4 | 0 | 2 | 2 | 0 | 39 | 1 | 1 | 1 | 2 |
| 5 | 0 | 2 | 8 | 2 | 40 | 1 | 1 | 8 | 0 |
| 6 | 0 | 3 | 3 | 0 | 50 | 1 | 7 | 1 | 0 |
| 7 | 0 | 3 | 9 | 2 | (56) | 1 | 10 | 4 | 0 |
| 8 | 0 | 4 | 4 | 0 | 60 | 1 | 12 | 6 | 0 |
| 9 | 0 | 4 | 10 | 2 | 70 | 1 | 17 | 11 | 0 |
| 10 | 0 | 5 | 5 | 0 | 80 | 2 | 3 | 4 | 0 |
| 11 | 0 | 5 | 11 | 2 | (84) | 2 | 5 | 6 | 0 |
| 12 | 0 | 6 | 6 | 0 | 90 | 2 | 8 | 9 | 0 |
| 13 | 0 | 7 | 0 | 2 | 100 | 2 | 14 | 2 | 0 |
| 14 | 0 | 7 | 7 | 0 | (112) | 3 | 0 | 8 | 0 |
| 15 | 0 | 8 | 1 | 2 | 200 | 5 | 8 | 4 | 0 |
| 16 | 0 | 8 | 8 | 0 | (224) | 6 | 1 | 4 | 0 |
| 17 | 0 | 9 | 2 | 2 | 300 | 8 | 2 | 6 | 0 |
| 18 | 0 | 9 | 9 | 0 | (336) | 9 | 2 | 0 | 0 |
| 19 | 0 | 10 | 3 | 2 | 400 | 10 | 16 | 8 | 0 |
| 20 | 0 | 10 | 10 | 0 | (448) | 12 | 2 | 8 | 0 |
| 21 | 0 | 11 | 4 | 2 | 500 | 13 | 10 | 10 | 0 |
| 22 | 0 | 11 | 11 | 0 | (560) | 15 | 3 | 4 | 0 |
| 23 | 0 | 12 | 5 | 2 | 600 | 16 | 5 | 0 | 0 |
| 24 | 0 | 13 | 0 | 0 | (672) | 18 | 4 | 0 | 0 |
| 25 | 0 | 13 | 6 | 2 | 700 | 18 | 19 | 2 | 0 |
| 26 | 0 | 14 | 1 | 0 | (784) | 21 | 4 | 8 | 0 |
| 27 | 0 | 14 | 7 | 2 | 800 | 21 | 13 | 4 | 0 |
| (28) | 0 | 15 | 2 | 0 | (896) | 24 | 5 | 4 | 0 |
| 29 | 0 | 15 | 8 | 2 | 900 | 24 | 7 | 6 | 0 |
| 30 | 0 | 16 | 3 | 0 | 1000 | 27 | 1 | 8 | 0 |
| 31 | 0 | 16 | 9 | 2 | 2000 | 54 | 3 | 4 | 0 |
| 32 | 0 | 17 | 4 | 0 | 3000 | 81 | 5 | 0 | 0 |
| 33 | 0 | 17 | 10 | 2 | 4000 | 108 | 6 | 8 | 0 |
| 34 | 0 | 18 | 5 | 0 | 5000 | 135 | 8 | 4 | 0 |
| 35 | 0 | 18 | 11 | 2 | 10000 | 270 | 16 | 8 | 0 |

## *Six-pence Three Farthings.*

| | l. | s. | d. | q. | | l. | s. | d. | q. |
|---|---|---|---|---|---|---|---|---|---|
| 1 | 0 | 0 | 6 | 3 | 36 | 1 | 0 | 3 | 0 |
| 2 | 0 | 1 | 1 | 2 | 37 | 1 | 0 | 9 | 3 |
| 3 | 0 | 1 | 8 | 1 | 38 | 1 | 1 | 4 | 2 |
| 4 | 0 | 2 | 3 | 0 | 39 | 1 | 1 | 11 | 1 |
| 5 | 0 | 2 | 9 | 3 | 40 | 1 | 2 | 6 | 0 |
| 6 | 0 | 3 | 4 | 2 | 50 | 1 | 8 | 1 | 2 |
| 7 | 0 | 3 | 11 | 1 | (56) | 1 | 11 | 6 | 0 |
| | 0 | 4 | 6 | 0 | 60 | 1 | 13 | 9 | 0 |
| | 0 | 5 | 0 | 3 | 70 | 1 | 19 | 4 | 2 |
| 10 | 0 | 5 | 7 | 2 | 80 | 2 | 5 | 0 | 0 |
| 11 | 0 | 6 | 2 | 1 | (84) | 2 | 7 | 3 | 0 |
| 12 | 0 | 6 | 9 | 0 | 90 | 2 | 10 | 7 | 2 |
| 13 | 0 | 7 | 3 | 3 | 100 | 2 | 16 | 3 | 0 |
| 14 | 0 | 7 | 10 | 2 | (112) | 3 | 3 | 0 | 0 |
| 15 | 0 | 8 | 5 | 1 | 200 | 5 | 12 | 6 | 0 |
| 16 | 0 | 9 | 0 | 0 | (224) | 6 | 6 | 0 | 0 |
| 17 | 0 | 9 | 6 | 3 | 300 | 8 | 8 | 9 | 0 |
| 18 | 0 | 10 | 1 | 2 | (336) | 9 | 9 | 0 | 0 |
| 19 | 0 | 10 | 8 | 1 | 400 | 11 | 5 | 0 | 0 |
| 20 | 0 | 11 | 3 | 0 | (448) | 12 | 12 | 0 | 0 |
| 21 | 0 | 11 | 9 | 3 | 500 | 14 | 1 | 3 | 0 |
| 22 | 0 | 12 | 4 | 2 | (560) | 15 | 15 | 0 | 0 |
| 23 | 0 | 12 | 11 | 1 | 600 | 16 | 17 | 6 | 0 |
| 24 | 0 | 13 | 6 | 0 | (672) | 18 | 18 | 0 | 0 |
| 25 | 0 | 14 | 0 | 3 | 700 | 19 | 13 | 9 | 0 |
| 26 | 0 | 14 | 7 | 2 | (784) | 22 | 1 | 0 | 0 |
| 27 | 0 | 15 | 2 | 1 | 800 | 22 | 10 | 0 | 0 |
| (28) | 0 | 15 | 9 | 0 | (896) | 25 | 4 | 0 | 0 |
| 29 | 0 | 16 | 3 | 3 | 900 | 25 | 6 | 3 | 0 |
| 30 | 0 | 16 | 10 | 2 | 1000 | 28 | 2 | 6 | 0 |
| 31 | 0 | 17 | 5 | 1 | 2000 | 56 | 5 | 0 | 0 |
| 32 | 0 | 18 | 0 | 0 | 3000 | 84 | 7 | 6 | 0 |
| 33 | 0 | 18 | 6 | 3 | 4000 | 112 | 10 | 0 | 0 |
| 34 | 0 | 19 | 1 | 2 | 5000 | 140 | 12 | 6 | 0 |
| 35 | 0 | 19 | 8 | 1 | 10000 | 281 | 5 | 0 | 0 |

## *Seven-Pence.*

| | l. | s. | d. | | l. | s. | d. |
|---|---|---|---|---|---|---|---|
| 1 | 0 | 0 | 7 | 36 | 1 | 1 | 0 |
| 2 | 0 | 1 | 2 | 37 | 1 | 1 | 7 |
| 3 | 0 | 1 | 9 | 38 | 1 | 2 | 2 |
| 4 | 0 | 2 | 4 | 39 | 1 | 2 | 9 |
| 5 | 0 | 2 | 11 | 40 | 1 | 3 | 4 |
| 6 | 0 | 3 | 6 | 50 | 1 | 9 | 2 |
| 7 | 0 | 4 | 1 | (56) | 1 | 12 | 8 |
| 8 | 0 | 4 | 8 | 60 | 1 | 15 | 0 |
| 9 | 0 | 5 | 3 | 70 | 2 | 0 | 10 |
| 10 | 0 | 5 | 10 | 80 | 2 | 6 | 8 |
| 11 | 0 | 6 | 5 | (84) | 2 | 9 | 0 |
| 12 | 0 | 7 | 0 | 90 | 2 | 12 | 6 |
| 13 | 0 | 7 | 7 | 100 | 2 | 18 | 4 |
| 14 | 0 | 8 | 2 | (112) | 3 | 5 | 4 |
| 15 | 0 | 8 | 9 | 200 | 5 | 16 | 8 |
| 16 | 0 | 9 | 4 | (224) | 6 | 10 | 8 |
| 17 | 0 | 9 | 11 | 300 | 8 | 15 | 0 |
| 18 | 0 | 10 | 6 | (336) | 9 | 16 | 0 |
| 19 | 0 | 11 | 1 | 400 | 11 | 13 | 4 |
| 20 | 0 | 11 | 8 | (448) | 13 | 1 | 4 |
| 21 | 0 | 12 | 3 | 500 | 14 | 11 | 8 |
| 22 | 0 | 12 | 10 | (560) | 16 | 6 | 8 |
| 23 | 0 | 13 | 5 | 600 | 17 | 10 | 0 |
| 24 | 0 | 14 | 0 | (672) | 19 | 12 | 0 |
| 25 | 0 | 14 | 7 | 700 | 20 | 8 | 4 |
| 26 | 0 | 15 | 2 | (784) | 22 | 17 | 4 |
| 27 | 0 | 15 | 9 | 800 | 23 | 6 | 8 |
| (28) | 0 | 16 | 4 | (896) | 26 | 2 | 8 |
| 29 | 0 | 16 | 11 | 900 | 26 | 5 | 0 |
| 30 | 0 | 17 | 6 | 1000 | 29 | 3 | 4 |
| 31 | 0 | 18 | 1 | 2000 | 58 | 6 | 8 |
| 32 | 0 | 18 | 8 | 3000 | 87 | 10 | 0 |
| 33 | 0 | 19 | 3 | 4000 | 116 | 13 | 4 |
| 34 | 0 | 19 | 10 | 5000 | 145 | 16 | 8 |
| 35 | 1 | 0 | 5 | 10000 | 291 | 13 | 4 |

## *Seven-pence Farthing.*

| | l. | s. | d. | q. | | l. | s. | d. | q. |
|---|---|---|---|---|---|---|---|---|---|
| 1 | 0 | 0 | 7 | 1 | 36 | 1 | 1 | 9 | 0 |
| [illegible] | 0 | 1 | 2 | 2 | 37 | 1 | 2 | 4 | 1 |
| [illegible] | 0 | 1 | 9 | 3 | 38 | 1 | 2 | 11 | 2 |
| [illegible] | 0 | 2 | 5 | 0 | 39 | 1 | 3 | 6 | 3 |
| [illegible] | 0 | 3 | 0 | 1 | 40 | 1 | 4 | 2 | 0 |
| [illegible] | 0 | 3 | 7 | 2 | 50 | 1 | 10 | 2 | 2 |
| [illegible] | 0 | 4 | 2 | 3 | (56) | 1 | 13 | 10 | 0 |
| [illegible] | 0 | 4 | 10 | 0 | 60 | 1 | 16 | 3 | 0 |
| 9 | 0 | 5 | 5 | 1 | 70 | 2 | 2 | 3 | 2 |
| 10 | 0 | 6 | 0 | 2 | 80 | 2 | 8 | 4 | 0 |
| 11 | 0 | 6 | 7 | 3 | (84) | 2 | 10 | 9 | 0 |
| 12 | 0 | 7 | 3 | 0 | 90 | 2 | 14 | 4 | 2 |
| 13 | 0 | 7 | 10 | 1 | 100 | 3 | 0 | 5 | 0 |
| 14 | 0 | 8 | 5 | 2 | (112) | 3 | 7 | 8 | 0 |
| 15 | 0 | 9 | 0 | 3 | 200 | 6 | 0 | 10 | 0 |
| 16 | 0 | 9 | 8 | 0 | (224) | 6 | 15 | 4 | 0 |
| 17 | 0 | 10 | 3 | 1 | 300 | 9 | 1 | 3 | 0 |
| 18 | 0 | 10 | 10 | 2 | (336) | 10 | 3 | 0 | 0 |
| 19 | 0 | 11 | 5 | 3 | 400 | 12 | 1 | 8 | 0 |
| 20 | 0 | 12 | 1 | 0 | (448) | 13 | 10 | 8 | 0 |
| 21 | 0 | 12 | 8 | 1 | 500 | 15 | 2 | 1 | 0 |
| 22 | 0 | 13 | 3 | 2 | (560) | 16 | 18 | 4 | 0 |
| 23 | 0 | 13 | 10 | 3 | 600 | 18 | 2 | 6 | 0 |
| 24 | 0 | 14 | 6 | 0 | (672) | 20 | 6 | 0 | 0 |
| 25 | 0 | 15 | 1 | 1 | 700 | 21 | 2 | 11 | 0 |
| 26 | 0 | 15 | 8 | 2 | (784) | 23 | 13 | 8 | 0 |
| 27 | 0 | 16 | 3 | 3 | 800 | 24 | 3 | 4 | 0 |
| (28) | 0 | 16 | 11 | 0 | (896) | 27 | 1 | 4 | 0 |
| 29 | 0 | 17 | 6 | 1 | 900 | 27 | 3 | 9 | 0 |
| 30 | 0 | 18 | 1 | 2 | 1000 | 30 | 4 | 2 | 0 |
| 31 | 0 | 18 | 8 | 3 | 2000 | 60 | 8 | 4 | 0 |
| 32 | 0 | 19 | 4 | 0 | 3000 | 90 | 12 | 6 | 0 |
| 33 | 0 | 19 | 11 | 1 | 4000 | 120 | 16 | 8 | 0 |
| 34 | 1 | 0 | 6 | 2 | 5000 | 151 | 0 | 10 | 0 |
| 35 | 1 | 1 | 1 | 3 | 10000 | 302 | 1 | 8 | 0 |

## Seven-pence Half-peny.

| | l. | s. | d. | q. | | l. | s. | d. | q. |
|---|---|---|---|---|---|---|---|---|---|
| 1 | 0 | 0 | 7 | 2 | 36 | 1 | 2 | 6 | 0 |
| 2 | 0 | 1 | 3 | 0 | 37 | 1 | 3 | 1 | 2 |
| 3 | 0 | 1 | 10 | 2 | 38 | 1 | 3 | 9 | 0 |
| 4 | 0 | 2 | 6 | 0 | 39 | 1 | 4 | 4 | 2 |
| 5 | 0 | 3 | 1 | 2 | 40 | 1 | 5 | 0 | 0 |
| 6 | 0 | 3 | 9 | 0 | 50 | 1 | 11 | 3 | 0 |
| 7 | 0 | 4 | 4 | 2 | (56) | 1 | 15 | 0 | 0 |
| 8 | 0 | 5 | 0 | 0 | 60 | 1 | 17 | 6 | 0 |
| 9 | 0 | 5 | 7 | 2 | 70 | 2 | 3 | 9 | 0 |
| 10 | 0 | 6 | 3 | 0 | 80 | 2 | 10 | 0 | 0 |
| 11 | 0 | 6 | 10 | 2 | (84) | 2 | 12 | 6 | 0 |
| 12 | 0 | 7 | 6 | 0 | 90 | 2 | 16 | 3 | 0 |
| 13 | 0 | 8 | 1 | 2 | 100 | 3 | 2 | 6 | 0 |
| 14 | 0 | 8 | 9 | 0 | (112) | 3 | 10 | 0 | 0 |
| 15 | 0 | 9 | 4 | 2 | 200 | 6 | 5 | 0 | 0 |
| 16 | 0 | 10 | 0 | 0 | (224) | 7 | 0 | 0 | 0 |
| 17 | 0 | 10 | 7 | 2 | 300 | 9 | 7 | 6 | 0 |
| 18 | 0 | 11 | 3 | 0 | (336) | 10 | 10 | 0 | 0 |
| 19 | 0 | 11 | 10 | 2 | 400 | 12 | 10 | 0 | 0 |
| 20 | 0 | 12 | 6 | 0 | (448) | 14 | 0 | 0 | 0 |
| 21 | 0 | 13 | 1 | 2 | 500 | 15 | 12 | 6 | 0 |
| 22 | 0 | 13 | 9 | 0 | (560) | 17 | 10 | 0 | 0 |
| 23 | 0 | 14 | 4 | 2 | 600 | 18 | 15 | 0 | 0 |
| 24 | 0 | 15 | 0 | 0 | (672) | 21 | 0 | 0 | 0 |
| 25 | 0 | 15 | 7 | 2 | 700 | 21 | 17 | 6 | 0 |
| 26 | 0 | 16 | 3 | 0 | (784) | 24 | 10 | 0 | 0 |
| 27 | 0 | 16 | 10 | 2 | 800 | 25 | 0 | 0 | 0 |
| (28) | 0 | 17 | 6 | 0 | (896) | 28 | 0 | 0 | 0 |
| 29 | 0 | 18 | 1 | 2 | 900 | 28 | 2 | 6 | 0 |
| 30 | 0 | 18 | 9 | 0 | 1000 | 31 | 5 | 0 | 0 |
| 31 | 0 | 19 | 4 | 2 | 2000 | 62 | 10 | 0 | 0 |
| 32 | 1 | 0 | 0 | 0 | 3000 | 93 | 15 | 0 | 0 |
| 33 | 1 | 0 | 7 | 2 | 4000 | 125 | 0 | 0 | 0 |
| 34 | 1 | 1 | 3 | 0 | 5000 | 156 | 5 | 0 | 0 |
| 35 | 1 | 1 | 10 | 2 | 10000 | 312 | 10 | 0 | 0 |

## Seven-pence Three Farthings.

| | l. | s. | d. | q. | | l. | s. | d. | q. |
|---|---|---|---|---|---|---|---|---|---|
| 1 | 0 | 0 | 7 | 3 | 36 | 1 | 3 | 3 | 0 |
| 2 | 0 | 1 | 3 | 2 | 37 | 1 | 3 | 10 | 3 |
| 3 | 0 | 1 | 11 | 1 | 38 | 1 | 4 | 6 | 2 |
| 4 | 0 | 2 | 7 | 0 | 39 | 1 | 5 | 2 | 1 |
| 5 | 0 | 3 | 2 | 3 | 40 | 1 | 5 | 10 | 0 |
| 6 | 0 | 3 | 10 | 2 | 50 | 1 | 12 | 3 | 2 |
| 7 | 0 | 4 | 6 | 1 | (56) | 1 | 16 | 2 | 0 |
| 8 | 0 | 5 | 2 | 0 | 60 | 1 | 18 | 9 | 0 |
| 9 | 0 | 5 | 9 | 3 | 70 | 2 | 5 | 2 | 2 |
| 10 | 0 | 6 | 5 | 2 | 80 | 2 | 11 | 8 | 0 |
| 11 | 0 | 7 | 1 | 1 | (84) | 2 | 14 | 3 | 0 |
| 12 | 0 | 7 | 9 | 0 | 90 | 2 | 18 | 1 | 2 |
| 13 | 0 | 8 | 4 | 3 | 100 | 3 | 4 | 7 | 0 |
| 14 | 0 | 9 | 0 | 2 | (112) | 3 | 12 | 4 | 0 |
| 15 | 0 | 9 | 8 | 1 | 200 | 6 | 9 | 2 | 0 |
| 16 | 0 | 10 | 4 | 0 | (224) | 7 | 4 | 8 | 0 |
| 17 | 0 | 10 | 11 | 3 | 300 | 9 | 13 | 9 | 0 |
| 18 | 0 | 11 | 7 | 2 | (336) | 10 | 17 | 0 | 0 |
| 19 | 0 | 12 | 3 | 1 | 400 | 12 | 18 | 4 | 0 |
| 20 | 0 | 12 | 11 | 0 | (448) | 14 | 9 | 4 | 0 |
| 21 | 0 | 13 | 6 | 3 | 500 | 16 | 2 | 11 | 0 |
| 22 | 0 | 14 | 2 | 2 | (560) | 18 | 1 | 8 | 0 |
| 23 | 0 | 14 | 10 | 1 | 600 | 19 | 7 | 6 | 0 |
| 24 | 0 | 15 | 6 | 0 | (672) | 21 | 14 | 0 | 0 |
| 25 | 0 | 16 | 1 | 3 | 700 | 22 | 12 | 1 | 0 |
| 26 | 0 | 16 | 9 | 2 | (784) | 25 | 6 | 4 | 0 |
| 27 | 0 | 17 | 5 | 1 | 800 | 25 | 16 | 8 | 0 |
| (28) | 0 | 18 | 1 | 0 | (896) | 28 | 18 | 8 | 0 |
| 29 | 0 | 18 | 8 | 3 | 900 | 29 | 1 | 3 | 0 |
| 30 | 0 | 19 | 4 | 2 | 1000 | 32 | 5 | 10 | 0 |
| 31 | 1 | 0 | 0 | 1 | 2000 | 64 | 11 | 8 | 0 |
| 32 | 1 | 0 | 8 | 0 | 3000 | 96 | 17 | 6 | 0 |
| 33 | 1 | 1 | 3 | 3 | 4000 | 129 | 3 | 4 | 0 |
| 34 | 1 | 1 | 11 | 2 | 5000 | 161 | 9 | 2 | 0 |
| 35 | 1 | 2 | 7 | 1 | 10000 | 322 | 18 | 4 | 0 |

## Eight-Pence.

| | l. | s. | d. | | l. | s. | d. |
|---|---|---|---|---|---|---|---|
| 1 | 0 | 0 | 8 | 36 | 1 | 4 | 0 |
| 2 | 0 | 1 | 4 | 37 | 1 | 4 | 8 |
| 3 | 0 | 2 | 0 | 38 | 1 | 5 | 4 |
| 4 | 0 | 2 | 8 | 39 | 1 | 6 | 0 |
| 5 | 0 | 3 | 4 | 40 | 1 | 6 | 8 |
| 6 | 0 | 4 | 0 | 50 | 1 | 13 | 4 |
| 7 | 0 | 4 | 8 | (56) | 1 | 17 | 4 |
| 8 | 0 | 5 | 4 | 60 | 2 | 0 | 0 |
| 9 | 0 | 6 | 0 | 70 | 2 | 6 | 8 |
| 10 | 0 | 6 | 8 | 80 | 2 | 13 | 4 |
| 11 | 0 | 7 | 4 | (84) | 2 | 16 | 0 |
| 12 | 0 | 8 | 0 | 90 | 3 | 0 | 0 |
| 13 | 0 | 8 | 8 | 100 | 3 | 6 | 8 |
| 14 | 0 | 9 | 4 | (112) | 3 | 14 | 8 |
| 15 | 0 | 10 | 0 | 200 | 6 | 13 | 4 |
| 16 | 0 | 10 | 8 | (224) | 7 | 9 | 4 |
| 17 | 0 | 11 | 4 | 300 | 10 | 0 | 0 |
| 18 | 0 | 12 | 0 | (336) | 11 | 4 | 0 |
| 19 | 0 | 12 | 8 | 400 | 13 | 6 | 8 |
| 20 | 0 | 13 | 4 | (448) | 14 | 18 | 8 |
| 21 | 0 | 14 | 0 | 500 | 16 | 13 | 4 |
| 22 | 0 | 14 | 8 | (560) | 18 | 13 | 4 |
| 23 | 0 | 15 | 4 | 600 | 20 | 0 | 0 |
| 24 | 0 | 16 | 0 | (672) | 22 | 8 | 0 |
| 25 | 0 | 16 | 8 | 700 | 23 | 6 | 8 |
| 26 | 0 | 17 | 4 | (784) | 26 | 2 | 8 |
| 27 | 0 | 18 | 0 | 800 | 26 | 13 | 4 |
| (28) | 0 | 18 | 8 | (896) | 29 | 17 | 4 |
| 29 | 0 | 19 | 4 | 900 | 30 | 0 | 0 |
| 30 | 1 | 0 | 0 | 1000 | 33 | 6 | 8 |
| 31 | 1 | 0 | 8 | 2000 | 66 | 13 | 4 |
| 32 | 1 | 1 | 4 | 3000 | 100 | 0 | 0 |
| 33 | 1 | 2 | 0 | 4000 | 133 | 6 | 8 |
| 34 | 1 | 2 | 8 | 5000 | 166 | 13 | 4 |
| 35 | 1 | 3 | 4 | 10000 | 333 | 6 | 8 |

## *Eight-pence Farthing.*

| | l. | s. | d. | q. | | l. | s. | d. | q. |
|---|---|---|---|---|---|---|---|---|---|
| 1 | 0 | 0 | 8 | 1 | 36 | 1 | 4 | 9 | 0 |
| 2 | 0 | 1 | 4 | 2 | 37 | 1 | 5 | 5 | 1 |
| 3 | 0 | 2 | 0 | 3 | 38 | 1 | 6 | 1 | 2 |
| 4 | 0 | 2 | 9 | 0 | 39 | 1 | 6 | 9 | 3 |
| 5 | 0 | 3 | 5 | 1 | 40 | 1 | 7 | 6 | 0 |
| 6 | 0 | 4 | 1 | 2 | 50 | 1 | 14 | 4 | 2 |
| 7 | 0 | 4 | 9 | 3 | (56) | 1 | 18 | 6 | 0 |
| 8 | 0 | 5 | 6 | 0 | 60 | 2 | 1 | 3 | 0 |
| 9 | 0 | 6 | 2 | 1 | 70 | 2 | 8 | 1 | 2 |
| 10 | 0 | 6 | 10 | 2 | 80 | 2 | 15 | 0 | 0 |
| 11 | 0 | 7 | 6 | 3 | (84) | 2 | 17 | 9 | 0 |
| 12 | 0 | 8 | 3 | 0 | 90 | 3 | 1 | 10 | 2 |
| 13 | 0 | 8 | 11 | 1 | 100 | 3 | 8 | 9 | 0 |
| 14 | 0 | 9 | 7 | 2 | (112) | 3 | 17 | 0 | 0 |
| 15 | 0 | 10 | 3 | 3 | 200 | 6 | 17 | 6 | 0 |
| 16 | 0 | 11 | 0 | 0 | (224) | 7 | 14 | 0 | 0 |
| 17 | 0 | 11 | 8 | 1 | 300 | 10 | 6 | 3 | 0 |
| 18 | 0 | 12 | 4 | 2 | (336) | 11 | 11 | 0 | 0 |
| 19 | 0 | 13 | 0 | 3 | 400 | 13 | 15 | 0 | 0 |
| 20 | 0 | 13 | 9 | 0 | (448) | 15 | 8 | 0 | 0 |
| 21 | 0 | 14 | 5 | 1 | 500 | 17 | 3 | 9 | 0 |
| 22 | 0 | 15 | 1 | 2 | (560) | 19 | 5 | 0 | 0 |
| 23 | 0 | 15 | 9 | 3 | 600 | 20 | 12 | 6 | 0 |
| 24 | 0 | 16 | 6 | 0 | (672) | 23 | 2 | 0 | 0 |
| 25 | 0 | 17 | 2 | 1 | 700 | 24 | 1 | 3 | 0 |
| 26 | 0 | 17 | 10 | 2 | (784) | 26 | 19 | 0 | 0 |
| 27 | 0 | 18 | 6 | 3 | 800 | 27 | 10 | 0 | 0 |
| (28) | 0 | 19 | 3 | 0 | (896) | 30 | 16 | 0 | 0 |
| 29 | 0 | 19 | 11 | 1 | 900 | 30 | 18 | 9 | 0 |
| 30 | 1 | 0 | 7 | 2 | 1000 | 34 | 7 | 6 | 0 |
| 31 | 1 | 1 | 3 | 3 | 2000 | 68 | 15 | 0 | 0 |
| 32 | 1 | 2 | 0 | 0 | 3000 | 103 | 2 | 6 | 0 |
| 33 | 1 | 2 | 8 | 1 | 4000 | 137 | 10 | 0 | 0 |
| 34 | 1 | 3 | 4 | 2 | 5000 | 171 | 17 | 6 | 0 |
| 35 | 1 | 4 | 0 | 3 | 10000 | 343 | 15 | 0 | 0 |

## *Eight-pence Half-peny.*

| | l. | s. | d. | q. | | l. | s. | d. | q. |
|---|---|---|---|---|---|---|---|---|---|
| 1 | 0 | 0 | 8 | 2 | 36 | 1 | 5 | 6 | 0 |
| 2 | 0 | 1 | 5 | 0 | 37 | 1 | 6 | 2 | 2 |
| 3 | 0 | 2 | 1 | 2 | 38 | 1 | 6 | 11 | 0 |
| 4 | 0 | 2 | 10 | 0 | 39 | 1 | 7 | 7 | 2 |
| 5 | 0 | 3 | 6 | 2 | 40 | 1 | 8 | 4 | 0 |
| 6 | 0 | 4 | 3 | 0 | 50 | 1 | 15 | 5 | 0 |
| 7 | 0 | 4 | 11 | 2 | (56) | 1 | 19 | 8 | 0 |
| 8 | 0 | 5 | 8 | 0 | 60 | 2 | 2 | 6 | 0 |
| 9 | 0 | 6 | 4 | 2 | 70 | 2 | 9 | 7 | 0 |
| 10 | 0 | 7 | 1 | 0 | 80 | 2 | 16 | 8 | 0 |
| 11 | 0 | 7 | 9 | 2 | (84) | 2 | 19 | 6 | 0 |
| 12 | 0 | 8 | 6 | 0 | 90 | 3 | 3 | 9 | 0 |
| 13 | 0 | 9 | 2 | 2 | 100 | 3 | 10 | 10 | 0 |
| 14 | 0 | 9 | 11 | 0 | (112) | 3 | 19 | 4 | 0 |
| 15 | 0 | 10 | 7 | 2 | 200 | 7 | 1 | 8 | 0 |
| 16 | 0 | 11 | 4 | 0 | (224) | 7 | 18 | 8 | 0 |
| 17 | 0 | 12 | 0 | 2 | 300 | 10 | 12 | 6 | 0 |
| 18 | 0 | 12 | 9 | 0 | (336) | 11 | 18 | 0 | 0 |
| 19 | 0 | 13 | 5 | 2 | 400 | 14 | 3 | 4 | 0 |
| 20 | 0 | 14 | 2 | 0 | (448) | 15 | 17 | 4 | 0 |
| 21 | 0 | 14 | 10 | 2 | 500 | 17 | 14 | 2 | 0 |
| 22 | 0 | 15 | 7 | 0 | (560) | 19 | 16 | 8 | 0 |
| 23 | 0 | 16 | 3 | 2 | 600 | 21 | 5 | 0 | 0 |
| 24 | 0 | 17 | 0 | 0 | (672) | 23 | 16 | 0 | 0 |
| 25 | 0 | 17 | 8 | 2 | 700 | 24 | 15 | 10 | 0 |
| 26 | 0 | 18 | 5 | 0 | (784) | 27 | 15 | 4 | 0 |
| 27 | 0 | 19 | 1 | 2 | 800 | 28 | 6 | 8 | 0 |
| (28) | 0 | 19 | 10 | 0 | (896) | 31 | 14 | 8 | 0 |
| 29 | 1 | 0 | 6 | 2 | 900 | 31 | 17 | 6 | 0 |
| 30 | 1 | 1 | 3 | 0 | 1000 | 35 | 8 | 4 | 0 |
| 31 | 1 | 1 | 11 | 2 | 2000 | 70 | 16 | 8 | 0 |
| 32 | 1 | 2 | 8 | 0 | 3000 | 106 | 5 | 0 | 0 |
| 33 | 1 | 3 | 4 | 2 | 4000 | 141 | 13 | 4 | 0 |
| 34 | 1 | 4 | 1 | 0 | 5000 | 177 | 1 | 8 | 0 |
| 35 | 1 | 4 | 9 | 2 | 10000 | 354 | 3 | 4 | 0 |

## *Eight-pence Three Farthings.*

| | l. | s. | d. | q. | | l. | s. | d. | q. |
|---|---|---|---|---|---|---|---|---|---|
| 1 | 0 | 0 | 8 | 3 | 36 | 1 | 6 | 3 | 0 |
| 2 | 0 | 1 | 5 | 2 | 37 | 1 | 6 | 11 | 3 |
| 3 | 0 | 2 | 2 | 1 | 38 | 1 | 7 | 8 | 2 |
| 4 | 0 | 2 | 11 | 0 | 39 | 1 | 8 | 5 | 1 |
| 5 | 0 | 3 | 7 | 3 | 40 | 1 | 9 | 2 | 0 |
| 6 | 0 | 4 | 4 | 2 | 50 | 1 | 16 | 5 | 2 |
| 7 | 0 | 5 | 1 | 1 | (56) | 2 | 0 | 10 | 0 |
| 8 | 0 | 5 | 10 | 0 | 60 | 2 | 3 | 9 | 0 |
| 9 | 0 | 6 | 6 | 3 | 70 | 2 | 11 | 0 | 2 |
| 10 | 0 | 7 | 3 | 2 | 80 | 2 | 18 | 4 | 0 |
| 11 | 0 | 8 | 0 | 1 | (84) | 3 | 1 | 3 | 0 |
| 12 | 0 | 8 | 9 | 0 | 90 | 3 | 5 | 7 | 2 |
| 13 | 0 | 9 | 5 | 3 | 100 | 3 | 12 | 11 | 0 |
| 14 | 0 | 10 | 2 | 2 | (112) | 4 | 1 | 8 | 0 |
| 15 | 0 | 10 | 11 | 1 | 200 | 7 | 5 | 10 | 0 |
| 16 | 0 | 11 | 8 | 0 | (224) | 8 | 3 | 4 | 0 |
| 17 | 0 | 12 | 4 | 3 | 300 | 10 | 18 | 9 | 0 |
| 18 | 0 | 13 | 1 | 2 | (336) | 12 | 5 | 0 | 0 |
| 19 | 0 | 13 | 10 | 1 | 400 | 14 | 11 | 8 | 0 |
| 20 | 0 | 14 | 7 | 0 | (448) | 16 | 6 | 8 | 0 |
| 21 | 0 | 15 | 3 | 3 | 500 | 18 | 4 | 7 | 0 |
| 22 | 0 | 16 | 0 | 2 | (560) | 20 | 8 | 4 | 0 |
| 23 | 0 | 16 | 9 | 1 | 600 | 21 | 17 | 6 | 0 |
| 24 | 0 | 17 | 6 | 0 | (672) | 24 | 10 | 0 | 0 |
| 25 | 0 | 18 | 2 | 3 | 700 | 25 | 10 | 5 | 0 |
| 26 | 0 | 18 | 11 | 2 | (784) | 28 | 11 | 8 | 0 |
| 27 | 0 | 19 | 8 | 1 | 800 | 29 | 3 | 4 | 0 |
| (28) | 1 | 0 | 5 | 0 | (896) | 32 | 13 | 4 | 0 |
| 29 | 1 | 1 | 1 | 3 | 900 | 32 | 16 | 3 | 0 |
| 30 | 1 | 1 | 10 | 2 | 1000 | 36 | 9 | 2 | 0 |
| 31 | 1 | 2 | 7 | 1 | 2000 | 72 | 18 | 4 | 0 |
| 32 | 1 | 3 | 4 | 0 | 3000 | 109 | 7 | 6 | 0 |
| 33 | 1 | 4 | 0 | 3 | 4000 | 145 | 16 | 8 | 0 |
| 34 | 1 | 4 | 9 | 2 | 5000 | 182 | 5 | 10 | 0 |
| 35 | 1 | 5 | 6 | 1 | 10000 | 364 | 11 | 8 | 0 |

## Nine-Pence.

| | l. | s. | d. | | l. | s. | d. |
|---|---|---|---|---|---|---|---|
| 1 | 0 | 0 | 9 | 36 | 1 | 7 | 0 |
| 2 | 0 | 1 | 6 | 37 | 1 | 7 | 9 |
| 3 | 0 | 2 | 3 | 38 | 1 | 8 | 6 |
| 4 | 0 | 3 | 0 | 39 | 1 | 9 | 3 |
| 5 | 0 | 3 | 9 | 40 | 1 | 10 | 0 |
| 6 | 0 | 4 | 6 | 50 | 1 | 17 | 6 |
| 7 | 0 | 5 | 3 | (56) | 2 | 2 | 0 |
| 8 | 0 | 6 | 0 | 60 | 2 | 5 | 0 |
| 9 | 0 | 6 | 9 | 70 | 2 | 12 | 6 |
| 10 | 0 | 7 | 6 | 80 | 3 | 0 | 0 |
| 11 | 0 | 8 | 3 | (84) | 3 | 3 | 0 |
| 12 | 0 | 9 | 0 | 90 | 3 | 7 | 6 |
| 13 | 0 | 9 | 9 | 100 | 3 | 15 | 0 |
| 14 | 0 | 10 | 6 | (112) | 4 | 4 | 0 |
| 15 | 0 | 11 | 3 | 200 | 7 | 10 | 0 |
| 16 | 0 | 12 | 0 | (224) | 8 | 8 | 0 |
| 17 | 0 | 12 | 9 | 300 | 11 | 5 | 0 |
| 18 | 0 | 13 | 6 | (336) | 12 | 12 | 0 |
| 19 | 0 | 14 | 3 | 400 | 15 | 0 | 0 |
| 20 | 0 | 15 | 0 | (448) | 16 | 16 | 0 |
| 21 | 0 | 15 | 9 | 500 | 18 | 15 | 0 |
| 22 | 0 | 16 | 6 | (560) | 21 | 0 | 0 |
| 23 | 0 | 17 | 3 | 600 | 22 | 10 | 0 |
| 24 | 0 | 18 | 0 | (672) | 25 | 4 | 0 |
| 25 | 0 | 18 | 9 | 700 | 26 | 5 | 0 |
| 26 | 0 | 19 | 6 | (784) | 29 | 8 | 0 |
| 27 | 1 | 0 | 3 | 800 | 30 | 0 | 0 |
| (28) | 1 | 1 | 0 | (896) | 33 | 12 | 0 |
| 29 | 1 | 1 | 9 | 900 | 33 | 15 | 0 |
| 30 | 1 | 2 | 6 | 1000 | 37 | 10 | 0 |
| 31 | 1 | 3 | 3 | 2000 | 75 | 0 | 0 |
| 32 | 1 | 4 | 0 | 3000 | 112 | 10 | 0 |
| 33 | 1 | 4 | 9 | 4000 | 150 | 0 | 0 |
| 34 | 1 | 5 | 6 | 5000 | 187 | 10 | 0 |
| 35 | 1 | 6 | 3 | 10000 | 375 | 0 | 0 |

## *Nine-pence Farthing.*

| | l. | s. | d. | q. | | l. | s. | d. | q. |
|---|---|---|---|---|---|---|---|---|---|
| 1 | 0 | 0 | 9 | 1 | 36 | 1 | 7 | 9 | 0 |
| 2 | 0 | 1 | 6 | 2 | 37 | 1 | 8 | 6 | 1 |
| 3 | 0 | 2 | 3 | 3 | 38 | 1 | 9 | 3 | 2 |
| 4 | 0 | 3 | 1 | 0 | 39 | 1 | 10 | 0 | 3 |
| 5 | 0 | 3 | 10 | 1 | 40 | 1 | 10 | 10 | 0 |
| 6 | 0 | 4 | 7 | 2 | 50 | 1 | 18 | 6 | 2 |
| 7 | 0 | 5 | 4 | 3 | (56) | 2 | 3 | 2 | 0 |
| 8 | 0 | 6 | 2 | 0 | 60 | 2 | 6 | 3 | 0 |
| 9 | 0 | 6 | 11 | 1 | 70 | 2 | 13 | 11 | 2 |
| 10 | 0 | 7 | 8 | 2 | 80 | 3 | 1 | 8 | 0 |
| 11 | 0 | 8 | 5 | 3 | (84) | 3 | 4 | 9 | 0 |
| 12 | 0 | 9 | 3 | 0 | 90 | 3 | 9 | 4 | 2 |
| 13 | 0 | 10 | 0 | 1 | 100 | 3 | 17 | 1 | 0 |
| 14 | 0 | 10 | 9 | 2 | (112) | 4 | 6 | 4 | 0 |
| 15 | 0 | 11 | 6 | 3 | 200 | 7 | 14 | 2 | 0 |
| 16 | 0 | 12 | 4 | 0 | (224) | 8 | 12 | 8 | 0 |
| 17 | 0 | 13 | 1 | 1 | 300 | 11 | 11 | 3 | 0 |
| 18 | 0 | 13 | 10 | 2 | (336) | 12 | 19 | 0 | 0 |
| 19 | 0 | 14 | 7 | 3 | 400 | 15 | 8 | 4 | 0 |
| 20 | 0 | 15 | 5 | 0 | (448) | 17 | 5 | 4 | 0 |
| 21 | 0 | 16 | 2 | 1 | 500 | 19 | 5 | 5 | 0 |
| 22 | 0 | 16 | 11 | 2 | (560) | 21 | 11 | 8 | 0 |
| 23 | 0 | 17 | 8 | 3 | 600 | 23 | 2 | 6 | 0 |
| 24 | 0 | 18 | 6 | 0 | (672) | 25 | 18 | 0 | 0 |
| 25 | 0 | 19 | 3 | 1 | 700 | 26 | 19 | 7 | 0 |
| 26 | 1 | 0 | 0 | 2 | (784) | 30 | 4 | 4 | 0 |
| 27 | 1 | 0 | 9 | 3 | 800 | 30 | 16 | 8 | 0 |
| (28) | 1 | 1 | 7 | 0 | (896) | 34 | 16 | 8 | 0 |
| 29 | 1 | 2 | 4 | 1 | 900 | 34 | 13 | 9 | 0 |
| 30 | 1 | 3 | 1 | 2 | 1000 | 38 | 10 | 10 | 0 |
| 31 | 1 | 3 | 10 | 3 | 2000 | 77 | 1 | 8 | 0 |
| 32 | 1 | 4 | 8 | 0 | 3000 | 115 | 12 | 6 | 0 |
| 33 | 1 | 5 | 5 | 1 | 4000 | 154 | 3 | 4 | 0 |
| 34 | 1 | 6 | 2 | 2 | 5000 | 192 | 14 | 2 | 0 |
| 35 | 1 | 6 | 11 | 3 | 10000 | 385 | 8 | 4 | 0 |

## *Nine-pence Half-peny.*

| | l. | s. | d. | q. | | l. | s. | d. | q. |
|---|---|---|---|---|---|---|---|---|---|
| 1 | 0 | 0 | 9 | 2 | 36 | 1 | 8 | 6 | 0 |
| 2 | 0 | 1 | 7 | 0 | 37 | 1 | 9 | 3 | 2 |
| 3 | 0 | 2 | 4 | 2 | 38 | 1 | 10 | 1 | 0 |
| 4 | 0 | 3 | 2 | 0 | 39 | 1 | 10 | 10 | 2 |
| 5 | 0 | 3 | 11 | 2 | 40 | 1 | 11 | 8 | 0 |
| 6 | 0 | 4 | 9 | 0 | 50 | 1 | 19 | 7 | 0 |
| 7 | 0 | 5 | 6 | 2 | (56) | 2 | 4 | 4 | 0 |
| 8 | 0 | 6 | 4 | 0 | 60 | 2 | 7 | 6 | 0 |
| 9 | 0 | 7 | 1 | 2 | 70 | 2 | 15 | 5 | 0 |
| 10 | 0 | 7 | 11 | 0 | 80 | 3 | 3 | 4 | 0 |
| 11 | 0 | 8 | 8 | 2 | (84) | 3 | 6 | 6 | 0 |
| 12 | 0 | 9 | 6 | 0 | 90 | 3 | 11 | 3 | 0 |
| 13 | 0 | 10 | 3 | 2 | 100 | 3 | 19 | 2 | 0 |
| 14 | 0 | 11 | 1 | 0 | (112) | 4 | 8 | 8 | 0 |
| 15 | 0 | 11 | 10 | 2 | 200 | 7 | 18 | 4 | 0 |
| 16 | 0 | 12 | 8 | 0 | (224) | 8 | 17 | 4 | 0 |
| 17 | 0 | 13 | 5 | 2 | 300 | 11 | 17 | 6 | 0 |
| 18 | 0 | 14 | 3 | 0 | (336) | 13 | 6 | 0 | 0 |
| 19 | 0 | 15 | 0 | 2 | 400 | 15 | 16 | 8 | 0 |
| 20 | 0 | 15 | 10 | 0 | (448) | 17 | 14 | 8 | 0 |
| 21 | 0 | 16 | 7 | 2 | 500 | 19 | 15 | 10 | 0 |
| 22 | 0 | 17 | 5 | 0 | (560) | 22 | 3 | 4 | 0 |
| 23 | 0 | 18 | 2 | 2 | 600 | 23 | 15 | 0 | 0 |
| 24 | 0 | 19 | 0 | 0 | (672) | 26 | 12 | 0 | 0 |
| 25 | 0 | 19 | 9 | 2 | 700 | 27 | 14 | 2 | 0 |
| 26 | 1 | 0 | 7 | 0 | (784) | 31 | 0 | 8 | 0 |
| 27 | 1 | 1 | 4 | 2 | 800 | 31 | 13 | 4 | 0 |
| (28) | 1 | 2 | 2 | 0 | (896) | 35 | 9 | 4 | 0 |
| 29 | 1 | 2 | 11 | 2 | 900 | 35 | 12 | 6 | 0 |
| 30 | 1 | 3 | 9 | 0 | 1000 | 39 | 11 | 8 | 0 |
| 31 | 1 | 4 | 6 | 2 | 2000 | 79 | 3 | 4 | 0 |
| 32 | 1 | 5 | 4 | 0 | 3000 | 118 | 15 | 0 | 0 |
| 33 | 1 | 6 | 1 | 2 | 4000 | 158 | 6 | 8 | 0 |
| 34 | 1 | 6 | 11 | 0 | 5000 | 197 | 18 | 4 | 0 |
| 35 | 1 | 7 | 8 | 2 | 10000 | 395 | 16 | 8 | 0 |

## *Nine-pence Three Farthings.*

| | l. | s. | d. | q. | | l. | s. | d. | q. |
|---|---|---|---|---|---|---|---|---|---|
| 1 | 0 | 0 | 9 | 3 | 36 | 1 | 9 | 3 | 0 |
| 2 | 0 | 1 | 7 | 2 | 37 | 1 | 10 | 0 | 3 |
| 3 | 0 | 2 | 5 | 1 | 38 | 1 | 10 | 10 | 2 |
| 4 | 0 | 3 | 3 | 0 | 39 | 1 | 11 | 8 | 1 |
| 5 | 0 | 4 | 0 | 3 | 40 | 1 | 12 | 6 | 0 |
| 6 | 0 | 4 | 10 | 2 | 50 | 2 | 0 | 7 | 2 |
| 7 | 0 | 5 | 8 | 1 | (56) | 2 | 5 | 6 | 0 |
| 8 | 0 | 6 | 6 | 0 | 60 | 2 | 8 | 9 | 0 |
| 9 | 0 | 7 | 3 | 3 | 70 | 2 | 16 | 10 | 2 |
| 10 | 0 | 8 | 1 | 2 | 80 | 3 | 5 | 0 | 0 |
| 11 | 0 | 8 | 11 | 1 | (84) | 3 | 8 | 3 | 0 |
| 12 | 0 | 9 | 9 | 0 | 90 | 3 | 13 | 1 | 2 |
| 13 | 0 | 10 | 6 | 3 | 100 | 4 | 1 | 3 | 0 |
| 14 | 0 | 11 | 4 | 2 | (112) | 4 | 11 | 0 | 0 |
| 15 | 0 | 12 | 2 | 1 | 200 | 8 | 2 | 6 | 0 |
| 16 | 0 | 13 | 0 | 0 | (224) | 9 | 2 | 0 | 0 |
| 17 | 0 | 13 | 9 | 3 | 300 | 12 | 3 | 9 | 0 |
| 18 | 0 | 14 | 7 | 2 | (336) | 13 | 13 | 0 | 0 |
| 19 | 0 | 15 | 5 | 1 | 400 | 16 | 5 | 0 | 0 |
| 20 | 0 | 16 | 3 | 0 | (448) | 18 | 4 | 0 | 0 |
| 21 | 0 | 17 | 0 | 3 | 500 | 20 | 6 | 3 | 0 |
| 22 | 0 | 17 | 10 | 2 | (560) | 22 | 15 | 0 | 0 |
| 23 | 0 | 18 | 8 | 1 | 600 | 24 | 7 | 6 | 0 |
| 24 | 0 | 19 | 6 | 0 | (672) | 27 | 6 | 0 | 0 |
| 25 | 1 | 0 | 3 | 3 | 700 | 28 | 8 | 9 | 0 |
| 26 | 1 | 1 | 1 | 2 | (784) | 31 | 17 | 0 | 0 |
| 27 | 1 | 1 | 11 | 1 | 800 | 32 | 10 | 0 | 0 |
| (28) | 1 | 2 | 9 | 0 | (896) | 36 | 8 | 0 | 0 |
| 29 | 1 | 3 | 6 | 3 | 900 | 36 | 11 | 3 | 0 |
| 30 | 1 | 4 | 4 | 2 | 1000 | 40 | 12 | 6 | 0 |
| 31 | 1 | 5 | 2 | 1 | 2000 | 81 | 5 | 0 | 0 |
| 32 | 1 | 6 | 0 | 0 | 3000 | 121 | 17 | 6 | 0 |
| 33 | 1 | 6 | 9 | 3 | 4000 | 162 | 10 | 0 | 0 |
| 34 | 1 | 7 | 7 | 2 | 5000 | 203 | 2 | 6 | 0 |
| 35 | 1 | 8 | 5 | 1 | 10000 | 406 | 5 | 0 | 0 |

## *Ten-Pence.*

| | l. | s. | d. | | l. | s. | d. |
|---|---|---|---|---|---|---|---|
| 1 | 0 | 0 | 10 | 36 | 1 | 10 | 0 |
| 2 | 0 | 1 | 8 | 37 | 1 | 10 | 10 |
| 3 | 0 | 2 | 6 | 38 | 1 | 11 | 8 |
| 4 | 0 | 3 | 4 | 39 | 1 | 12 | 6 |
| 5 | 0 | 4 | 2 | 40 | 1 | 13 | 4 |
| 6 | 0 | 5 | 0 | 50 | 2 | 1 | 8 |
| 7 | 0 | 5 | 10 | (56) | 2 | 6 | 8 |
| 8 | 0 | 6 | 8 | 60 | 2 | 10 | 0 |
| 9 | 0 | 7 | 6 | 70 | 2 | 18 | 4 |
| 10 | 0 | 8 | 4 | 80 | 3 | 6 | 8 |
| 11 | 0 | 9 | 2 | (84) | 3 | 10 | 0 |
| 12 | 0 | 10 | 0 | 90 | 3 | 15 | 0 |
| 13 | 0 | 10 | 10 | 100 | 4 | 3 | 4 |
| 14 | 0 | 11 | 8 | (112) | 4 | 13 | 4 |
| 15 | 0 | 12 | 6 | 200 | 8 | 6 | 8 |
| 16 | 0 | 13 | 4 | (224) | 9 | 6 | 8 |
| 17 | 0 | 14 | 2 | 300 | 12 | 10 | 0 |
| 18 | 0 | 15 | 0 | (336) | 14 | 0 | 0 |
| 19 | 0 | 15 | 10 | 400 | 16 | 13 | 4 |
| 20 | 0 | 16 | 8 | (448) | 18 | 13 | 4 |
| 21 | 0 | 17 | 6 | 500 | 20 | 16 | 8 |
| 22 | 0 | 18 | 4 | (560) | 23 | 6 | 8 |
| 23 | 0 | 19 | 2 | 600 | 25 | 0 | 0 |
| 24 | 1 | 0 | 0 | (672) | 28 | 0 | 0 |
| 25 | 1 | 0 | 10 | 700 | 29 | 3 | 4 |
| 26 | 1 | 1 | 8 | (784) | 32 | 13 | 4 |
| 27 | 1 | 2 | 6 | 800 | 33 | 6 | 8 |
| (28) | 1 | 3 | 4 | (896) | 37 | 6 | 8 |
| 29 | 1 | 4 | 2 | 900 | 37 | 10 | 0 |
| 30 | 1 | 5 | 0 | 1000 | 41 | 13 | 4 |
| 31 | 1 | 5 | 10 | 2000 | 83 | 6 | 8 |
| 32 | 1 | 6 | 8 | 3000 | 125 | 0 | 0 |
| 33 | 1 | 7 | 6 | 4000 | 166 | 13 | 4 |
| 34 | 1 | 8 | 4 | 5000 | 208 | 6 | 8 |
| 35 | 1 | 9 | 2 | 10000 | 416 | 13 | 4 |

## *Ten-pence Farthing.*

| | l. | s. | d. | q. | | l. | s. | d. | q. |
|---|---|---|---|---|---|---|---|---|---|
| 1 | 0 | 0 | 10 | 1 | 36 | 1 | 10 | 9 | 0 |
| 2 | 0 | 1 | 8 | 2 | 37 | 1 | 11 | 7 | 1 |
| 3 | 0 | 2 | 6 | 3 | 38 | 1 | 12 | 5 | 2 |
| 4 | 0 | 3 | 5 | 0 | 39 | 1 | 13 | 3 | 3 |
| 5 | 0 | 4 | 3 | 1 | 40 | 1 | 14 | 2 | 0 |
| 6 | 0 | 5 | 1 | 2 | 50 | 2 | 2 | 8 | 2 |
| 7 | 0 | 5 | 11 | 3 | (56) | 2 | 7 | 10 | 0 |
| 8 | 0 | 6 | 10 | 0 | 60 | 2 | 11 | 3 | 0 |
| 9 | 0 | 7 | 8 | 1 | 70 | 2 | 19 | 9 | 2 |
| 10 | 0 | 8 | 6 | 2 | 80 | 3 | 8 | 4 | 0 |
| 11 | 0 | 9 | 4 | 3 | (84) | 3 | 11 | 9 | 0 |
| 12 | 0 | 10 | 3 | 0 | 90 | 3 | 16 | 10 | 2 |
| 13 | 0 | 11 | 1 | 1 | 100 | 4 | 5 | 5 | 0 |
| 14 | 0 | 11 | 11 | 2 | (112) | 4 | 15 | 8 | 0 |
| 15 | 0 | 12 | 9 | 3 | 200 | 8 | 10 | 10 | 0 |
| 16 | 0 | 13 | 8 | 0 | (224) | 9 | 11 | 4 | 0 |
| 17 | 0 | 14 | 6 | 1 | 300 | 12 | 16 | 3 | 0 |
| 18 | 0 | 15 | 4 | 2 | (336) | 14 | 7 | 0 | 0 |
| 19 | 0 | 16 | 2 | 3 | 400 | 17 | 1 | 8 | 0 |
| 20 | 0 | 17 | 1 | 0 | (448) | 19 | 2 | 8 | 0 |
| 21 | 0 | 17 | 11 | 1 | 500 | 21 | 7 | 1 | 0 |
| 22 | 0 | 18 | 9 | 2 | (560) | 23 | 18 | 4 | 0 |
| 23 | 0 | 19 | 7 | 3 | 600 | 25 | 12 | 6 | 0 |
| 24 | 1 | 0 | 6 | 0 | (672) | 28 | 14 | 0 | 0 |
| 25 | 1 | 1 | 4 | 1 | 700 | 29 | 17 | 11 | 0 |
| 26 | 1 | 2 | 2 | 2 | (784) | 33 | 9 | 8 | 0 |
| 27 | 1 | 3 | 0 | 3 | 800 | 34 | 3 | 4 | 0 |
| (28) | 1 | 3 | 11 | 0 | (896) | 38 | 5 | 4 | 0 |
| 29 | 1 | 4 | 9 | 1 | 900 | 38 | 8 | 9 | 0 |
| 30 | 1 | 5 | 7 | 2 | 1000 | 42 | 14 | 2 | 0 |
| 31 | 1 | 6 | 5 | 3 | 2000 | 85 | 8 | 4 | 0 |
| 32 | 1 | 7 | 4 | 0 | 3000 | 128 | 2 | 6 | 0 |
| 33 | 1 | 8 | 2 | 1 | 4000 | 170 | 16 | 8 | 0 |
| 34 | 1 | 9 | 0 | 2 | 5000 | 213 | 10 | 10 | 0 |
| 35 | 1 | 9 | 10 | 3 | 10000 | 427 | 1 | 8 | 0 |

## Ten-pence Half-peny.

| | l. | s. | d. | q. | | l. | s. | d. | q. |
|---|---|---|---|---|---|---|---|---|---|
| 1 | 0 | 0 | 10 | 2 | 36 | 1 | 11 | 6 | 0 |
| 2 | 0 | 1 | 9 | 0 | 37 | 1 | 12 | 4 | 2 |
| 3 | 0 | 2 | 7 | 2 | 38 | 1 | 13 | 3 | 0 |
| 4 | 0 | 3 | 6 | 0 | 39 | 1 | 14 | 1 | 2 |
| 5 | 0 | 4 | 4 | 2 | 40 | 1 | 15 | 0 | 0 |
| 6 | 0 | 5 | 3 | 0 | 50 | 2 | 3 | 9 | 0 |
| 7 | 0 | 6 | 1 | 2 | (56) | 2 | 9 | 0 | 0 |
| 8 | 0 | 7 | 0 | 0 | 60 | 2 | 12 | 6 | 0 |
| 9 | 0 | 7 | 10 | 2 | 70 | 3 | 1 | 3 | 0 |
| 10 | 0 | 8 | 9 | 0 | 80 | 3 | 10 | 0 | 0 |
| 11 | 0 | 9 | 7 | 2 | (84) | 3 | 13 | 6 | 0 |
| 12 | 0 | 10 | 6 | 0 | 90 | 3 | 18 | 9 | 0 |
| 13 | 0 | 11 | 4 | 2 | 100 | 4 | 7 | 6 | 0 |
| 14 | 0 | 12 | 3 | 0 | (112) | 4 | 18 | 0 | 0 |
| 15 | 0 | 13 | 1 | 2 | 200 | 8 | 15 | 0 | 0 |
| 16 | 0 | 14 | 0 | 0 | (224) | 9 | 16 | 0 | 0 |
| 17 | 0 | 14 | 10 | 2 | 300 | 13 | 2 | 6 | 0 |
| 18 | 0 | 15 | 9 | 0 | (336) | 14 | 14 | 0 | 0 |
| 19 | 0 | 16 | 7 | 2 | 400 | 17 | 10 | 0 | 0 |
| 20 | 0 | 17 | 6 | 0 | (448) | 19 | 12 | 0 | 0 |
| 21 | 0 | 18 | 4 | 2 | 500 | 21 | 17 | 6 | 0 |
| 22 | 0 | 19 | 3 | 0 | (560) | 24 | 10 | 0 | 0 |
| 23 | 1 | 0 | 1 | 2 | 600 | 26 | 5 | 0 | 0 |
| 24 | 1 | 1 | 0 | 0 | (672) | 29 | 8 | 0 | 0 |
| 25 | 1 | 1 | 10 | 2 | 700 | 30 | 12 | 6 | 0 |
| 26 | 1 | 2 | 9 | 0 | (784) | 34 | 6 | 0 | 0 |
| 27 | 1 | 3 | 7 | 2 | 800 | 35 | 0 | 0 | 0 |
| (28) | 1 | 4 | 6 | 0 | (896) | 39 | 4 | 0 | 0 |
| 29 | 1 | 5 | 4 | 2 | 900 | 39 | 7 | 6 | 0 |
| 30 | 1 | 6 | 3 | 0 | 1000 | 43 | 15 | 0 | 0 |
| 31 | 1 | 7 | 1 | 2 | 2000 | 87 | 10 | 0 | 0 |
| 32 | 1 | 8 | 0 | 0 | 3000 | 131 | 5 | 0 | 0 |
| 33 | 1 | 8 | 10 | 2 | 4000 | 175 | 0 | 0 | 0 |
| 34 | 1 | 9 | 9 | 0 | 5000 | 218 | 15 | 0 | 0 |
| 35 | 1 | 10 | 7 | 2 | 10000 | 437 | 10 | 0 | 0 |

## *Ten-pence Three Farthings.*

| | l. | s. | d. | q. | | l. | s. | d. | q. |
|---|---|---|---|---|---|---|---|---|---|
| 1 | 0 | 0 | 10 | 3 | 36 | 1 | 12 | 3 | 0 |
| 2 | 0 | 1 | 9 | 2 | 37 | 1 | 13 | 1 | 3 |
| 3 | 0 | 2 | 8 | 1 | 38 | 1 | 14 | 0 | 2 |
| 4 | 0 | 3 | 7 | 0 | 39 | 1 | 14 | 11 | 1 |
| 5 | 0 | 4 | 5 | 3 | 40 | 1 | 15 | 10 | 0 |
| 6 | 0 | 5 | 4 | 2 | 50 | 2 | 4 | 9 | 2 |
| 7 | 0 | 6 | 3 | 1 | (56) | 2 | 10 | 2 | 0 |
| 8 | 0 | 7 | 2 | 0 | 60 | 2 | 13 | 9 | 0 |
| 9 | 0 | 8 | 0 | 3 | 70 | 3 | 2 | 8 | 2 |
| 10 | 0 | 8 | 11 | 2 | 80 | 3 | 11 | 8 | 0 |
| 11 | 0 | 9 | 10 | 1 | (84) | 3 | 15 | 3 | 0 |
| 12 | 0 | 10 | 9 | 0 | 90 | 4 | 0 | 7 | 2 |
| 13 | 0 | 11 | 7 | 3 | 100 | 4 | 9 | 7 | 0 |
| 14 | 0 | 12 | 6 | 2 | (112) | 5 | 0 | 4 | 0 |
| 15 | 0 | 13 | 5 | 1 | 200 | 8 | 19 | 2 | 0 |
| 16 | 0 | 14 | 4 | 0 | (224) | 10 | 0 | 8 | 0 |
| 17 | 0 | 15 | 2 | 3 | 300 | 13 | 8 | 9 | 0 |
| 18 | 0 | 16 | 1 | 2 | (336) | 15 | 1 | 0 | 0 |
| 19 | 0 | 17 | 0 | 1 | 400 | 17 | 18 | 4 | 0 |
| 20 | 0 | 17 | 11 | 0 | (448) | 20 | 1 | 4 | 0 |
| 21 | 0 | 18 | 9 | 3 | 500 | 22 | 7 | 11 | 0 |
| 22 | 0 | 19 | 8 | 2 | (560) | 25 | 1 | 8 | 0 |
| 23 | 1 | 0 | 7 | 1 | 600 | 26 | 17 | 6 | 0 |
| 24 | 1 | 1 | 6 | 0 | (672) | 30 | 2 | 0 | 0 |
| 25 | 1 | 2 | 4 | 3 | 700 | 31 | 7 | 1 | 0 |
| 26 | 1 | 3 | 3 | 2 | (784) | 35 | 2 | 4 | 0 |
| 27 | 1 | 4 | 2 | 1 | 800 | 35 | 16 | 8 | 0 |
| (28) | 1 | 5 | 1 | 0 | (896) | 40 | 2 | 8 | 0 |
| 29 | 1 | 5 | 11 | 3 | 900 | 40 | 6 | 3 | 0 |
| 30 | 1 | 6 | 10 | 2 | 1000 | 44 | 15 | 10 | 0 |
| 31 | 1 | 7 | 9 | 1 | 2000 | 89 | 11 | 8 | 0 |
| 32 | 1 | 8 | 8 | 0 | 3000 | 134 | 7 | 6 | 0 |
| 33 | 1 | 9 | 6 | 3 | 4000 | 179 | 3 | 4 | 0 |
| 34 | 1 | 10 | 5 | 2 | 5000 | 223 | 19 | 2 | 0 |
| 35 | 1 | 11 | 4 | 1 | 10000 | 447 | 18 | 4 | 0 |

## Eleven-Pence.

| | l. | s. | d. | | l. | s. | d. |
|---|---|---|---|---|---|---|---|
| 1 | 0 | 0 | 11 | 36 | 1 | 13 | 0 |
| 2 | 0 | 1 | 10 | 37 | 1 | 13 | 11 |
| 3 | 0 | 2 | 9 | 38 | 1 | 14 | 10 |
| 4 | 0 | 3 | 8 | 39 | 1 | 15 | 9 |
| 5 | 0 | 4 | 7 | 40 | 1 | 16 | 8 |
| 6 | 0 | 5 | 6 | 50 | 2 | 5 | 10 |
| 7 | 0 | 6 | 5 | (56) | 2 | 11 | 4 |
| 8 | 0 | 7 | 4 | 60 | 2 | 15 | 0 |
| 9 | 0 | 8 | 3 | 70 | 3 | 4 | 2 |
| 10 | 0 | 9 | 2 | 80 | 3 | 13 | 4 |
| 11 | 0 | 10 | 1 | (84) | 3 | 17 | 0 |
| 12 | 0 | 11 | 0 | 90 | 4 | 2 | 6 |
| 13 | 0 | 11 | 11 | 100 | 4 | 11 | 8 |
| 14 | 0 | 12 | 10 | (112) | 5 | 2 | 8 |
| 15 | 0 | 13 | 9 | 200 | 9 | 3 | 4 |
| 16 | 0 | 14 | 8 | (224) | 10 | 5 | 4 |
| 17 | 0 | 15 | 7 | 300 | 13 | 15 | 0 |
| 18 | 0 | 16 | 6 | (336) | 15 | 8 | 0 |
| 19 | 0 | 17 | 5 | 400 | 18 | 6 | 8 |
| 20 | 0 | 18 | 4 | (448) | 20 | 10 | 8 |
| 21 | 0 | 19 | 3 | 500 | 22 | 18 | 4 |
| 22 | 1 | 0 | 2 | (560) | 25 | 13 | 4 |
| 23 | 1 | 1 | 1 | 600 | 27 | 10 | 0 |
| 24 | 1 | 2 | 0 | (672) | 30 | 16 | 0 |
| 25 | 1 | 2 | 11 | 700 | 32 | 1 | 8 |
| 26 | 1 | 3 | 10 | (784) | 35 | 18 | 8 |
| 27 | 1 | 4 | 9 | 800 | 36 | 13 | 4 |
| (28) | 1 | 5 | 8 | (896) | 41 | 1 | 4 |
| 29 | 1 | 6 | 7 | 900 | 41 | 5 | 0 |
| 30 | 1 | 7 | 6 | 1000 | 45 | 16 | 8 |
| 31 | 1 | 8 | 5 | 2000 | 91 | 13 | 4 |
| 32 | 1 | 9 | 4 | 3000 | 137 | 10 | 0 |
| 33 | 1 | 10 | 3 | 4000 | 183 | 6 | 8 |
| 34 | 1 | 11 | 2 | 5000 | 229 | 3 | 4 |
| 35 | 1 | 12 | 1 | 10000 | 458 | 6 | 8 |

## *Eleven-pence Farthing.*

| | l. | s. | d. | q. | | l. | s. | d. | q. |
|---|---|---|---|---|---|---|---|---|---|
| 1 | 0 | 0 | 11 | 1 | 36 | 1 | 13 | 9 | 0 |
| 2 | 0 | 1 | 10 | 2 | 37 | 1 | 14 | 8 | 1 |
| 3 | 0 | 2 | 9 | 3 | 38 | 1 | 15 | 7 | 2 |
| 4 | 0 | 3 | 9 | 0 | 39 | 1 | 16 | 6 | 3 |
| 5 | 0 | 4 | 8 | 1 | 40 | 1 | 17 | 6 | 0 |
| 6 | 0 | 5 | 7 | 2 | 50 | 2 | 6 | 10 | 2 |
| 7 | 0 | 6 | 6 | 3 | (56) | 2 | 12 | 6 | 0 |
| 8 | 0 | 7 | 6 | 0 | 60 | 2 | 16 | 3 | 0 |
| 9 | 0 | 8 | 5 | 1 | 70 | 3 | 5 | 7 | 2 |
| 10 | 0 | 9 | 4 | 2 | 80 | 3 | 15 | 0 | 0 |
| 11 | 0 | 10 | 3 | 3 | (84) | 3 | 18 | 9 | 0 |
| 12 | 0 | 11 | 3 | 0 | 90 | 4 | 4 | 4 | 2 |
| 13 | 0 | 12 | 2 | 1 | 100 | 4 | 13 | 9 | 0 |
| 14 | 0 | 13 | 1 | 2 | (112) | 5 | 5 | 0 | 0 |
| 15 | 0 | 14 | 0 | 3 | 200 | 9 | 7 | 6 | 0 |
| 16 | 0 | 15 | 0 | 0 | (224) | 10 | 10 | 0 | 0 |
| 17 | 0 | 15 | 11 | 1 | 300 | 14 | 1 | 3 | 0 |
| 18 | 0 | 16 | 10 | 2 | (336) | 15 | 15 | 0 | 0 |
| 19 | 0 | 17 | 9 | 3 | 400 | 18 | 15 | 0 | 0 |
| 20 | 0 | 18 | 9 | 0 | (448) | 21 | 0 | 0 | 0 |
| 21 | 0 | 19 | 8 | 1 | 500 | 23 | 8 | 9 | 0 |
| 22 | 1 | 0 | 7 | 2 | (560) | 26 | 5 | 0 | 0 |
| 23 | 1 | 1 | 6 | 3 | 600 | 28 | 2 | 6 | 0 |
| 24 | 1 | 2 | 6 | 0 | (672) | 31 | 10 | 0 | 0 |
| 25 | 1 | 3 | 5 | 1 | 700 | 32 | 16 | 3 | 0 |
| 26 | 1 | 4 | 4 | 2 | (784) | 36 | 15 | 0 | 0 |
| 27 | 1 | 5 | 3 | 3 | 800 | 37 | 10 | 0 | 0 |
| (28) | 1 | 6 | 3 | 0 | (896) | 42 | 0 | 0 | 0 |
| 29 | 1 | 7 | 2 | 1 | 900 | 42 | 3 | 9 | 0 |
| 30 | 1 | 8 | 1 | 2 | 1000 | 46 | 17 | 6 | 0 |
| 31 | 1 | 9 | 0 | 3 | 2000 | 93 | 15 | 0 | 0 |
| 32 | 1 | 10 | 0 | 0 | 3000 | 140 | 12 | 6 | 0 |
| 33 | 1 | 10 | 11 | 1 | 4000 | 187 | 10 | 0 | 0 |
| 34 | 1 | 11 | 10 | 2 | 5000 | 234 | 7 | 6 | 0 |
| 35 | 1 | 12 | 9 | 3 | 10000 | 468 | 15 | 0 | 0 |

## *Eleven-pence Half-peny.*

| | l. | s. | d. | q. | | l. | s. | d. | q. |
|---|---|---|---|---|---|---|---|---|---|
| 1 | 0 | 0 | 11 | 2 | 36 | 1 | 14 | 6 | 0 |
| 2 | 0 | 1 | 11 | 0 | 37 | 1 | 15 | 5 | 2 |
| 3 | 0 | 2 | 10 | 2 | 38 | 1 | 16 | 5 | 0 |
| 4 | 0 | 3 | 10 | 0 | 39 | 1 | 17 | 4 | 2 |
| 5 | 0 | 4 | 9 | 2 | 40 | 1 | 18 | 4 | 0 |
| 6 | 0 | 5 | 9 | 0 | 50 | 2 | 7 | 11 | 0 |
| 7 | 0 | 6 | 8 | 2 | (56) | 2 | 13 | 8 | 0 |
| 8 | 0 | 7 | 8 | 0 | 60 | 2 | 17 | 6 | 0 |
| 9 | 0 | 8 | 7 | 2 | 70 | 3 | 7 | 1 | 0 |
| 10 | 0 | 9 | 7 | 0 | 80 | 3 | 16 | 8 | 0 |
| 11 | 0 | 10 | 6 | 2 | (84) | 4 | 0 | 6 | 0 |
| 12 | 0 | 11 | 6 | 0 | 90 | 4 | 6 | 3 | 0 |
| 13 | 0 | 12 | 5 | 2 | 100 | 4 | 15 | 10 | 0 |
| 14 | 0 | 13 | 5 | 0 | (112) | 5 | 7 | 4 | 0 |
| 15 | 0 | 14 | 4 | 2 | 200 | 9 | 11 | 8 | 0 |
| 16 | 0 | 15 | 4 | 0 | (224) | 10 | 14 | 8 | 0 |
| 17 | 0 | 16 | 3 | 2 | 300 | 14 | 7 | 6 | 0 |
| 18 | 0 | 17 | 3 | 0 | (336) | 16 | 2 | 0 | 0 |
| 19 | 0 | 18 | 2 | 2 | 400 | 19 | 3 | 4 | 0 |
| 20 | 0 | 19 | 2 | 0 | (448) | 21 | 9 | 4 | 0 |
| 21 | 1 | 0 | 1 | 2 | 500 | 23 | 19 | 2 | 0 |
| 22 | 1 | 1 | 1 | 0 | (560) | 26 | 16 | 8 | 0 |
| 23 | 1 | 2 | 0 | 2 | 600 | 28 | 15 | 0 | 0 |
| 24 | 1 | 3 | 0 | 0 | (672) | 32 | 4 | 0 | 0 |
| 25 | 1 | 3 | 11 | 2 | 700 | 33 | 10 | 10 | 0 |
| 26 | 1 | 4 | 11 | 0 | (784) | 37 | 11 | 4 | 0 |
| 27 | 1 | 5 | 10 | 2 | 800 | 38 | 6 | 8 | 0 |
| (28) | 1 | 6 | 10 | 0 | (896) | 42 | 18 | 8 | 0 |
| 29 | 1 | 7 | 9 | 2 | 900 | 43 | 2 | 6 | 0 |
| 30 | 1 | 8 | 9 | 0 | 1000 | 47 | 18 | 4 | 0 |
| 31 | 1 | 9 | 8 | 2 | 2000 | 95 | 16 | 8 | 0 |
| 32 | 1 | 10 | 8 | 0 | 3000 | 143 | 15 | 0 | 0 |
| 33 | 1 | 11 | 7 | 2 | 4000 | 191 | 13 | 4 | 0 |
| 34 | 1 | 12 | 7 | 0 | 5000 | 239 | 11 | 8 | 0 |
| 35 | 1 | 13 | 6 | 2 | 10000 | 479 | 3 | 4 | 0 |

## *Eleven-pence Three Farthings.*

| | l. | s. | d. | q. | | l. | s. | d. | q. |
|---|---|---|---|---|---|---|---|---|---|
| 1 | 0 | 0 | 11 | 3 | 36 | 1 | 15 | 3 | 0 |
| 2 | 0 | 1 | 11 | 2 | 37 | 1 | 16 | 2 | 3 |
| 3 | 0 | 2 | 11 | 1 | 38 | 1 | 17 | 2 | 2 |
| 4 | 0 | 3 | 11 | 0 | 39 | 1 | 18 | 2 | 1 |
| 5 | 0 | 4 | 10 | 3 | 40 | 1 | 19 | 2 | 0 |
| 6 | 0 | 5 | 10 | 2 | 50 | 2 | 8 | 11 | 2 |
| 7 | 0 | 6 | 10 | 1 | (56) | 2 | 14 | 10 | 0 |
| 8 | 0 | 7 | 10 | 0 | 60 | 2 | 18 | 9 | 0 |
| 9 | 0 | 8 | 9 | 3 | 70 | 3 | 8 | 6 | 2 |
| 10 | 0 | 9 | 9 | 2 | 80 | 3 | 18 | 4 | 0 |
| 11 | 0 | 10 | 9 | 1 | (84) | 4 | 2 | 3 | 0 |
| 12 | 0 | 11 | 9 | 0 | 90 | 4 | 8 | 1 | 2 |
| 13 | 0 | 12 | 8 | 3 | 100 | 4 | 17 | 11 | 0 |
| 14 | 0 | 13 | 8 | 2 | (112) | 5 | 9 | 8 | 0 |
| 15 | 0 | 14 | 8 | 1 | 200 | 9 | 15 | 10 | 0 |
| 16 | 0 | 15 | 8 | 0 | (224) | 10 | 19 | 4 | 0 |
| 17 | 0 | 16 | 7 | 3 | 300 | 14 | 13 | 9 | 0 |
| 18 | 0 | 17 | 7 | 2 | (336) | 16 | 9 | 0 | 0 |
| 19 | 0 | 18 | 7 | 1 | 400 | 19 | 11 | 8 | 0 |
| 20 | 0 | 19 | 7 | 0 | (448) | 21 | 18 | 8 | 0 |
| 21 | 1 | 0 | 6 | 3 | 500 | 24 | 9 | 7 | 0 |
| 22 | 1 | 1 | 6 | 2 | (560) | 27 | 8 | 4 | 0 |
| 23 | 1 | 2 | 6 | 1 | 600 | 29 | 7 | 6 | 0 |
| 24 | 1 | 3 | 6 | 0 | (672) | 32 | 18 | 0 | 0 |
| 25 | 1 | 4 | 5 | 3 | 700 | 34 | 5 | 5 | 0 |
| 26 | 1 | 5 | 5 | 2 | (784) | 38 | 7 | 8 | 0 |
| 27 | 1 | 6 | 5 | 1 | 800 | 39 | 3 | 4 | 0 |
| (28) | 1 | 7 | 5 | 0 | (896) | 43 | 17 | 4 | 0 |
| 29 | 1 | 8 | 4 | 3 | 900 | 44 | 1 | 3 | 0 |
| 30 | 1 | 9 | 4 | 2 | 1000 | 48 | 19 | 2 | 0 |
| 31 | 1 | 10 | 4 | 1 | 2000 | 97 | 18 | 4 | 0 |
| 32 | 1 | 11 | 4 | 0 | 3000 | 146 | 17 | 6 | 0 |
| 33 | 1 | 12 | 3 | 3 | 4000 | 195 | 16 | 8 | 0 |
| 34 | 1 | 13 | 3 | 2 | 5000 | 244 | 15 | 10 | 0 |
| 35 | 1 | 14 | 3 | 1 | 10000 | 489 | 11 | 8 | 0 |

## Twelve-pence, or a Shilling.

| | l. | s. | | l. | s. |
|---|---|---|---|---|---|
| 1 | 0 | 1 | 36 | 1 | 16 |
| 2 | 0 | 2 | 37 | 1 | 17 |
| 3 | 0 | 3 | 38 | 1 | 18 |
| 4 | 0 | 4 | 39 | 1 | 19 |
| 5 | 0 | 5 | 40 | 2 | 0 |
| 6 | 0 | 6 | 50 | 2 | 10 |
| 7 | 0 | 7 | (56) | 2 | 16 |
| 8 | 0 | 8 | 60 | 3 | 0 |
| 9 | 0 | 9 | 70 | 3 | 10 |
| 10 | 0 | 10 | 80 | 4 | 0 |
| 11 | 0 | 11 | (84) | 4 | 4 |
| 12 | 0 | 12 | 90 | 4 | 10 |
| 13 | 0 | 13 | 100 | 5 | 0 |
| 14 | 0 | 14 | (112) | 5 | 12 |
| 15 | 0 | 15 | 200 | 10 | 0 |
| 16 | 0 | 16 | (224) | 11 | 4 |
| 17 | 0 | 17 | 300 | 15 | 0 |
| 18 | 0 | 18 | (336) | 16 | 16 |
| 19 | 0 | 19 | 400 | 20 | 0 |
| 20 | 1 | 0 | (448) | 22 | 8 |
| 21 | 1 | 1 | 500 | 25 | 0 |
| 22 | 1 | 2 | (560) | 28 | 0 |
| 23 | 1 | 3 | 600 | 30 | 0 |
| 24 | 1 | 4 | (672) | 33 | 12 |
| 25 | 1 | 5 | 700 | 35 | 0 |
| 26 | 1 | 6 | (784) | 39 | 4 |
| 27 | 1 | 7 | 800 | 40 | 0 |
| (28) | 1 | 8 | (896) | 44 | 16 |
| 29 | 1 | 9 | 900 | 45 | 0 |
| 30 | 1 | 10 | 1000 | 50 | 0 |
| 31 | 1 | 11 | 2000 | 100 | 0 |
| 32 | 1 | 12 | 3000 | 150 | 0 |
| 33 | 1 | 13 | 4000 | 200 | 0 |
| 34 | 1 | 14 | 5000 | 250 | 0 |
| 35 | 1 | 15 | 10000 | 500 | 0 |

## Thirteen-Pence.

| | l. | s. | d. | | l. | s. | d. |
|---|---|---|---|---|---|---|---|
| 1 | 0 | 1 | 1 | 36 | 1 | 19 | 0 |
| 2 | 0 | 2 | 2 | 37 | 2 | 0 | 1 |
| 3 | 0 | 3 | 3 | 38 | 2 | 1 | 2 |
| 4 | 0 | 4 | 4 | 39 | 2 | 2 | 3 |
| 5 | 0 | 5 | 5 | 40 | 2 | 3 | 4 |
| 6 | 0 | 6 | 6 | 50 | 2 | 14 | 2 |
| 7 | 0 | 7 | 7 | (56) | 3 | 0 | 8 |
| 8 | 0 | 8 | 8 | 60 | 3 | 5 | 0 |
| 9 | 0 | 9 | 9 | 70 | 3 | 15 | 10 |
| 10 | 0 | 10 | 10 | 80 | 4 | 6 | 8 |
| 11 | 0 | 11 | 11 | (84) | 4 | 11 | 0 |
| 12 | 0 | 13 | 0 | 90 | 4 | 17 | 6 |
| 13 | 0 | 14 | 1 | 100 | 5 | 8 | 4 |
| 14 | 0 | 15 | 2 | (112) | 6 | 1 | 4 |
| 15 | 0 | 16 | 3 | 200 | 10 | 16 | 8 |
| 16 | 0 | 17 | 4 | (224) | 12 | 2 | 8 |
| 17 | 0 | 18 | 5 | 300 | 16 | 5 | 0 |
| 18 | 0 | 19 | 6 | (336) | 18 | 4 | 0 |
| 19 | 1 | 0 | 7 | 400 | 21 | 13 | 4 |
| 20 | 1 | 1 | 8 | (448) | 24 | 5 | 4 |
| 21 | 1 | 2 | 9 | 500 | 27 | 1 | 8 |
| 22 | 1 | 3 | 10 | (560) | 30 | 6 | 8 |
| 23 | 1 | 4 | 11 | 600 | 32 | 10 | 0 |
| 24 | 1 | 6 | 0 | (672) | 36 | 8 | 0 |
| 25 | 1 | 7 | 1 | 700 | 37 | 18 | 4 |
| 26 | 1 | 8 | 2 | (784) | 42 | 9 | 4 |
| 27 | 1 | 9 | 3 | 800 | 43 | 6 | 8 |
| (28) | 1 | 10 | 4 | (896) | 48 | 10 | 8 |
| 29 | 1 | 11 | 5 | 900 | 48 | 15 | 0 |
| 30 | 1 | 12 | 6 | 1000 | 54 | 3 | 4 |
| 31 | 1 | 13 | 7 | 2000 | 108 | 6 | 8 |
| 32 | 1 | 14 | 8 | 3000 | 162 | 10 | 0 |
| 33 | 1 | 15 | 9 | 4000 | 216 | 13 | 4 |
| 34 | 1 | 16 | 10 | 5000 | 270 | 16 | 8 |
| 35 | 1 | 17 | 11 | 10000 | 541 | 13 | 4 |

## *Thirteen-pence Half-peny.*

| | l. | s. | d. | q. | | l. | s. | d. | q. |
|---|---|---|---|---|---|---|---|---|---|
| 1 | 0 | 1 | 1 | 2 | 36 | 2 | 0 | 6 | 0 |
| 2 | 0 | 2 | 3 | 0 | 37 | 2 | 1 | 7 | 2 |
| 3 | 0 | 3 | 4 | 2 | 38 | 2 | 2 | 9 | 0 |
| 4 | 0 | 4 | 6 | 0 | 39 | 2 | 3 | 10 | 2 |
| 5 | 0 | 5 | 7 | 2 | 40 | 2 | 5 | 0 | 0 |
| 6 | 0 | 6 | 9 | 0 | 50 | 2 | 16 | 3 | 0 |
| 7 | 0 | 7 | 10 | 2 | (56) | 3 | 3 | 0 | 0 |
| 8 | 0 | 9 | 0 | 0 | 60 | 3 | 7 | 6 | 0 |
| 9 | 0 | 10 | 1 | 2 | 70 | 3 | 18 | 9 | 0 |
| 10 | 0 | 11 | 3 | 0 | 80 | 4 | 10 | 0 | 0 |
| 11 | 0 | 12 | 4 | 2 | (84) | 4 | 14 | 6 | 0 |
| 12 | 0 | 13 | 6 | 0 | 90 | 5 | 1 | 3 | 0 |
| 13 | 0 | 14 | 7 | 2 | 100 | 5 | 12 | 6 | 0 |
| 14 | 0 | 15 | 9 | 0 | (112) | 6 | 6 | 0 | 0 |
| 15 | 0 | 16 | 10 | 2 | 200 | 11 | 5 | 0 | 0 |
| 16 | 0 | 18 | 0 | 0 | (224) | 12 | 12 | 0 | 0 |
| 17 | 0 | 19 | 1 | 2 | 300 | 16 | 17 | 6 | 0 |
| 18 | 1 | 0 | 3 | 0 | (336) | 18 | 18 | 0 | 0 |
| 19 | 1 | 1 | 4 | 2 | 400 | 22 | 10 | 0 | 0 |
| 20 | 1 | 2 | 6 | 0 | (448) | 25 | 4 | 0 | 0 |
| 21 | 1 | 3 | 7 | 2 | 500 | 28 | 2 | 6 | 0 |
| 22 | 1 | 4 | 9 | 0 | (560) | 31 | 10 | 0 | 0 |
| 23 | 1 | 5 | 10 | 2 | 600 | 33 | 15 | 0 | 0 |
| 24 | 1 | 7 | 0 | 0 | (672) | 37 | 16 | 0 | 0 |
| 25 | 1 | 8 | 1 | 2 | 700 | 39 | 7 | 6 | 0 |
| 26 | 1 | 9 | 3 | 0 | (784) | 44 | 2 | 0 | 0 |
| 27 | 1 | 10 | 4 | 2 | 800 | 45 | 0 | 0 | 0 |
| (28) | 1 | 11 | 6 | 0 | (896) | 50 | 8 | 0 | 0 |
| 29 | 1 | 12 | 7 | 2 | 900 | 50 | 12 | 6 | 0 |
| 30 | 1 | 13 | 9 | 0 | 1000 | 56 | 5 | 0 | 0 |
| 31 | 1 | 14 | 10 | 2 | 2000 | 112 | 10 | 0 | 0 |
| 32 | 1 | 16 | 0 | 0 | 3000 | 168 | 15 | 0 | 0 |
| 33 | 1 | 17 | 1 | 2 | 4000 | 225 | 0 | 0 | 0 |
| 34 | 1 | 18 | 3 | 0 | 5000 | 281 | 5 | 0 | 0 |
| 35 | 1 | 19 | 4 | 2 | 10000 | 562 | 10 | 0 | 0 |

## *Fourteen-Pence.*

| | l. | s. | d. | | l. | s. | d. |
|---|---|---|---|---|---|---|---|
| 1 | 0 | 1 | 2 | 36 | 2 | 2 | 0 |
| 2 | 0 | 2 | 4 | 37 | 2 | 3 | 2 |
| 3 | 0 | 3 | 6 | 38 | 2 | 4 | 4 |
| 4 | 0 | 4 | 8 | 39 | 2 | 5 | 6 |
| 5 | 0 | 5 | 10 | 40 | 2 | 6 | 8 |
| 6 | 0 | 7 | 0 | 50 | 2 | 18 | 4 |
| 7 | 0 | 8 | 2 | (56) | 3 | 5 | 4 |
| 8 | 0 | 9 | 4 | 60 | 3 | 10 | 0 |
| 9 | 0 | 10 | 6 | 70 | 4 | 1 | 8 |
| 10 | 0 | 11 | 8 | 80 | 4 | 13 | 4 |
| 11 | 0 | 12 | 10 | (84) | 4 | 18 | 0 |
| 12 | 0 | 14 | 0 | 90 | 5 | 5 | 0 |
| 13 | 0 | 15 | 2 | 100 | 5 | 16 | 8 |
| 14 | 0 | 16 | 4 | (112) | 6 | 10 | 8 |
| 15 | 0 | 17 | 6 | 200 | 11 | 13 | 4 |
| 16 | 0 | 18 | 8 | (224) | 13 | 1 | 4 |
| 17 | 0 | 19 | 10 | 300 | 17 | 10 | 0 |
| 18 | 1 | 1 | 0 | (336) | 19 | 12 | 0 |
| 19 | 1 | 2 | 2 | 400 | 23 | 6 | 8 |
| 20 | 1 | 3 | 4 | (448) | 26 | 2 | 8 |
| 21 | 1 | 4 | 6 | 500 | 29 | 3 | 4 |
| 22 | 1 | 5 | 8 | (560) | 32 | 13 | 4 |
| 23 | 1 | 6 | 10 | 600 | 35 | 0 | 0 |
| 24 | 1 | 8 | 0 | (672) | 39 | 4 | 0 |
| 25 | 1 | 9 | 2 | 700 | 40 | 16 | 8 |
| 26 | 1 | 10 | 4 | (784) | 45 | 14 | 8 |
| 27 | 1 | 11 | 6 | 800 | 46 | 13 | 4 |
| (28) | 1 | 12 | 8 | (896) | 52 | 5 | 4 |
| 29 | 1 | 13 | 10 | 900 | 52 | 10 | 0 |
| 30 | 1 | 15 | 0 | 1000 | 58 | 6 | 8 |
| 31 | 1 | 16 | 2 | 2000 | 116 | 13 | 4 |
| 32 | 1 | 17 | 4 | 3000 | 175 | 0 | 0 |
| 33 | 1 | 18 | 6 | 4000 | 233 | 6 | 8 |
| 34 | 1 | 19 | 8 | 5000 | 291 | 13 | 4 |
| 35 | 2 | 0 | 10 | 10000 | 583 | 6 | 8 |

## *Fifteen-Pence.*

| | l. | s. | d. | | l. | s. | d. |
|---|---|---|---|---|---|---|---|
| 1 | 0 | 1 | 3 | 36 | 2 | 5 | 0 |
| 2 | 0 | 2 | 6 | 37 | 2 | 6 | 3 |
| 3 | 0 | 3 | 9 | 38 | 2 | 7 | 6 |
| 4 | 0 | 5 | 0 | 39 | 2 | 8 | 9 |
| 5 | 0 | 6 | 3 | 40 | 2 | 10 | 0 |
| 6 | 0 | 7 | 6 | 50 | 3 | 2 | 6 |
| 7 | 0 | 8 | 9 | (56) | 3 | 10 | 0 |
| 8 | 0 | 10 | 0 | 60 | 3 | 15 | 0 |
| 9 | 0 | 11 | 3 | 70 | 4 | 7 | 6 |
| 10 | 0 | 12 | 6 | 80 | 5 | 0 | 0 |
| 11 | 0 | 13 | 9 | (84) | 5 | 5 | 0 |
| 12 | 0 | 15 | 0 | 90 | 5 | 12 | 6 |
| 13 | 0 | 16 | 3 | 100 | 6 | 5 | 0 |
| 14 | 0 | 17 | 6 | (112) | 7 | 0 | 0 |
| 15 | 0 | 18 | 9 | 200 | 12 | 10 | 0 |
| 16 | 1 | 0 | 0 | (224) | 14 | 0 | 0 |
| 17 | 1 | 1 | 3 | 300 | 18 | 15 | 0 |
| 18 | 1 | 2 | 6 | (336) | 21 | 0 | 0 |
| 19 | 1 | 3 | 9 | 400 | 25 | 0 | 0 |
| 20 | 1 | 5 | 0 | (448) | 28 | 0 | 0 |
| 21 | 1 | 6 | 3 | 500 | 31 | 5 | 0 |
| 22 | 1 | 7 | 6 | (560) | 35 | 0 | 0 |
| 23 | 1 | 8 | 9 | 600 | 37 | 10 | 0 |
| 24 | 1 | 10 | 0 | (672) | 42 | 0 | 0 |
| 25 | 1 | 11 | 3 | 700 | 43 | 15 | 0 |
| 26 | 1 | 12 | 6 | (784) | 49 | 0 | 0 |
| 27 | 1 | 13 | 9 | 800 | 50 | 0 | 0 |
| (28) | 1 | 15 | 0 | (896) | 56 | 0 | 0 |
| 29 | 1 | 16 | 3 | 900 | 56 | 5 | 0 |
| 30 | 1 | 17 | 6 | 1000 | 62 | 10 | 0 |
| 31 | 1 | 18 | 9 | 2000 | 125 | 0 | 0 |
| 32 | 2 | 0 | 0 | 3000 | 187 | 10 | 0 |
| 33 | 2 | 1 | 3 | 4000 | 250 | 0 | 0 |
| 34 | 2 | 2 | 6 | 5000 | 312 | 10 | 0 |
| 35 | 2 | 3 | 9 | 10000 | 625 | 0 | 0 |

## *Sixteen-Pence.*

| | l. | s. | d. | | l. | s. | d. |
|---|---|---|---|---|---|---|---|
| 1 | 0 | 1 | 4 | 36 | 2 | 8 | 0 |
| 2 | 0 | 2 | 8 | 37 | 2 | 9 | 4 |
| 3 | 0 | 4 | 0 | 38 | 2 | 10 | 8 |
| 4 | 0 | 5 | 4 | 39 | 2 | 12 | 0 |
| 5 | 0 | 6 | 8 | 40 | 2 | 13 | 4 |
| 6 | 0 | 8 | 0 | 50 | 3 | 6 | 8 |
| 7 | 0 | 9 | 4 | (56) | 3 | 14 | 8 |
| 8 | 0 | 10 | 8 | 60 | 4 | 0 | 0 |
| 9 | 0 | 12 | 0 | 70 | 4 | 13 | 4 |
| 10 | 0 | 13 | 4 | 80 | 5 | 6 | 8 |
| 11 | 0 | 14 | 8 | (84) | 5 | 12 | 0 |
| 12 | 0 | 16 | 0 | 90 | 6 | 0 | 0 |
| 13 | 0 | 17 | 4 | 100 | 6 | 13 | 4 |
| 14 | 0 | 18 | 8 | (112) | 7 | 9 | 4 |
| 15 | 1 | 0 | 0 | 200 | 13 | 6 | 8 |
| 16 | 1 | 1 | 4 | (224) | 14 | 18 | 8 |
| 17 | 1 | 2 | 8 | 300 | 20 | 0 | 0 |
| 18 | 1 | 4 | 0 | (336) | 22 | 8 | 0 |
| 19 | 1 | 5 | 4 | 400 | 26 | 13 | 4 |
| 20 | 1 | 6 | 8 | (448) | 29 | 17 | 4 |
| 21 | 1 | 8 | 0 | 500 | 33 | 6 | 8 |
| 22 | 1 | 9 | 4 | (560) | 37 | 6 | 8 |
| 23 | 1 | 10 | 8 | 600 | 40 | 0 | 0 |
| 24 | 1 | 12 | 0 | (672) | 44 | 16 | 0 |
| 25 | 1 | 13 | 4 | 700 | 46 | 13 | 4 |
| 26 | 1 | 14 | 8 | (784) | 52 | 5 | 4 |
| 27 | 1 | 16 | 0 | 800 | 53 | 6 | 8 |
| (28) | 1 | 17 | 4 | (896) | 59 | 14 | 8 |
| 29 | 1 | 18 | 8 | 900 | 60 | 0 | 0 |
| 30 | 2 | 0 | 0 | 1000 | 66 | 13 | 4 |
| 31 | 2 | 1 | 4 | 2000 | 133 | 6 | 8 |
| 32 | 2 | 2 | 8 | 3000 | 200 | 0 | 0 |
| 33 | 2 | 4 | 0 | 4000 | 266 | 13 | 4 |
| 34 | 2 | 5 | 4 | 5000 | 333 | 6 | 8 |
| 35 | 2 | 6 | 8 | 10000 | 666 | 13 | 4 |

## Seventeen-Pence.

| | l. | s. | d. | | l. | s. | d. |
|---|---|---|---|---|---|---|---|
| 1 | 0 | 1 | 5 | 36 | 2 | 11 | 0 |
| 2 | 0 | 2 | 10 | 37 | 2 | 12 | 5 |
| 3 | 0 | 4 | 3 | 38 | 2 | 13 | 10 |
| 4 | 0 | 5 | 8 | 39 | 2 | 15 | 3 |
| 5 | 0 | 7 | 1 | 40 | 2 | 16 | 8 |
| 6 | 0 | 8 | 6 | 50 | 3 | 10 | 10 |
| 7 | 0 | 9 | 11 | (56) | 3 | 19 | 4 |
| 8 | 0 | 11 | 4 | 60 | 4 | 5 | 0 |
| 9 | 0 | 12 | 9 | 70 | 4 | 19 | 2 |
| 10 | 0 | 14 | 2 | 80 | 5 | 13 | 4 |
| 11 | 0 | 15 | 7 | (84) | 5 | 19 | 0 |
| 12 | 0 | 17 | 0 | 90 | 6 | 7 | 6 |
| 13 | 0 | 18 | 5 | 100 | 7 | 1 | 8 |
| 14 | 0 | 19 | 10 | (112) | 7 | 18 | 8 |
| 15 | 1 | 1 | 3 | 200 | 14 | 3 | 4 |
| 16 | 1 | 2 | 8 | (224) | 15 | 17 | 4 |
| 17 | 1 | 4 | 1 | 300 | 21 | 5 | 0 |
| 18 | 1 | 5 | 6 | (336) | 23 | 16 | 0 |
| 19 | 1 | 6 | 11 | 400 | 28 | 6 | 8 |
| 20 | 1 | 8 | 4 | (448) | 31 | 14 | 8 |
| 21 | 1 | 9 | 9 | 500 | 35 | 8 | 4 |
| 22 | 1 | 11 | 2 | (560) | 39 | 13 | 4 |
| 23 | 1 | 12 | 7 | 600 | 42 | 10 | 0 |
| 24 | 1 | 14 | 0 | (672) | 47 | 12 | 0 |
| 25 | 1 | 15 | 5 | 700 | 49 | 11 | 8 |
| 26 | 1 | 16 | 10 | (784) | 55 | 10 | 8 |
| 27 | 1 | 18 | 3 | 800 | 56 | 13 | 4 |
| (28) | 1 | 19 | 8 | (896) | 63 | 9 | 4 |
| 29 | 2 | 1 | 1 | 900 | 63 | 15 | 0 |
| 30 | 2 | 2 | 6 | 1000 | 70 | 16 | 8 |
| 31 | 2 | 3 | 11 | 2000 | 141 | 13 | 4 |
| 32 | 2 | 5 | 4 | 3000 | 212 | 10 | 0 |
| 33 | 2 | 6 | 9 | 4000 | 283 | 6 | 8 |
| 34 | 2 | 8 | 2 | 5000 | 354 | 3 | 4 |
| 35 | 2 | 9 | 7 | 10000 | 708 | 6 | 8 |

## Eighteen-Pence.

| | l. | s. | d. | | l. | s. | d. |
|---|---|---|---|---|---|---|---|
| 1 | 0 | 1 | 6 | 36 | 2 | 14 | 0 |
| 2 | 0 | 3 | 0 | 37 | 2 | 15 | 6 |
| 3 | 0 | 4 | 6 | 38 | 2 | 17 | 0 |
| 4 | 0 | 6 | 0 | 39 | 2 | 18 | 6 |
| 5 | 0 | 7 | 6 | 40 | 3 | 0 | 0 |
| 6 | 0 | 9 | 0 | 50 | 3 | 15 | 0 |
| 7 | 0 | 10 | 6 | (56) | 4 | 4 | 0 |
| 8 | 0 | 12 | 0 | 60 | 4 | 10 | 0 |
| 9 | 0 | 13 | 6 | 70 | 5 | 5 | 0 |
| 10 | 0 | 15 | 0 | 80 | 6 | 0 | 0 |
| 11 | 0 | 16 | 6 | (84) | 6 | 6 | 0 |
| 12 | 0 | 18 | 0 | 90 | 6 | 15 | 0 |
| 13 | 0 | 19 | 6 | 100 | 7 | 10 | 0 |
| 14 | 1 | 1 | 0 | (112) | 8 | 8 | 0 |
| 15 | 1 | 2 | 6 | 200 | 15 | 0 | 0 |
| 16 | 1 | 4 | 0 | (224) | 16 | 16 | 0 |
| 17 | 1 | 5 | 6 | 300 | 22 | 10 | 0 |
| 18 | 1 | 7 | 0 | (336) | 25 | 4 | 0 |
| 19 | 1 | 8 | 6 | 400 | 30 | 0 | 0 |
| 20 | 1 | 10 | 0 | (448) | 33 | 12 | 0 |
| 21 | 1 | 11 | 6 | 500 | 37 | 10 | 0 |
| 22 | 1 | 13 | 0 | (560) | 42 | 0 | 0 |
| 23 | 1 | 14 | 6 | 600 | 45 | 0 | 0 |
| 24 | 1 | 16 | 0 | (672) | 50 | 8 | 0 |
| 25 | 1 | 17 | 6 | 700 | 52 | 10 | 0 |
| 26 | 1 | 19 | 0 | (784) | 58 | 16 | 0 |
| 27 | 2 | 0 | 6 | 800 | 60 | 0 | 0 |
| (28) | 2 | 2 | 0 | (896) | 67 | 4 | 0 |
| 29 | 2 | 3 | 6 | 900 | 67 | 10 | 0 |
| 30 | 2 | 5 | 0 | 1000 | 75 | 0 | 0 |
| 31 | 2 | 6 | 6 | 2000 | 150 | 0 | 0 |
| 32 | 2 | 8 | 0 | 3000 | 225 | 0 | 0 |
| 33 | 2 | 9 | 6 | 4000 | 300 | 0 | 0 |
| 34 | 2 | 11 | 0 | 5000 | 375 | 0 | 0 |
| 35 | 2 | 12 | 6 | 10000 | 750 | 0 | 0 |

## Nineteen-Pence.

| | l. | s. | d. | | l. | s. | d. |
|---|---|---|---|---|---|---|---|
| 1 | 0 | 1 | 7 | 36 | 2 | 17 | 0 |
| 2 | 0 | 3 | 2 | 37 | 2 | 18 | 7 |
| 3 | 0 | 4 | 9 | 38 | 3 | 0 | 2 |
| 4 | 0 | 6 | 4 | 39 | 3 | 1 | 9 |
| 5 | 0 | 7 | 11 | 40 | 3 | 3 | 4 |
| 6 | 0 | 9 | 6 | 50 | 3 | 19 | 2 |
| 7 | 0 | 11 | 1 | (56) | 4 | 8 | 8 |
| 8 | 0 | 12 | 8 | 60 | 4 | 15 | 0 |
| 9 | 0 | 14 | 3 | 70 | 5 | 10 | 10 |
| 10 | 0 | 15 | 10 | 80 | 6 | 6 | 8 |
| 11 | 0 | 17 | 5 | (84) | 6 | 13 | 0 |
| 12 | 0 | 19 | 0 | 90 | 7 | 2 | 6 |
| 13 | 1 | 0 | 7 | 100 | 7 | 18 | 4 |
| 14 | 1 | 2 | 2 | (112) | 8 | 17 | 4 |
| 15 | 1 | 3 | 9 | 200 | 15 | 16 | 8 |
| 16 | 1 | 5 | 4 | (224) | 17 | 14 | 8 |
| 17 | 1 | 6 | 11 | 300 | 23 | 15 | 0 |
| 18 | 1 | 8 | 6 | (336) | 26 | 12 | 0 |
| 19 | 1 | 10 | 1 | 400 | 31 | 13 | 4 |
| 20 | 1 | 11 | 8 | (448) | 35 | 9 | 4 |
| 21 | 1 | 13 | 3 | 500 | 39 | 11 | 8 |
| 22 | 1 | 14 | 10 | (560) | 44 | 6 | 8 |
| 23 | 1 | 16 | 5 | 600 | 47 | 10 | 0 |
| 24 | 1 | 18 | 0 | (672) | 53 | 4 | 0 |
| 25 | 1 | 19 | 7 | 700 | 55 | 8 | 4 |
| 26 | 2 | 1 | 2 | (784) | 62 | 1 | 4 |
| 27 | 2 | 2 | 9 | 800 | 63 | 6 | 8 |
| (28) | 2 | 4 | 4 | (896) | 70 | 18 | 8 |
| 29 | 2 | 5 | 11 | 900 | 71 | 5 | 0 |
| 30 | 2 | 7 | 6 | 1000 | 79 | 3 | 4 |
| 31 | 2 | 9 | 1 | 2000 | 158 | 6 | 8 |
| 32 | 2 | 10 | 8 | 3000 | 237 | 10 | 0 |
| 33 | 2 | 12 | 3 | 4000 | 316 | 13 | 4 |
| 34 | 2 | 13 | 10 | 5000 | 395 | 16 | 8 |
| 35 | 2 | 15 | 5 | 10000 | 791 | 13 | 4 |

## Five-Groats, or Twenty-Pence.

| | l. | s. | d. | | l. | s. | d. |
|---|---|---|---|---|---|---|---|
| 1 | 0 | 1 | 8 | 36 | 3 | 0 | 0 |
| 2 | 0 | 3 | 4 | 37 | 3 | 1 | 8 |
| 3 | 0 | 5 | 0 | 38 | 3 | 3 | 4 |
| 4 | 0 | 6 | 8 | 39 | 3 | 5 | 0 |
| 5 | 0 | 8 | 4 | 40 | 3 | 6 | 8 |
| 6 | 0 | 10 | 0 | 50 | 4 | 3 | 4 |
| 7 | 0 | 11 | 8 | (56) | 4 | 13 | 4 |
| 8 | 0 | 13 | 4 | 60 | 5 | 0 | 0 |
| 9 | 0 | 15 | 0 | 70 | 5 | 16 | 8 |
| 10 | 0 | 16 | 8 | 80 | 6 | 13 | 4 |
| 11 | 0 | 18 | 4 | (84) | 7 | 0 | 0 |
| 12 | 1 | 0 | 0 | 90 | 7 | 10 | 0 |
| 13 | 1 | 1 | 8 | 100 | 8 | 6 | 8 |
| 14 | 1 | 3 | 4 | (112) | 9 | 6 | 8 |
| 15 | 1 | 5 | 0 | 200 | 16 | 13 | 4 |
| 16 | 1 | 6 | 8 | (224) | 18 | 13 | 4 |
| 17 | 1 | 8 | 4 | 300 | 25 | 0 | 0 |
| 18 | 1 | 10 | 0 | (336) | 28 | 0 | 0 |
| 19 | 1 | 11 | 8 | 400 | 33 | 6 | 8 |
| 20 | 1 | 13 | 4 | (448) | 37 | 6 | 8 |
| 21 | 1 | 15 | 0 | 500 | 41 | 13 | 4 |
| 22 | 1 | 16 | 8 | (560) | 46 | 13 | 4 |
| 23 | 1 | 18 | 4 | 600 | 50 | 0 | 0 |
| 24 | 2 | 0 | 0 | (672) | 56 | 0 | 0 |
| 25 | 2 | 1 | 8 | 700 | 58 | 6 | 8 |
| 26 | 2 | 3 | 4 | (784) | 65 | 6 | 8 |
| 27 | 2 | 5 | 0 | 800 | 66 | 13 | 4 |
| (28) | 2 | 6 | 8 | (896) | 74 | 13 | 4 |
| 29 | 2 | 8 | 4 | 900 | 75 | 0 | 0 |
| 30 | 2 | 10 | 0 | 1000 | 83 | 6 | 8 |
| 31 | 2 | 11 | 8 | 2000 | 166 | 13 | 4 |
| 32 | 2 | 13 | 4 | 3000 | 250 | 0 | 0 |
| 33 | 2 | 15 | 0 | 4000 | 333 | 6 | 8 |
| 34 | 2 | 16 | 8 | 5000 | 416 | 13 | 4 |
| 35 | 2 | 18 | 4 | 10000 | 833 | 6 | 8 |

## One and Twenty-Pence.

| | l. | s. | d. | | l. | s. | d. |
|---|---|---|---|---|---|---|---|
| 1 | 0 | 1 | 9 | 36 | 3 | 3 | 0 |
| 2 | 0 | 3 | 6 | 37 | 3 | 4 | 9 |
| 3 | 0 | 5 | 3 | 38 | 3 | 6 | 6 |
| 4 | 0 | 7 | 0 | 39 | 3 | 8 | 3 |
| 5 | 0 | 8 | 9 | 40 | 3 | 10 | 0 |
| 6 | 0 | 10 | 6 | 50 | 4 | 7 | 6 |
| 7 | 0 | 12 | 3 | (56) | 4 | 18 | 0 |
| 8 | 0 | 14 | 0 | 60 | 5 | 5 | 0 |
| 9 | 0 | 15 | 9 | 70 | 6 | 2 | 6 |
| 10 | 0 | 17 | 6 | 80 | 7 | 0 | 0 |
| 11 | 0 | 19 | 3 | (84) | 7 | 7 | 0 |
| 12 | 1 | 1 | 0 | 90 | 7 | 17 | 6 |
| 13 | 1 | 2 | 9 | 100 | 8 | 15 | 0 |
| 14 | 1 | 4 | 6 | (112) | 9 | 16 | 0 |
| 15 | 1 | 6 | 3 | 200 | 17 | 10 | 0 |
| 16 | 1 | 8 | 0 | (224) | 19 | 12 | 0 |
| 17 | 1 | 9 | 9 | 300 | 26 | 5 | 0 |
| 18 | 1 | 11 | 6 | (336) | 29 | 8 | 0 |
| 19 | 1 | 13 | 3 | 400 | 35 | 0 | 0 |
| 20 | 1 | 15 | 0 | (448) | 39 | 4 | 0 |
| 21 | 1 | 16 | 9 | 500 | 43 | 15 | 0 |
| 22 | 1 | 18 | 6 | (560) | 49 | 0 | 0 |
| 23 | 2 | 0 | 3 | 600 | 52 | 10 | 0 |
| 24 | 2 | 2 | 0 | (672) | 58 | 16 | 0 |
| 25 | 2 | 3 | 9 | 700 | 61 | 5 | 0 |
| 26 | 2 | 5 | 6 | (784) | 68 | 12 | 0 |
| 27 | 2 | 7 | 3 | 800 | 70 | 0 | 0 |
| (28) | 2 | 9 | 0 | (896) | 78 | 8 | 0 |
| 29 | 2 | 10 | 9 | 900 | 78 | 15 | 0 |
| 30 | 2 | 12 | 6 | 1000 | 87 | 10 | 0 |
| 31 | 2 | 14 | 3 | 2000 | 175 | 0 | 0 |
| 32 | 2 | 16 | 0 | 3000 | 262 | 10 | 0 |
| 33 | 2 | 17 | 9 | 4000 | 350 | 0 | 0 |
| 34 | 2 | 19 | 6 | 5000 | 437 | 10 | 0 |
| 35 | 3 | 1 | 3 | 10000 | 875 | 0 | 0 |

## Two and Twenty-Pence.

| | l. | s. | d. | | l. | s. | d. |
|---|---|---|---|---|---|---|---|
| 1 | 0 | 1 | 10 | 36 | 3 | 6 | 0 |
| 2 | 0 | 3 | 8 | 37 | 3 | 7 | 10 |
| 3 | 0 | 5 | 6 | 38 | 3 | 9 | 8 |
| 4 | 0 | 7 | 4 | 39 | 3 | 11 | 6 |
| 5 | 0 | 9 | 2 | 40 | 3 | 13 | 4 |
| 6 | 0 | 11 | 0 | 50 | 4 | 11 | 8 |
| 7 | 0 | 12 | 10 | (56) | 5 | 2 | 8 |
| 8 | 0 | 14 | 8 | 60 | 5 | 10 | 0 |
| 9 | 0 | 16 | 6 | 70 | 6 | 8 | 4 |
| 10 | 0 | 18 | 4 | 80 | 7 | 6 | 8 |
| 11 | 1 | 0 | 2 | (84) | 7 | 14 | 0 |
| 12 | 1 | 2 | 0 | 90 | 8 | 5 | 0 |
| 13 | 1 | 3 | 10 | 100 | 9 | 3 | 4 |
| 14 | 1 | 5 | 8 | (112) | 10 | 5 | 4 |
| 15 | 1 | 7 | 6 | 200 | 18 | 6 | 8 |
| 16 | 1 | 9 | 4 | (224) | 20 | 10 | 8 |
| 17 | 1 | 11 | 2 | 300 | 27 | 10 | 0 |
| 18 | 1 | 13 | 0 | (336) | 30 | 16 | 0 |
| 19 | 1 | 14 | 10 | 400 | 36 | 13 | 4 |
| 20 | 1 | 16 | 8 | (448) | 41 | 1 | 4 |
| 21 | 1 | 18 | 6 | 500 | 45 | 16 | 8 |
| 22 | 2 | 0 | 4 | (560) | 51 | 6 | 8 |
| 23 | 2 | 2 | 2 | 600 | 55 | 0 | 0 |
| 24 | 2 | 4 | 0 | (672) | 61 | 12 | 0 |
| 25 | 2 | 5 | 10 | 700 | 64 | 3 | 4 |
| 26 | 2 | 7 | 8 | (784) | 71 | 17 | 4 |
| 27 | 2 | 9 | 6 | 800 | 73 | 6 | 8 |
| (28) | 2 | 11 | 4 | (896) | 82 | 2 | 8 |
| 29 | 2 | 13 | 2 | 900 | 82 | 10 | 0 |
| 30 | 2 | 15 | 0 | 1000 | 91 | 13 | 4 |
| 31 | 2 | 16 | 10 | 2000 | 183 | 6 | 8 |
| 32 | 2 | 18 | 8 | 3000 | 275 | 0 | 0 |
| 33 | 3 | 0 | 6 | 4000 | 366 | 13 | 4 |
| 34 | 3 | 2 | 4 | 5000 | 458 | 6 | 8 |
| 35 | 3 | 4 | 2 | 10000 | 916 | 13 | 4 |

## *Three and Twenty-Pence.*

| | l. | s. | d. | | l. | s. | d. |
|---|---|---|---|---|---|---|---|
| 1 | 0 | 1 | 11 | 36 | 3 | 9 | 0 |
| 2 | 0 | 3 | 10 | 37 | 3 | 10 | 11 |
| 3 | 0 | 5 | 9 | 38 | 3 | 12 | 10 |
| 4 | 0 | 7 | 8 | 39 | 3 | 14 | 9 |
| 5 | 0 | 9 | 7 | 40 | 3 | 16 | 8 |
| 6 | 0 | 11 | 6 | 50 | 4 | 15 | 10 |
| 7 | 0 | 13 | 5 | (56) | 5 | 7 | 4 |
| 8 | 0 | 15 | 4 | 60 | 5 | 15 | 0 |
| 9 | 0 | 17 | 3 | 70 | 6 | 14 | 2 |
| 10 | 0 | 19 | 2 | 80 | 7 | 13 | 4 |
| 11 | 1 | 1 | 1 | (84) | 8 | 1 | 0 |
| 12 | 1 | 3 | 0 | 90 | 8 | 12 | 6 |
| 13 | 1 | 4 | 11 | 100 | 9 | 11 | 8 |
| 14 | 1 | 6 | 10 | (112) | 10 | 14 | 8 |
| 15 | 1 | 8 | 9 | 200 | 19 | 3 | 4 |
| 16 | 1 | 10 | 8 | (224) | 21 | 9 | 4 |
| 17 | 1 | 12 | 7 | 300 | 28 | 15 | 0 |
| 18 | 1 | 14 | 6 | (336) | 32 | 4 | 0 |
| 19 | 1 | 16 | 5 | 400 | 38 | 6 | 8 |
| 20 | 1 | 18 | 4 | (448) | 42 | 18 | 8 |
| 21 | 2 | 0 | 3 | 500 | 47 | 18 | 4 |
| 22 | 2 | 2 | 2 | (560) | 53 | 13 | 4 |
| 23 | 2 | 4 | 1 | 600 | 57 | 10 | 0 |
| 24 | 2 | 6 | 0 | (672) | 64 | 8 | 0 |
| 25 | 2 | 7 | 11 | 700 | 67 | 1 | 8 |
| 26 | 2 | 9 | 10 | (784) | 75 | 2 | 8 |
| 27 | 2 | 11 | 9 | 800 | 76 | 13 | 4 |
| (28) | 2 | 13 | 8 | (896) | 85 | 17 | 4 |
| 29 | 2 | 15 | 7 | 900 | 86 | 5 | 0 |
| 30 | 2 | 17 | 6 | 1000 | 95 | 16 | 8 |
| 31 | 2 | 19 | 5 | 2000 | 191 | 13 | 4 |
| 32 | 3 | 1 | 4 | 3000 | 287 | 10 | 0 |
| 33 | 3 | 3 | 3 | 4000 | 383 | 6 | 8 |
| 34 | 3 | 5 | 2 | 5000 | 479 | 3 | 4 |
| 35 | 3 | 7 | 1 | 10000 | 958 | 6 | 8 |

## *Two Shillings.*

|  | l. | s. |  | l. | s. |
|---|---|---|---|---|---|
| 1 | 0 | 2 | 36 | 3 | 12 |
| 2 | 0 | 4 | 37 | 3 | 14 |
| 3 | 0 | 6 | 38 | 3 | 16 |
| 4 | 0 | 8 | 39 | 3 | 18 |
| 5 | 0 | 10 | 40 | 4 | 0 |
| 6 | 0 | 12 | 50 | 5 | 0 |
| 7 | 0 | 14 | (56) | 5 | 12 |
| 8 | 0 | 16 | 60 | 6 | 0 |
| 9 | 0 | 18 | 70 | 7 | 0 |
| 10 | 1 | 0 | 80 | 8 | 0 |
| 11 | 1 | 2 | (84) | 8 | 8 |
| 12 | 1 | 4 | 90 | 9 | 0 |
| 13 | 1 | 6 | 100 | 10 | 0 |
| 14 | 1 | 8 | (112) | 11 | 4 |
| 15 | 1 | 10 | 200 | 20 | 0 |
| 16 | 1 | 12 | (224) | 22 | 8 |
| 17 | 1 | 14 | 300 | 30 | 0 |
| 18 | 1 | 16 | (336) | 33 | 12 |
| 19 | 1 | 18 | 400 | 40 | 0 |
| 20 | 2 | 0 | (448) | 44 | 16 |
| 21 | 2 | 2 | 500 | 50 | 0 |
| 22 | 2 | 4 | (560) | 56 | 0 |
| 23 | 2 | 6 | 600 | 60 | 0 |
| 24 | 2 | 8 | (672) | 67 | 4 |
| 25 | 2 | 10 | 700 | 70 | 0 |
| 26 | 2 | 12 | (784) | 78 | 8 |
| 27 | 2 | 14 | 800 | 80 | 0 |
| (28) | 2 | 16 | (896) | 89 | 12 |
| 29 | 2 | 18 | 900 | 90 | 0 |
| 30 | 3 | 0 | 1000 | 100 | 0 |
| 31 | 3 | 2 | 2000 | 200 | 0 |
| 32 | 3 | 4 | 3000 | 300 | 0 |
| 33 | 3 | 6 | 4000 | 400 | 0 |
| 34 | 3 | 8 | 5000 | 500 | 0 |
| 35 | 3 | 10 | 10000 | 1000 | 0 |

## *Two Shillings and a Peny.*

| | l. | s. | d. | | l. | s. | d. |
|---|---|---|---|---|---|---|---|
| 1 | 0 | 2 | 1 | 36 | 3 | 15 | 0 |
| 2 | 0 | 4 | 2 | 37 | 3 | 17 | 1 |
| 3 | 0 | 6 | 3 | 38 | 3 | 19 | 2 |
| 4 | 0 | 8 | 4 | 39 | 4 | 1 | 3 |
| 5 | 0 | 10 | 5 | 40 | 4 | 3 | 4 |
| 6 | 0 | 12 | 6 | 50 | 5 | 4 | 2 |
| 7 | 0 | 14 | 7 | (56) | 5 | 16 | 8 |
| 8 | 0 | 16 | 8 | 60 | 6 | 5 | 0 |
| 9 | 0 | 18 | 9 | 70 | 7 | 5 | 10 |
| 10 | 1 | 0 | 10 | 80 | 8 | 6 | 8 |
| 11 | 1 | 2 | 11 | (84) | 8 | 15 | 0 |
| 12 | 1 | 5 | 0 | 90 | 9 | 7 | 6 |
| 13 | 1 | 7 | 1 | 100 | 10 | 8 | 4 |
| 14 | 1 | 9 | 2 | (112) | 11 | 13 | 4 |
| 15 | 1 | 11 | 3 | 200 | 20 | 16 | 8 |
| 16 | 1 | 13 | 4 | (224) | 23 | 6 | 8 |
| 17 | 1 | 15 | 5 | 300 | 31 | 5 | 0 |
| 18 | 1 | 17 | 6 | (336) | 35 | 0 | 0 |
| 19 | 1 | 19 | 7 | 400 | 41 | 13 | 4 |
| 20 | 2 | 1 | 8 | (448) | 46 | 13 | 4 |
| 21 | 2 | 3 | 9 | 500 | 52 | 1 | 8 |
| 22 | 2 | 5 | 10 | (560) | 58 | 6 | 8 |
| 23 | 2 | 7 | 11 | 600 | 62 | 10 | 0 |
| 24 | 2 | 10 | 0 | (672) | 70 | 0 | 0 |
| 25 | 2 | 12 | 1 | 700 | 72 | 18 | 4 |
| 26 | 2 | 14 | 2 | (784) | 81 | 13 | 4 |
| 27 | 2 | 16 | 3 | 800 | 83 | 6 | 8 |
| (28) | 2 | 18 | 4 | (896) | 93 | 6 | 8 |
| 29 | 3 | 0 | 5 | 900 | 93 | 15 | 0 |
| 30 | 3 | 2 | 6 | 1000 | 104 | 3 | 4 |
| 31 | 3 | 4 | 7 | 2000 | 208 | 6 | 8 |
| 32 | 3 | 6 | 8 | 3000 | 312 | 10 | 0 |
| 33 | 3 | 8 | 9 | 4000 | 416 | 13 | 4 |
| 34 | 3 | 10 | 10 | 5000 | 520 | 16 | 8 |
| 35 | 3 | 12 | 11 | 10000 | 1041 | 13 | 4 |

## Two Shillings and Two-pence.

| | l. | s. | d. |
|---|---|---|---|
| 1 | 0 | 2 | 2 |
| 2 | 0 | 4 | 4 |
| 3 | 0 | 6 | 6 |
| 4 | 0 | 8 | 8 |
| 5 | 0 | 10 | 10 |
| 6 | 0 | 13 | 0 |
| 7 | 0 | 15 | 2 |
| 8 | 0 | 17 | 4 |
| 9 | 0 | 19 | 6 |
| 10 | 1 | 1 | 8 |
| 11 | 1 | 3 | 10 |
| 12 | 1 | 6 | 0 |
| 13 | 1 | 8 | 2 |
| 14 | 1 | 10 | 4 |
| 15 | 1 | 12 | 6 |
| 16 | 1 | 14 | 8 |
| 17 | 1 | 16 | 10 |
| 18 | 1 | 19 | 0 |
| 19 | 2 | 1 | 2 |
| 20 | 2 | 3 | 4 |
| 21 | 2 | 5 | 6 |
| 22 | 2 | 7 | 8 |
| 23 | 2 | 9 | 10 |
| 24 | 2 | 12 | 0 |
| 25 | 2 | 14 | 2 |
| 26 | 2 | 16 | 4 |
| 27 | 2 | 18 | 6 |
| (28) | 3 | 0 | 8 |
| 29 | 3 | 2 | 10 |
| 30 | 3 | 5 | 0 |
| 31 | 3 | 7 | 2 |
| 32 | 3 | 9 | 4 |
| 33 | 3 | 11 | 6 |
| 34 | 3 | 13 | 8 |
| 35 | 3 | 15 | 10 |
| 36 | 3 | 18 | 0 |
| 37 | 4 | 0 | 2 |
| 38 | 4 | 2 | 4 |
| 39 | 4 | 4 | 6 |
| 40 | 4 | 6 | 8 |
| 50 | 5 | 8 | 4 |
| (56) | 6 | 1 | 4 |
| 60 | 6 | 10 | 0 |
| 70 | 7 | 11 | 8 |
| 80 | 8 | 13 | 4 |
| (84) | 9 | 2 | 0 |
| 90 | 9 | 15 | 0 |
| 100 | 10 | 16 | 8 |
| (112) | 12 | 2 | 8 |
| 200 | 21 | 13 | 4 |
| (224) | 24 | 5 | 4 |
| 300 | 32 | 10 | 0 |
| (336) | 36 | 8 | 0 |
| 400 | 43 | 6 | 8 |
| (448) | 48 | 10 | 8 |
| 500 | 54 | 3 | 4 |
| (560) | 60 | 13 | 4 |
| 600 | 65 | 0 | 0 |
| (672) | 72 | 16 | 0 |
| 700 | 75 | 16 | 8 |
| (784) | 84 | 18 | 8 |
| 800 | 86 | 13 | 4 |
| (896) | 97 | 1 | 4 |
| 900 | 97 | 10 | 0 |
| 1000 | 108 | 6 | 8 |
| 2000 | 216 | 13 | 4 |
| 3000 | 325 | 0 | 0 |
| 4000 | 433 | 6 | 8 |
| 5000 | 541 | 13 | 4 |
| 10000 | 1083 | 6 | 8 |

## Two Shillings and Three-Pence.

| | l. | s. | d. | | l. | s. | d. |
|---|---|---|---|---|---|---|---|
| 1 | 0 | 2 | 3 | 36 | 4 | 1 | 0 |
| 2 | 0 | 4 | 6 | 37 | 4 | 3 | 3 |
| 3 | 0 | 6 | 9 | 38 | 4 | 5 | 6 |
| 4 | 0 | 9 | 0 | 39 | 4 | 7 | 9 |
| 5 | 0 | 11 | 3 | 40 | 4 | 10 | 0 |
| 6 | 0 | 13 | 6 | 50 | 5 | 12 | 6 |
| 7 | 0 | 15 | 9 | (56) | 6 | 6 | 0 |
| 8 | 0 | 18 | 0 | 60 | 6 | 15 | 0 |
| 9 | 1 | 0 | 3 | 70 | 7 | 17 | 6 |
| 10 | 1 | 2 | 6 | 80 | 9 | 0 | 0 |
| 11 | 1 | 4 | 9 | (84) | 9 | 9 | 0 |
| 12 | 1 | 7 | 0 | 90 | 10 | 2 | 6 |
| 13 | 1 | 9 | 3 | 100 | 11 | 5 | 0 |
| 14 | 1 | 11 | 6 | (112) | 12 | 12 | 0 |
| 15 | 1 | 13 | 9 | 200 | 22 | 10 | 0 |
| 16 | 1 | 16 | 0 | (224) | 25 | 4 | 0 |
| 17 | 1 | 18 | 3 | 300 | 33 | 15 | 0 |
| 18 | 2 | 0 | 6 | (336) | 37 | 16 | 0 |
| 19 | 2 | 2 | 9 | 400 | 45 | 0 | 0 |
| 20 | 2 | 5 | 0 | (448) | 50 | 8 | 0 |
| 21 | 2 | 7 | 3 | 500 | 56 | 5 | 0 |
| 22 | 2 | 9 | 6 | (560) | 63 | 0 | 0 |
| 23 | 2 | 11 | 9 | 600 | 67 | 10 | 0 |
| 24 | 2 | 14 | 0 | (672) | 75 | 12 | 0 |
| 25 | 2 | 16 | 3 | 700 | 78 | 15 | 0 |
| 26 | 2 | 18 | 6 | (784) | 88 | 4 | 0 |
| 27 | 3 | 0 | 9 | 800 | 90 | 0 | 0 |
| (28) | 3 | 3 | 0 | (896) | 100 | 16 | 0 |
| 29 | 3 | 5 | 3 | 900 | 101 | 5 | 0 |
| 30 | 3 | 7 | 6 | 1000 | 112 | 10 | 0 |
| 31 | 3 | 9 | 9 | 2000 | 225 | 0 | 0 |
| 32 | 3 | 12 | 0 | 3000 | 337 | 10 | 0 |
| 33 | 3 | 14 | 3 | 4000 | 450 | 0 | 0 |
| 34 | 3 | 16 | 6 | 5000 | 562 | 10 | 0 |
| 35 | 3 | 18 | 9 | 10000 | 1125 | 0 | 0 |

## Two Shillings Four-Pence, or Seven Groats.

| | l. | s. | d. | | l. | s. | d. |
|---|---|---|---|---|---|---|---|
| 1 | 0 | 2 | 4 | 36 | 4 | 4 | 0 |
| 2 | 0 | 4 | 8 | 37 | 4 | 6 | 4 |
| 3 | 0 | 7 | 0 | 38 | 4 | 8 | 8 |
| 4 | 0 | 9 | 4 | 39 | 4 | 11 | 0 |
| 5 | 0 | 11 | 8 | 40 | 4 | 13 | 4 |
| 6 | 0 | 14 | 0 | 50 | 5 | 16 | 8 |
| 7 | 0 | 16 | 4 | (56) | 6 | 10 | 8 |
| 8 | 0 | 18 | 8 | 60 | 7 | 0 | 0 |
| 9 | 1 | 1 | 0 | 70 | 8 | 3 | 4 |
| 10 | 1 | 3 | 4 | 80 | 9 | 6 | 8 |
| 11 | 1 | 5 | 8 | (84) | 9 | 16 | 0 |
| 12 | 1 | 8 | 0 | 90 | 10 | 10 | 0 |
| 13 | 1 | 10 | 4 | 100 | 11 | 13 | 4 |
| 14 | 1 | 12 | 8 | (112) | 13 | 1 | 4 |
| 15 | 1 | 15 | 0 | 200 | 23 | 6 | 8 |
| 16 | 1 | 17 | 4 | (224) | 26 | 2 | 8 |
| 17 | 1 | 19 | 8 | 300 | 35 | 0 | 0 |
| 18 | 2 | 2 | 0 | (336) | 39 | 4 | 0 |
| 19 | 2 | 4 | 4 | 400 | 46 | 13 | 4 |
| 20 | 2 | 6 | 8 | (448) | 52 | 5 | 4 |
| 21 | 2 | 9 | 0 | 500 | 58 | 6 | 8 |
| 22 | 2 | 11 | 4 | (560) | 65 | 6 | 8 |
| 23 | 2 | 13 | 8 | 600 | 70 | 0 | 0 |
| 24 | 2 | 16 | 0 | (672) | 78 | 8 | 0 |
| 25 | 2 | 18 | 4 | 700 | 81 | 13 | 4 |
| 26 | 3 | 0 | 8 | (784) | 91 | 9 | 4 |
| 27 | 3 | 3 | 0 | 800 | 93 | 6 | 8 |
| (28) | 3 | 5 | 4 | (896) | 104 | 10 | 8 |
| 29 | 3 | 7 | 8 | 900 | 105 | 0 | 0 |
| 30 | 3 | 10 | 0 | 1000 | 116 | 13 | 4 |
| 31 | 3 | 12 | 4 | 2000 | 233 | 6 | 8 |
| 32 | 3 | 14 | 8 | 3000 | 350 | 0 | 0 |
| 33 | 3 | 17 | 0 | 4000 | 466 | 13 | 4 |
| 34 | 3 | 19 | 4 | 5000 | 583 | 6 | 8 |
| 35 | 4 | 1 | 8 | 10000 | 1166 | 13 | 4 |

## *Two Shillings and Five-Pence.*

| | l. | s. | d. |
|---|---|---|---|
| 1 | 0 | 2 | 5 |
| 2 | 0 | 4 | 10 |
| 3 | 0 | 7 | 3 |
| 4 | 0 | 9 | 8 |
| 5 | 0 | 12 | 1 |
| 6 | 0 | 14 | 6 |
| 7 | 0 | 16 | 11 |
| 8 | 0 | 19 | 4 |
| 9 | 1 | 1 | 9 |
| 10 | 1 | 4 | 2 |
| 11 | 1 | 6 | 7 |
| 12 | 1 | 9 | 0 |
| 13 | 1 | 11 | 5 |
| 14 | 1 | 13 | 10 |
| 15 | 1 | 16 | 3 |
| 16 | 1 | 18 | 8 |
| 17 | 2 | 1 | 1 |
| 18 | 2 | 3 | 6 |
| 19 | 2 | 5 | 11 |
| 20 | 2 | 8 | 4 |
| 21 | 2 | 10 | 9 |
| 22 | 2 | 13 | 2 |
| 23 | 2 | 15 | 7 |
| 24 | 2 | 18 | 0 |
| 25 | 3 | 0 | 5 |
| 26 | 3 | 2 | 10 |
| 27 | 3 | 5 | 3 |
| (28) | 3 | 7 | 8 |
| 29 | 3 | 10 | 1 |
| 30 | 3 | 12 | 6 |
| 31 | 3 | 14 | 11 |
| 32 | 3 | 17 | 4 |
| 33 | 3 | 19 | 9 |
| 34 | 4 | 2 | 2 |
| 35 | 4 | 4 | 7 |

| | l. | s. | d. |
|---|---|---|---|
| 36 | 4 | 7 | 0 |
| 37 | 4 | 9 | 5 |
| 38 | 4 | 11 | 10 |
| 39 | 4 | 14 | 3 |
| 40 | 4 | 16 | 8 |
| 50 | 6 | 0 | 10 |
| (56) | 6 | 15 | 4 |
| 60 | 7 | 5 | 0 |
| 70 | 8 | 9 | 2 |
| 80 | 9 | 13 | 4 |
| (84) | 10 | 3 | 0 |
| 90 | 10 | 17 | 6 |
| 100 | 12 | 1 | 8 |
| (112) | 13 | 10 | 8 |
| 200 | 24 | 3 | 4 |
| (224) | 27 | 1 | 4 |
| 300 | 36 | 5 | 0 |
| (336) | 40 | 12 | 0 |
| 400 | 48 | 6 | 8 |
| (448) | 54 | 2 | 8 |
| 500 | 60 | 8 | 4 |
| (560) | 67 | 13 | 4 |
| 600 | 72 | 10 | 0 |
| (672) | 81 | 4 | 0 |
| 700 | 84 | 11 | 8 |
| (784) | 94 | 14 | 8 |
| 800 | 96 | 13 | 4 |
| (896) | 108 | 5 | 4 |
| 900 | 108 | 15 | 0 |
| 1000 | 120 | 16 | 8 |
| 2000 | 241 | 13 | 4 |
| 3000 | 362 | 10 | 0 |
| 4000 | 483 | 6 | 8 |
| 5000 | 604 | 3 | 4 |
| 10000 | 1208 | 6 | 8 |

## Two Shillings Six-Pence, or Half a Crown.

| | l. | s. | d. | | l. | s. | d. |
|---|---|---|---|---|---|---|---|
| 1 | 0 | 2 | 6 | 36 | 4 | 10 | 0 |
| 2 | 0 | 5 | 0 | 37 | 4 | 12 | 6 |
| 3 | 0 | 7 | 6 | 38 | 4 | 15 | 0 |
| 4 | 0 | 10 | 0 | 39 | 4 | 17 | 6 |
| 5 | 0 | 12 | 6 | 40 | 5 | 0 | 0 |
| 6 | 0 | 15 | 0 | 50 | 6 | 5 | 0 |
| 7 | 0 | 17 | 6 | (56) | 7 | 0 | 0 |
| 8 | 1 | 0 | 0 | 60 | 7 | 10 | 0 |
| 9 | 1 | 2 | 6 | 70 | 8 | 15 | 0 |
| 10 | 1 | 5 | 0 | 80 | 10 | 0 | 0 |
| 11 | 1 | 7 | 6 | (84) | 10 | 10 | 0 |
| 12 | 1 | 10 | 0 | 90 | 11 | 5 | 0 |
| 13 | 1 | 12 | 6 | 100 | 12 | 10 | 0 |
| 14 | 1 | 15 | 0 | (112) | 14 | 0 | 0 |
| 15 | 1 | 17 | 6 | 200 | 25 | 0 | 0 |
| 16 | 2 | 0 | 0 | (224) | 28 | 0 | 0 |
| 17 | 2 | 2 | 6 | 300 | 37 | 10 | 0 |
| 18 | 2 | 5 | 0 | (336) | 42 | 0 | 0 |
| 19 | 2 | 7 | 6 | 400 | 50 | 0 | 0 |
| 20 | 2 | 10 | 0 | (448) | 56 | 0 | 0 |
| 21 | 2 | 12 | 6 | 500 | 62 | 10 | 0 |
| 22 | 2 | 15 | 0 | (560) | 70 | 0 | 0 |
| 23 | 2 | 17 | 6 | 600 | 75 | 0 | 0 |
| 24 | 3 | 0 | 0 | (672) | 84 | 0 | 0 |
| 25 | 3 | 2 | 6 | 700 | 87 | 10 | 0 |
| 26 | 3 | 5 | 0 | (784) | 98 | 0 | 0 |
| 27 | 3 | 7 | 6 | 800 | 100 | 0 | 0 |
| (28) | 3 | 10 | 0 | (896) | 112 | 0 | 0 |
| 29 | 3 | 12 | 6 | 900 | 112 | 10 | 0 |
| 30 | 3 | 15 | 0 | 1000 | 125 | 0 | 0 |
| 31 | 3 | 17 | 6 | 2000 | 250 | 0 | 0 |
| 32 | 4 | 0 | 0 | 3000 | 375 | 0 | 0 |
| 33 | 4 | 2 | 6 | 4000 | 500 | 0 | 0 |
| 34 | 4 | 5 | 0 | 5000 | 625 | 0 | 0 |
| 35 | 4 | 7 | 6 | 10000 | 1250 | 0 | 0 |

# Two Shillings and Seven Pence.

| | l. | s. | d. | | l. | s. | d. |
|---|---|---|---|---|---|---|---|
| 1 | 0 | 2 | 7 | 36 | 4 | 13 | 0 |
| 2 | 0 | 5 | 2 | 37 | 4 | 15 | 7 |
| 3 | 0 | 7 | 9 | 38 | 4 | 18 | 2 |
| 4 | 0 | 10 | 4 | 39 | 5 | 0 | 9 |
| 5 | 0 | 12 | 11 | 40 | 5 | 3 | 4 |
| 6 | 0 | 15 | 6 | 50 | 6 | 9 | 2 |
| 7 | 0 | 18 | 1 | (56) | 7 | 4 | 8 |
| 8 | 1 | 0 | 8 | 60 | 7 | 15 | 0 |
| 9 | 1 | 3 | 3 | 70 | 9 | 0 | 10 |
| 10 | 1 | 5 | 10 | 80 | 10 | 6 | 8 |
| 11 | 1 | 8 | 5 | (84) | 10 | 17 | 0 |
| 12 | 1 | 11 | 0 | 90 | 11 | 12 | 6 |
| 13 | 1 | 13 | 7 | 100 | 12 | 18 | 4 |
| 14 | 1 | 16 | 2 | (112) | 14 | 9 | 4 |
| 15 | 1 | 18 | 9 | 200 | 25 | 16 | 8 |
| 16 | 2 | 1 | 4 | (224) | 28 | 18 | 8 |
| 17 | 2 | 3 | 11 | 300 | 38 | 15 | 0 |
| 18 | 2 | 6 | 6 | (336) | 43 | 8 | 0 |
| 19 | 2 | 9 | 1 | 400 | 51 | 13 | 4 |
| 20 | 2 | 11 | 8 | (448) | 57 | 17 | 4 |
| 21 | 2 | 14 | 3 | 500 | 64 | 11 | 8 |
| 22 | 2 | 16 | 10 | (560) | 72 | 6 | 8 |
| 23 | 2 | 19 | 5 | 600 | 77 | 10 | 0 |
| 24 | 3 | 2 | 0 | (672) | 86 | 16 | 0 |
| 25 | 3 | 4 | 7 | 700 | 90 | 8 | 4 |
| 26 | 3 | 7 | 2 | (784) | 101 | 5 | 4 |
| 27 | 3 | 9 | 9 | 800 | 103 | 6 | 8 |
| (28) | 3 | 12 | 4 | (896) | 115 | 14 | 8 |
| 29 | 3 | 14 | 11 | 900 | 116 | 5 | 0 |
| 30 | 3 | 17 | 6 | 1000 | 129 | 3 | 4 |
| 31 | 4 | 0 | 1 | 2000 | 258 | 6 | 8 |
| 32 | 4 | 2 | 8 | 3000 | 387 | 10 | 0 |
| 33 | 4 | 5 | 3 | 4000 | 516 | 13 | 4 |
| 34 | 4 | 7 | 10 | 5000 | 645 | 16 | 8 |
| 35 | 4 | 10 | 5 | 10000 | 1291 | 13 | 4 |

## Two Shillings Eight Pence, or Eight Groats.

| | l. | s. | d. | | l. | s. | d. |
|---|---|---|---|---|---|---|---|
| 1 | 0 | 2 | 8 | 36 | 4 | 16 | 0 |
| 2 | 0 | 5 | 4 | 37 | 4 | 18 | 8 |
| 3 | 0 | 8 | 0 | 38 | 5 | 1 | 4 |
| 4 | 0 | 10 | 8 | 39 | 5 | 4 | 0 |
| 5 | 0 | 13 | 4 | 40 | 5 | 6 | 8 |
| 6 | 0 | 16 | 0 | 50 | 6 | 13 | 4 |
| 7 | 0 | 18 | 8 | (56) | 7 | 9 | 4 |
| 8 | 1 | 1 | 4 | 60 | 8 | 0 | 0 |
| 9 | 1 | 4 | 0 | 70 | 9 | 6 | 8 |
| 10 | 1 | 6 | 8 | 80 | 10 | 13 | 4 |
| 11 | 1 | 9 | 4 | (84) | 11 | 4 | 0 |
| 12 | 1 | 12 | 0 | 90 | 12 | 0 | 0 |
| 13 | 1 | 14 | 8 | 100 | 13 | 6 | 8 |
| 14 | 1 | 17 | 4 | (112) | 14 | 18 | 8 |
| 15 | 2 | 0 | 0 | 200 | 26 | 13 | 4 |
| 16 | 2 | 2 | 8 | (224) | 29 | 17 | 4 |
| 17 | 2 | 5 | 4 | 300 | 40 | 0 | 0 |
| 18 | 2 | 8 | 0 | (336) | 44 | 16 | 0 |
| 19 | 2 | 10 | 8 | 400 | 53 | 6 | 8 |
| 20 | 2 | 13 | 4 | (448) | 59 | 14 | 8 |
| 21 | 2 | 16 | 0 | 500 | 66 | 13 | 4 |
| 22 | 2 | 18 | 8 | (560) | 74 | 13 | 4 |
| 23 | 3 | 1 | 4 | 600 | 80 | 0 | 0 |
| 24 | 3 | 4 | 0 | (672) | 89 | 12 | 0 |
| 25 | 3 | 6 | 8 | 700 | 93 | 6 | 8 |
| 26 | 3 | 9 | 4 | (784) | 104 | 10 | 8 |
| 27 | 3 | 12 | 0 | 800 | 106 | 13 | 4 |
| 28 | 3 | 14 | 8 | (896) | 119 | 9 | 4 |
| 29 | 3 | 17 | 4 | 900 | 120 | 0 | 0 |
| 30 | 4 | 0 | 0 | 1000 | 133 | 6 | 8 |
| 31 | 4 | 2 | 8 | 2000 | 266 | 13 | 4 |
| 32 | 4 | 5 | 4 | 3000 | 400 | 0 | 0 |
| 33 | 4 | 8 | 0 | 4000 | 533 | 6 | 8 |
| 34 | 4 | 10 | 8 | 5000 | 666 | 13 | 4 |
| 35 | 4 | 13 | 4 | 10000 | 1333 | 6 | 8 |

## Two Shillings and Nine-Pence.

| | l. | s. | d. | | l. | s. | d. |
|---|---|---|---|---|---|---|---|
| 1 | 0 | 2 | 9 | 36 | 4 | 19 | 0 |
| 2 | 0 | 5 | 6 | 37 | 5 | 1 | 9 |
| 3 | 0 | 8 | 3 | 38 | 5 | 4 | 6 |
| 4 | 0 | 11 | 0 | 39 | 5 | 7 | 3 |
| 5 | 0 | 13 | 9 | 40 | 5 | 10 | 0 |
| 6 | 0 | 16 | 6 | 50 | 6 | 17 | 6 |
| 7 | 0 | 19 | 3 | (56) | 7 | 14 | 0 |
| 8 | 1 | 2 | 0 | 60 | 8 | 5 | 0 |
| 9 | 1 | 4 | 9 | 70 | 9 | 12 | 6 |
| 10 | 1 | 7 | 6 | 80 | 11 | 0 | 0 |
| 11 | 1 | 10 | 3 | (84) | 11 | 11 | 0 |
| 12 | 1 | 13 | 0 | 90 | 12 | 7 | 6 |
| 13 | 1 | 15 | 9 | 100 | 13 | 15 | 0 |
| 14 | 1 | 18 | 6 | (112) | 15 | 8 | 0 |
| 15 | 2 | 1 | 3 | 200 | 27 | 10 | 0 |
| 16 | 2 | 4 | 0 | (224) | 30 | 16 | 0 |
| 17 | 2 | 6 | 9 | 300 | 41 | 5 | 0 |
| 18 | 2 | 9 | 6 | (336) | 46 | 4 | 0 |
| 19 | 2 | 12 | 3 | 400 | 55 | 0 | 0 |
| 20 | 2 | 15 | 0 | (448) | 61 | 12 | 0 |
| 21 | 2 | 17 | 9 | 500 | 68 | 15 | 0 |
| 22 | 3 | 0 | 6 | (560) | 77 | 0 | 0 |
| 23 | 3 | 3 | 3 | 600 | 82 | 10 | 0 |
| 24 | 3 | 6 | 0 | (672) | 92 | 8 | 0 |
| 25 | 3 | 8 | 9 | 700 | 96 | 5 | 0 |
| 26 | 3 | 11 | 6 | (784) | 107 | 16 | 0 |
| 27 | 3 | 14 | 3 | 800 | 110 | 0 | 0 |
| (28) | 3 | 17 | 0 | (896) | 123 | 4 | 0 |
| 29 | 3 | 19 | 9 | 900 | 123 | 15 | 9 |
| 30 | 4 | 2 | 6 | 1000 | 137 | 10 | 0 |
| 31 | 4 | 5 | 3 | 2000 | 275 | 0 | 0 |
| 32 | 4 | 8 | 0 | 3000 | 412 | 10 | 0 |
| 33 | 4 | 10 | 9 | 4000 | 550 | 0 | 0 |
| 34 | 4 | 13 | 6 | 5000 | 687 | 10 | 0 |
| 35 | 4 | 16 | 3 | 10000 | 1375 | 0 | 0 |

## *Two Shillings and Ten-Pence.*

| | l. | s. | d. | | l. | s. | d. |
|---|---|---|---|---|---|---|---|
| 1 | 0 | 2 | 10 | 36 | 5 | 2 | 0 |
| 2 | 0 | 5 | 8 | 37 | 5 | 4 | 10 |
| 3 | 0 | 8 | 6 | 38 | 5 | 7 | 8 |
| 4 | 0 | 11 | 4 | 39 | 5 | 10 | 6 |
| 5 | 0 | 14 | 2 | 40 | 5 | 13 | 4 |
| 6 | 0 | 17 | 0 | 50 | 7 | 1 | 8 |
| 7 | 0 | 19 | 10 | (56) | 7 | 18 | 8 |
| 8 | 1 | 2 | 8 | 60 | 8 | 10 | 0 |
| 9 | 1 | 5 | 6 | 70 | 9 | 18 | 4 |
| 10 | 1 | 8 | 4 | 80 | 11 | 6 | 8 |
| 11 | 1 | 11 | 2 | (84) | 11 | 18 | 0 |
| 12 | 1 | 14 | 0 | 90 | 12 | 15 | 0 |
| 13 | 1 | 16 | 10 | 100 | 14 | 3 | 4 |
| 14 | 1 | 19 | 8 | (112) | 15 | 17 | 4 |
| 15 | 2 | 2 | 6 | 200 | 28 | 6 | 8 |
| 16 | 2 | 5 | 4 | (224) | 31 | 14 | 8 |
| 17 | 2 | 8 | 2 | 300 | 42 | 10 | 0 |
| 18 | 2 | 11 | 0 | (336) | 47 | 12 | 0 |
| 19 | 2 | 13 | 10 | 400 | 56 | 13 | 4 |
| 20 | 2 | 16 | 8 | (448) | 63 | 9 | 4 |
| 21 | 2 | 19 | 6 | 500 | 70 | 16 | 8 |
| 22 | 3 | 2 | 4 | (560) | 79 | 6 | 8 |
| 23 | 3 | 5 | 2 | 600 | 85 | 0 | 0 |
| 24 | 3 | 8 | 0 | (672) | 95 | 4 | 0 |
| 25 | 3 | 10 | 10 | 700 | 99 | 3 | 4 |
| 26 | 3 | 13 | 8 | (784) | 111 | 1 | 4 |
| 27 | 3 | 16 | 6 | 800 | 113 | 6 | 8 |
| (28) | 3 | 19 | 4 | (896) | 126 | 18 | 8 |
| 29 | 4 | 2 | 2 | 900 | 127 | 10 | 0 |
| 30 | 4 | 5 | 0 | 1000 | 141 | 13 | 4 |
| 31 | 4 | 7 | 10 | 2000 | 283 | 6 | 8 |
| 32 | 4 | 10 | 8 | 3000 | 425 | 0 | 0 |
| 33 | 4 | 13 | 6 | 4000 | 566 | 13 | 4 |
| 34 | 4 | 16 | 4 | 5000 | 708 | 6 | 8 |
| 35 | 4 | 19 | 2 | 10000 | 1416 | 13 | 4 |

## *Two Shillings and Eleven-Pence.*

| | l. | s. | d. | | l. | s. | d. |
|---|---|---|---|---|---|---|---|
| 1 | 0 | 2 | 11 | 36 | 5 | 5 | 0 |
| 2 | 0 | 5 | 10 | 37 | 5 | 7 | 11 |
| 3 | 0 | 8 | 9 | 38 | 5 | 10 | 10 |
| 4 | 0 | 11 | 8 | 39 | 5 | 13 | 9 |
| 5 | 0 | 14 | 7 | 40 | 5 | 16 | 8 |
| 6 | 0 | 17 | 6 | 50 | 7 | 5 | 10 |
| 7 | 1 | 0 | 5 | (56) | 8 | 3 | 4 |
| 8 | 1 | 3 | 4 | 60 | 8 | 15 | 0 |
| 9 | 1 | 6 | 3 | 70 | 10 | 4 | 2 |
| 10 | 1 | 9 | 2 | 80 | 11 | 13 | 4 |
| 11 | 1 | 12 | 1 | (84) | 12 | 5 | 0 |
| 12 | 1 | 15 | 0 | 90 | 13 | 2 | 6 |
| 13 | 1 | 17 | 11 | 100 | 14 | 11 | 8 |
| 14 | 2 | 0 | 10 | (112) | 16 | 6 | 8 |
| 15 | 2 | 3 | 9 | 200 | 29 | 3 | 4 |
| 16 | 2 | 6 | 8 | (224) | 32 | 13 | 4 |
| 17 | 2 | 9 | 7 | 300 | 43 | 15 | 0 |
| 18 | 2 | 12 | 6 | (336) | 49 | 0 | 0 |
| 19 | 2 | 15 | 5 | 400 | 58 | 6 | 8 |
| 20 | 2 | 18 | 4 | (448) | 65 | 6 | 8 |
| 21 | 3 | 1 | 3 | 500 | 72 | 18 | 4 |
| 22 | 3 | 4 | 2 | (560) | 81 | 13 | 4 |
| 23 | 3 | 7 | 1 | 600 | 87 | 10 | 0 |
| 24 | 3 | 10 | 0 | (672) | 98 | 0 | 0 |
| 25 | 3 | 12 | 11 | 700 | 102 | 1 | 8 |
| 26 | 3 | 15 | 10 | (784) | 114 | 6 | 8 |
| 27 | 3 | 18 | 9 | 800 | 116 | 13 | 4 |
| (28) | 4 | 1 | 8 | (896) | 130 | 13 | 4 |
| 29 | 4 | 4 | 7 | 900 | 131 | 5 | 0 |
| 30 | 4 | 7 | 6 | 1000 | 145 | 16 | 8 |
| 31 | 4 | 10 | 5 | 2000 | 291 | 13 | 4 |
| 32 | 4 | 13 | 4 | 3000 | 437 | 10 | 0 |
| 33 | 4 | 16 | 3 | 4000 | 583 | 6 | 8 |
| 34 | 4 | 19 | 2 | 5000 | 729 | 3 | 4 |
| 35 | 5 | 2 | 1 | 10000 | 1458 | 6 | 8 |

## Three Shillings.

| | l. | s. | | l. | s. |
|---|---|---|---|---|---|
| 1 | 0 | 3 | 36 | 5 | 8 |
| 2 | 0 | 6 | 37 | 5 | 11 |
| 3 | 0 | 9 | 38 | 5 | 14 |
| 4 | 0 | 12 | 39 | 5 | 17 |
| 5 | 0 | 15 | 40 | 6 | 0 |
| 6 | 0 | 18 | 50 | 7 | 10 |
| 7 | 1 | 1 | (56) | 8 | 8 |
| 8 | 1 | 4 | 60 | 9 | 0 |
| 9 | 1 | 7 | 70 | 10 | 10 |
| 10 | 1 | 10 | 80 | 12 | 0 |
| 11 | 1 | 13 | (84) | 12 | 12 |
| 12 | 1 | 16 | 90 | 13 | 10 |
| 13 | 1 | 19 | 100 | 15 | 0 |
| 14 | 2 | 2 | (112) | 16 | 16 |
| 15 | 2 | 5 | 200 | 30 | 0 |
| 16 | 2 | 8 | (224) | 33 | 12 |
| 17 | 2 | 11 | 300 | 45 | 0 |
| 18 | 2 | 14 | (336) | 50 | 8 |
| 19 | 2 | 17 | 400 | 60 | 0 |
| 20 | 3 | 0 | (448) | 67 | 4 |
| 21 | 3 | 3 | 500 | 75 | 0 |
| 22 | 3 | 6 | (560) | 84 | 0 |
| 23 | 3 | 9 | 600 | 90 | 0 |
| 24 | 3 | 12 | (672) | 100 | 16 |
| 25 | 3 | 15 | 700 | 105 | 0 |
| 26 | 3 | 18 | (784) | 117 | 12 |
| 27 | 4 | 1 | 800 | 120 | 0 |
| (28) | 4 | 4 | (896) | 134 | 8 |
| 29 | 4 | 7 | 900 | 135 | 0 |
| 30 | 4 | 10 | 1000 | 150 | 0 |
| 31. | 4 | 13 | 2000 | 300 | 0 |
| 32 | 4 | 16 | 3000 | 450 | 0 |
| 33 | 4 | 19 | 4000 | 600 | 0 |
| 34 | 5 | 2 | 5000 | 750 | 0 |
| 35 | 5 | 5 | 10000. | 1500. | 0 |

## *Three Shillings and Six-Pence.*

| | l. | s. | d. | | l. | s. | d. |
|---|---|---|---|---|---|---|---|
| 1 | 0 | 3 | 6 | 36 | 6 | 6 | 0 |
| 2 | 0 | 7 | 0 | 37 | 6 | 9 | 6 |
| 3 | 0 | 10 | 6 | 38 | 6 | 13 | 0 |
| 4 | 0 | 14 | 0 | 39 | 6 | 16 | 6 |
| 5 | 0 | 17 | 6 | 40 | 7 | 0 | 0 |
| 6 | 1 | 1 | 0 | 50 | 8 | 15 | 0 |
| 7 | 1 | 4 | 6 | (56) | 9 | 16 | 0 |
| 8 | 1 | 8 | 0 | 60 | 10 | 10 | 0 |
| 9 | 1 | 11 | 6 | 70 | 12 | 5 | 0 |
| 10 | 1 | 15 | 0 | 80 | 1[illegible] | 0 | 0 |
| 11 | 1 | 18 | 6 | (84) | 14 | 14 | 0 |
| 12 | 2 | 2 | 0 | 90 | 15 | 15 | 0 |
| 13 | 2 | 5 | 6 | 100 | 17 | 10 | 0 |
| 14 | 2 | 9 | 0 | (112) | 19 | 12 | 0 |
| 15 | 2 | 12 | 6 | 200 | 35 | 0 | 0 |
| 16 | 2 | 16 | 0 | (224) | 39 | 4 | 0 |
| 17 | 2 | 19 | 6 | 300 | 52 | 10 | 0 |
| 18 | 3 | 3 | 0 | (336) | 58 | 16 | 0 |
| 19 | 3 | 6 | 6 | 400 | 70 | 0 | 0 |
| 20 | 3 | 10 | 0 | (448) | 78 | 8 | 0 |
| 21 | 3 | 13 | 6 | 500 | 87 | 10 | 0 |
| 22 | 3 | 17 | 0 | (560) | 98 | 0 | 0 |
| 23 | 4 | 0 | 6 | 600 | 105 | 0 | 0 |
| 24 | 4 | 4 | 0 | (672) | 117 | 12 | 0 |
| 25 | 4 | 7 | 6 | 700 | 122 | 10 | 0 |
| 26 | 4 | 11 | 0 | (784) | 137 | 4 | 0 |
| 27 | 4 | 14 | 6 | 800 | 140 | 0 | 0 |
| (28) | 4 | 18 | 0 | (896) | 156 | 16 | 0 |
| 29 | 5 | 1 | 6 | 900 | 157 | 10 | 0 |
| 30 | 5 | 5 | 0 | 1000 | 175 | 0 | 0 |
| 31 | 5 | 8 | 6 | 2000 | 350 | 0 | 0 |
| 32 | 5 | 12 | 0 | 3000 | 525 | 0 | 0 |
| 33 | 5 | 15 | 6 | 4000 | 700 | 0 | 0 |
| 34 | 5 | 19 | 0 | 5000 | 875 | 0 | 0 |
| 35 | 6 | 2 | 6 | 10000 | 1750 | 0 | 0 |

## Four Shillings.

| | l. | s. | | l. | s. |
|---|---|---|---|---|---|
| 1 | 0 | 4 | 36 | 7 | 4 |
| 2 | 0 | 8 | 37 | 7 | 8 |
| 3 | 0 | 12 | 38 | 7 | 12 |
| 4 | 0 | 16 | 39 | 7 | 16 |
| 5 | 1 | 0 | 40 | 8 | 0 |
| 6 | 1 | 4 | 50 | 10 | 0 |
| 7 | 1 | 8 | (56) | 11 | 4 |
| 8 | 1 | 12 | 60 | 12 | 0 |
| 9 | 1 | 16 | 70 | 14 | 0 |
| 10 | [illegible] | 0 | 80 | 16 | 0 |
| 11 | 2 | 4 | (84) | 16 | 16 |
| 12 | 2 | 8 | 90 | 18 | 0 |
| 13 | 2 | 12 | 100 | 20 | 0 |
| 14 | 2 | 16 | (112) | 22 | 8 |
| 15 | 3 | 0 | 200 | 40 | 0 |
| 16 | 3 | 4 | (224) | 44 | 16 |
| 17 | 3 | 8 | 300 | 60 | 0 |
| 18 | 3 | 12 | (336) | 67 | 4 |
| 19 | 3 | 16 | 400 | 80 | 0 |
| 20 | 4 | 0 | (448) | 89 | 12 |
| 21 | 4 | 4 | 500 | 100 | 0 |
| 22 | 4 | 8 | (560) | 112 | 0 |
| 23 | 4 | 12 | 600 | 120 | 0 |
| 24 | 4 | 16 | (672) | 134 | 8 |
| 25 | 5 | 0 | 700 | 140 | 0 |
| 26 | 5 | 4 | (784) | 156 | 16 |
| 27 | 5 | 8 | 800 | 160 | 0 |
| (28) | 5 | 12 | (896) | 179 | 4 |
| 29 | 5 | 16 | 900 | 180 | 0 |
| 30 | 6 | 0 | 1000 | 200 | 0 |
| 31 | 6 | 4 | 2000 | 400 | 0 |
| 32 | 6 | 8 | 3000 | 600 | 0 |
| 33 | 6 | 12 | 4000 | 800 | 0 |
| 34 | 6 | 16 | 5000 | 1000 | 0 |
| 35 | 7 | 0 | 10000 | 2000 | 0 |

## Four Shillings and Six-Pence.

| | l. | s. | d. | | l. | s. | d. |
|---|---|---|---|---|---|---|---|
| 1 | 0 | 4 | 6 | 36 | 8 | 2 | 0 |
| 2 | 0 | 9 | 0 | 37 | 8 | 6 | 6 |
| 3 | 0 | 13 | 6 | 38 | 8 | 11 | 0 |
| 4 | 0 | 18 | 0 | 39 | 8 | 15 | 6 |
| 5 | 1 | 2 | 6 | 40 | 9 | 0 | 0 |
| 6 | 1 | 7 | 0 | 50 | 11 | 5 | 0 |
| 7 | 1 | 11 | 6 | (56) | 12 | 12 | 0 |
| 8 | 1 | 16 | 0 | 60 | 13 | 10 | 0 |
| 9 | 2 | 0 | 6 | 70 | 15 | 15 | 0 |
| 10 | 2 | 5 | 0 | 80 | 18 | 0 | 0 |
| 11 | 2 | 9 | 6 | (84) | 18 | 18 | 0 |
| 12 | 2 | 14 | 0 | 90 | 20 | 5 | 0 |
| 13 | 2 | 18 | 6 | 100 | 22 | 10 | 0 |
| 14 | 3 | 3 | 0 | (112) | 25 | 4 | 0 |
| 15 | 3 | 7 | 6 | 200 | 45 | 0 | 0 |
| 16 | 3 | 12 | 0 | (224) | 50 | 8 | 0 |
| 17 | 3 | 16 | 6 | 300 | 67 | 10 | 0 |
| 18 | 4 | 1 | 0 | (336) | 75 | 12 | 0 |
| 19 | 4 | 5 | 6 | 400 | 90 | 0 | 0 |
| 20 | 4 | 10 | 0 | (448) | 100 | 16 | 0 |
| 21 | 4 | 14 | 6 | 500 | 112 | 10 | 0 |
| 22 | 4 | 19 | 0 | (560) | 126 | 0 | 0 |
| 23 | 5 | 3 | 6 | 600 | 135 | 0 | 0 |
| 24 | 5 | 8 | 0 | (672) | 151 | 4 | 0 |
| 25 | 5 | 12 | 6 | 700 | 157 | 10 | 0 |
| 26 | 5 | 17 | 0 | (784) | 176 | 8 | 0 |
| 27 | 6 | 1 | 6 | 800 | 180 | 0 | 0 |
| (28) | 6 | 6 | 0 | (896) | 201 | 12 | 0 |
| 29 | 6 | 10 | 6 | 900 | 202 | 10 | 0 |
| 30 | 6 | 15 | 0 | 1000 | 225 | 0 | 0 |
| 31 | 6 | 19 | 6 | 2000 | 450 | 0 | 0 |
| 32 | 7 | 4 | 0 | 3000 | 675 | 0 | 0 |
| 33 | 7 | 8 | 6 | 4000 | 900 | 0 | 0 |
| 34 | 7 | 13 | 0 | 5000 | 1125 | 0 | 0 |
| 35 | 7 | 17 | 6 | 10000 | 2250 | 0 | 0 |

## *Five Shillings, or a Crown.*

| | l. | s. | | l. | s. |
|---|---|---|---|---|---|
| 1 | 0 | 5 | 36 | 9 | 0 |
| 2 | 0 | 10 | 37 | 9 | 5 |
| 3 | 0 | 15 | 38 | 9 | 10 |
| 4 | 1 | 0 | 39 | 9 | 15 |
| 5 | 1 | 5 | 40 | 10 | 0 |
| 6 | 1 | 10 | 50 | 12 | 10 |
| 7 | 1 | 15 | (56) | 14 | 0 |
| 8 | 2 | 0 | 60 | 15 | 0 |
| 9 | 2 | 5 | 70 | 17 | 10 |
| 10 | 2 | 10 | 80 | 20 | 0 |
| 11 | 2 | 15 | (84) | 21 | 0 |
| 12 | 3 | 0 | 90 | 22 | 10 |
| 13 | 3 | 5 | 100 | 25 | 0 |
| 14 | 3 | 10 | (112) | 28 | 0 |
| 15 | 3 | 15 | 200 | 50 | 0 |
| 16 | 4 | 0 | (224) | 56 | 0 |
| 17 | 4 | 5 | 300 | 75 | 0 |
| 18 | 4 | 10 | (336) | 84 | 0 |
| 19 | 4 | 15 | 400 | 100 | 0 |
| 20 | 5 | 0 | (448) | 112 | 0 |
| 21 | 5 | 5 | 500 | 125 | 0 |
| 22 | 5 | 10 | (560) | 140 | 0 |
| 23 | 5 | 15 | 600 | 150 | 0 |
| 24 | 6 | 0 | (672) | 168 | 0 |
| 25 | 6 | 5 | 700 | 175 | 0 |
| 26 | 6 | 10 | (784) | 196 | 0 |
| 27 | 6 | 15 | 800 | 200 | 0 |
| (28) | 7 | 0 | (896) | 224 | 0 |
| 29 | 7 | 5 | 900 | 225 | 0 |
| 30 | 7 | 10 | 1000 | 250 | 0 |
| 31 | 7 | 15 | 2000 | 500 | 0 |
| 32 | 8 | 0 | 3000 | 750 | 0 |
| 33 | 8 | 5 | 4000 | 1000 | 0 |
| 34 | 8 | 10 | 5000 | 1250 | 0 |
| 35 | 8 | 15 | 10000 | 2500 | 0 |

## Five Shillings and Six-Pence.

| | l. | s. | d. | | l. | s. | d. |
|---|---|---|---|---|---|---|---|
| 1 | 0 | 5 | 6 | 36 | 9 | 18 | 0 |
| 2 | 0 | 11 | 0 | 37 | 10 | 3 | 6 |
| 3 | 0 | 16 | 6 | 38 | 10 | 9 | 0 |
| 4 | 1 | 2 | 0 | 39 | 10 | 14 | 6 |
| 5 | 1 | 7 | 6 | 40 | 11 | 0 | 0 |
| 6 | 1 | 13 | 0 | 50 | 13 | 15 | 0 |
| 7 | 1 | 18 | 6 | (56) | 15 | 8 | 0 |
| 8 | 2 | 4 | 0 | 60 | 16 | 10 | 0 |
| 9 | 2 | 9 | 6 | 70 | 19 | 5 | 0 |
| 10 | 2 | 15 | 0 | 80 | 22 | 0 | 0 |
| 11 | 3 | 0 | 6 | (84) | 23 | 2 | 0 |
| 12 | 3 | 6 | 0 | 90 | 24 | 15 | 0 |
| 13 | 3 | 11 | 6 | 100 | 27 | 10 | 0 |
| 14 | 3 | 17 | 0 | (112) | 30 | 16 | 0 |
| 15 | 4 | 2 | 6 | 200 | 55 | 0 | 0 |
| 16 | 4 | 8 | 0 | (224) | 61 | 12 | 0 |
| 17 | 4 | 13 | 6 | 300 | 82 | 10 | 0 |
| 18 | 4 | 19 | 0 | (336) | 92 | 8 | 0 |
| 19 | 5 | 4 | 6 | 400 | 110 | 0 | 0 |
| 20 | 5 | 10 | 0 | (448) | 123 | 4 | 0 |
| 21 | 5 | 15 | 6 | 500 | 137 | 10 | 0 |
| 22 | 6 | 1 | 0 | (560) | 154 | 0 | 0 |
| 23 | 6 | 6 | 6 | 600 | 165 | 0 | 0 |
| 24 | 6 | 12 | 0 | (672) | 184 | 16 | 0 |
| 25 | 6 | 17 | 6 | 700 | 192 | 10 | 0 |
| 26 | 7 | 3 | 0 | (784) | 215 | 12 | 0 |
| 27 | 7 | 8 | 6 | 800 | 220 | 0 | 0 |
| (28) | 7 | 14 | 0 | (896) | 246 | 8 | 0 |
| 29 | 7 | 19 | 6 | 900 | 247 | 10 | 0 |
| 30 | 8 | 5 | 0 | 1000 | 275 | 0 | 0 |
| 31 | 8 | 10 | 6 | 2000 | 550 | 0 | 0 |
| 32 | 8 | 16 | 0 | 3000 | 825 | 0 | 0 |
| 33 | 9 | 1 | 6 | 4000 | 1100 | 0 | 0 |
| 34 | 9 | [illegible] | 0 | 5000 | 1375 | 0 | 0 |
| 35 | 9 | 12 | 6 | 10000 | 2750 | 0 | 0 |

## Six Shillings.

| | l. | s. | | l. | s. |
|---|---|---|---|---|---|
| 1 | 0 | 6 | 36 | 10 | 16 |
| 2 | 0 | 12 | 37 | 11 | 2 |
| 3 | 0 | 18 | 38 | 11 | 8 |
| 4 | 1 | 4 | 39 | 11 | 14 |
| 5 | 1 | 10 | 40 | 12 | 0 |
| 6 | 1 | 16 | 50 | 15 | 0 |
| 7 | 2 | 2 | (56) | 16 | 16 |
| 8 | 2 | 8 | 60 | 18 | 0 |
| 9 | 2 | 14 | 70 | 21 | 0 |
| 10 | 3 | 0 | 80 | 24 | 0 |
| 11 | 3 | 6 | (84) | 25 | 4 |
| 12 | 3 | 12 | 90 | 27 | 0 |
| 13 | 3 | 18 | 100 | 30 | 0 |
| 14 | 4 | 4 | (112) | 33 | 12 |
| 15 | 4 | 10 | 200 | 60 | 0 |
| 16 | 4 | 16 | (224) | 67 | 4 |
| 17 | 5 | 2 | 300 | 90 | 0 |
| 18 | 5 | 8 | (336) | 100 | 16 |
| 19 | 5 | 14 | 400 | 120 | 0 |
| 20 | 6 | 0 | (448) | 134 | 8 |
| 21 | 6 | 6 | 500 | 150 | 0 |
| 22 | 6 | 12 | (560) | 168 | 0 |
| 23 | 6 | 18 | 600 | 180 | 0 |
| 24 | 7 | 4 | (672) | 201 | 12 |
| 25 | 7 | 10 | 700 | 210 | 0 |
| 26 | 7 | 16 | (784) | 235 | 4 |
| 27 | 8 | 2 | 800 | 240 | 0 |
| (28) | 8 | 8 | (896) | 268 | 16 |
| 29 | 8 | 14 | 900 | 270 | 0 |
| 30 | 9 | 0 | 1000 | 300 | 0 |
| 31 | 9 | 6 | 2000 | 600 | 0 |
| 32 | 9 | 12 | 3000 | 900 | 0 |
| 33 | 9 | 18 | 4000 | 1200 | 0 |
| 34 | 10 | 4 | 5000 | 1500 | 0 |
| 35 | 10 | 10 | 10000 | 3000 | 0 |

## *Six Shillings and Six-Pence.*

| | *l.* | *s.* | *d.* | | *l.* | *s.* | *d.* |
|---|---|---|---|---|---|---|---|
| 1 | 0 | 6 | 6 | 36 | 11 | 14 | 0 |
| 2 | 0 | 13 | 0 | 37 | 12 | 0 | 6 |
| 3 | 0 | 19 | 6 | 38 | 12 | 7 | 0 |
| 4 | 1 | 6 | 0 | 39 | 12 | 13 | 6 |
| 5 | 1 | 12 | 6 | 40 | 13 | 0 | 0 |
| 6 | 1 | 19 | 0 | 50 | 16 | 5 | 0 |
| 7 | 2 | 5 | 6 | (56) | 18 | 4 | 0 |
| 8 | 2 | 12 | 0 | 60 | 19 | 10 | 0 |
| 9 | 2 | 18 | 6 | 70 | 22 | 15 | 0 |
| 10 | 3 | 5 | 0 | 80 | 26 | 0 | 0 |
| 11 | 3 | 11 | 6 | (84) | 27 | 6 | 0 |
| 12 | 3 | 18 | 0 | 90 | 29 | 5 | 0 |
| 13 | 4 | 4 | 6 | 100 | 32 | 10 | 0 |
| 14 | 4 | 11 | 0 | (112) | 36 | 8 | 0 |
| 15 | 4 | 17 | 6 | 200 | 65 | 0 | 0 |
| 16 | 5 | 4 | 0 | (224) | 72 | 16 | 0 |
| 17 | 5 | 10 | 6 | 300 | 97 | 10 | 0 |
| 18 | 5 | 17 | 0 | (336) | 109 | 4 | 0 |
| 19 | 6 | 3 | 6 | 400 | 130 | 0 | 0 |
| 20 | 6 | 10 | 0 | (448) | 145 | 12 | 0 |
| 21 | 6 | 16 | 6 | 500 | 162 | 10 | 0 |
| 22 | 7 | 3 | 0 | (560) | 182 | 0 | 0 |
| 23 | 7 | 9 | 6 | 600 | 195 | 0 | 0 |
| 24 | 7 | 16 | 0 | (672) | 218 | 8 | 0 |
| 25 | 8 | 2 | 6 | 700 | 227 | 10 | 0 |
| 26 | 8 | 9 | 0 | (784) | 254 | 16 | 0 |
| 27 | 8 | 15 | 6 | 800 | 260 | 0 | 0 |
| (28) | 9 | 2 | 0 | (896) | 291 | 4 | 0 |
| 29 | 9 | 8 | 6 | 900 | 292 | 10 | 0 |
| 30 | 9 | 15 | 0 | 1000 | 325 | 0 | 0 |
| 31 | 10 | 1 | 6 | 2000 | 650 | 0 | 0 |
| 32 | 10 | 8 | 0 | 3000 | 975 | 0 | 0 |
| 33 | 10 | 14 | 6 | 4000 | 1300 | 0 | 0 |
| 34 | 11 | 1 | 0 | 5000 | 1625 | 0 | 0 |
| 35 | 11 | 7 | 6 | 10000 | 3250 | 0 | 0 |

## *Seven Shillings.*

| | l. | s. | | l. | s. |
|---|---|---|---|---|---|
| 1 | 0 | 7 | 36 | 12 | 12 |
| 2 | 0 | 14 | 37 | 12 | 19 |
| 3 | 1 | 1 | 38 | 13 | 6 |
| 4 | 1 | 8 | 39 | 13 | 13 |
| 5 | 1 | 15 | 40 | 14 | 0 |
| 6 | 2 | 2 | 50 | 17 | 10 |
| 7 | 2 | 9 | (56) | 19 | 12 |
| 8 | 2 | 16 | 60 | 21 | 0 |
| 9 | 3 | 3 | 70 | 24 | 10 |
| 10 | 3 | 10 | 80 | 28 | 0 |
| 11 | 3 | 17 | (84) | 29 | 8 |
| 12 | 4 | 4 | 90 | 31 | 10 |
| 13 | 4 | 11 | 100 | 35 | 0 |
| 14 | 4 | 18 | (112) | 39 | 4 |
| 15 | 5 | 5 | 200 | 70 | 0 |
| 16 | 5 | 12 | (224) | 78 | 8 |
| 17 | 5 | 19 | 300 | 105 | 0 |
| 18 | 6 | 6 | (336) | 117 | 12 |
| 19 | 6 | 13 | 400 | 140 | 0 |
| 20 | 7 | 0 | (448) | 156 | 16 |
| 21 | 7 | 7 | 500 | 175 | 0 |
| 22 | 7 | 14 | (560) | 196 | 0 |
| 23 | 8 | 1 | 600 | 210 | 0 |
| 24 | 8 | 8 | (672) | 235 | 4 |
| 25 | 8 | 15 | 700 | 245 | 0 |
| 26 | 9 | 2 | (784) | 274 | 8 |
| 27 | 9 | 9 | 800 | 280 | 0 |
| (28) | 9 | 16 | (896) | 313 | 12 |
| 29 | 10 | 3 | 900 | 315 | 0 |
| 30 | 10 | 10 | 1000 | 350 | 0 |
| 31 | 10 | 17 | 2000 | 700 | 0 |
| 32 | 11 | 4 | 3000 | 1050 | 0 |
| 33 | 11 | 11 | 4000 | 1400 | 0 |
| 34 | 11 | 18 | 5000 | 1750 | 0 |
| 35 | 12 | 5 | 10000 | 3500 | 0 |

## *Seven Shillings and Six-Pence.*

| | l. | s. | d. | | l. | s. | d. |
|---|---|---|---|---|---|---|---|
| 1 | 0 | 7 | 6 | 36 | 13 | 10 | 0 |
| 2 | 0 | 15 | 0 | 37 | 13 | 17 | 6 |
| 3 | 1 | 2 | 6 | 38 | 14 | 5 | 0 |
| 4 | 1 | 10 | 0 | 39 | 14 | 12 | 6 |
| 5 | 1 | 17 | 6 | 40 | 15 | 0 | 0 |
| 6 | 2 | 5 | 0 | 50 | 18 | 15 | 0 |
| 7 | 2 | 12 | 6 | (56) | 21 | 0 | 0 |
| 8 | 3 | 0 | 0 | 60 | 22 | 10 | 0 |
| 9 | 3 | 7 | 6 | 70 | 26 | 5 | 0 |
| 10 | 3 | 15 | 0 | 80 | 30 | 0 | 0 |
| 11 | 4 | 2 | 6 | (84) | 31 | 10 | 0 |
| 12 | 4 | 10 | 0 | 90 | 33 | 15 | 0 |
| 13 | 4 | 17 | 6 | 100 | 37 | 10 | 0 |
| 14 | 5 | 5 | 0 | (112) | 42 | 0 | 0 |
| 15 | 5 | 12 | 6 | 200 | 75 | 0 | 0 |
| 16 | 6 | 0 | 0 | (224) | 84 | 0 | 0 |
| 17 | 6 | 7 | 6 | 300 | 112 | 10 | 0 |
| 18 | 6 | 15 | 0 | (336) | 126 | 0 | 0 |
| 19 | 7 | 2 | 6 | 400 | 150 | 0 | 0 |
| 20 | 7 | 10 | 0 | (448) | 168 | 0 | 0 |
| 21 | 7 | 17 | 6 | 500 | 187 | 10 | 0 |
| 22 | 8 | 5 | 0 | (560) | 210 | 0 | 0 |
| 23 | 8 | 12 | 6 | 600 | 225 | 0 | 0 |
| 24 | 9 | 0 | 0 | (672) | 252 | 0 | 0 |
| 25 | 9 | 7 | 6 | 700 | 262 | 10 | 0 |
| 26 | 9 | 15 | 0 | (784) | 294 | 0 | 0 |
| 27 | 10 | 2 | 6 | 800 | 300 | 0 | 0 |
| (28) | 10 | 10 | 0 | (896) | 336 | 0 | 0 |
| 29 | 10 | 17 | 6 | 900 | 337 | 10 | 0 |
| 30 | 11 | 5 | 0 | 1000 | 375 | 0 | 0 |
| 31 | 11 | 12 | 6 | 2000 | 750 | 0 | 0 |
| 32 | 12 | 0 | 0 | 3000 | 1125 | 0 | 0 |
| 33 | 12 | 7 | 6 | 4000 | 1500 | 0 | 0 |
| 34 | 12 | 15 | 0 | 5000 | 1875 | 0 | 0 |
| 35 | 13 | 2 | 6 | 10000 | 3750 | 0 | 0 |

## *Eight Shillings.*

| | l. | s. | | l. | s. |
|---|---|---|---|---|---|
| 1 | 0 | 8 | 36 | 14 | 8 |
| 2 | 0 | 16 | 37 | 14 | 16 |
| 3 | 1 | 4 | 38 | 15 | 4 |
| 4 | 1 | 12 | 39 | 15 | 12 |
| 5 | 2 | 0 | 40 | 16 | 0 |
| 6 | 2 | 8 | 50 | 20 | 0 |
| 7 | 2 | 16 | (56) | 22 | 8 |
| 8 | 3 | 4 | 60 | 24 | 0 |
| 9 | 3 | 12 | 70 | 28 | 0 |
| 10 | 4 | 0 | 80 | 32 | 0 |
| 11 | 4 | 8 | (84) | 33 | 12 |
| 12 | 4 | 16 | 90 | 36 | 0 |
| 13 | 5 | 4 | 100 | 40 | 0 |
| 14 | 5 | 12 | (112) | 44 | 16 |
| 15 | 6 | 0 | 200 | 80 | 0 |
| 16 | 6 | 8 | (224) | 89 | 12 |
| 17 | 6 | 16 | 300 | 120 | 0 |
| 18 | 7 | 4 | (336) | 134 | 8 |
| 19 | 7 | 12 | 400 | 160 | 0 |
| 20 | 8 | 0 | (448) | 179 | 4 |
| 21 | 8 | 8 | 500 | 200 | 0 |
| 22 | 8 | 16 | (560) | 224 | 0 |
| 23 | 9 | 4 | 600 | 240 | 0 |
| 24 | 9 | 12 | (672) | 268 | 16 |
| 25 | 10 | 0 | 700 | 280 | 0 |
| 26 | 10 | 8 | (784) | 313 | 12 |
| 27 | 10 | 16 | 800 | 320 | 0 |
| (28) | 11 | 4 | (896) | 358 | 8 |
| 29 | 11 | 12 | 900 | 360 | 0 |
| 30 | 12 | 0 | 1000 | 400 | 0 |
| 31 | 12 | 8 | 2000 | 800 | 0 |
| 32 | 12 | 16 | 3000 | 1200 | 0 |
| 33 | 13 | 4 | 4000 | 1600 | 0 |
| 34 | 13 | 12 | 5000 | 2000 | 0 |
| 35 | 14 | 0 | 10000 | 4000 | 0 |

## *Eight Shillings and Six-Pence.*

| | l. | s. | d. | | l. | s. | d. |
|---|---|---|---|---|---|---|---|
| 1 | 0 | 8 | 6 | 36 | 15 | 6 | 0 |
| 2 | 0 | 17 | 0 | 37 | 15 | 14 | 6 |
| 3 | 1 | 5 | 6 | 38 | 16 | 3 | 0 |
| 4 | 1 | 14 | 0 | 39 | 16 | 11 | 6 |
| 5 | 2 | 2 | 6 | 40 | 17 | 0 | 0 |
| 6 | 2 | 11 | 0 | 50 | 21 | 5 | 0 |
| 7 | 2 | 19 | 6 | (56) | 23 | 16 | 0 |
| 8 | 3 | 8 | 0 | 60 | 25 | 10 | 0 |
| 9 | 3 | 16 | 6 | 70 | 29 | 15 | 0 |
| 10 | 4 | 5 | 0 | 80 | 34 | 0 | 0 |
| 11 | 4 | 13 | 6 | (84) | 35 | 14 | 0 |
| 12 | 5 | 2 | 0 | 90 | 38 | 5 | 0 |
| 13 | 5 | 10 | 6 | 100 | 42 | 10 | 0 |
| 14 | 5 | 19 | 0 | (112) | 47 | 12 | 0 |
| 15 | 6 | 7 | 6 | 200 | 85 | 0 | 0 |
| 16 | 6 | 16 | 0 | (224) | 95 | 4 | 0 |
| 17 | 7 | 4 | 6 | 300 | 127 | 10 | 0 |
| 18 | 7 | 13 | 0 | (336) | 142 | 16 | 0 |
| 19 | 8 | 1 | 6 | 400 | 170 | 0 | 0 |
| 20 | 8 | 10 | 0 | (448) | 190 | 8 | 0 |
| 21 | 8 | 18 | 6 | 500 | 212 | 10 | 0 |
| 22 | 9 | 7 | 0 | (560) | 238 | 0 | 0 |
| 23 | 9 | 15 | 6 | 600 | 255 | 0 | 0 |
| 24 | 10 | 4 | 0 | (672) | 285 | 12 | 0 |
| 25 | 10 | 12 | 6 | 700 | 297 | 10 | 0 |
| 26 | 11 | 1 | 0 | (784) | 333 | 4 | 0 |
| 27 | 11 | 9 | 6 | 800 | 340 | 0 | 0 |
| (28) | 11 | 18 | 0 | (896) | 380 | 16 | 0 |
| 29 | 12 | 6 | 6 | 900 | 382 | 10 | 0 |
| 30 | 12 | 15 | 0 | 1000 | 425 | 0 | 0 |
| 31 | 13 | 3 | 6 | 2000 | 850 | 0 | 0 |
| 32 | 13 | 12 | 0 | 3000 | 1275 | 0 | 0 |
| 33 | 14 | 0 | 6 | 4000 | 1700 | 0 | 0 |
| 34 | 14 | 9 | 0 | 5000 | 2125 | 0 | 0 |
| 35 | 14 | 17 | 6 | 10000 | 4250 | 0 | 0 |

## Nine Shillings.

| | l. | s. | | l. | s. |
|---|---|---|---|---|---|
| 1 | 0 | 9 | 36 | 16 | 4 |
| 2 | 0 | 18 | 37 | 16 | 13 |
| 3 | 1 | 7 | 38 | 17 | 2 |
| 4 | 1 | 16 | 39 | 17 | 11 |
| 5 | 2 | 5 | 40 | 18 | 0 |
| 6 | 2 | 14 | 50 | 22 | 10 |
| 7 | 3 | 3 | (56) | 25 | 4 |
| 8 | 3 | 12 | 60 | 27 | 0 |
| 9 | 4 | 1 | 70 | 31 | 10 |
| 10 | 4 | 10 | 80 | 36 | 0 |
| 11 | 4 | 19 | (84) | 37 | 16 |
| 12 | 5 | 8 | 90 | 40 | 10 |
| 13 | 5 | 17 | 100 | 45 | 0 |
| 14 | 6 | 6 | (112) | 50 | 8 |
| 15 | 6 | 15 | 200 | 90 | 0 |
| 16 | 7 | 4 | (224) | 100 | 16 |
| 17 | 7 | 13 | 300 | 135 | 0 |
| 18 | 8 | 2 | (336) | 151 | 4 |
| 19 | 8 | 11 | 400 | 180 | 0 |
| 20 | 9 | 0 | (448) | 201 | 12 |
| 21 | 9 | 9 | 500 | 225 | 0 |
| 22 | 9 | 18 | (560) | 252 | 0 |
| 23 | 10 | 7 | 600 | 270 | 0 |
| 24 | 10 | 16 | (672) | 302 | 8 |
| 25 | 11 | 5 | 700 | 315 | 0 |
| 26 | 11 | 14 | (784) | 352 | 16 |
| 27 | 12 | 3 | 800 | 360 | 0 |
| (28) | 12 | 12 | (896) | 403 | 4 |
| 29 | 13 | 1 | 900 | 405 | 0 |
| 30 | 13 | 10 | 1000 | 450 | 0 |
| 31 | 13 | 19 | 2000 | 900 | 0 |
| 32 | 14 | 8 | 3000 | 1350 | 0 |
| 33 | 14 | 17 | 4000 | 1800 | 0 |
| 34 | 15 | 6 | 5000 | 2250 | 0 |
| 35 | 15 | 15 | 10000 | 4500 | 0 |

## *Nine Shillings and Six-Pence.*

| | l. | s. | d. | | l. | s. | d. |
|---|---|---|---|---|---|---|---|
| 1 | 0 | 9 | 6 | 36 | 17 | 2 | 0 |
| 2 | 0 | 19 | 0 | 37 | 17 | 11 | 6 |
| 3 | 1 | 8 | 6 | 38 | 18 | 1 | 0 |
| 4 | 1 | 18 | 0 | 39 | 18 | 10 | 6 |
| 5 | 2 | 7 | 6 | 40 | 19 | 0 | 0 |
| 6 | 2 | 17 | 0 | 50 | 23 | 15 | 0 |
| 7 | 3 | 6 | 6 | (56) | 26 | 12 | 0 |
| 8 | 3 | 16 | 0 | 60 | 28 | 10 | 0 |
| 9 | 4 | 5 | 6 | 70 | 33 | 5 | 0 |
| 10 | 4 | 15 | 0 | 80 | 38 | 0 | 0 |
| 11 | 5 | 4 | 6 | (84) | 39 | 18 | 0 |
| 12 | 5 | 14 | 0 | 90 | 42 | 15 | 0 |
| 13 | 6 | 3 | 6 | 100 | 47 | 10 | 0 |
| 14 | 6 | 13 | 0 | (112) | 53 | 4 | 0 |
| 15 | 7 | 2 | 6 | 200 | 95 | 0 | 0 |
| 16 | 7 | 12 | 0 | (224) | 106 | 8 | 0 |
| 17 | 8 | 1 | 6 | 300 | 142 | 10 | 0 |
| 18 | 8 | 11 | 0 | (336) | 159 | 12 | 0 |
| 19 | 9 | 0 | 6 | 400 | 190 | 0 | 0 |
| 20 | 9 | 10 | 0 | (448) | 212 | 16 | 0 |
| 21 | 9 | 19 | 6 | 500 | 237 | 10 | 0 |
| 22 | 10 | 9 | 0 | (560) | 266 | 0 | 0 |
| 23 | 10 | 18 | 6 | 600 | 285 | 0 | 0 |
| 24 | 11 | 8 | 0 | (672) | 319 | 4 | 0 |
| 25 | 11 | 17 | 6 | 700 | 332 | 10 | 0 |
| 26 | 12 | 7 | 0 | (784) | 372 | 8 | 0 |
| 27 | 12 | 16 | 6 | 800 | 380 | 0 | 0 |
| (28) | 13 | 6 | 0 | (896) | 425 | 12 | 0 |
| 29 | 13 | 15 | 6 | 900 | 427 | 10 | 0 |
| 39 | 14 | 5 | 0 | 1000 | 475 | 0 | 0 |
| 31 | 14 | 14 | 6 | 2000 | 950 | 0 | 0 |
| 32 | 15 | 4 | 0 | 3000 | 1425 | 0 | 0 |
| 33 | 15 | 13 | 6 | 4000 | 1900 | 0 | 0 |
| 34 | 16 | 3 | 0 | 5000 | 2375 | 0 | 0 |
| 35 | 16 | 12 | 6 | 10000 | 4750 | 0 | 0 |

## *Ten Shillings.*

| | l. | s. | | l. | s. |
|---|---|---|---|---|---|
| 1 | 0 | 10 | 36 | 18 | 0 |
| 2 | 1 | 0 | 37 | 18 | 10 |
| 3 | 1 | 10 | 38 | 19 | 0 |
| 4 | 2 | 0 | 39 | 19 | 10 |
| 5 | 2 | 10 | 40 | 20 | 0 |
| 6 | 3 | 0 | 50 | 25 | 0 |
| 7 | 3 | 10 | (56) | 28 | 0 |
| 8 | 4 | 0 | 60 | 30 | 0 |
| 9 | 4 | 10 | 70 | 35 | 0 |
| 10 | 5 | 0 | 80 | 40 | 0 |
| 11 | 5 | 10 | (84) | 42 | 0 |
| 12 | 6 | 0 | 90 | 45 | 0 |
| 13 | 6 | 10 | 100 | 50 | 0 |
| 14 | 7 | 0 | (112) | 56 | 0 |
| 15 | 7 | 10 | 200 | 100 | 0 |
| 16 | 8 | 0 | (224) | 112 | 0 |
| 17 | 8 | 10 | 300 | 150 | 0 |
| 18 | 9 | 0 | (336) | 168 | 0 |
| 19 | 9 | 10 | 400 | 200 | 0 |
| 20 | 10 | 0 | (448) | 224 | 0 |
| 21 | 10 | 10 | 500 | 250 | 0 |
| 22 | 11 | 0 | (560) | 280 | 0 |
| 23 | 11 | 10 | 600 | 300 | 0 |
| 24 | 12 | 0 | (672) | 336 | 0 |
| 25 | 12 | 10 | 700 | 350 | 0 |
| 26 | 13 | 0 | (784) | 392 | 0 |
| 27 | 13 | 10 | 800 | 400 | 0 |
| (28) | 14 | 0 | (896) | 448 | 0 |
| 29 | 14 | 10 | 900 | 450 | 0 |
| 30 | 15 | 0 | 1000 | 500 | 0 |
| 31 | 15 | 10 | 2000 | 1000 | 0 |
| 32 | 16 | 0 | 3000 | 1500 | 0 |
| 33 | 16 | 10 | 4000 | 2000 | 0 |
| 34 | 17 | 0 | 5000 | 2500 | 0 |
| 35 | 17 | 10 | 10000 | 5000 | 0 |

## *Ten Shillings and Six-Pence.*

| | l. | s. | d. | | l. | s. | d. |
|---|---|---|---|---|---|---|---|
| 1 | 0 | 10 | 6 | 36 | 18 | 18 | 0 |
| 2 | 1 | 1 | 0 | 37 | 19 | 8 | 6 |
| 3 | 1 | 11 | 6 | 38 | 19 | 19 | 0 |
| 4 | 2 | 2 | 0 | 39 | 20 | 9 | 6 |
| 5 | 2 | 12 | 6 | 40 | 21 | 0 | 0 |
| 6 | 3 | 3 | 0 | 50 | 26 | 5 | 0 |
| 7 | 3 | 13 | 6 | (56) | 29 | 8 | 0 |
| 8 | 4 | 4 | 0 | 60 | 31 | 10 | 0 |
| 9 | 4 | 14 | 6 | 70 | 36 | 15 | 0 |
| 10 | 5 | 5 | 0 | 80 | 42 | 0 | 0 |
| 11 | 5 | 15 | 6 | (84) | 44 | 2 | 0 |
| 12 | 6 | 6 | 0 | 90 | 47 | 5 | 0 |
| 13 | 6 | 16 | 6 | 100 | 52 | 10 | 0 |
| 14 | 7 | 7 | 0 | (112) | 58 | 16 | 0 |
| 15 | 7 | 17 | 6 | 200 | 105 | 0 | 0 |
| 16 | 8 | 8 | 0 | (224) | 117 | 12 | 0 |
| 17 | 8 | 18 | 6 | 300 | 157 | 10 | 0 |
| 18 | 9 | 9 | 0 | (336) | 176 | 8 | 0 |
| 19 | 9 | 19 | 6 | 400 | 210 | 0 | 0 |
| 20 | 10 | 10 | 0 | (448) | 235 | 4 | 0 |
| 21 | 11 | 0 | 6 | 500 | 262 | 10 | 0 |
| 22 | 11 | 11 | 0 | (560) | 294 | 0 | 0 |
| 23 | 12 | 1 | 6 | 600 | 315 | 0 | 0 |
| 24 | 12 | 12 | 0 | (672) | 352 | 16 | 0 |
| 25 | 13 | 2 | [illegible] | 700 | 367 | 10 | 0 |
| 26 | 13 | 13 | 0 | (784) | 411 | 12 | 0 |
| 27 | 14 | 3 | 6 | 800 | 420 | 0 | 0 |
| (28) | 14 | 14 | 0 | (896) | 470 | 8 | 0 |
| 29 | 15 | 4 | 6 | 900 | 472 | 10 | 0 |
| 30 | 15 | 15 | 0 | 1000 | 525 | 0 | 0 |
| 31 | 16 | 5 | 6 | 2000 | 1050 | 0 | 0 |
| 32 | 16 | 16 | 0 | 3000 | 1575 | 0 | 0 |
| 33 | 17 | 6 | 6 | 4000 | 2100 | 0 | 0 |
| 34 | 17 | 17 | 0 | 5000 | 2625 | 0 | 0 |
| 35 | 18 | 7 | 6 | 10000 | 5250 | 0 | 0 |

## Eleven, Twelve, and Thirteen Shillings.

| | 11 Shillings. | | 12 Shillings. | | 13 Shillings. | |
|---|---|---|---|---|---|---|
| | l. | s. | l. | s. | l. | s. |
| 1 | 0 | 11 | 0 | 12 | 0 | 13 |
| 2 | 1 | 2 | 1 | 4 | 1 | 6 |
| 3 | 1 | 13 | 1 | 16 | 1 | 19 |
| 4 | 2 | 4 | 2 | 8 | 2 | 12 |
| 5 | 2 | 15 | 3 | 0 | 3 | 5 |
| 6 | 3 | 6 | 3 | 12 | 3 | 18 |
| 7 | 3 | 17 | 4 | 4 | 4 | 11 |
| 8 | 4 | 8 | 4 | 16 | 5 | 4 |
| 9 | 4 | 19 | 5 | 8 | 5 | 17 |
| 10 | 5 | 10 | 6 | 0 | 6 | 10 |
| 11 | 6 | 1 | 6 | 12 | 7 | 3 |
| 12 | 6 | 12 | 7 | 4 | 7 | 16 |
| 13 | 7 | 3 | 7 | 16 | 8 | 9 |
| 14 | 7 | 14 | 8 | 8 | 9 | 2 |
| 15 | 8 | 5 | 9 | 0 | 9 | 15 |
| 16 | 8 | 16 | 9 | 12 | 10 | 8 |
| 17 | 9 | 7 | 10 | 4 | 11 | 1 |
| 18 | 9 | 18 | 10 | 16 | 11 | 14 |
| 19 | 10 | 9 | 11 | 8 | 12 | 7 |
| 20 | 11 | 0 | 12 | 0 | 13 | 0 |
| 30 | 16 | 10 | 18 | 0 | 19 | 10 |
| 40 | 22 | 0 | 24 | 0 | 26 | 0 |
| 50 | 27 | 10 | 30 | 0 | 32 | 10 |
| 60 | 33 | 0 | 36 | 0 | 39 | 0 |
| 70 | 38 | 10 | 42 | 0 | 45 | 10 |
| 80 | 44 | 0 | 48 | 0 | 52 | 0 |
| 90 | 49 | 10 | 54 | 0 | 58 | 10 |
| 100 | 55 | 0 | 60 | 0 | 65 | 0 |
| 200 | 110 | 0 | 120 | 0 | 130 | 0 |
| 300 | 165 | 0 | 180 | 0 | 195 | 0 |
| 400 | 220 | 0 | 240 | 0 | 260 | 0 |
| 500 | 275 | 0 | 300 | 0 | 325 | 0 |
| 1000 | 550 | 0 | 600 | 0 | 650 | 0 |
| 5000 | 2750 | 0 | 3000 | 0 | 3250 | 0 |

## *Fourteen, Fifteen, and Sixteen Shillings.*

| | 14 Shillings. | | 15 Shillings. | | 16 Shillings. | |
|---|---|---|---|---|---|---|
| | *l.* | *s.* | *l.* | *s.* | *l.* | *s.* |
| 1 | 0 | 14 | 0 | 15 | 0 | 16 |
| 2 | 1 | 8 | 1 | 10 | 1 | 12 |
| 3 | 2 | 2 | 2 | [illegible] | 2 | 8 |
| 4 | 2 | 16 | 3 | 0 | 3 | 4 |
| 5 | 3 | 10 | 3 | 15 | 4 | 0 |
| 6 | 4 | 4 | 4 | 10 | 4 | 16 |
| 7 | 4 | 18 | 5 | 5 | 5 | 12 |
| 8 | 5 | 12 | 6 | 0 | 6 | 8 |
| 9 | 6 | 6 | 6 | 15 | 7 | 4 |
| 10 | 7 | 0 | 7 | 10 | 8 | 0 |
| 11 | 7 | 14 | 8 | 5 | 8 | 16 |
| 12 | 8 | 8 | 9 | 0 | 9 | 12 |
| 13 | 9 | 2 | 9 | 15 | 10 | 8 |
| 14 | 9 | 16 | 10 | 10 | 11 | 4 |
| 15 | 10 | 10 | 11 | 5 | 12 | 0 |
| 16 | 11 | 4 | 12 | 0 | 12 | 16 |
| 17 | 11 | 18 | 12 | 15 | 13 | 12 |
| 18 | 12 | 12 | 13 | 10 | 14 | 8 |
| 19 | 13 | 6 | 14 | 5 | 15 | 4 |
| 20 | 14 | 0 | 15 | 0 | 16 | 0 |
| 30 | 21 | 0 | 22 | 10 | 24 | 0 |
| 40 | 28 | 0 | 30 | 0 | 32 | 0 |
| 50 | 35 | 0 | 37 | 10 | 40 | 0 |
| 60 | 42 | 0 | 45 | 0 | 48 | 0 |
| 70 | 49 | 0 | 52 | 10 | 56 | 0 |
| 80 | 56 | 0 | 60 | 0 | 64 | 0 |
| 90 | 63 | 0 | 67 | 10 | 72 | 0 |
| 100 | 70 | 0 | 75 | 0 | 80 | 0 |
| 200 | 140 | 0 | 150 | 0 | 160 | 0 |
| 300 | 210 | 0 | 225 | 0 | 240 | 0 |
| 400 | 280 | 0 | 300 | 0 | 320 | 0 |
| 500 | 350 | 0 | 375 | 0 | 400 | 0 |
| 1000 | 700 | 0 | 750 | 0 | 800 | 0 |
| 5000 | 3500 | 0 | 3750 | 0 | 4000 | 0 |

## *Seventeen, Eighteen, and Nineteen Shillings.*

| | 17 Shillings. | | 18 Shillings. | | 19 Shillings. | |
|---|---|---|---|---|---|---|
| | *l.* | *s.* | *l.* | *s.* | *l.* | *s.* |
| 1 | 0 | 17 | 0 | 18 | 0 | 19 |
| 2 | 1 | 14 | 1 | 16 | 1 | 18 |
| 3 | 2 | [illegible]1 | 2 | 14 | 2 | 17 |
| 4 | 3 | 8 | 3 | 12 | 3 | 16 |
| 5 | 4 | 5 | 4 | 10 | 4 | 15 |
| 6 | 5 | 2 | 5 | 8 | 5 | 14 |
| 7 | 5 | 19 | 6 | 6 | 6 | 13 |
| 8 | 6 | 16 | 7 | 4 | 7 | 12 |
| 9 | 7 | 13 | 8 | 2 | 8 | 11 |
| 10 | 8 | 10 | 9 | 0 | 9 | 10 |
| 11 | 9 | 7 | 9 | 18 | 10 | 9 |
| 12 | 10 | 4 | 10 | 16 | 11 | 8 |
| 13 | 11 | 1 | 11 | 14 | 12 | 7 |
| 14 | 11 | 18 | 12 | 12 | 13 | 6 |
| 15 | 12 | 15 | 13 | 10 | 14 | 5 |
| 16 | 13 | 12 | 14 | 8 | 15 | 4 |
| 17 | 14 | 9 | 15 | 6 | 16 | 3 |
| 18 | 15 | 6 | 16 | 4 | 17 | 2 |
| 19 | 16 | 3 | 17 | 2 | 18 | 1 |
| 20 | 17 | 0 | 18 | 0 | 19 | 0 |
| 30 | 25 | 10 | 27 | 0 | 28 | 10 |
| 40 | 34 | 0 | 36 | 0 | 38 | 0 |
| 50 | 42 | 10 | 45 | 0 | 47 | 10 |
| 60 | 51 | 0 | 54 | 0 | 57 | 0 |
| 70 | 59 | 10 | 63 | 0 | 66 | 10 |
| 80 | 68 | 0 | 72 | 0 | 76 | 0 |
| 90 | 76 | 10 | 81 | 0 | 85 | 10 |
| 100 | 85 | 0 | 90 | 0 | 95 | 0 |
| 200 | 170 | 0 | 180 | 0 | 190 | 0 |
| 300 | 255 | 0 | 270 | 0 | 285 | 0 |
| 400 | 340 | 0 | 360 | 0 | 380 | 0 |
| 500 | 425 | 0 | 450 | 0 | 475 | 0 |
| 1000 | 850 | 0 | 900 | 0 | 950 | 0 |
| 5000 | 4250 | 0 | 4500 | 0 | 4750 | 0 |

## *The Use of this* Table.

THis Table is of great Uſe, whereof I will only give you ſome few Examples: It is ſo plain and eaſie to be underſtood, that it will be needleſs to ſay much by way of Explanation, only this I would have you take notice, That the firſt and third Columns are the Multiplicators, in all the Pages from a Farthing to Eleven Shillings, and the ſecond and fourth Columns ſhew the value of the ſum multiplied; alſo that thoſe Numbers within Parentheſes relate chiefly to the Great Hundred Weight, as (28) (56) (84) (112), are the Quarter, Half, Three Quarters, and Whole Great Hundred, (224) is 2 C. (336) is 3 C. *&c.* When you are paſt Ten Shillings Six-pence, the firſt Column contains all the Multipicators, and the other three ſhew the value of the ſum multiplied.

*Example* 1.

*If* 1 *Yard of Tape coſt* 3 *Farthings, I deſire to know what* 600 *Yards will amount unto at the ſame rate?*

I ſeek for the Page that has *Three Farthings* for the Title, which I find to be page 44, then I look for the Number 600 in the Third Column (that being a continuation of the Numbers or Multiplicators in the firſt Column 'till the Table exceeds Ten Shillings,) and againſt it in the Fourth Column I find 1 *l.* 17 *s.* 6 *d.* and ſo much will 600 Yards of Tape coſt at Three Farthings the Yard.

*Example* 2

*If* 1 *Ell of Canvas coſt* 7 d. 2 q. *what will* 527 *Ells coſt?*

I ſeek in Page 71 (that has for its Title *Seven-pence Half peny*) for the Number 527, but becauſe I cannot find it at once, I firſt ſeek for the Hundreds, *viz.* 500, which

which I find in the Third Column, and againſt it in the Fourth 15 *l.* 12 *s.* 6 *d.* and then for the broken Number or part of an Hundred, *viz.* 27, which I find in the firſt Column, and againſt it in the ſecond 16 *s.* 10 *d* 2 *q.* which added to 15 *l.* 12 *s.* 6 *d.* gives 16 *l.* 9 *s.* 4 *d.* 2 *q.* and ſo much will 527 Ells coſt.

*Example* 3.

*If* 1 *Pound of Sugar coſt* 10 d. ¼ q. *what will* 8 C. *weight* Averdupois *coſt?*

I ſeek in the Page whoſe Title is *Ten-pence Farthing* for (896) (there being ſo many neat Pounds in 8 C. *Averdupois*) and againſt it I find 38 *l.* 5 *s.* 4 *d.* which anſwers the Queſtion.

*Example* 4.

*If* 1 *Pound of Cheeſe coſt* 3 d. 3 q. *what will* 2 C. 3 Qrs 22 lb. *coſt?*

| | *l.* | *s* | *d.* | *q.* |
|---|---|---|---|---|
| Firſt, 2 C. or 224 times 3 *d.* 3 *q.* comes to | 3 | 10 | 0 | 0 |
| Then 3 Quarters of 1 C. or 84 lb. comes to | 1 | 6 | 3 | 0 |
| And laſtly, 22 lb. or 22 times 3 *d.* 3 *q.* comes to | 0 | 6 | 10 | 2 |
| Which added together, makes | 5 | 3 | 1 | 2 |

And ſo much will 2 Hundred, 3 Quarters, and 22 Pound of Cheeſe coſt at 3 *d* 3 *q.* the Pound.

By theſe Examples you may not only underſtand the Uſe of this Table, but alſo of the Table for Marks and Nobles, and that of Guinneys and Broad Gold, which follow next.

A

# A TABLE

FOR

The ready Casting up any Number

OF

*NOBLES and MARKS*,

From One to Five Thousand.

## Multiplication of a Noble and a Mark.

| | 6 Shillings 8 Pence. | | | 13 Shillings 4 Pence. | | |
|---|---|---|---|---|---|---|
| | l. | s. | d. | l. | s. | d. |
| 1 | 0 | 6 | 8 | 0 | 13 | 4 |
| 2 | 0 | 13 | 4 | 1 | 6 | 8 |
| 3 | 1 | 0 | 0 | 2 | 0 | 0 |
| 4 | 1 | 6 | 8 | 2 | 13 | 4 |
| 5 | 1 | 13 | 4 | 3 | 6 | 8 |
| 6 | 2 | 0 | 0 | 4 | 0 | 0 |
| 7 | 2 | 6 | 8 | 4 | 13 | 4 |
| 8 | 2 | 13 | 4 | 5 | 6 | 8 |
| 9 | 3 | 0 | 0 | 6 | 0 | 0 |
| 10 | 3 | 6 | 8 | 6 | 13 | 4 |
| 11 | 3 | 13 | 4 | 7 | 6 | 8 |
| 12 | 4 | 0 | 0 | 8 | 0 | 0 |
| 13 | 4 | 6 | 8 | 8 | 13 | 4 |
| 14 | 4 | 13 | 4 | 9 | 6 | 8 |
| 15 | 5 | 0 | 0 | 10 | 0 | 0 |
| 16 | 5 | 6 | 8 | 10 | 13 | 4 |
| 17 | 5 | 13 | 4 | 11 | 6 | 8 |
| 18 | 6 | 0 | 0 | 12 | 0 | 0 |
| 19 | 6 | 6 | 8 | 12 | 13 | 4 |
| 20 | 6 | 13 | 4 | 13 | 6 | 8 |
| 30 | 10 | 0 | 0 | 20 | 0 | 0 |
| 40 | 13 | 6 | 8 | 26 | 13 | 4 |
| 50 | 16 | 13 | 4 | 33 | 6 | 8 |
| 60 | 20 | 0 | 0 | 40 | 0 | 0 |
| 70 | 23 | 6 | 8 | 46 | 13 | 4 |
| 80 | 26 | 13 | 4 | 53 | 6 | 8 |
| 90 | 30 | 0 | 0 | 60 | 0 | 0 |
| 100 | 33 | 6 | 8 | 66 | 13 | 4 |
| 200 | 66 | 13 | 4 | 133 | 6 | 8 |
| 300 | 100 | 0 | 0 | 200 | 0 | 0 |
| 400 | 133 | 6 | 8 | 266 | 13 | 4 |
| 500 | 166 | 13 | 4 | 333 | 6 | 8 |
| 1000 | 333 | 6 | 8 | 666 | 13 | 4 |
| 5000 | 1666 | 13 | 4 | 3333 | 6 | 8 |

# Sir *SAMUEL MORLAND's*

# TABLE

*FOR*

The ready Casting up any Number

*OF*

# GUINNEYS,

*AT ANY RATE*

From Eighteen-Pence to Two Shillings:

ALSO

# *BROAD GOLD,*

AT

Three Shillings, and Three Shillings and Six-Pence; and Five Shillings, and Five Shillings and Six-Pence.

## Multiplication of Guinneys, at

| | Eighteen Pence. | | | 18 Pence Farthing. | | | |
|---|---|---|---|---|---|---|---|
| | l. | s. | d. | l. | s. | d. | q. |
| 1 | 1 | 1 | 6 | 1 | 1 | 6 | 1 |
| 2 | 2 | 3 | 0 | 2 | 3 | 0 | 2 |
| 3 | 3 | 4 | 6 | 3 | 4 | 6 | 3 |
| 4 | 4 | 6 | 0 | 4 | 6 | 1 | 0 |
| 5 | 5 | 7 | 6 | 5 | 7 | 7 | 1 |
| 6 | 6 | 9 | 0 | 6 | 9 | 1 | 2 |
| 7 | 7 | 10 | 6 | 7 | 10 | 7 | 3 |
| 8 | 8 | 12 | 0 | 8 | 12 | 2 | 0 |
| 9 | 9 | 13 | 6 | 9 | 13 | 8 | 1 |
| 10 | 10 | 15 | 0 | 10 | 15 | 2 | 2 |
| 11 | 11 | 16 | 6 | 11 | 16 | 8 | 3 |
| 12 | 12 | 18 | 0 | 12 | 18 | 3 | 0 |
| 13 | 13 | 19 | 6 | 13 | 19 | 9 | 1 |
| 14 | 15 | 1 | 0 | 15 | 1 | 3 | 2 |
| 15 | 16 | 2 | 6 | 16 | 2 | 9 | 3 |
| 16 | 17 | 4 | 0 | 17 | 4 | 4 | 0 |
| 17 | 18 | 5 | 6 | 18 | 5 | 10 | 1 |
| 18 | 19 | 7 | 0 | 19 | 7 | 4 | 2 |
| 19 | 20 | 8 | 6 | 20 | 8 | 10 | 3 |
| 20 | 21 | 10 | 0 | 21 | 10 | 5 | 0 |
| 30 | 32 | 5 | 0 | 32 | 5 | 7 | 2 |
| 40 | 43 | 0 | 0 | 43 | 0 | 10 | 0 |
| 50 | 53 | 15 | 0 | 53 | 16 | 9 | 2 |
| 60 | 64 | 10 | 0 | 64 | 11 | 3 | 0 |
| 70 | 75 | 5 | 0 | 75 | 6 | 5 | 2 |
| 80 | 86 | 0 | 0 | 86 | 1 | 8 | 0 |
| 90 | 96 | 15 | 0 | 96 | 16 | 10 | 2 |
| 100 | 107 | 10 | 0 | 107 | 12 | 1 | 0 |
| 200 | 215 | 0 | 0 | 215 | 4 | 2 | 0 |
| 300 | 322 | 10 | 0 | 322 | 16 | 3 | 0 |
| 400 | 430 | 0 | 0 | 430 | 8 | 4 | 0 |
| 500 | 537 | 10 | 0 | 538 | 0 | 5 | 0 |
| 1000 | 1075 | 0 | 0 | 1076 | 0 | 10 | 0 |
| 5000 | 5375 | 0 | 0 | 5380 | 4 | 2 | 0 |

## *Multiplication of Guinneys, at*

| | 18 Pence Half-peny. | | | | 18 Pence 3 Farthings. | | | |
|---|---|---|---|---|---|---|---|---|
| | *l.* | *s.* | *d.* | *q.* | *l.* | *s.* | *d.* | *q.* |
| 1 | 1 | 1 | 6 | 2 | 1 | 1 | 6 | 3 |
| 2 | 2 | 3 | 1 | 0 | 2 | 3 | 1 | 2 |
| 3 | 3 | 4 | 7 | 2 | 3 | 4 | 8 | 1 |
| 4 | 4 | 6 | 2 | 0 | 4 | 6 | 3 | 0 |
| 5 | 5 | 7 | 8 | 2 | 5 | 7 | 9 | 3 |
| 6 | 6 | 9 | 3 | 0 | 6 | 9 | 4 | 2 |
| 7 | 7 | 10 | 9 | 2 | 7 | 10 | 11 | 1 |
| 8 | 8 | 12 | 4 | 0 | 8 | 12 | 6 | 0 |
| 9 | 9 | 13 | 10 | 2 | 9 | 14 | 0 | 3 |
| 10 | 10 | 15 | 5 | 0 | 10 | 15 | 7 | 2 |
| 11 | 11 | 16 | 11 | 2 | 11 | 17 | 2 | 1 |
| 12 | 12 | 18 | 6 | 0 | 12 | 18 | 9 | 0 |
| 13 | 14 | 0 | 0 | 2 | 14 | 0 | 3 | 3 |
| 14 | 15 | 1 | 7 | 0 | 15 | 1 | 10 | 2 |
| 15 | 16 | 3 | 1 | 2 | 16 | 3 | 5 | 1 |
| 16 | 17 | 4 | 8 | 0 | 17 | 5 | 0 | 0 |
| 17 | 18 | 6 | 2 | 2 | 18 | 6 | 6 | 3 |
| 18 | 19 | 7 | 9 | 0 | 19 | 8 | 1 | 2 |
| 19 | 20 | 9 | 3 | 2 | 20 | 9 | 8 | 1 |
| 20 | 21 | 10 | 10 | 0 | 21 | 11 | 3 | 0 |
| 30 | 32 | 6 | 3 | 0 | 32 | 6 | 10 | 2 |
| 40 | 43 | 1 | 8 | 0 | 43 | 2 | 6 | 0 |
| 50 | 53 | 17 | 1 | 0 | 53 | 18 | 1 | 2 |
| 60 | 64 | 12 | 6 | 0 | 64 | 13 | 9 | 0 |
| 70 | 75 | 7 | 11 | 0 | 75 | 9 | 4 | 2 |
| 80 | 86 | 3 | 4 | 0 | 86 | 5 | 9 | 0 |
| 90 | 96 | 18 | 9 | 0 | 97 | 0 | 7 | 2 |
| 100 | 107 | 11 | 2 | 0 | 107 | 18 | 3 | 0 |
| 200 | 215 | 8 | 4 | 0 | 215 | 12 | 6 | 0 |
| 300 | 323 | 2 | 6 | 0 | 323 | 8 | 9 | 0 |
| 400 | 430 | 16 | 8 | 0 | 431 | 5 | 0 | 0 |
| 500 | 538 | 10 | 10 | 0 | 539 | 1 | 3 | 0 |
| 1000 | 1077 | 1 | 8 | 0 | 1078 | 2 | 6 | 0 |
| 5000 | 5385 | 8 | 4 | 0 | 5390 | 12 | 6 | 0 |

## *Multiplication of Guinneys, at*

| | Nineteen Pence. | | | 19 Pence Farthing. | | | |
|---|---|---|---|---|---|---|---|
| | *l.* | *s.* | *d.* | *l.* | *s.* | *d.* | *q.* |
| 1 | 1 | 1 | 7 | 1 | 1 | 7 | 1 |
| 2 | 2 | 3 | 2 | 2 | 3 | 2 | 2 |
| 3 | 3 | 4 | 9 | 3 | 4 | 9 | 3 |
| 4 | 4 | 6 | 4 | 4 | 6 | 5 | 0 |
| 5 | 5 | 7 | 11 | 5 | 8 | 0 | 1 |
| 6 | 6 | 9 | 6 | 6 | 9 | 7 | 2 |
| 7 | 7 | 11 | 1 | 7 | 11 | 2 | 3 |
| 8 | 8 | 12 | 8 | 8 | 12 | 10 | 0 |
| 9 | 9 | 14 | 3 | 9 | 14 | 5 | 1 |
| 10 | 10 | 15 | 10 | 10 | 16 | 0 | 2 |
| 11 | 11 | 17 | 5 | 11 | 17 | 7 | 3 |
| 12 | 12 | 19 | 0 | 12 | 19 | 3 | 0 |
| 13 | 14 | 0 | 7 | 14 | 0 | 10 | 1 |
| 14 | 15 | 2 | 2 | 15 | 2 | 5 | 2 |
| 15 | 16 | 3 | 9 | 16 | 4 | 0 | 3 |
| 16 | 17 | 5 | 4 | 17 | 5 | 8 | 0 |
| 17 | 18 | 6 | 11 | 18 | 7 | 3 | 1 |
| 18 | 19 | 8 | 6 | 19 | 8 | 10 | 2 |
| 19 | 20 | 10 | 1 | 20 | 10 | 5 | 3 |
| 20 | 21 | 11 | 8 | 21 | 12 | 1 | 0 |
| 30 | 32 | 7 | 6 | 32 | 8 | 1 | 2 |
| 40 | 43 | 3 | 4 | 43 | 4 | 2 | 0 |
| 50 | 53 | 19 | 2 | 54 | 0 | 2 | 2 |
| 60 | 64 | 15 | 0 | 64 | 16 | 3 | 0 |
| 70 | 75 | 10 | 10 | 75 | 12 | 3 | 2 |
| 80 | 86 | 6 | 8 | 86 | 8 | 4 | 0 |
| 90 | 97 | 2 | 6 | 97 | 4 | 4 | 2 |
| 100 | 107 | 18 | 4 | 108 | 0 | 5 | 0 |
| 200 | 215 | 16 | 8 | 216 | 0 | 10 | 0 |
| 300 | 323 | 15 | 0 | 324 | 1 | 3 | 0 |
| 400 | 431 | 13 | 4 | 432 | 1 | 8 | 0 |
| 500 | 539 | 11 | 8 | 540 | 2 | 1 | 0 |
| 1000 | 1079 | 3 | 4 | 1080 | 4 | 2 | 0 |
| 5000 | 5395 | 16 | 8 | 5401 | 0 | 10 | 0 |

# *Multiplication of Guinneys, at*

| | 19 Pence Half-peny. | | | | 19 Pence 3 Farthings. | | | |
|---|---|---|---|---|---|---|---|---|
| | *l.* | *s.* | *d.* | *q.* | *l.* | *s.* | *d.* | *q.* |
| 1 | 1 | 1 | 7 | 2 | 1 | 1 | 7 | 3 |
| 2 | 2 | 3 | 3 | 0 | 2 | 3 | 3 | 2 |
| 3 | 3 | 4 | 10 | 2 | 3 | 4 | 11 | 1 |
| 4 | 4 | 6 | 6 | 0 | 4 | 6 | 7 | 0 |
| 5 | 5 | 8 | 1 | 2 | 5 | 8 | 2 | 3 |
| 6 | 6 | 9 | 9 | 0 | 6 | 9 | 10 | 2 |
| 7 | 7 | 11 | 4 | 2 | 7 | 11 | 6 | 1 |
| 8 | 8 | 13 | 0 | 0 | 8 | 13 | 2 | 0 |
| 9 | 9 | 14 | 7 | 2 | 9 | 14 | 9 | 3 |
| 10 | 10 | 16 | 3 | 0 | 10 | 16 | 5 | 2 |
| 11 | 11 | 17 | 10 | 2 | 11 | 18 | 1 | 1 |
| 12 | 12 | 19 | 6 | 0 | 12 | 19 | 9 | 0 |
| 13 | 14 | 1 | 1 | 2 | 14 | 1 | 4 | 3 |
| 14 | 15 | 2 | 9 | 0 | 15 | 3 | 0 | 2 |
| 15 | 16 | 4 | 4 | 2 | 16 | 4 | 8 | 1 |
| 16 | 17 | 6 | 0 | 0 | 17 | 6 | 4 | 0 |
| 17 | 18 | 7 | 7 | 2 | 18 | 7 | 11 | 3 |
| 18 | 19 | 9 | 3 | 0 | 19 | 9 | 7 | 2 |
| 19 | 20 | 10 | 10 | 2 | 20 | 11 | 3 | 1 |
| 20 | 21 | 12 | 6 | 0 | 21 | 12 | 11 | 0 |
| 30 | 32 | 8 | 9 | 0 | 32 | 9 | 4 | 2 |
| 40 | 43 | 5 | 0 | 0 | 43 | 5 | 10 | 0 |
| 50 | 54 | 1 | 3 | 0 | 54 | 2 | 3 | 2 |
| 60 | 64 | 17 | 6 | 0 | 64 | 18 | 9 | 0 |
| 70 | 75 | 13 | 9 | 0 | 75 | 15 | 2 | 2 |
| 80 | 86 | 10 | 0 | 0 | 86 | 11 | 8 | 0 |
| 90 | 97 | 6 | 3 | 0 | 97 | 8 | 1 | 2 |
| 100 | 108 | 2 | 6 | 0 | 108 | 4 | 7 | 0 |
| 200 | 216 | 5 | 0 | 0 | 216 | 9 | 2 | 0 |
| 300 | 324 | 7 | 6 | 0 | 324 | 13 | 9 | 0 |
| 400 | 432 | 10 | 0 | 0 | 432 | 18 | 4 | 0 |
| 500 | 540 | 12 | 6 | 0 | 541 | 2 | 11 | 0 |
| 1000 | 1081 | 5 | 0 | 0 | 1082 | 5 | 10 | 0 |
| 5000 | 5406 | 5 | 0 | 0 | 5411 | 9 | 2 | 0 |

**Multiplication of Guinneys, at**

| | Twenty Pence. | | | 20 Pence Farthing | | | |
|---|---|---|---|---|---|---|---|
| | *l.* | *s.* | *d.* | *l.* | *s.* | *d.* | *q.* |
| 1 | 1 | 1 | 8 | 1 | 1 | 8 | 1 |
| 2 | 2 | 3 | 4 | 2 | 3 | 4 | 2 |
| 3 | 3 | 5 | 0 | 3 | 5 | 0 | 3 |
| 4 | 4 | 6 | 8 | 4 | 6 | 9 | 0 |
| 5 | 5 | 8 | 4 | 5 | 8 | 5 | 1 |
| 6 | 6 | 10 | 0 | 6 | 10 | 1 | 2 |
| 7 | 7 | 11 | 8 | 7 | 11 | 9 | 3 |
| 8 | 8 | 13 | 4 | 8 | 13 | 6 | 0 |
| 9 | 9 | 15 | 0 | 9 | 15 | 2 | 1 |
| 10 | 10 | 16 | 8 | 10 | 16 | 10 | 2 |
| 11 | 11 | 18 | 4 | 11 | 18 | 6 | 3 |
| 12 | 13 | 0 | 0 | 13 | 0 | 3 | 0 |
| 13 | 14 | 1 | 8 | 14 | 1 | 11 | 1 |
| 14 | 15 | 3 | 4 | 15 | 3 | 7 | 2 |
| 15 | 16 | 5 | 0 | 16 | 5 | 3 | 3 |
| 16 | 17 | 6 | 8 | 17 | 7 | 0 | 0 |
| 17 | 18 | 8 | 4 | 18 | 8 | 8 | 1 |
| 18 | 19 | 10 | 0 | 19 | 10 | 4 | 2 |
| 19 | 20 | 11 | 8 | 20 | 12 | 0 | 3 |
| 20 | 21 | 13 | 4 | 21 | 13 | 9 | 0 |
| 30 | 32 | 10 | 0 | 32 | 10 | 7 | 2 |
| 40 | 43 | 6 | 8 | 43 | 7 | 6 | 0 |
| 50 | 54 | 3 | 4 | 54 | 4 | 4 | 2 |
| 60 | 65 | 0 | 0 | 65 | 1 | 3 | 0 |
| 70 | 75 | 16 | 8 | 75 | 18 | 1 | 2 |
| 80 | 86 | 13 | 4 | 86 | 15 | 0 | 0 |
| 90 | 97 | 10 | 0 | 97 | 11 | 10 | 2 |
| 100 | 108 | 6 | 8 | 108 | 8 | 9 | 0 |
| 200 | 216 | 13 | 4 | 216 | 17 | 6 | 0 |
| 300 | 325 | 0 | 0 | 325 | 6 | 3 | 0 |
| 400 | 433 | 6 | 8 | 433 | 15 | 0 | 0 |
| 500 | 541 | 13 | 4 | 542 | 3 | 9 | 0 |
| 1000 | 1083 | 6 | 8 | 1084 | 7 | 6 | 0 |
| 5000 | 5416 | 13 | 4 | 5421 | 17 | 6 | 0 |

## Multiplication of Guineas, at

| | 20 Pence Half-peny. | | | | 20 Pence 3 Farthings. | | | |
|---|---|---|---|---|---|---|---|---|
| | l. | s. | d. | q. | l. | s. | d. | q. |
| 1 | 1 | 1 | 8 | 2 | 1 | 1 | 8 | 3 |
| 2 | 2 | 3 | 5 | 0 | 2 | 3 | 5 | 2 |
| 3 | 3 | 5 | 1 | 2 | 3 | 5 | 2 | 1 |
| 4 | 4 | 6 | 10 | 0 | 4 | 6 | 11 | 0 |
| 5 | 5 | 8 | 6 | 2 | 5 | 8 | 7 | 3 |
| 6 | 6 | 10 | 3 | 0 | 6 | 10 | 4 | 2 |
| 7 | 7 | 11 | 11 | 2 | 7 | 12 | 1 | 1 |
| 8 | 8 | 13 | 8 | 0 | 8 | 13 | 10 | 0 |
| 9 | 9 | 15 | 4 | 2 | 9 | 15 | 6 | 3 |
| 10 | 10 | 17 | 1 | 0 | 10 | 17 | 3 | 2 |
| 11 | 11 | 18 | 9 | 2 | 11 | 19 | 0 | 1 |
| 12 | 13 | 0 | 6 | 0 | 13 | 0 | 9 | 0 |
| 13 | 14 | 2 | 2 | 2 | 14 | 2 | 5 | 3 |
| 14 | 15 | 3 | 11 | 0 | 15 | 4 | 2 | 2 |
| 15 | 16 | 5 | 7 | 2 | 16 | 5 | 11 | 1 |
| 16 | 17 | 7 | 4 | 0 | 17 | 7 | 8 | 0 |
| 17 | 18 | 9 | 0 | 2 | 18 | 9 | 4 | 3 |
| 18 | 19 | 10 | 9 | 0 | 19 | 11 | 1 | 2 |
| 19 | 20 | 12 | 5 | 2 | 20 | 12 | 10 | 1 |
| 20 | 21 | 14 | 2 | 0 | 21 | 14 | 7 | 0 |
| 30 | 32 | 11 | 3 | 0 | 32 | 11 | 10 | 2 |
| 40 | 43 | 8 | 4 | 0 | 43 | 9 | 2 | 0 |
| 50 | 54 | 5 | 5 | 0 | 54 | 6 | 5 | 2 |
| 60 | 65 | 2 | 6 | 0 | 65 | 3 | 9 | 0 |
| 70 | 75 | 19 | 7 | 0 | 76 | 1 | 0 | 2 |
| 80 | 86 | 16 | 8 | 0 | 86 | 18 | 4 | 0 |
| 90 | 97 | 13 | 9 | 0 | 97 | 15 | 7 | 2 |
| 100 | 108 | 10 | 10 | 0 | 108 | 12 | 11 | 0 |
| 200 | 217 | 1 | 8 | 0 | 217 | 5 | 10 | 0 |
| 300 | 325 | 12 | 6 | 0 | 325 | 18 | 9 | 0 |
| 400 | 434 | 3 | 4 | 0 | 434 | 11 | 8 | 0 |
| 500 | 542 | 14 | 2 | 0 | 543 | 4 | 7 | 0 |
| 1000 | 1085 | 8 | 4 | 0 | 1086 | 9 | 2 | 0 |
| 5000 | 5427 | 1 | 8 | 0 | 5432 | 5 | 10 | 0 |

## Multiplication of Guinneys, at

| | One & Twenty Pence. | | | 21 Pence Farthing. | | | |
|---|---|---|---|---|---|---|---|
| | l. | s. | d. | l. | s. | d. | q. |
| 1 | 1 | 1 | 9 | 1 | 1 | 9 | 1 |
| 2 | 2 | 3 | 6 | 2 | 3 | 6 | 2 |
| 3 | 3 | 5 | 3 | 3 | 5 | 3 | 3 |
| 4 | 4 | 7 | 0 | 4 | 7 | 1 | 0 |
| 5 | 5 | 8 | 9 | 5 | 8 | 10 | 1 |
| 6 | 6 | 10 | 6 | 6 | 10 | 7 | 2 |
| 7 | 7 | 12 | 3 | 7 | 12 | 4 | 3 |
| 8 | 8 | 14 | 0 | 8 | 14 | 2 | 0 |
| 9 | 9 | 15 | 9 | 9 | 15 | 11 | 1 |
| 10 | 10 | 17 | 6 | 10 | 17 | 8 | 2 |
| 11 | 11 | 19 | 3 | 11 | 19 | 5 | 3 |
| 12 | 13 | 1 | 0 | 13 | 1 | 3 | 0 |
| 13 | 14 | 2 | 9 | 14 | 3 | 0 | 1 |
| 14 | 15 | 4 | 6 | 15 | 4 | 9 | 2 |
| 15 | 16 | 6 | 3 | 16 | 6 | 6 | 3 |
| 16 | 17 | 8 | 0 | 17 | 8 | 4 | 0 |
| 17 | 18 | 9 | 9 | 18 | 10 | 1 | 1 |
| 18 | 19 | 11 | 6 | 19 | 11 | 10 | 2 |
| 19 | 20 | 13 | 3 | 20 | 13 | 7 | 3 |
| 20 | 21 | 15 | 0 | 21 | 15 | 5 | 0 |
| 30 | 32 | 12 | 6 | 32 | 13 | 1 | 2 |
| 40 | 43 | 10 | 0 | 43 | 10 | 10 | 0 |
| 50 | 54 | 7 | 6 | 54 | 8 | 6 | 2 |
| 60 | 65 | 5 | 0 | 65 | 6 | 3 | 0 |
| 70 | 76 | 2 | 6 | 76 | 3 | 11 | 2 |
| 80 | 87 | 0 | 0 | 87 | 1 | 8 | 0 |
| 90 | 97 | 17 | 6 | 97 | 19 | 4 | 2 |
| 100 | 108 | 15 | 0 | 108 | 17 | 1 | 0 |
| 200 | 217 | 10 | 0 | 217 | 14 | 2 | 0 |
| 300 | 326 | 5 | 0 | 326 | 11 | 3 | 0 |
| 400 | 435 | 0 | 0 | 435 | 8 | 4 | 0 |
| 500 | 543 | 15 | 0 | 544 | 5 | 5 | 0 |
| 1000 | 1087 | 10 | 0 | 1088 | 10 | 10 | 0 |
| 5000 | 5437 | 10 | 0 | 5442 | 14 | 2 | 0 |

## *Multiplication of Guinneys, at*

| | 21 Pence Half-peny. | | | | 21 Pence 3 Farthings. | | | |
|---|---|---|---|---|---|---|---|---|
| | l. | s. | d. | q. | l. | s. | d. | q. |
| 1 | 1 | 1 | 9 | 2 | 1 | 1 | 9 | 3 |
| 2 | 2 | 3 | 7 | 0 | 2 | 3 | 7 | 2 |
| 3 | 3 | 5 | 4 | 2 | 3 | 5 | 5 | 1 |
| 4 | 4 | 7 | 2 | 0 | 4 | 7 | 3 | 0 |
| 5 | 5 | 8 | 11 | 2 | 5 | 9 | 0 | 3 |
| 6 | 6 | 10 | 9 | 0 | 6 | 10 | 10 | 2 |
| 7 | 7 | 12 | 6 | 2 | 7 | 12 | 8 | 1 |
| 8 | 8 | 14 | 4 | 0 | 8 | 14 | 6 | 0 |
| 9 | 9 | 16 | 1 | 2 | 9 | 16 | 3 | 3 |
| 10 | 10 | 17 | 11 | 0 | 10 | 18 | 1 | 2 |
| 11 | 11 | 19 | 8 | 2 | 11 | 19 | 11 | 1 |
| 12 | 13 | 1 | 6 | 0 | 13 | 1 | 9 | 0 |
| 13 | 14 | 3 | 3 | 2 | 14 | 3 | 6 | 3 |
| 14 | 15 | 5 | 1 | 0 | 15 | 5 | 4 | 2 |
| 15 | 16 | 6 | 10 | 2 | 16 | 7 | 2 | 1 |
| 16 | 17 | 8 | 8 | 0 | 17 | 9 | 0 | 0 |
| 17 | 18 | 10 | 5 | 2 | 18 | 10 | 9 | 3 |
| 18 | 19 | 12 | 3 | 0 | 19 | 12 | 7 | 2 |
| 19 | 20 | 14 | 0 | 2 | 20 | 14 | 5 | 1 |
| 20 | 21 | 15 | 10 | 0 | 21 | 16 | 3 | 0 |
| 30 | 32 | 13 | 9 | 0 | 32 | 14 | 4 | 2 |
| 40 | 43 | 11 | 8 | 0 | 43 | 12 | 6 | 0 |
| 50 | 54 | 9 | 7 | 0 | 54 | 10 | 7 | 2 |
| 60 | 65 | 7 | 6 | 0 | 65 | 8 | 9 | 0 |
| 70 | 76 | 5 | 5 | 0 | 76 | 6 | 10 | 2 |
| 80 | 87 | 3 | 4 | 0 | 87 | 5 | 0 | 0 |
| 90 | 98 | 1 | 3 | 0 | 98 | 3 | 1 | 2 |
| 100 | 108 | 19 | 2 | 0 | 109 | 1 | 3 | 0 |
| 200 | 217 | 18 | 4 | 0 | 218 | 2 | 6 | 0 |
| 300 | 326 | 17 | 6 | 0 | 327 | 3 | 9 | 0 |
| 400 | 435 | 16 | 8 | 0 | 436 | 5 | 0 | 0 |
| 500 | 544 | 15 | 10 | 0 | 545 | 6 | 3 | 0 |
| 1000 | 1089 | 11 | 8 | 0 | 1090 | 12 | 6 | 0 |
| 5000 | 5447 | 18 | 4 | 0 | 5453 | 2 | 6 | 0 |

# Multiplication of Guinneys, at

| | Two & Twenty-pence. | | | 22 Pence, Farthing. | | | |
|---|---|---|---|---|---|---|---|
| | l. | s. | d. | l. | s. | d. | q. |
| 1 | 1 | 1 | 10 | 1 | 1 | 10 | 1 |
| 2 | 2 | 3 | 8 | 2 | 3 | 8 | 2 |
| 3 | 3 | 5 | 6 | 3 | 5 | 6 | 3 |
| 4 | 4 | 7 | 4 | 4 | 7 | 5 | 0 |
| 5 | 5 | 9 | 2 | 5 | 9 | 3 | 1 |
| 6 | 6 | 11 | 0 | 6 | 11 | 1 | 2 |
| 7 | 7 | 12 | 10 | 7 | 12 | 11 | 3 |
| 8 | 8 | 14 | 8 | 8 | 14 | 10 | 0 |
| 9 | 9 | 16 | 6 | 9 | 16 | 8 | 1 |
| 10 | 10 | 18 | 4 | 10 | 18 | 6 | 2 |
| 11 | 12 | 0 | 2 | 12 | 0 | 4 | 3 |
| 12 | 13 | 2 | 0 | 13 | 2 | 3 | 0 |
| 13 | 14 | 3 | 10 | 14 | 4 | 1 | 1 |
| 14 | 15 | 5 | 8 | 15 | 5 | 11 | 2 |
| 15 | 16 | 7 | 6 | 16 | 7 | 9 | 3 |
| 16 | 17 | 9 | 4 | 17 | 9 | 8 | 0 |
| 17 | 18 | 11 | 2 | 18 | 11 | 6 | 1 |
| 18 | 19 | 13 | 0 | 19 | 13 | 4 | 2 |
| 19 | 20 | 14 | 10 | 20 | 15 | 2 | 3 |
| 20 | 21 | 16 | 8 | 21 | 17 | 1 | 0 |
| 30 | 32 | 15 | 0 | 32 | 15 | 7 | 2 |
| 40 | 43 | 13 | 4 | 43 | 14 | 2 | 0 |
| 50 | 54 | 11 | 8 | 54 | 12 | 8 | 2 |
| 60 | 65 | 10 | 0 | 65 | 11 | 3 | 0 |
| 70 | 76 | 8 | 4 | 76 | 9 | 9 | 2 |
| 80 | 87 | 6 | 8 | 87 | 8 | 4 | 0 |
| 90 | 98 | 5 | 0 | 98 | 6 | 10 | 2 |
| 100 | 109 | 3 | 4 | 109 | 5 | 5 | 0 |
| 200 | 218 | 6 | 8 | 218 | 10 | 10 | 0 |
| 300 | 327 | 10 | 0 | 327 | 16 | 3 | 0 |
| 400 | 436 | 13 | 4 | 437 | 1 | 8 | 0 |
| 500 | 545 | 16 | 8 | 546 | 7 | 1 | 0 |
| 1000 | 1091 | 13 | 4 | 1092 | 14 | 2 | 0 |
| 5000 | 5458 | 6 | 8 | 5463 | 10 | 10 | 0 |

## Multiplication of Guinneys.

| | 22 Pence Half-peny. | | | | 22 Pence 2 Farthings. | | | |
|---|---|---|---|---|---|---|---|---|
| | *l.* | *s.* | *d.* | *q.* | *l.* | *s.* | *d.* | *q.* |
| 1 | 1 | 1 | 10 | 2 | 1 | 1 | 10 | 3 |
| 2 | 2 | 3 | 9 | 0 | 2 | 3 | 9 | 2 |
| 3 | 3 | 5 | 7 | 2 | 3 | 5 | 8 | 1 |
| 4 | 4 | 7 | 6 | 0 | 4 | 7 | 7 | 0 |
| 5 | 5 | 9 | 4 | 2 | 5 | 9 | 5 | 3 |
| 6 | 6 | 11 | 3 | 0 | 6 | 11 | 4 | 2 |
| 7 | 7 | 13 | 1 | 2 | 7 | 13 | 3 | 1 |
| 8 | 8 | 15 | 0 | 0 | 8 | 15 | 2 | 0 |
| 9 | 9 | 16 | 10 | 2 | 9 | 17 | 0 | 3 |
| 10 | 10 | 18 | 9 | 0 | 10 | 18 | 11 | 2 |
| 11 | 12 | 0 | 7 | 2 | 12 | 0 | 10 | 1 |
| 12 | 13 | 2 | 6 | 0 | 13 | 2 | 9 | 0 |
| 13 | 14 | 4 | 4 | 2 | 14 | 4 | 7 | 3 |
| 14 | 15 | 6 | 3 | 0 | 15 | 6 | 6 | 2 |
| 15 | 16 | 8 | 1 | 2 | 16 | 8 | 5 | 1 |
| 16 | 17 | 10 | 0 | 0 | 17 | 10 | 4 | 0 |
| 17 | 18 | 11 | 10 | 2 | 18 | 12 | 2 | 3 |
| 18 | 19 | 13 | 9 | 0 | 19 | 14 | 1 | 2 |
| 19 | 20 | 15 | 7 | 2 | 20 | 16 | 0 | 1 |
| 20 | 21 | 17 | 6 | 0 | 21 | 17 | 11 | 0 |
| 30 | 32 | 16 | 3 | 0 | 32 | 16 | 10 | 2 |
| 40 | 43 | 15 | 0 | 0 | 43 | 15 | 10 | 0 |
| 50 | 54 | 13 | 9 | 0 | 54 | 14 | 9 | 2 |
| 60 | 65 | 12 | 6 | 0 | 65 | 13 | 9 | 0 |
| 70 | 76 | 11 | 3 | 0 | 76 | 12 | 8 | 2 |
| 80 | 87 | 10 | 0 | 0 | 87 | 11 | 8 | 0 |
| 90 | 98 | 8 | 9 | 0 | 98 | 10 | 7 | 2 |
| 100 | 109 | 7 | 6 | 0 | 109 | 9 | 7 | 0 |
| 200 | 218 | 15 | 0 | 0 | 218 | 19 | 2 | 0 |
| 300 | 328 | 2 | 6 | 0 | 328 | 8 | 9 | 0 |
| 400 | 437 | 10 | 0 | 0 | 437 | 18 | 4 | 0 |
| 500 | 546 | 17 | 6 | 0 | 547 | 7 | 11 | 0 |
| 1000 | 1093 | 15 | 0 | 0 | 1094 | 15 | 10 | 0 |
| 5000 | 5468 | 15 | 0 | 0 | 5473 | 19 | 2 | 0 |

## *Multiplication of Guinneys, at*

| | Three & twenty-pence. | | | 23 Pence Farthing. | | | |
|---|---|---|---|---|---|---|---|
| | *l.* | *s.* | *d.* | *l.* | *s.* | *d.* | *q.* |
| 1 | 1 | 1 | 11 | 1 | 1 | 11 | 1 |
| 2 | 2 | 3 | 10 | 2 | 3 | 10 | 2 |
| 3 | 3 | 5 | 9 | 3 | 5 | 9 | 3 |
| 4 | 4 | 7 | 8 | 4 | 7 | 9 | 0 |
| 5 | 5 | 9 | 7 | 5 | 9 | 8 | 1 |
| 6 | 6 | 11 | 6 | 6 | 11 | 7 | 2 |
| 7 | 7 | 13 | 5 | 7 | 13 | 6 | 3 |
| 8 | 8 | 15 | 4 | 8 | 15 | 6 | 0 |
| 9 | 9 | 17 | 3 | 9 | 17 | 5 | 1 |
| 10 | 10 | 19 | 2 | 10 | 19 | 4 | 2 |
| 11 | 12 | 1 | 1 | 12 | 1 | 3 | 3 |
| 12 | 13 | 3 | 0 | 13 | 3 | 3 | 0 |
| 13 | 14 | 4 | 11 | 14 | 5 | 2 | 1 |
| 14 | 15 | 6 | 10 | 15 | 7 | 1 | 2 |
| 15 | 16 | 8 | 9 | 16 | 9 | 0 | 3 |
| 16 | 17 | 10 | 8 | 17 | 11 | 0 | 0 |
| 17 | 18 | 12 | 7 | 18 | 12 | 11 | 1 |
| 18 | 19 | 14 | 6 | 19 | 14 | 10 | 2 |
| 19 | 20 | 16 | 5 | 20 | 16 | 9 | 3 |
| 20 | 21 | 18 | 4 | 21 | 18 | 9 | 0 |
| 30 | 33 | 17 | 6 | 32 | 18 | 1 | 2 |
| 40 | 43 | 16 | 8 | 43 | 17 | 6 | 0 |
| 50 | 54 | 15 | 10 | 54 | 16 | 10 | 2 |
| 60 | 65 | 15 | 0 | 65 | 16 | 3 | 0 |
| 70 | 76 | 14 | 2 | 76 | 15 | 7 | 2 |
| 80 | 87 | 13 | 4 | 87 | 15 | 0 | 0 |
| 90 | 98 | 12 | 6 | 98 | 14 | 4 | 2 |
| 100 | 109 | 11 | 8 | 109 | 13 | 9 | 0 |
| 200 | 219 | 3 | 4 | 219 | 7 | 6 | 0 |
| 300 | 328 | 15 | 0 | 329 | 1 | 3 | 0 |
| 400 | 438 | 6 | 8 | 438 | 15 | 0 | 0 |
| 500 | 547 | 18 | 4 | 548 | 8 | 9 | 0 |
| 1000 | 1095 | 16 | 8 | 1096 | 17 | 6 | 0 |
| 5000 | 5479 | 3 | 4 | 5484 | 7 | 6 | 0 |

## *Multiplication of Guinneys, &c.*

| | 23 Pence Half-peny. | | | | 23 Pence 3 Farthings. | | | |
|---|---|---|---|---|---|---|---|---|
| | l. | s. | d. | q | l. | s. | d. | q. |
| 1 | 1 | 1 | 11 | 2 | 1 | 1 | 11 | 3 |
| 2 | 2 | 3 | 11 | 0 | 2 | 3 | 11 | 2 |
| 3 | 3 | 5 | 10 | 2 | 3 | 5 | 11 | 1 |
| 4 | 4 | 7 | 10 | 0 | 4 | 7 | 11 | 0 |
| 5 | 5 | 9 | 9 | 2 | 5 | 9 | 10 | 3 |
| 6 | 6 | 11 | 9 | 0 | 6 | 11 | 10 | 2 |
| 7 | 7 | 13 | 8 | 2 | 7 | 13 | 10 | 1 |
| 8 | 8 | 15 | 8 | 0 | 8 | 15 | 10 | 0 |
| 9 | 9 | 17 | 7 | 2 | 9 | 17 | 9 | 3 |
| 10 | 10 | 19 | 7 | 0 | 10 | 19 | 9 | 2 |
| 11 | 12 | 1 | 6 | 2 | 12 | 1 | 9 | 1 |
| 12 | 13 | 3 | 6 | 0 | 13 | 3 | 9 | 0 |
| 13 | 14 | 5 | 5 | 2 | 14 | 5 | 8 | 3 |
| 14 | 15 | 7 | 5 | 0 | 15 | 7 | 8 | 2 |
| 15 | 16 | 9 | 4 | 2 | 16 | 9 | 8 | 1 |
| 16 | 17 | 11 | 4 | 0 | 17 | 11 | 8 | 0 |
| 17 | 18 | 13 | 3 | 2 | 18 | 13 | 7 | 3 |
| 18 | 19 | 15 | 3 | 0 | 19 | 15 | 7 | 2 |
| 19 | 20 | 17 | 2 | 2 | 20 | 17 | 7 | 1 |
| 20 | 21 | 19 | 2 | 0 | 21 | 19 | 7 | 0 |
| 30 | 32 | 18 | 9 | 0 | 32 | 19 | 4 | 2 |
| 40 | 43 | 18 | 4 | 0 | 43 | 19 | 2 | 0 |
| 50 | 54 | 17 | 11 | 0 | 54 | 18 | 11 | 2 |
| 60 | 65 | 17 | 6 | 0 | 65 | 18 | 9 | 0 |
| 70 | 76 | 17 | 1 | 0 | 76 | 18 | 6 | 2 |
| 80 | 87 | 16 | 8 | 0 | 87 | 18 | 4 | 0 |
| 90 | 98 | 16 | 3 | 0 | 98 | 18 | 1 | 2 |
| 100 | 109 | 15 | 10 | 0 | 109 | 17 | 11 | 0 |
| 200 | 219 | 11 | 8 | 0 | 219 | 15 | 10 | 0 |
| 300 | 329 | 7 | 6 | 0 | 329 | 13 | 9 | 0 |
| 400 | 439 | 3 | 4 | 0 | 439 | 11 | 8 | 0 |
| 500 | 548 | 19 | 2 | 0 | 549 | 9 | 7 | 0 |
| 1000 | 1097 | 18 | 4 | 0 | 1098 | 19 | 2 | 0 |
| 5000 | 5489 | 11 | 8 | 0 | 5494 | 15 | 10 | 0 |

*Multiplication of Guinneys, at 22 Shillings.*

| | *l.* | *s.* | | *l.* | *s.* |
|---|---|---|---|---|---|
| 1 | 1 | 2 | 30 | 33 | 0 |
| 2 | 2 | 4 | 40 | 44 | 0 |
| 3 | 3 | 6 | 50 | 55 | 0 |
| 4 | 4 | 8 | 60 | 66 | 0 |
| 5 | 5 | 10 | 70 | 77 | 0 |
| 6 | 6 | 12 | 80 | 88 | 0 |
| 7 | 7 | 14 | 90 | 99 | 0 |
| 8 | 8 | 16 | 100 | 110 | 0 |
| 9 | 9 | 18 | 200 | 220 | 0 |
| 10 | 11 | 0 | 300 | 330 | 0 |
| 11 | 12 | 2 | 400 | 440 | 0 |
| 12 | 13 | 4 | 500 | 550 | 0 |
| 13 | 14 | 6 | 600 | 660 | 0 |
| 14 | 15 | 8 | 700 | 770 | 0 |
| 15 | 16 | 10 | 800 | 880 | 0 |
| 16 | 17 | 12 | 900 | 990 | 0 |
| 17 | 18 | 14 | 1000 | 1100 | 0 |
| 18 | 19 | 16 | 2000 | 2200 | 0 |
| 19 | 20 | 18 | 5000 | 5500 | 0 |
| 20 | 22 | 0 | 10000 | 11000 | 0 |

## Example of this TABLE.

*What comes* 500 *Guinneys to at* 1 l. 1 s. 8 d. 3 q. per *Guinney.*

I seek for 20 Pence 3 Farthings at the top of the Table, which I find over the third Column in pag. 143; then I seek for 500 in the first Column, and right against it in the third Column I find 543 *l.* 4 *s.* 7 *d.* which answers the Question.

*Multi-*

# Multiplication of Broad-Gold, at

| | 23 Shillings. | | 23 Shillings 6 Pence. | | |
|---|---|---|---|---|---|
| | l. | s. | l. | s. | d. |
| 1 | 1 | 3 | 1 | 3 | 6 |
| 2 | 2 | 6 | 2 | 7 | 0 |
| 3 | 3 | 9 | 3 | 10 | 6 |
| 4 | 4 | 12 | 4 | 14 | 0 |
| 5 | 5 | 15 | 5 | 17 | 6 |
| 6 | 6 | 18 | 7 | 1 | 0 |
| 7 | 8 | 1 | 8 | 4 | 6 |
| 8 | 9 | 4 | 9 | 8 | 0 |
| 9 | 10 | 7 | 10 | 11 | 6 |
| 10 | 11 | 10 | 11 | 15 | 0 |
| 11 | 12 | 13 | 12 | 18 | 6 |
| 12 | 13 | 16 | 14 | 2 | 0 |
| 13 | 14 | 19 | 15 | 5 | 6 |
| 14 | 16 | 2 | 16 | 9 | 0 |
| 15 | 17 | 5 | 17 | 12 | 6 |
| 16 | 18 | 8 | 18 | 16 | 0 |
| 17 | 19 | 11 | 19 | 19 | 6 |
| 18 | 20 | 14 | 21 | 3 | 0 |
| 19 | 21 | 17 | 22 | 6 | 6 |
| 20 | 23 | 0 | 23 | 10 | 0 |
| 30 | 34 | 10 | 35 | 5 | 0 |
| 40 | 46 | 0 | 47 | 0 | 0 |
| 50 | 57 | 10 | 58 | 15 | 0 |
| 60 | 69 | 0 | 70 | 10 | 0 |
| 70 | 80 | 10 | 82 | 5 | 0 |
| 80 | 92 | 0 | 94 | 0 | 0 |
| 90 | 103 | 10 | 105 | 15 | 0 |
| 100 | 115 | 0 | 117 | 10 | 0 |
| 200 | 230 | 0 | 235 | 0 | 0 |
| 300 | 345 | 0 | 352 | 10 | 0 |
| 400 | 460 | 0 | 470 | 0 | 0 |
| 500 | 575 | 0 | 587 | 10 | 0 |
| 1000 | 1150 | 0 | 1175 | 0 | 0 |
| 5000 | 5750 | 0 | 5875 | 0 | 0 |

## Multiplication of Broad-Gold, at

| | 25 Shillings. | | 25 Shillings 6 Pence. | | |
|---|---|---|---|---|---|
| | l. | s. | l. | s. | d. |
| 1 | 1 | 5 | 1 | 5 | 6 |
| 2 | 2 | 10 | 2 | 11 | 0 |
| 3 | 3 | 15 | 3 | 16 | 6 |
| 4 | 5 | 0 | 5 | 2 | 0 |
| 5 | 6 | 5 | 6 | 7 | 6 |
| 6 | 7 | 10 | 7 | 13 | 0 |
| 7 | 8 | 15 | 8 | 18 | 6 |
| 8 | 10 | 0 | 10 | 4 | 0 |
| 9 | 11 | 5 | 11 | 9 | 6 |
| 10 | 12 | 10 | 12 | 15 | 0 |
| 11 | 13 | 15 | 14 | 0 | 6 |
| 12 | 15 | 0 | 15 | 6 | 0 |
| 13 | 16 | 5 | 16 | 11 | 6 |
| 14 | 17 | 10 | 17 | 17 | 0 |
| 15 | 18 | 15 | 19 | 2 | 6 |
| 16 | 20 | 0 | 20 | 8 | 0 |
| 17 | 21 | 5 | 21 | 13 | 6 |
| 18 | 22 | 10 | 22 | 19 | 0 |
| 19 | 23 | 15 | 24 | 4 | 6 |
| 20 | 25 | 0 | 25 | 10 | 0 |
| 30 | 37 | 10 | 38 | 5 | 0 |
| 40 | 50 | 0 | 51 | 0 | 0 |
| 50 | 62 | 10 | 63 | 15 | 0 |
| 60 | 75 | 0 | 76 | 10 | 0 |
| 70 | 87 | 10 | 89 | 5 | 0 |
| 80 | 100 | 0 | 102 | 0 | 0 |
| 90 | 112 | 10 | 114 | 15 | 0 |
| 100 | 125 | 0 | 127 | 10 | 0 |
| 200 | 250 | 0 | 255 | 0 | 0 |
| 300 | 375 | 0 | 382 | 10 | 0 |
| 400 | 500 | 0 | 510 | 0 | 0 |
| 500 | 625 | 0 | 637 | 10 | 0 |
| 1000 | 1250 | 0 | 1275 | 0 | 0 |
| 5000 | 6250 | 0 | 6375 | 0 | 0 |

# A TABLE

SHEWING

## The Intereſt of any Sum of Money At 6 *per Cent.* Simple Intereſt.

*Example.*

*What is the Intereſt of* 336 l. *for* 9 *Months?*

Firſt I find the Intereſt of 300 *l.* then of 30 *l.* and laſtly of 6 *l.* in the Column under 9 Months, thus:

| *l.* | *l.* | *s.* | *d.* |
|---|---|---|---|
| 300 | 13 | 10 | 00.0 |
| 30 | 1 | 7 | 00.0 |
| 6 | 0 | 5 | 04.8 |
| | 15 | 2 | 04.8 |

The Anſwer is 15 *l.* 2 *s.* 4 *d.* 3 *q.*

# *Simple Interest,*

| | | 1 Month. | | | 2 Months. | | | 3 Months. | | |
|---|---|---|---|---|---|---|---|---|---|---|
| | | *l.* | *s.* | *d.* | *l.* | *s.* | *d.* | *l.* | *s.* | *d.* |
| s. | 5 | 0 | 0 | 0.3 | 0 | 0 | 0.6 | 0 | 0 | 0.9 |
| | 10 | 0 | 0 | 0.6 | 0 | 0 | 1.2 | 0 | 0 | 1.8 |
| | 15 | 0 | 0 | 0.9 | 0 | 0 | 1.8 | 0 | 0 | 2.7 |
| l. | 1 | 0 | 0 | 1.2 | 0 | 0 | 2.4 | 0 | 0 | 3.6 |
| | 2 | 0 | 0 | 2.4 | 0 | 0 | 4.8 | 0 | 0 | 7.2 |
| | 3 | 0 | 0 | 3.6 | 0 | 0 | 7.2 | 0 | 0 | 10.8 |
| | 4 | 0 | 0 | 4.8 | 0 | 0 | 9.6 | 0 | 1 | 2.4 |
| | 5 | 0 | 0 | 6.0 | 0 | 1 | 0.0 | 0 | 1 | 6.0 |
| | 6 | 0 | 0 | 7.2 | 0 | 1 | 2.4 | 0 | 1 | 9.6 |
| | 7 | 0 | 0 | 8.4 | 0 | 1 | 4.8 | 0 | 2 | 1.2 |
| | 8 | 0 | 0 | 9.6 | 0 | 1 | 7.2 | 0 | 2 | 4.8 |
| | 9 | 0 | 0 | 10.8 | 0 | 1 | 9.6 | 0 | 2 | 8.4 |
| | 10 | 0 | 1 | 0.0 | 0 | 2 | 0.0 | 0 | 3 | 0.0 |
| | 20 | 0 | 2 | 0.0 | | 4 | 0.0 | 0 | 6 | 0.0 |
| | 30 | 0 | 3 | 0.0 | | 6 | 0.0 | 0 | 9 | 0.0 |
| | 40 | 0 | 4 | 0.0 | 0 | 8 | 0.0 | 0 | 12 | 0.0 |
| | 50 | 0 | 5 | 0.0 | 0 | 10 | 0.0 | 0 | 15 | 0.0 |
| | 60 | 0 | 6 | 0.0 | 0 | 12 | 0.0 | 0 | 18 | 0.0 |
| | 70 | 0 | 7 | 0.0 | 0 | 14 | 0.0 | 1 | 1 | 0.0 |
| | 80 | 0 | 8 | 0.0 | 0 | 16 | 0.0 | 1 | 4 | 0.0 |
| | 90 | 0 | 9 | 0.0 | 0 | 18 | 0.0 | 1 | 7 | 0.0 |
| | 100 | 0 | 10 | 0.0 | 1 | 0 | 0.0 | 1 | 10 | 0.0 |
| | 200 | 1 | 0 | 0.0 | 2 | 0 | 0.0 | 3 | 0 | 0.0 |
| | 300 | 1 | 10 | 0.0 | 3 | 0 | 0.0 | 4 | 10 | 0.0 |
| | 400 | 2 | 0 | 0.0 | 4 | 0 | 0.0 | 6 | 0 | 0.0 |
| | 500 | 2 | 10 | 0.0 | 5 | 0 | 0.0 | 7 | 10 | 0.0 |
| | 600 | 3 | 0 | 0.0 | 6 | 0 | 0.0 | 9 | 0 | 0.0 |
| | 700 | 3 | 10 | 0 0 | 7 | 0 | 0.0 | 10 | 10 | 0.0 |
| | 800 | 4 | 0 | 0.0 | 8 | 0 | 0.0 | 12 | 0 | 0. |
| | 900 | 4 | 10 | 0.0 | 9 | 0 | 0.0 | 13 | 10 | 0. |
| | 1000 | 5 | 0 | 0.0 | 10 | 0 | 0.0 | 15 | 0 | 0. |
| | 2000 | 10 | 0 | 0.0 | 20 | 0 | 0.0 | 30 | 0 | 0. |
| | 3000 | 15 | 0 | 0.0 | 30 | 0 | 0.0 | 45 | 0 | 0. |
| | 5000 | 25 | 0 | 0.0 | 50 | 0 | 0.0 | 75 | 0 | 0. |

## at 6 per Cent.

| | 4 Months. | | | 5 Months. | | | 6 Months. | | |
|---|---|---|---|---|---|---|---|---|---|
| | l. | s. | d. | l. | s. | d. | l. | s. | d. |
| s. 5 | 0 | 0 | 1.2 | 0 | 0 | 1.5 | 0 | 0 | 1.8 |
| 10 | 0 | 0 | 2.4 | 0 | 0 | 3.0 | 0 | 0 | 3.6 |
| 15 | 0 | 0 | 3.6 | 0 | 0 | 4.5 | 0 | 0 | 5.4 |
| l. 1 | 0 | 0 | 4.8 | 0 | 0 | 6.0 | 0 | 0 | 7.2 |
| 2 | 0 | 0 | 9.6 | 0 | 1 | 0.0 | 0 | 1 | 2.4 |
| 3 | 0 | 1 | 2.4 | 0 | 1 | 6.0 | 0 | 1 | 9.6 |
| 4 | 0 | 1 | 7.2 | 0 | 2 | 0.0 | 0 | 2 | 4.8 |
| 5 | 0 | 2 | 0.0 | 0 | 2 | 6.0 | 0 | 3 | 0.0 |
| 6 | 0 | 2 | 4.8 | 0 | 3 | 0.0 | 0 | 3 | 7.2 |
| 7 | 0 | 2 | 9.6 | 0 | 3 | 6.0 | 0 | 4 | 2.4 |
| 8 | 0 | 3 | 2.4 | 0 | 4 | 0.0 | 0 | 4 | 9.6 |
| 9 | 0 | 3 | 7.2 | 0 | 4 | 6.0 | 0 | 5 | 4.8 |
| 10 | 0 | 4 | 0.0 | 0 | 5 | 0.0 | 0 | 6 | 0.0 |
| 20 | 0 | 8 | 0.0 | 0 | 10 | 0.0 | 0 | 12 | 0 0 |
| 30 | 0 | 12 | 0.0 | 0 | 15 | 0.0 | 0 | 18 | 0.0 |
| 40 | 0 | 16 | 0.0 | 1 | 0 | 0.0 | 1 | 4 | 0.0 |
| 50 | 1 | 0 | 0.0 | 1 | 5 | 0.0 | 1 | 10 | 0.0 |
| 60 | 1 | 4 | 0.0 | 1 | 10 | 0.0 | 1 | 16 | 0.0 |
| 70 | 1 | 8 | 0.0 | 1 | 15 | 0.0 | 2 | 2 | 0.0 |
| 80 | 1 | 12 | 0.0 | 2 | 0 | 0.0 | 2 | 8 | 0.0 |
| 90 | 1 | 16 | 0.0 | 2 | 5 | 0.0 | 2 | 14 | 0.0 |
| 100 | 2 | 0 | 0.0 | 2 | 10 | 0.0 | 3 | 0 | 0.0 |
| 200 | 4 | 0 | 0.0 | 5 | 0 | 0.0 | 6 | 0 | 0.0 |
| 300 | 6 | 0 | 0.0 | 7 | 10 | 0.0 | 9 | 0 | 0.0 |
| 400 | 8 | 0 | 0.0 | 10 | 0 | 0.0 | 12 | 0 | 0.0 |
| 500 | 10 | 0 | 0.0 | 12 | 10 | 0.0 | 15 | 0 | 0.0 |
| 600 | 12 | 0 | 0.0 | 15 | 0 | 0.0 | 18 | 0 | 0.0 |
| 700 | 14 | 0 | 0.0 | 17 | 10 | 0.0 | 21 | 0 | 0.0 |
| 800 | 16 | 0 | 0 0 | 20 | 0 | 0.0 | 24 | 0 | 0.0 |
| 900 | 18 | 0 | 0.0 | 22 | 10 | 0.0 | 27 | 0 | 0.0 |
| 1000 | 20 | 0 | 0.0 | 25 | 0 | 0.0 | 30 | 0 | 0.0 |
| 2000 | 40 | 0 | 0.0 | 50 | 0 | 0.0 | 60 | 0 | 0.0 |
| 3000 | 60 | 0 | 0.0 | 75 | 0 | 0.0 | 90 | 0 | 0.0 |
| 5000 | 100 | 0 | 0.0 | 125 | 0 | 0.0 | 150 | 0 | 0.0 |

## *Simple Interest,*

| | 7 Months. | | | 8 Months. | | | 9 Months. | | |
|---|---|---|---|---|---|---|---|---|---|
| | *l.* | *s.* | *d.* | *l.* | *s.* | *d.* | *l.* | *s.* | *d.* |
| s. 5 | 0 | 0 | 2.1 | 0 | 0 | 2.4 | 0 | 0 | 2.7 |
| 10 | 0 | 0 | 4.2 | 0 | 0 | 4.8 | 0 | 0 | 5.4 |
| 15 | 0 | 0 | 6.3 | 0 | 0 | 7.2 | 0 | 0 | 8.1 |
| l. 1 | 0 | 0 | 8.4 | 0 | 0 | 9.6 | 0 | 0 | 10.8 |
| 2 | 0 | 1 | 4.8 | 0 | 1 | 7.2 | 0 | 1 | 9.6 |
| 3 | 0 | 2 | 1.2 | 0 | 2 | 4.8 | 0 | 2 | 8.4 |
| 4 | 0 | 2 | 9.6 | 0 | 3 | 2.4 | 0 | 3 | 7.2 |
| 5 | 0 | 3 | 6.0 | 0 | 4 | 0.0 | 0 | 4 | 6.0 |
| 6 | 0 | 4 | 2.4 | 0 | 4 | 9.6 | 0 | 5 | 4.8 |
| 7 | 0 | 4 | 10.8 | 0 | 5 | 7.2 | 0 | 6 | 3.6 |
| 8 | 0 | 5 | 7.2 | 0 | 6 | 4.8 | 0 | 7 | 2.4 |
| 9 | 0 | 6 | 3.6 | 0 | 7 | 2.4 | 0 | 8 | 1.2 |
| 10 | 0 | 7 | 0.0 | 0 | 8 | 0.0 | 0 | 9 | 0.0 |
| 20 | 0 | 14 | 0.0 | 0 | 16 | 0.0 | 0 | 18 | 0.0 |
| 30 | 1 | 1 | 0.0 | 1 | 4 | 0.0 | 1 | 7 | 0.0 |
| 40 | 1 | 8 | 0.0 | 1 | 12 | 0.0 | 1 | 16 | 0.0 |
| 50 | 1 | 15 | 0.0 | 2 | 0 | 0.0 | 2 | 5 | 0.0 |
| 60 | 2 | 2 | 0.0 | 2 | 8 | 0.0 | 2 | 14 | 0.0 |
| 70 | 2 | 9 | 0.0 | 2 | 16 | 0.0 | 3 | 3 | 0.0 |
| 80 | 2 | 16 | 0.0 | 3 | 4 | 0.0 | 3 | 12 | 0.0 |
| 90 | 3 | 3 | 0.0 | 3 | 12 | 0.0 | 4 | 1 | 0.0 |
| 100 | 3 | 10 | 0.0 | 4 | 0 | 0.0 | 4 | 10 | 0.0 |
| 200 | 7 | 0 | 0.0 | 8 | 0 | 0.0 | 9 | 0 | 0.0 |
| 300 | 10 | 10 | 0.0 | 12 | 0 | 0.0 | 13 | 10 | 0.0 |
| 400 | 14 | 0 | 0.0 | 16 | 0 | 0.0 | 18 | 0 | 0.0 |
| 500 | 17 | 10 | 0.0 | 20 | 0 | 0.0 | 22 | 10 | 0.0 |
| 600 | 21 | 0 | 0.0 | 24 | 0 | 0.0 | 27 | 0 | 0.0 |
| 700 | 24 | 10 | 0.0 | 28 | 0 | 0.0 | 31 | 10 | 0.0 |
| 800 | 28 | 0 | 0.0 | 32 | 0 | 0.0 | 36 | 0 | 0.0 |
| 900 | 31 | 10 | 0.0 | 36 | 0 | 0.0 | 40 | 10 | 0.0 |
| 1000 | 35 | 0 | 0.0 | 40 | 0 | 0.0 | 45 | 0 | 0.0 |
| 2000 | 70 | 0 | 0.0 | 80 | 0 | 0.0 | 90 | 0 | 0.0 |
| 3000 | 105 | 0 | 0.0 | 120 | 0 | 0.0 | 135 | 0 | 0.0 |
| 5000 | 175 | 0 | 0.0 | 200 | 0 | 0.0 | 225 | 0 | 0.0 |

## at 6 per Cent.

| | 10 Months. | | | 11 Months. | | | 12 Months. | | |
|---|---|---|---|---|---|---|---|---|---|
| | l. | s. | d. | l. | s. | d. | l. | s. | d. |
| s. 5 | 0 | 0 | 3.0 | 0 | 0 | 3.3 | 0 | 0 | 3.6 |
| 10 | 0 | 0 | 6.0 | 0 | 0 | 6.6 | 0 | 0 | 7.2 |
| 15 | 0 | 0 | 9.0 | 0 | 0 | 9.9 | 0 | 0 | 10.8 |
| l. 1 | 0 | 1 | 0.0 | 0 | 1 | 1.2 | 0 | 1 | 2.4 |
| 2 | 0 | 2 | 0.0 | 0 | 2 | 2.4 | 0 | 2 | 4.8 |
| 3 | 0 | 3 | 0.0 | 0 | 3 | 3.6 | 0 | 3 | 7.2 |
| 4 | 0 | 4 | 0.0 | 0 | 4 | 4.8 | 0 | 4 | 9.6 |
| 5 | 0 | 5 | 0.0 | 0 | 5 | 6.0 | 0 | 6 | 0.0 |
| 6 | 0 | 6 | 0.0 | 0 | 6 | 7.2 | 0 | 7 | 2.4 |
| 7 | 0 | 7 | 0.0 | 0 | 7 | 8.4 | 0 | 8 | 4.8 |
| 8 | 0 | 8 | 0.0 | 0 | 8 | 9.6 | 0 | 9 | 7.2 |
| 9 | 0 | 9 | 0.0 | 0 | 9 | 10.8 | 0 | 10 | 9.6 |
| 10 | 0 | 10 | 0.0 | 0 | 11 | 0.0 | 0 | 12 | 0.0 |
| 20 | 1 | 0 | 0.0 | 1 | 2 | 0.0 | 1 | 4 | 0.0 |
| 30 | 1 | 10 | 0.0 | 1 | 13 | 0.0 | 1 | 16 | 0.0 |
| 40 | 2 | 0 | 0.0 | 2 | 4 | 0.0 | 2 | 8 | 0.0 |
| 50 | 2 | 10 | 0.0 | 2 | 15 | 0.0 | 3 | 0 | 0.0 |
| 60 | 3 | 0 | 0.0 | 3 | 6 | 0.0 | 3 | 12 | 0.0 |
| 70 | 3 | 10 | 0.0 | 3 | 17 | 0.0 | 4 | 4 | 0.0 |
| 80 | 4 | 0 | 0.0 | 4 | 8 | 0.0 | 4 | 16 | 0.0 |
| 90 | 4 | 10 | 0.0 | 4 | 19 | 0.0 | 5 | 8 | 0.0 |
| 100 | 5 | 0 | 0.0 | 5 | 10 | 0.0 | 6 | 0 | 0.0 |
| 200 | 10 | 0 | 0.0 | 11 | 0 | 0.0 | 12 | 0 | 0.0 |
| 300 | 15 | 0 | 0.0 | 16 | 10 | 0.0 | 18 | 0 | 0.0 |
| 400 | 20 | 0 | 0.0 | 22 | 0 | 0.0 | 24 | 0 | 0.0 |
| 500 | 25 | 0 | 0.0 | 27 | 10 | 0.0 | 30 | 0 | 0.0 |
| 600 | 30 | 0 | 0.0 | 33 | 0 | 0.0 | 36 | 6 | 0.0 |
| 700 | 35 | 0 | 0.0 | 38 | 10 | 0.0 | 42 | 0 | 0.0 |
| 800 | 40 | 0 | 0.0 | 44 | 0 | 0.0 | 48 | 0 | 0.0 |
| 900 | 45 | 0 | 0.0 | 49 | 10 | 0.0 | 54 | 0 | 0.0 |
| 1000 | 50 | 0 | 0.0 | 55 | 0 | 0.0 | 60 | 0 | 0.0 |
| 2000 | 100 | 0 | 0.0 | 110 | 0 | 0.0 | 120 | 0 | 0.0 |
| 3000 | 150 | 0 | 0.0 | 165 | 0 | 0.0 | 180 | 0 | 0.0 |
| 5000 | 250 | 0 | 0.0 | 275 | 0 | 0.0 | 300 | 0 | 0.0 |

## *Intereſt of Money for Days.*

TO find the Intereſt of any ſum of Money for any Number of Days at any Rate of Intereſt, the Rule is,

Multiply the Principal by the Rate, and the Product by the Number of Days, and it gives a Dividend, which divided by 36500 (the Common Diviſor for all Rates) anſwers the Queſtion.

Example 1. *What is the Intereſt of* 500 l. *at* 6 *per* Cent. *for* 200 *Days?*

The Principal 500
The Rate 6
3000
Days 200

Common Diviſor 36500) 600000 (16.438

Anſwer 16 *l.* 8 *s.* 9 *d.*

Example 2. *What is the Intereſt of* 1000 l. *at* 8 per Cent. *for* 365 *Days?*

Principal 1000
Rate 8
8000
365

Common Diviſor 36500) 2920000 (80 *l.* Anſwer.

And thus may you readily find the Intereſt of any ſum of Money at any other Rate, for any Number of Days.

| | |
|---|---|
| 1 | 36500 |
| 2 | 73000 |
| 3 | 109500 |
| 4 | 146000 |
| 5 | 182500 |
| 6 | 219000 |
| 7 | 255500 |
| 8 | 292000 |
| 9 | 328500 |

For the eaſing you in your Diviſion, I have here inſerted a Table of the Multiplication of the Common Diviſor, whereby you may at firſt ſight perceive how many times the Diviſor is contained in the Dividend.

*A Table*

# A TABLE OF THE *DISCOMPT* or *REBATE* OF MONEYS

## At 6 *per Cent.* Simple Intereſt.

*SHEWING*

The preſent Value of a Sum of Money due at the End of 1,2,3,4,5,6,7,8,9,10,11,12,24, or 36 Months.

*Example.*

I have bought Goods amounting to 155 *l.* to be paid at the end of 3 Months, I deſire to know how much Money paid down preſently will ſatisfie this ſum, diſcompting after the Rate of 6 *per Cent.*

Here I muſt ſeek for the ſum in three parts thus,

| *l.* | | *l.* | *s.* | *q.* |
|---|---|---|---|---|
| 100 | Due at 3 Months end, worth preſently | 98. | 10 | 5.32 |
| 50 | | 49 | 5 | 2.66 |
| 5 | | 4 | 18 | 6.27 |
| | | 152 | 14 | 2.25 |

So that it appears by the Table that 152 *l.* 14 *s.* and 2 *d.* 1 *q.* paid down preſently, will ſatisfie for 155 *l.* due at 3 Months end.

## Discompt, or Rebate,

| | 1 Month. | | | 2 Months. | | |
|---|---|---|---|---|---|---|
| | l. | s. | d. | l. | s. | d |
| s. 5 | 0 | 4 | 11.70 | 0 | 4 | 11.41 |
| 10 | 0 | 9 | 11.40 | 0 | 9 | 10.81 |
| 15 | 0 | 14 | 11.10 | 0 | 14 | 10.22 |
| l. 1 | 0 | 19 | 10.81 | 0 | 19 | 9.63 |
| 2 | 1 | 19 | 9.61 | 1 | 19 | 7.25 |
| 3 | 2 | 19 | 8.42 | 2 | 19 | 4.87 |
| 4 | 3 | 19 | 7.22 | 3 | 19 | 2.50 |
| 5 | 4 | 19 | 6.03 | 4 | 19 | 0.12 |
| 6 | 5 | 19 | 4.84 | 5 | 18 | 9.74 |
| 7 | 6 | 19 | 3.64 | 6 | 18 | 7.37 |
| 8 | 7 | 19 | 2.45 | 7 | 18 | 4.99 |
| 9 | 8 | 19 | 1.25 | 8 | 18 | 2.61 |
| 10 | 9 | 19 | 0.06 | 9 | 18 | 0.24 |
| 20 | 19 | 18 | 0.12 | 19 | 16 | 0.48 |
| 30 | 29 | 17 | 0.18 | 29 | 14 | 0.71 |
| 40 | 39 | 16 | 0.24 | 39 | 12 | 0.95 |
| 50 | 49 | 15 | 0.30 | 49 | 10 | 1.19 |
| 60 | 59 | 14 | 0.36 | 59 | 8 | 1.43 |
| 70 | 69 | 13 | 0.42 | 69 | 6 | 1.66 |
| 80 | 79 | 12 | 0.48 | 79 | 4 | 1.90 |
| 90 | 89 | 11 | 0.54 | 89 | 2 | 2.14 |
| 100 | 99 | 10 | 0.60 | 99 | 0 | 2.38 |
| 200 | 199 | 0 | 1.19 | 198 | 0 | 4.75 |
| 300 | 298 | 10 | 1.79 | 297 | 0 | 7.13 |
| 400 | 398 | 0 | 2.39 | 396 | 0 | 9.50 |
| 500 | 497 | 10 | 2.99 | 495 | 0 | 11.88 |
| 600 | 597 | 0 | 3.58 | 594 | 1 | 2.26 |
| 700 | 696 | 10 | 4.18 | 693 | 1 | 4.63 |
| 800 | 796 | 0 | 4.78 | 792 | 1 | 7.01 |
| 900 | 895 | 0 | 5.37 | 891 | 1 | 9.39 |
| 1000 | 995 | 0 | 5.97 | 990 | 1 | 11.76 |
| 2000 | 1990 | 0 | 11.94 | 1980 | 3 | 11.52 |
| 3000 | 2985 | 1 | 5.91 | 2970 | 5 | 11.29 |
| 5000 | 4975 | 2 | 5.85 | 4950 | 9 | 10.81 |

## at 6 per Cent.

| | 3 Months. | | | 4 Months. | | |
|---|---|---|---|---|---|---|
| | *l.* | *s.* | *d.* | *l.* | *s.* | *d.* |
| s. 5 | 0 | 4 | 11.11 | 0 | 4 | 10.82 |
| 10 | 0 | 9 | 10.23 | 0 | 9 | 9.65 |
| 15 | 0 | 14 | 9.34 | 0 | 14 | 8.47 |
| l. 1 | 0 | 19 | 8.45 | 0 | 19 | 7.29 |
| 2 | 1 | 19 | 4.91 | 1 | 19 | 2.59 |
| 3 | 2 | 19 | 1.36 | 2 | 18 | 9.88 |
| 4 | 3 | 18 | 9.81 | 3 | 18 | 5.18 |
| 5 | 4 | 18 | 6.27 | 4 | 18 | 0.47 |
| 6 | 5 | 18 | 2.72 | 5 | 17 | 7.76 |
| 7 | 6 | 17 | 11.17 | 6 | 17 | 3.06 |
| 8 | 7 | 17 | 7.63 | 7 | 16 | 10.35 |
| 9 | 8 | 17 | 4.08 | 8 | 16 | 5.65 |
| 10 | 9 | 17 | 0.53 | 9 | 16 | 0.94 |
| 20 | 19 | 14 | 1.06 | 19 | 12 | 1.88 |
| 30 | 29 | 11 | 1.60 | 29 | 8 | 2.82 |
| 40 | 39 | 8 | 2.13 | 39 | 4 | 3.76 |
| 50 | 49 | 5 | 2.66 | 49 | 0 | 4.71 |
| 60 | 59 | 2 | 3.19 | 58 | 16 | 5.65 |
| 70 | 68 | 19 | 3.72 | 68 | 12 | 6.59 |
| 80 | 78 | 16 | 4.26 | 78 | 8 | 7.53 |
| 90 | 88 | 13 | 4.79 | 88 | 4 | 8.47 |
| 100 | 98 | 10 | 5.32 | 98 | 0 | 9.41 |
| 200 | 197 | 0 | 10.64 | 196 | 1 | 6.82 |
| 300 | 295 | 11 | 3.96 | 294 | 2 | 4.24 |
| 400 | 394 | 1 | 9.28 | 392 | 3 | 1.65 |
| 500 | 492 | 12 | 2.60 | 490 | 3 | 11.06 |
| 600 | 591 | 2 | 7.92 | 588 | 4 | 8.47 |
| 700 | 689 | 13 | 1.24 | 686 | 5 | 5.88 |
| 800 | 788 | 3 | 6.56 | 784 | 6 | 3.29 |
| 900 | 886 | 13 | 11.88 | 882 | 7 | 0.71 |
| 1000 | 985 | 4 | 5.20 | 980 | 7 | 10.12 |
| 2000 | 1970 | 8 | 10.40 | 1960 | 15 | 8.24 |
| 3000 | 2955 | 13 | 3.61 | 2941 | 3 | 6.35 |
| 5000 | 4926 | 2 | 2.01 | 4901 | 19 | 2.59 |

## *Discompt, or Rebate,*

| | 5 Months. | | | 6 Months. | | |
|---|---|---|---|---|---|---|
| | *l.* | *s.* | *d.* | *l.* | *s.* | *d.* |
| *s.* 5 | 0 | 4 | 10.54 | 0 | 4 | 10.25 |
| 10 | 0 | 9 | 9.07 | 0 | 9 | 8.51 |
| 15 | 0 | 14 | 7.61 | 0 | 14 | 6.76 |
| *l.* 1 | 0 | 19 | 6.15 | 0 | 19 | 5.01 |
| 2 | 1 | 19 | 0.29 | 1 | 18 | 10.02 |
| 3 | 2 | 18 | 6.44 | 2 | 18 | 3.03 |
| 4 | 3 | 18 | 0.59 | 3 | 17 | 8.04 |
| 5 | 4 | 17 | 6.73 | 4 | 17 | 1.05 |
| 6 | 5 | 17 | 0.88 | 5 | 16 | 6.06 |
| 7 | 6 | 16 | 7.02 | 6 | 15 | 11.07 |
| 8 | 7 | 16 | 1.17 | 7 | 15 | 4.08 |
| 9 | 8 | 15 | 7.32 | 8 | 14 | 9.09 |
| 10 | 9 | 15 | 1.46 | 9 | 14 | 2.10 |
| 20 | 19 | 10 | 2.93 | 19 | 8 | 4.19 |
| 30 | 29 | 5 | 4.39 | 29 | 2 | 6.29 |
| 40 | 39 | 0 | 5.85 | 38 | 16 | 8.39 |
| 50 | 48 | 15 | 7.32 | 48 | 10 | 10.48 |
| 60 | 58 | 10 | 8.78 | 58 | 5 | 0.58 |
| 70 | 68 | 5 | 10.24 | 67 | 19 | 2.68 |
| 80 | 78 | 0 | 11.71 | 77 | 13 | 4.78 |
| 90 | 87 | 16 | 1.17 | 87 | 7 | 6.87 |
| 100 | 97 | 11 | 2.63 | 97 | 1 | 8.97 |
| 200 | 195 | 2 | 5.27 | 194 | 3 | 5.94 |
| 300 | 292 | 13 | 7.90 | 291 | 5 | 2.91 |
| 400 | 390 | 4 | 10.54 | 388 | 6 | 11.88 |
| 500 | 487 | 16 | 1.17 | 485 | 8 | 8.85 |
| 600 | 585 | 7 | 3.80 | 582 | 10 | 5.82 |
| 700 | 682 | 18 | 6.44 | 679 | 12 | 2.79 |
| 800 | 780 | 9 | 9.07 | 776 | 13 | 11.77 |
| 900 | 878 | 0 | 11.71 | 873 | 15 | 8.74 |
| 1000 | 975 | 12 | 2.34 | 970 | 17 | 5.71 |
| 2000 | 1951 | 4 | 4.68 | 1941 | 14 | 11.42 |
| 3000 | 2926 | 16 | 7.02 | 2912 | 12 | 5.13 |
| 5000 | 4878 | 0 | 11.71 | 4854 | 7 | 4.54 |

## at 6 per Cent.

| | 7 Months. | | | 8 Months. | | |
|---|---|---|---|---|---|---|
| | l. | s. | d. | l. | s. | d. |
| s. 5 | 0 | 4 | 9.97 | 0 | 4 | 9.69 |
| 10 | 0 | 9 | 7.94 | 0 | 9 | 7.38 |
| 15 | 0 | 14 | 5.91 | 0 | 14 | 5.07 |
| l. 1 | 0 | 19 | 3.88 | 0 | 19 | 2.77 |
| 2 | 1 | 18 | 7.77 | 1 | 18 | 5.54 |
| 3 | 2 | 17 | 11.65 | 2 | 17 | 8.31 |
| 4 | 3 | 17 | 3.54 | 3 | 16 | 11.08 |
| 5 | 4 | 16 | 7.42 | 4 | 16 | 1.85 |
| 6 | 5 | 15 | 11.30 | 5 | 15 | 4.61 |
| 7 | 6 | 15 | 3.19 | 6 | 14 | 7.38 |
| 8 | 7 | 14 | 7.07 | 7 | 13 | 10.15 |
| 9 | 8 | 13 | 10.96 | 8 | 13 | 0.92 |
| 10 | 9 | 13 | 2.84 | 9 | 12 | 3.69 |
| 20 | 19 | 6 | 5.68 | 19 | 4 | 7.38 |
| 30 | 28 | 19 | 8.52 | 28 | 16 | 11.08 |
| 40 | 38 | 12 | 11.36 | 38 | 9 | 2.77 |
| 50 | 48 | 6 | 2.20 | 48 | 1 | 6.46 |
| 60 | 57 | 19 | 5.04 | 57 | 13 | 10.15 |
| 70 | 67 | 12 | 7.88 | 67 | 6 | 1.85 |
| 80 | 77 | 5 | 10.72 | 76 | 18 | 5.54 |
| 90 | 86 | 19 | 1.57 | 86 | 10 | 9.23 |
| 100 | 96 | 12 | 4.41 | 96 | 3 | 0.92 |
| 200 | 193 | 4 | 8.81 | 192 | 6 | 1.84 |
| 300 | 289 | 17 | 1.22 | 288 | 9 | 2.76 |
| 400 | 386 | 9 | 5.62 | 384 | 12 | 3.69 |
| 500 | 483 | 1 | 10.03 | 480 | 15 | 4.61 |
| 600 | 579 | 14 | 2.43 | 576 | 18 | 5.54 |
| 700 | 676 | 6 | 6.84 | 673 | 1 | 6.46 |
| 800 | 772 | 18 | 11.25 | 769 | 4 | 7.38 |
| 900 | 869 | 11 | 3.65 | 865 | 7 | 8.31 |
| 1000 | 966 | 3 | 8.06 | 961 | 10 | 9.23 |
| 2000 | 1932 | 7 | 4.12 | 1923 | 1 | 6.46 |
| 3000 | 2898 | 11 | 0.17 | 2884 | 12 | 3.69 |
| 5000 | 4830 | 18 | 4.29 | 4807 | 13 | 10.15 |

## *Discompt, or Rebate,*

| | 9 Months. | | | 10 Months. | | |
|---|---|---|---|---|---|---|
| | *l.* | *s.* | *d.* | *l.* | *s.* | *d.* |
| s. 5 | 0 | 4 | 9.42 | 0 | 4 | 9.14 |
| 10 | 0 | 9 | 6.83 | 0 | 9 | 6.28 |
| 15 | 0 | 14 | 4.25 | 0 | 14 | 3.42 |
| l. 1 | 0 | 19 | 1.67 | 0 | 19 | 0.57 |
| 2 | 1 | 18 | 3.33 | 1 | 18 | 1.14 |
| 3 | 2 | 17 | 4.99 | 2 | 17 | 1.71 |
| 4 | 3 | 16 | 6.66 | 3 | 16 | 2.29 |
| 5 | 4 | 15 | 8.33 | 4 | 15 | 2.86 |
| 6 | 5 | 14 | 9.99 | 5 | 14 | 3.43 |
| 7 | 6 | 13 | 11.66 | 6 | 13 | 4.90 |
| 8 | 7 | 13 | 1.32 | 7 | 12 | 4.57 |
| 9 | 8 | 12 | 2.99 | 8 | 11 | 5.14 |
| 10 | 9 | 11 | 4.65 | 9 | 10 | 5.71 |
| 20 | 19 | 2 | 9.30 | 19 | 0 | 11.43 |
| 30 | 28 | 14 | 1.95 | 28 | 11 | 5.14 |
| 40 | 38 | 5 | 6.60 | 38 | 1 | 10.86 |
| 50 | 47 | 16 | 11.25 | 47 | 12 | 4.57 |
| 60 | 57 | 8 | 3.90 | 57 | 2 | 10.29 |
| 70 | 66 | 19 | 8.56 | 66 | 13 | 4.00 |
| 80 | 76 | 11 | 1.21 | 76 | 3 | 9.71 |
| 90 | 86 | 2 | 5.86 | 85 | 14 | 3.43 |
| 100 | 95 | 13 | 10.51 | 95 | 4 | 9.14 |
| 200 | 191 | 7 | 9.01 | 190 | 9 | 6.29 |
| 300 | 287 | 1 | 7.52 | 285 | 14 | 3.43 |
| 400 | 382 | 15 | 6.03 | 380 | 19 | 0.57 |
| 500 | 478 | 9 | 4.54 | 476 | 3 | 9.71 |
| 600 | 574 | 3 | 3.04 | 571 | 8 | 6.86 |
| 700 | 669 | 17 | 1.55 | 666 | 13 | 4.00 |
| 800 | 765 | 11 | 0.06 | 761 | 18 | 1.14 |
| 900 | 861 | 4 | 10.56 | 857 | 2 | 10.29 |
| 1000 | 956 | 18 | 9.07 | 952 | 7 | 7.43 |
| 2000 | 1913 | 17 | 6.14 | 1904 | 15 | 2.86 |
| 3000 | 2870 | 16 | 3.22 | 2857 | 2 | 10.29 |
| 5000 | 4784 | 13 | 9.36 | 4761 | 18 | 1.14 |

## at 6 per Cent.

| | 11 Months. | | | 12 Months. | | |
|---|---|---|---|---|---|---|
| | l. | s. | d. | l. | s. | d. |
| s. 5 | 0 | 4 | 8.87 | 0 | 4 | 8.60 |
| 10 | 0 | 9 | 5.74 | 0 | 9 | 5.21 |
| 15 | 0 | 14 | 2.61 | 0 | 14 | 1.81 |
| l. 1 | 0 | 18 | 11.49 | 0 | 18 | 10.42 |
| 2 | 1 | 17 | 10.98 | 1 | 17 | 8.83 |
| 3 | 2 | 16 | 10.46 | 2 | 16 | 7.25 |
| 4 | 3 | 15 | 9.95 | 3 | 15 | 5.66 |
| 5 | 4 | 14 | 9.44 | 4 | 14 | 4.08 |
| 6 | 5 | 13 | 8.93 | 5 | 13 | 2.49 |
| 7 | 6 | 12 | 8.42 | 6 | 12 | 0.91 |
| 8 | 7 | 11 | 7.91 | 7 | 10 | 11.32 |
| 9 | 8 | 10 | 7.39 | 8 | 9 | 9.74 |
| 10 | 9 | 9 | 6.88 | 9 | 8 | 8.15 |
| 20 | 18 | 19 | 1.76 | 18 | 17 | 4.30 |
| 30 | 28 | 8 | 8.64 | 28 | 6 | 0.45 |
| 40 | 37 | 18 | 3.53 | 37 | 14 | 8.60 |
| 50 | 47 | 7 | 10.41 | 47 | 3 | 4.75 |
| 60 | 56 | 17 | 5.29 | 56 | 12 | 0.91 |
| 70 | 66 | 7 | 0.17 | 66 | 0 | 9.06 |
| 80 | 75 | 16 | 7.05 | 75 | 9 | 5.21 |
| 90 | 85 | 6 | 1.93 | 84 | 18 | 1.36 |
| 100 | 94 | 15 | 8.82 | 94 | 6 | 9.51 |
| 200 | 189 | 11 | 5.63 | 188 | 13 | 7.01 |
| 300 | 284 | 7 | 2.45 | 283 | 0 | 4.53 |
| 400 | 379 | 2 | 1.26 | 377 | 7 | 2.04 |
| 500 | 473 | 18 | 8.08 | 471 | 13 | 11.55 |
| 600 | 568 | 14 | 4.89 | 566 | 0 | 9.06 |
| 700 | 663 | 10 | 1.71 | 660 | 7 | 6.57 |
| 800 | 758 | 5 | 10.52 | 754 | 14 | 4.08 |
| 900 | 853 | 1 | 7.34 | 849 | 1 | 1.58 |
| 1000 | 947 | 17 | 4.15 | 943 | 7 | 11.09 |
| 2000 | 1895 | 14 | 8.30 | 1886 | 15 | 10.19 |
| 3000 | 2843 | 12 | 0.45 | 2830 | 3 | 9.28 |
| 5000 | 4739 | 6 | 8.76 | 4716 | 19 | 7.47 |

## *Rebate at* 6 per Cent.

| | 24 Months. | | | 36 Months. | | |
|---|---|---|---|---|---|---|
| | *l.* | *s.* | *d.* | *l.* | *s.* | *d.* |
| s. 5 | 0 | 4 | 5.57 | 0 | 4 | 2.85 |
| 10 | 0 | 8 | 11.14 | 0 | 8 | 5.70 |
| 15 | 0 | 13 | 4.71 | 0 | 12 | 8.55 |
| l. 1 | 0 | 17 | 10.28 | 0 | 16 | 11.39 |
| 2 | 1 | 15 | 8.57 | 1 | 13 | 10.78 |
| 3 | 2 | 13 | 6.86 | 2 | 10 | 10.17 |
| 4 | 3 | 11 | 5.14 | 3 | 7 | 9.56 |
| 5 | 4 | 9 | 3.43 | 4 | 4 | 8.95 |
| 6 | 5 | 7 | 1.71 | 5 | 1 | 8.34 |
| 7 | 6 | 5 | 0.00 | 5 | 18 | 7.73 |
| 8 | 7 | 2 | 10.28 | 6 | 15 | 7.12 |
| 9 | 8 | 0 | 8.57 | 7 | 12 | 6.51 |
| 10 | 8 | 18 | 6.86 | 8 | 9 | 5.90 |
| 20 | 17 | 17 | 1.71 | 16 | 18 | 11.79 |
| 30 | 26 | 15 | 8.57 | 25 | 8 | 5.69 |
| 40 | 35 | 14 | 3.43 | 33 | 17 | 11.59 |
| 50 | 44 | 12 | 10.28 | 42 | 7 | 5.49 |
| 60 | 53 | 11 | 5.14 | 50 | 16 | 11.39 |
| 70 | 62 | 10 | 0.00 | 59 | 6 | 5.29 |
| 80 | 71 | 8 | 6.86 | 67 | 15 | 11.19 |
| 90 | 80 | 7 | 1.71 | 76 | 5 | 5.08 |
| 100 | 89 | 5 | 8.57 | 84 | 14 | 10.98 |
| 200 | 178 | 11 | 5.14 | 169 | 9 | 9.97 |
| 300 | 267 | 17 | 1.71 | 254 | 4 | 8.95 |
| 400 | 357 | 2 | 10.28 | 338 | 19 | 7.93 |
| 500 | 446 | 8 | 6.86 | 423 | 14 | 6.91 |
| 600 | 535 | 14 | 3.43 | 508 | 9 | 5.90 |
| 700 | 625 | 0 | 0.00 | 593 | 4 | 4.88 |
| 800 | 714 | 5 | 8.57 | 677 | 19 | 3.86 |
| 900 | 803 | 11 | 5.14 | 762 | 14 | 2.85 |
| 1000 | 892 | 17 | 1.71 | 847 | 9 | 1.83 |
| 2000 | 1785 | 14 | 3.43 | 1694 | 18 | 3.66 |
| 3000 | 2678 | 11 | 5.14 | 2542 | 7 | 5.49 |
| 5000 | 4464 | 5 | 8.57 | 4237 | 5 | 9.15 |

# TABLES

*FOR THE*

## Forbearance, Difcompt, and Purchafe

*OF*

# ANNUITIES,

For 1, 3, 5, 7, 10, 14, 20, and 21 Years, at 6 *per Cent.* Compound Intereft.

*SHEWING,*

1. What an Annuity, Rent, or Penfion, forborn any of thofe Numbers of Years amounts to.
2. What an Annuity, to continue any of thofe Numbers of Years, is worth in ready Money.
3. What Annuity any fum of Money will purchafe to continue any of the abovefaid Numbers of Years.

*Note*, That you have two years inftead of one year purpofely fet down in the Forbearance of Annuities, becaufe the Annuity is not due till the end of one year, and therefore cannot be confidered as forborn that time.

*Forbearance of Annuities,*

| Pounds | 2 Years. | | | 3 Years. | | |
|---|---|---|---|---|---|---|
| | l. | s. | d. | l. | s. | d. |
| 1 | 2 | 1 | 2.40 | 3 | 3 | 8.06 |
| 2 | 4 | 2 | 4.80 | 6 | 7 | 4.13 |
| 3 | 6 | 3 | 7.20 | 9 | 11 | 0.19 |
| 4 | 8 | 4 | 9.60 | 12 | 14 | 8.26 |
| 5 | 10 | 6 | 0.00 | 15 | 18 | 4.32 |
| 6 | 12 | 7 | 2.40 | 19 | 2 | 0.38 |
| 7 | 14 | 8 | 4.80 | 22 | 5 | 8.45 |
| 8 | 16 | 9 | 7.20 | 25 | 9 | 4.51 |
| 9 | 18 | 10 | 9.60 | 28 | 13 | 0.58 |
| 10 | 20 | 12 | 0.00 | 31 | 16 | 8.64 |
| 20 | 41 | 4 | 0.00 | 63 | 13 | 5.28 |
| 30 | 61 | 16 | 0.00 | 95 | 10 | 1.93 |
| 40 | 82 | 8 | 0.00 | 127 | 6 | 10.56 |
| 50 | 103 | 0 | 0.00 | 159 | 3 | 7.20 |
| 60 | 123 | 12 | 0.00 | 191 | 0 | 3.84 |
| 70 | 144 | 4 | 0.00 | 222 | 17 | 0.48 |
| 80 | 164 | 6 | 0.00 | 254 | 13 | 9.12 |
| 90 | 185 | 8 | 0.00 | 286 | 10 | 5.76 |
| 100 | 206 | 0 | 0.00 | 318 | 7 | 2.40 |
| 200 | 412 | 0 | 0.00 | 636 | 14 | 4.80 |
| 300 | 618 | 0 | 0.00 | 955 | 1 | 7.20 |
| 400 | 824 | 0 | 0.00 | 1273 | 8 | 9.60 |
| 500 | 1030 | 0 | 0.00 | 1591 | 16 | 0.00 |
| 600 | 1236 | 0 | 0.00 | 1910 | 3 | 2.40 |
| 700 | 1442 | 0 | 0.00 | 2228 | 10 | 4.80 |
| 800 | 1648 | 0 | 0.00 | 2546 | 17 | 7.20 |
| 900 | 1854 | 0 | 0.00 | 2865 | 4 | 9.60 |
| 1000 | 2060 | 0 | 0.00 | 3183 | 12 | 0.00 |
| 2000 | 4120 | 0 | 0.00 | 6367 | 4 | 0.00 |
| 3000 | 6180 | 0 | 0.00 | 9550 | 16 | 0.00 |
| 4000 | 8240 | 0 | 0.00 | 12734 | 8 | 0.00 |
| 5000 | 10300 | 0 | 0.00 | 15918 | 0 | 0.00 |
| 10000 | 20600 | 0 | 0.00 | 31836 | 0 | 0.00 |

## at 6 per Cent.

| Pounds | 5 Years. | | | 7 Years. | | |
|---|---|---|---|---|---|---|
| | l. | s. | d. | l. | s. | d. |
| 1 | 5 | 12 | 8.90 | 8 | 7 | 10.52 |
| 2 | 11 | 5 | 5.80 | 16 | 15 | 9.04 |
| 3 | 16 | 18 | 2.71 | 25 | 3 | 7.56 |
| 4 | 22 | 10 | 11.61 | 33 | 11 | 6.08 |
| 5 | 28 | 3 | 8.51 | 41 | 19 | 4.60 |
| 6 | 33 | 16 | 5.41 | 50 | 7 | 3.13 |
| 7 | 39 | 9 | 2.32 | 58 | 15 | 1.65 |
| 8 | 45 | 1 | 11.22 | 67 | 3 | 0.17 |
| 9 | 50 | 14 | 8.12 | 75 | 10 | 10.69 |
| 10 | 56 | 7 | 5.02 | 83 | 18 | 9.21 |
| 20 | 112 | 14 | 10.05 | 167 | 17 | 6.42 |
| 30 | 169 | 2 | 3.07 | 251 | 16 | 3.63 |
| 40 | 225 | 9 | 8.09 | 335 | 15 | 0.84 |
| 50 | 281 | 17 | 1.12 | 419 | 13 | 10.04 |
| 60 | 338 | 4 | 6.14 | 503 | 12 | 7.25 |
| 70 | 394 | 11 | 11.16 | 587 | 11 | 4.46 |
| 80 | 450 | 19 | 4.19 | 671 | 10 | 1.67 |
| 90 | 507 | 6 | 9.21 | 755 | 8 | 10.89 |
| 100 | 563 | 14 | 2.23 | 839 | 7 | 8.09 |
| 200 | 1127 | 8 | 4.46 | 1678 | 15 | 4.18 |
| 300 | 1691 | 2 | 6.70 | 2518 | 3 | 0.26 |
| 400 | 2254 | 16 | 8.93 | 3357 | 10 | 8.35 |
| 500 | 2818 | 10 | 11.16 | 4196 | 18 | 4.44 |
| 600 | 3382 | 5 | 1.39 | 5036 | 6 | 0.53 |
| 700 | 3945 | 19 | 3.62 | 5875 | 13 | 8.62 |
| 800 | 4509 | 13 | 5.86 | 6715 | 1 | 4.70 |
| 900 | 5073 | 7 | 8.09 | 7554 | 9 | 0.79 |
| 1000 | 5637 | 1 | 10.32 | 8393 | 16 | 8.88 |
| 2000 | 11274 | 3 | 8.64 | 16787 | 13 | 5.76 |
| 3000 | 16911 | 5 | 6.96 | 25181 | 10 | 2.64 |
| 4000 | 22548 | 7 | 5.28 | 33575 | 6 | 11.52 |
| 5000 | 28185 | 9 | 3.60 | 41969 | 3 | 8.40 |
| 10000 | 56370 | 18 | 7.20 | 83938 | 7 | 4.80 |

## *Forbearance of Annuities,*

| Pounds | 10 Years. | | | 14 Years. | | |
|---|---|---|---|---|---|---|
| | l. | s. | d. | l. | s. | d. |
| 1 | 13 | 3 | 7.40 | 21 | 0 | 3.61 |
| 2 | 26 | 7 | 2.80 | 42 | 0 | 7.23 |
| 3 | 39 | 10 | 10.20 | 63 | 0 | 10.85 |
| 4 | 52 | 14 | 5.60 | 84 | 1 | 2.46 |
| 5 | 65 | 18 | 0.95 | 105 | 1 | 6.08 |
| 6 | 79 | 1 | 8.34 | 126 | 1 | 9.69 |
| 7 | 92 | 5 | 3 73 | 147 | 2 | 1.31 |
| 8 | 105 | 8 | 11.13 | 168 | 2 | 4.93 |
| 9 | 118 | 12 | 6.52 | 189 | 2 | 8.54 |
| 10 | 131 | 16 | 1.92 | 210 | 3 | 0.16 |
| 20 | 263 | 12 | 3.84 | 420 | 6 | 0.31 |
| 30 | 395 | 8 | 5.75 | 630 | 9 | 0.47 |
| 40 | 527 | 4 | 7.67 | 840 | 12 | 0.62 |
| 50 | 659 | 0 | 9.59 | 1050 | 15 | 0.78 |
| 60 | 790 | 16 | 11.51 | 1260 | 18 | 0.94 |
| 70 | 922 | 13 | 1.42 | 1471 | 1 | 1.09 |
| 80 | 1054 | 9 | 3.34 | 1681 | 4 | 1.25 |
| 90 | 1186 | 5 | 5.26 | 1891 | 7 | 1.40 |
| 100 | 1318 | 1 | 7.18 | 2101 | 10 | 1.56 |
| 200 | 2636 | 3 | 2.35 | 4203 | 0 | 3.12 |
| 300 | 3954 | 4 | 9.53 | 6304 | 10 | 4.68 |
| 400 | 5272 | 6 | 4.70 | 8406 | 0 | 6.24 |
| 500 | 6590 | 7 | 11.88 | 10507 | 10 | 7.80 |
| 600 | 7908 | 9 | 7.06 | 12609 | 0 | 9.36 |
| 700 | 9226 | 11 | 2.23 | 14710 | 10 | 10.92 |
| 800 | 10544 | 12 | 9.41 | 16812 | 1 | 0.48 |
| 900 | 11862 | 14 | 4.58 | 18913 | 11 | 2.04 |
| 1000 | 13180 | 15 | 11.76 | 21015 | 1 | 3.60 |
| 2000 | 26361 | 11 | 11.52 | 42030 | 2 | 7.20 |
| 3000 | 39542 | 7 | 11.28 | 63045 | 3 | 10.80 |
| 4090 | 52723 | 3 | 11.04 | 84060 | 5 | 2.40 |
| 5000 | 65903 | 19 | 10.80 | 105075 | 6 | 6.00 |
| 10000 | 131807 | 18 | 9.60 | 210150 | 13 | 0.00 |

## at 6 per Cent.

| Pounds | 20 Years. | | | 21 Years. | | |
|---|---|---|---|---|---|---|
| | l. | s. | d. | l. | s. | d. |
| 1 | 36 | 15 | 8.54 | 39 | 19 | 10.25 |
| 2 | 73 | 11 | 5.98 | 79 | 19 | 8.51 |
| 3 | 110 | 7 | 1.63 | 119 | 19 | 6.76 |
| 4 | 147 | 2 | 10.17 | 159 | 19 | 5.02 |
| 5 | 183 | 18 | 6.71 | 199 | 19 | 3.27 |
| 6 | 220 | 14 | 3.25 | 239 | 19 | 1.53 |
| 7 | 257 | 9 | 11.79 | 279 | 18 | 11.78 |
| 8 | 294 | 5 | 8.34 | 319 | 18 | 10.04 |
| 9 | 331 | 1 | 4.88 | 359 | 18 | 8.29 |
| 10 | 367 | 17 | 1.42 | 399 | 18 | 6.54 |
| 20 | 735 | 14 | 2.83 | 799 | 17 | 1.08 |
| 30 | 1103 | 11 | 4.25 | 1199 | 15 | 7.62 |
| 40 | 1471 | 8 | 5.66 | 1599 | 14 | 2.16 |
| 50 | 1839 | 5 | 7.08 | 1999 | 12 | 8.70 |
| 60 | 2207 | 2 | 8.50 | 2399 | 11 | 3.24 |
| 70 | 2574 | 19 | 9.91 | 2799 | 9 | 9.78 |
| 80 | 2942 | 16 | 11.33 | 3199 | 8 | 4.32 |
| 90 | 3310 | 14 | 0.74 | 3599 | 6 | 10.86 |
| 100 | 3678 | 11 | 2.16 | 3999 | 5 | 5.40 |
| 200 | 7357 | 2 | 4.32 | 7998 | 10 | 10.80 |
| 300 | 11035 | 13 | 6.48 | 11997 | 16 | 4.20 |
| 400 | 14714 | 4 | 8.64 | 15997 | 1 | 9.60 |
| 500 | 18392 | 15 | 10.80 | 19996 | 7 | 3.00 |
| 600 | 22071 | 7 | 0.96 | 23995 | 12 | 8.40 |
| 700 | 25749 | 18 | 3.12 | 27994 | 18 | 1.80 |
| 800 | 29428 | 9 | 5.28 | 31994 | 3 | 7.20 |
| 900 | 33107 | 0 | 7.44 | 35993 | 9 | 0.60 |
| 1000 | 36785 | 11 | 9.60 | 39992 | 14 | 6.00 |
| 2000 | 73571 | 3 | 7.20 | 79985 | 9 | 0.00 |
| 3000 | 110356 | 15 | 4.80 | 119978 | 3 | 6.00 |
| 4000 | 147142 | 7 | 2.40 | 159970 | 18 | 0.00 |
| 5000 | 183927 | 19 | 0.00 | 199963 | 12 | 6.00 |
| 10000 | 367855 | 18 | 0.00 | 399927 | 5 | 0.00 |

## *Discompt of Annuities,*

| Pounds | 1 Year. | | | 3 Years. | | |
|---|---|---|---|---|---|---|
| | *l.* | *s.* | *d.* | *l.* | *s.* | *d.* |
| 1 | 0 | 18 | 10.41 | 2 | 13 | 5.52 |
| 2 | 1 | 17 | 8.83 | 5 | 6 | 11.05 |
| 3 | 2 | 16 | 7.25 | 8 | 0 | 4.57 |
| 4 | 3 | 15 | 5.67 | 10 | 13 | 10.09 |
| 5 | 4 | 14 | 4.08 | 13 | 7 | 3.61 |
| 6 | 5 | 13 | 2.49 | 16 | 0 | 9.14 |
| 7 | 6 | 12 | 0.91 | 18 | 14 | 2.66 |
| 8 | 7 | 10 | 11.32 | 21 | 7 | 8.18 |
| 9 | 8 | 9 | 9.74 | 24 | 1 | 1.71 |
| 10 | 9 | 8 | 8.15 | 26 | 14 | 7.23 |
| 20 | 18 | 17 | 4.30 | 53 | 9 | 2.46 |
| 30 | 28 | 6 | 0.45 | 80 | 3 | 9.69 |
| 40 | 37 | 14 | 8.60 | 106 | 18 | 4.92 |
| 50 | 47 | 3 | 4.75 | 133 | 13 | 0.14 |
| 60 | 56 | 12 | 0.90 | 160 | 7 | 7.37 |
| 70 | 66 | 0 | 9.05 | 187 | 2 | 2.60 |
| 80 | 75 | 9 | 5.20 | 213 | 16 | 9.83 |
| 90 | 84 | 18 | 1.35 | 240 | 11 | 5.06 |
| 100 | 94 | 6 | 9.50 | 267 | 6 | 0.29 |
| 200 | 188 | 13 | 7.01 | 534 | 12 | 0.58 |
| 300 | 283 | 0 | 4.51 | 801 | 18 | 0.86 |
| 400 | 377 | 7 | 2.02 | 1069 | 4 | 1.15 |
| 500 | 471 | 13 | 11.52 | 1336 | 10 | 1.44 |
| 600 | 566 | 0 | 9.02 | 1603 | 16 | 1.73 |
| 700 | 660 | 7 | 6.53 | 1871 | 2 | 2.02 |
| 800 | 754 | 14 | 4.03 | 2138 | 8 | 2.30 |
| 900 | 849 | 1 | 1.54 | 2405 | 14 | 2.59 |
| 1000 | 943 | 7 | 11.04 | 2673 | 0 | 2.88 |
| 2000 | 1886 | 15 | 10.08 | 5346 | 0 | 5.76 |
| 3000 | 2830 | 3 | 9.12 | 8019 | 0 | 8.64 |
| 4000 | 3773 | 11 | 8.16 | 10692 | 0 | 11.52 |
| 5000 | 4716 | 19 | 7.20 | 13365 | 1 | 2.40 |
| 10000 | 9433 | 19 | 2.40 | 26730 | 2 | 4.80 |

## at 6 per Cent.

| Pounds | 5 Years. | | | 7 Years. | | |
|---|---|---|---|---|---|---|
| | *l.* | *s.* | *d.* | *l.* | *s.* | *d.* |
| 1 | 4 | 4 | 2.97 | 5 | 11 | 7.77 |
| 2 | 8 | 8 | 5.93 | 11 | 3 | 3.54 |
| 3 | 12 | 12 | 8.90 | 16 | 14 | 11.31 |
| 4 | 16 | 16 | 11.87 | 22 | 6 | 7.09 |
| 5 | 21 | 1 | 2.84 | 27 | 18 | 2.86 |
| 6 | 25 | 5 | 5.80 | 33 | 9 | 10.63 |
| 7 | 29 | 9 | 8.77 | 39 | 1 | 6.40 |
| 8 | 33 | 13 | 11.74 | 44 | 13 | 2.17 |
| 9 | 37 | 18 | 2.71 | 50 | 4 | 9.94 |
| 10 | 42 | 2 | 5.67 | 55 | 16 | 5.71 |
| 20 | 84 | 4 | 11.34 | 111 | 12 | 11.43 |
| 30 | 126 | 7 | 5.01 | 167 | 9 | 5.14 |
| 40 | 168 | 9 | 10.68 | 223 | 5 | 10.86 |
| 50 | 210 | 12 | 4.36 | 279 | 2 | 4.57 |
| 60 | 252 | 14 | 10.03 | 334 | 18 | 10.29 |
| 70 | 294 | 17 | 3.70 | 390 | 15 | 4.00 |
| 80 | 336 | 19 | 9.37 | 446 | 11 | 9.72 |
| 90 | 379 | 2 | 3.04 | 502 | 8 | 3.43 |
| 100 | 421 | 4 | 8.71 | 558 | 4 | 9.15 |
| 200 | 842 | 9 | 5.42 | 1116 | 9 | 6.29 |
| 300 | 1263 | 14 | 2.14 | 1674 | 14 | 3.43 |
| 400 | 1684 | 18 | 10.85 | 2232 | 19 | 0.58 |
| 500 | 2106 | 3 | 7.56 | 2791 | 3 | 9.72 |
| 600 | 2527 | 8 | 4.27 | 3349 | 8 | 6.86 |
| 700 | 2948 | 13 | 0.98 | 3907 | 13 | 4.01 |
| 800 | 3369 | 17 | 9.70 | 4465 | 18 | 1.15 |
| 900 | 3791 | 2 | 6.41 | 5024 | 2 | 10.30 |
| 1000 | 4212 | 7 | 3.12 | 5582 | 7 | 7.44 |
| 2000 | 8424 | 14 | 6.24 | 11164 | 15 | 2.88 |
| 3000 | 12637 | 1 | 9.36 | 16747 | 2 | 10.32 |
| 4000 | 16849 | 9 | 0.48 | 22329 | 10 | 5.76 |
| 5000 | 21061 | 16 | 3.60 | 27911 | 18 | 1.20 |
| 10000 | 42123 | 12 | 7.20 | 55823 | 16 | 2.40 |

## *Discompt of Annuities,*

| Pounds | 10 Years. | | | 14 Years. | | |
|---|---|---|---|---|---|---|
| | *l.* | *s.* | *d.* | *l.* | *s.* | *d.* |
| 1 | 7 | 7 | 2.42 | 9 | 5 | 10.80 |
| 2 | 14 | 14 | 4.84 | 18 | 11 | 9.59 |
| 3 | 22 | 1 | 7.26 | 27 | 17 | 8.39 |
| 4 | 29 | 8 | 9.68 | 37 | 3 | 7.19 |
| 5 | 36 | 16 | 0.10 | 46 | 9 | 5.98 |
| 6 | 44 | 3 | 2.53 | 55 | 15 | 4.78 |
| 7 | 51 | 10 | 4.95 | 65 | 1 | 3.57 |
| 8 | 58 | 17 | 7.37 | 74 | 7 | 2.37 |
| 9 | 66 | 4 | 9.79 | 83 | 13 | 1.17 |
| 10 | 73 | 12 | 0.21 | 92 | 18 | 11.96 |
| 20 | 147 | 4 | 0.41 | 185 | 17 | 11.92 |
| 30 | 220 | 16 | 0.62 | 278 | 16 | 11.88 |
| 40 | 294 | 8 | 0.83 | 371 | 15 | 11.84 |
| 50 | 368 | 0 | 1.03 | 464 | 14 | 11.80 |
| 60 | 441 | 12 | 1.24 | 557 | 13 | 11.76 |
| 70 | 515 | 4 | 1.44 | 650 | 12 | 11.71 |
| 80 | 588 | 16 | 1.65 | 743 | 11 | 11.67 |
| 90 | 662 | 8 | 1.86 | 836 | 10 | 11.63 |
| 100 | 736 | 0 | 2.06 | 929 | 9 | 11.59 |
| 200 | 1472 | 0 | 4.13 | 1858 | 19 | 11.18 |
| 300 | 2208 | 0 | 6.19 | 2788 | 9 | 10.78 |
| 400 | 2944 | 0 | 8.26 | 3717 | 19 | 10.37 |
| 500 | 3680 | 0 | 10.32 | 4647 | 9 | 9.96 |
| 600 | 4416 | 1 | 0.38 | 5576 | 19 | 9.55 |
| 700 | 5152 | 1 | 2.45 | 6506 | 9 | 9.14 |
| 800 | 5888 | 1 | 4.51 | 7435 | 19 | 8.74 |
| 900 | 6624 | 1 | 6.58 | 8365 | 9 | 8.33 |
| 1000 | 7360 | 1 | 8.64 | 9294 | 19 | 7.92 |
| 2000 | 14720 | 3 | 5.28 | 18589 | 19 | 3.84 |
| 3000 | 22080 | 5 | 1.92 | 27884 | 18 | 11.76 |
| 4000 | 29440 | 6 | 10.56 | 37179 | 18 | 7.68 |
| 5000 | 36800 | 8 | 7.20 | 46474 | 18 | 3.60 |
| 10000 | 73600 | 17 | 2.40 | 92949 | 16 | 7.20 |

## at 6 per Cent.

| Pounds | 20 Years. | | | 21 Years. | | |
|---|---|---|---|---|---|---|
| | l. | s. | d. | l. | s. | d. |
| 1 | 11 | 9 | 4.78 | 11 | 15 | 3.38 |
| 2 | 22 | 18 | 9.56 | 23 | 10 | 6.76 |
| 3 | 34 | 8 | 2.34 | 35 | 5 | 10.14 |
| 4 | 45 | 17 | 7.12 | 47 | 1 | 1.51 |
| 5 | 57 | 6 | 11.91 | 58 | 16 | 4.89 |
| 6 | 68 | 16 | 4.69 | 70 | 11 | 8.27 |
| 7 | 80 | 5 | 9.47 | 82 | 6 | 11.65 |
| 8 | 91 | 15 | 2.25 | 94 | 2 | 3.03 |
| 9 | 103 | 4 | 7.03 | 105 | 17 | 6.41 |
| 10 | 114 | 13 | 11.81 | 117 | 12 | 9.78 |
| 20 | 229 | 7 | 11.62 | 235 | 5 | 7.56 |
| 30 | 344 | 1 | 11.43 | 352 | 18 | 5.34 |
| 40 | 458 | 15 | 11.23 | 470 | 11 | 3.12 |
| 50 | 573 | 9 | 11.04 | 588 | 4 | 0.90 |
| 60 | 688 | 3 | 10.85 | 705 | 16 | 10.68 |
| 70 | 802 | 17 | 10,66 | 823 | 9 | 8.46 |
| 80 | 917 | 11 | 10.46 | 941 | 2 | 6.24 |
| 90 | 1032 | 5 | 10,27 | 1058 | 15 | 4.02 |
| 100 | 1146 | 19 | 10.08 | 1176 | 8 | 1.80 |
| 200 | 2293 | 19 | 8.16 | 2352 | 16 | 3.60 |
| 300 | 3440 | 19 | 6.24 | 3529 | 4 | 5.40 |
| 400 | 4587 | 19 | 4.32 | 4705 | 12 | 7.20 |
| 500 | 5734 | 19 | 2.40 | 5882 | 0 | 9.00 |
| 600 | 6881 | 19 | 0.48 | 7058 | 8 | 10.80 |
| 700 | 8028 | 18 | 10.56 | 8234 | 17 | 0.60 |
| 800 | 9175 | 18 | 8 64 | 9411 | 5 | 2.40 |
| 900 | 10322 | 18 | 6.72 | 10587 | 13 | 4.20 |
| 1000 | 11469 | 18 | 4.80 | 11764 | 1 | 6.00 |
| 2000 | 22939 | 16 | 9.60 | 23528 | 3 | 0.00 |
| 3000 | 34409 | 15 | 2.40 | 35292 | 4 | 6.00 |
| 4000 | 45879 | 13 | 7.20 | 47056 | 6 | 0.00 |
| 5000 | 57349 | 12 | 0.00 | 58820 | 7 | 6.00 |
| 10000 | 114699 | 4 | 0.00 | 117640 | 15 | 0.00 |

## *Purchase of Annuities,*

| Pounds | 1 Year. | | | 3 Years. | | |
|---|---|---|---|---|---|---|
| | *l.* | *s.* | *d.* | *l.* | *s.* | *d.* |
| 1 | 1 | 1 | 2.40 | 0 | 7 | 5.79 |
| 2 | 2 | 2 | 4.80 | 0 | 14 | 11.57 |
| 3 | 3 | 3 | 7.20 | 1 | 2 | 5.36 |
| 4 | 4 | 4 | 9.60 | 1 | 9 | 11.14 |
| 5 | 5 | 6 | 0.00 | 1 | 17 | 4.93 |
| 6 | 6 | 7 | 2.40 | 2 | 4 | 10.72 |
| 7 | 7 | 8 | 4.80 | 2 | 12 | 4.50 |
| 8 | 8 | 9 | 7.20 | 2 | 19 | 10.29 |
| 9 | 9 | 10 | 9.60 | 3 | 7 | 4.08 |
| 10 | 10 | 12 | 0.00 | 3 | 14 | 9.86 |
| 20 | 21 | 4 | 0.00 | 7 | 9 | 7.73 |
| 30 | 31 | 16 | 0.00 | 11 | 4 | 5.59 |
| 40 | 42 | 8 | 0.00 | 14 | 19 | 3.46 |
| 50 | 53 | 0 | 0.00 | 18 | 14 | 1.32 |
| 60 | 63 | 12 | 0.00 | 22 | 8 | 11.18 |
| 70 | 74 | 4 | 0.00 | 26 | 3 | 9.05 |
| 80 | 84 | 16 | 0.00 | 29 | 18 | 6.91 |
| 90 | 95 | 8 | 0.00 | 33 | 13 | 4.78 |
| 100 | 106 | 0 | 0.00 | 37 | 8 | 2.64 |
| 200 | 212 | 0 | 0.00 | 74 | 16 | 5.28 |
| 300 | 318 | 0 | 0.00 | 112 | 4 | 7.92 |
| 400 | 424 | 0 | 0.00 | 149 | 12 | 10.56 |
| 500 | 530 | 0 | 0.00 | 187 | 1 | 1.20 |
| 600 | 636 | 0 | 0.00 | 224 | 9 | 3.84 |
| 700 | 742 | 0 | 0.00 | 261 | 17 | 6.48 |
| 800 | 848 | 0 | 0.00 | 299 | 5 | 9.12 |
| 900 | 954 | 0 | 0.00 | 336 | 13 | 11.76 |
| 1000 | 1060 | 0 | 0.00 | 374 | 2 | 2.40 |
| 2000 | 2120 | 0 | 0.00 | 748 | 4 | 4.80 |
| 3000 | 3180 | 0 | 0.00 | 1122 | 6 | 7.20 |
| 4000 | 4240 | 0 | 0.00 | 1496 | 8 | 9.60 |
| 5000 | 5300 | 0 | 0.00 | 1870 | 11 | 0.00 |
| 10000 | 10600 | 0 | 0.00 | 3741 | 2 | 0.00 |

## *at* 6 per Cent.

| Pounds | 5 Years. | | | 7 Years. | | |
|---|---|---|---|---|---|---|
| | *l.* | *s.* | *d.* | *l.* | *s.* | *d.* |
| 1 | 0 | 4 | 8.97 | 0 | 3 | 6.99 |
| 2 | 0 | 9 | 5.95 | 0 | 7 | 1.98 |
| 3 | 0 | 14 | 2.93 | 0 | 10 | 8.98 |
| 4 | 0 | 18 | 11.90 | 0 | 14 | 3.97 |
| 5 | 1 | 3 | 8.88 | 0 | 17 | 10.96 |
| 6 | 1 | 8 | 5.85 | 1 | 1 | 5.95 |
| 7 | 1 | 13 | 2.83 | 1 | 5 | 0.95 |
| 8 | 1 | 17 | 11.80 | 1 | 8 | 7.94 |
| 9 | 2 | 2 | 8.78 | 1 | 12 | 2.93 |
| 10 | 2 | 7 | 5.75 | 1 | 15 | 9.92 |
| 20 | 4 | 14 | 11.50 | 3 | 11 | 7 85 |
| 30 | 7 | 2 | 5.25 | 5 | 7 | 5.77 |
| 40 | 9 | 9 | 11.00 | 7 | 3 | 3.70 |
| 50 | 11 | 17 | 4.75 | 8 | 19 | 1.62 |
| 60 | 14 | 4 | 10.50 | 10 | 14 | 11.54 |
| 70 | 16 | 12 | 4.25 | 12 | 10 | 9.47 |
| 80 | 18 | 19 | 10.00 | 14 | 6 | 7.39 |
| 90 | 21 | 7 | 3 75 | 16 | 2 | 5.32 |
| 100 | 23 | 14 | 9.50 | 17 | 18 | 3.24 |
| 200 | 47 | 9 | 7.00 | 35 | 16 | 6.48 |
| 300 | 71 | 4 | 4.51 | 53 | 14 | 9.72 |
| 400 | 94 | 19 | 2.02 | 71 | 13 | 0.96 |
| 500 | 118 | 13 | 11.52 | 89 | 11 | 4.20 |
| 600 | 142 | 8 | 9.02 | 107 | 9 | 7.44 |
| 700 | 166 | 3 | 6.53 | 125 | 7 | 10.68 |
| 800 | 189 | 18 | 4.03 | 143 | 6 | 1.92 |
| 900 | 213 | 13 | 1.54 | 161 | 4 | 5.16 |
| 1000 | 237 | 7 | 11.04 | 179 | 2 | 8.40 |
| 2000 | 474 | 15 | 10.08 | 358 | 5 | 4.80 |
| 3000 | 712 | 3 | 9.12 | 537 | 8 | 1.20 |
| 4000 | 949 | 11 | 8.16 | 716 | 10 | 9.60 |
| 5000 | 1186 | 19 | 7.20 | 895 | 13 | 6.00 |
| 10000 | 2373 | 19 | 2.40 | 1791 | 7 | 0.00 |

*Purchase of Annuities,*

| Pounds | 10 Years. | | | 14 Years. | | |
|---|---|---|---|---|---|---|
| | *l.* | *s.* | *d.* | *l.* | *s.* | *d.* |
| 1 | 0 | 2 | 8.61 | 0 | 2 | 1.82 |
| 2 | 0 | 5 | 5.22 | 0 | 4 | 3.64 |
| 3 | 0 | 8 | 1.82 | 0 | 6 | 5.46 |
| 4 | 0 | 10 | 10.43 | 0 | 8 | 7.28 |
| 5 | 0 | 13 | 7.04 | 0 | 10 | 9.10 |
| 6 | 0 | 16 | 3.65 | 0 | 12 | 10.92 |
| 7 | 0 | 19 | 0.26 | 0 | 15 | 0.74 |
| 8 | 1 | 1 | 8.87 | 0 | 17 | 2.56 |
| 9 | 1 | 4 | 5.47 | 0 | 19 | 4.38 |
| 10 | 1 | 7 | 2.08 | 1 | 1 | 6.20 |
| 20 | 2 | 14 | 4.17 | 2 | 3 | 0.41 |
| 30 | 4 | 1 | 6.25 | 3 | 4 | 6.61 |
| 40 | 5 | 8 | 8.33 | 4 | 6 | 0.82 |
| 50 | 6 | 15 | 10.42 | 5 | 7 | 7.02 |
| 60 | 8 | 3 | 0.50 | 6 | 9 | 1.22 |
| 70 | 9 | 10 | 2.58 | 7 | 10 | 7.43 |
| 80 | 10 | 17 | 4.67 | 8 | 12 | 1.63 |
| 90 | 12 | 4 | 6.75 | 9 | 13 | 7.84 |
| 100 | 13 | 11 | 8.83 | 10 | 15 | 2.04 |
| 200 | 27 | 3 | 5.66 | 21 | 10 | 4.08 |
| 300 | 40 | 15 | 2.50 | 32 | 5 | 6.12 |
| 400 | 54 | 6 | 11.33 | 43 | 0 | 8.16 |
| 500 | 67 | 18 | 8.16 | 53 | 15 | 10.20 |
| 600 | 81 | 10 | 4.99 | 64 | 11 | 0.24 |
| 700 | 95 | 2 | 1.82 | 75 | 6 | 2.28 |
| 800 | 108 | 13 | 10.66 | 86 | 1 | 432 |
| 900 | 122 | 5 | 7.49 | 96 | 16 | 6.36 |
| 1000 | 135 | 17 | 4.32 | 107 | 11 | 8.40 |
| 2000 | 271 | 14 | 8.64 | 215 | 3 | 4.80 |
| 3000 | 407 | 12 | 0.96 | 322 | 15 | 1.20 |
| 4000 | 543 | 9 | 5.28 | 430 | 6 | 9.60 |
| 5000 | 679 | 6 | 9.60 | 537 | 18 | 6.00 |
| 10000 | 1358 | 13 | 7.20 | 1075 | 17 | 0.00 |

## at 6 per Cent.

| Pounds | 20 Years. | | | 21 Years. | | |
|---|---|---|---|---|---|---|
| | l. | s. | d. | l. | s. | d. |
| 1 | 0 | 1 | 8.92 | 0 | 1 | 8.40 |
| 2 | 0 | 3 | 5.84 | 0 | 3 | 4.80 |
| 3 | 0 | 5 | 2.77 | 0 | 5 | 1.20 |
| 4 | 0 | 6 | 11.70 | 0 | 6 | 9.60 |
| 5 | 0 | 8 | 8.62 | 0 | 8 | 6.00 |
| 6 | 0 | 10 | 5.55 | 0 | 10 | 2.41 |
| 7 | 0 | 12 | 2.47 | 0 | 11 | 10.81 |
| 8 | 0 | 13 | 11.39 | 0 | 13 | 7.21 |
| 9 | 0 | 15 | 8.32 | 0 | 15 | 3.61 |
| 10 | 0 | 17 | 5.24 | 0 | 17 | 0.01 |
| 20 | 1 | 14 | 10.48 | 1 | 14 | 0 02 |
| 30 | 2 | 12 | 3.72 | 2 | 11 | 0.03 |
| 40 | 3 | 9 | 8.97 | 3 | 8 | 0.04 |
| 50 | 4 | 7 | 2.21 | 4 | 5 | 0.05 |
| 60 | 5 | 4 | 7.45 | 5 | 2 | 0.06 |
| 70 | 6 | 2 | 0.69 | 5 | 19 | 0.07 |
| 80 | 6 | 19 | 5.93 | 6 | 16 | 0 08 |
| 90 | 7 | 16 | 11.17 | 7 | 13 | 0.09 |
| 100 | 8 | 14 | 4.42 | 8 | 10 | 0.10 |
| 200 | 17 | 8 | 8.83 | 17 | 0 | 0.19 |
| 300 | 26 | 3 | 1.25 | 25 | 10 | 0 29 |
| 400 | 34 | 17 | 5.66 | 34 | 0 | 0.39 |
| 500 | 43 | 11 | 10.08 | 42 | 10 | 0.48 |
| 600 | 52 | 6 | 2 50 | 51 | 0 | 0.58 |
| 700 | 61 | 0 | 6.91 | 59 | 10 | 0.67 |
| 800 | 69 | 14 | 11.33 | 68 | 0 | 0.77 |
| 900 | 78 | 9 | 3.74 | 76 | 10 | 0.86 |
| 1000 | 87 | 3 | 8.16 | 85 | 0 | 0.96 |
| 2000 | 174 | 7 | 4.32 | 170 | 0 | 1.92 |
| 3000 | 261 | 11 | 0.48 | 255 | 0 | 2.88 |
| 4000 | 348 | 14 | 8.64 | 340 | 0 | 3.84 |
| 5000 | 435 | 18 | 4.80 | 425 | 0 | 4.80 |
| 10000 | 871 | 16 | 9.60 | 850 | 0 | 9.60 |

THese Tables are so plain in themselves, that they need no Example to illustrate them: But because Questions only of the particular Years mentioned at the top of each Column can be resolved by them, I shall in the next Page insert a Table, whereby you may try any Number in the foregoing Tables, and answer any Question belonging either to Forbearance, Discompt, or Purchase of Annuities, (as also to the Rebate of Money) at 6 *per Cent.* Compound Interest, for any Number of Years, not exceeding 40. To do which, this is the Rule:

Multiply that Number in the Table which stands right against the Number of Years proposed (and in the Column to which the Question belongs, whether for Forbearance, Discompt, or Purchase of Annuities, or Rebate of Money) by the Annuity to be forborn, discompted, or purchased, or by the sum to be rebated, and from the Product cut off six Figures to the right hand, the Figures remaining to the left hand are Pounds, and the Figures cut off are the Decimal Parts of a Pound.

One Example will be sufficient to explain the whole Table, which shall be this:

*If* 500 l. *Annuity be forborn* 21 *Years, what will it amount to?*

Tabular Number against 21, and under *Forbearance of Annuities* —— } 39992725

Annuity forborn — 500

19996|362500

Answer 19996 *l.* and .362500 Decimal Parts of a Pound, which being reduced is 7 *s.* 3 *d.* And this agrees exactly with the foregoing Table of the Forbearance of Annuities.

And after this manner are all Questions belonging to the following Table resolved.

*A Table*

*A Table shewing the Value of a Decimal Fraction, the Integer being One Pound, or Twenty Shillings.*

| d. | q. | Dec. of 1 l | d. | q. | Dec. of 1 l. | s. | d. | q. | Dec. of 1 l. |
|---|---|---|---|---|---|---|---|---|---|
| 0 | 1 | .0010416 | 5 | 3 | .0239583 | 0 | 11 | 1 | .046875 |
| 0 | 2 | .0020833 | 6 | 0 | .025 | 0 | 11 | 2 | .0479166 |
| 0 | 3 | .003125 | 6 | 1 | .0260416 | 0 | 11 | 3 | .0489583 |
| 1 | 0 | .0041666 | 6 | 2 | .0270833 | 1 | 0 | 0 | .05 |
| 1 | 1 | .0052083 | 6 | 3 | .028125 | 2 | 0 | 0 | .1 |
| 1 | 2 | .00625 | 7 | 0 | .0291666 | 3 | 0 | 0 | .15 |
| 1 | 3 | .0072916 | 7 | 1 | .0302083 | 4 | 0 | 0 | .2 |
| 2 | 0 | .0083333 | 7 | 2 | .03125 | 5 | 0 | 0 | .25 |
| 2 | 1 | .009375 | 7 | 3 | .0322916 | 6 | 0 | 0 | .3 |
| 2 | 2 | .0104166 | 8 | 0 | .0333333 | 7 | 0 | 0 | .35 |
| 2 | 3 | .0114583 | 8 | 1 | .0343750 | 8 | 0 | 0 | .4 |
| 3 | 0 | .0125 | 8 | 2 | .0353166 | 9 | 0 | 0 | .45 |
| 3 | 1 | .0135416 | 8 | 3 | .0364583 | 10 | 0 | 0 | .5 |
| 3 | 2 | .0145833 | 9 | 0 | .0375 | 11 | 0 | 0 | .55 |
| 3 | 3 | .015625 | 9 | 1 | .0385416 | 12 | 0 | 0 | .6 |
| 4 | 0 | .0166666 | 9 | 2 | .0395833 | 13 | 0 | 0 | .65 |
| 4 | 1 | .0177083 | 9 | 3 | .040625 | 14 | 0 | 0 | .7 |
| 4 | 2 | .01875 | 10 | 0 | .0416666 | 15 | 0 | 0 | .75 |
| 4 | 3 | .0197916 | 10 | 1 | .0427082 | 16 | 0 | 0 | 8 |
| 5 | 0 | .0208333 | 10 | 2 | .04375 | 17 | 0 | 0 | .85 |
| 5 | 1 | .021875 | 10 | 3 | .0447916 | 18 | 0 | 0 | .9 |
| 5 | 2 | .0229166 | 11 | 0 | .0458333 | 19 | 0 | 0 | .95 |

To find the foregoing Fraction .3625 by this Table, you must do thus; seek for the Decimal Fraction in the Table that is nearest to it, (since you cannot at once find all the Figures) which is .35, against which on the left hand you have the value of it, *viz.* 7 *s.* subtract this from .3625, and there will remain .0125, which being found in the Table, against it stands 3 *d.* which added to 7 *s.* gives 7 *s.* 3 *d.* for the value of .3625 of a Pound.

And thus may you find the Value of any Fraction of a Pound by this Table.

*To*

# *To find the Value of a* DECIMAL FRACTION.

IN the foregoing Tables of Intereſt, &c. inſtead of expreſſing the Parts of a Peny in Farthings, I have done it in Decimal Fractions, which is more exact, and more eaſie for Addition, &c. the nature of which perhaps you may not underſtand, and to give you a particular Conſtruction of them in this place would ſwell this Book into more Sheets than I have reſolved to confine it to, however to render them uſeful to you, I ſhall ſhew you a ready and eaſie way to find the Value of them.

In Decimals, all Cyphers to the right hand having no Figure after them, neither increaſe or diminiſh the Value of the Fraction; but every Cypher to the left hand at the beginning of ſuch Fraction leſſens the Value ten times, as if this were the Fraction .1, which is 1 Tenth, if a Cypher were placed before it thus .01, it would be but 1 Hundredth, if two Cyphers .001, but 1 Thouſandth Part, &c.

The Decimal Fraction .25 is equal to the Vulgar Fraction $\frac{1}{4}$, .50 to $\frac{1}{2}$, and .75 to $\frac{3}{4}$, ſo that in the aforeſaid Tables, where the Decimals are Parts of a Peny, you may preſently perceive how many Farthings the Decimal conſiſts of, for .25 is exactly 1 Farthing, .50 is 2 Farthings, and .75 is 3 Farthings; and if the Fractions be more or leſs than either of theſe, you may take that which is neareſt to it, as if it be 7.34, then you may value it to be 7 *d.* 1 *q.*

But if your Decimal Fraction be Parts of a Pound ſterling, as they happen to be in reſolving Queſtions by the laſt Table, then to find the Value thereof, you muſt multiply it by 20, the Shillings contained in a Pound, and ſo many Figures as you have in your Product more than in your Multiplicand, cut off to the left hand, and the Figures ſo cut off are Shillings, and thoſe remaining to the right hand are the Decimal Parts of a Shilling.

*Example.*

### *Example.*

*What is the Value of the Decimal Fraction in the Example preceding the last Table, viz. .3625?*

The Fraction .3625 multiplied by 20 produces 72500, which is one Figure more than the Fraction propounded, wherefore I cut off one Figure to the left hand thus, 7|2500, which is 7 Shillings, and .25 Decimal Parts of a Shilling: The whole Work will stand thus:

```
 .3625
    20
------
7|2500
```

If your Decimal Fraction be Parts of a Shilling, then you must multiply it by 12,(the Pence therein contained) cutting off the Excess to the left hand for Pence as before for Shillings.

*Example.*

```
  .25
   12
-----
 3|00
```

Here there is no remainder, or Fraction of a Peny, and therefore the exact value of the foregoing Fraction .3625 of a Pound, is found to be 7 *s.* 3 *d.*

If your Decimal be Parts of a Peny, as .753 Parts of a Peny, you must multiply it by 4, (the Farthings contained in a Peny) and the Figures cut off will be Farthings.

*Example.*

```
 .753
    4
-----
3|012
```

And so this Fraction is found to be 3 *q.* and somewhat more, but so inconsiderable (being not 2 Hundred parts of a Farthing) that it is not worth notifying.

After this manner you may find the Value of any Fraction, but for your more ease, I will here set down a Decimal Table for Money, the Integer being 1 *l.*

*A Table*

*A Table supplying the Defect of Years in the Three last Tables, as also shewing the Rebate of Money, at 6 per Cent. Compound Interest.*

| *Years.* | *Forbearance of Annuities.* | *Discompt of Annuities.* | *Purchase of Annuities.* | *Rebate of Money.* |
|---|---|---|---|---|
| 1 | 1000000 | 943396 | 1060000 | 943396 |
| 2 | 2060000 | 1833392 | 545437 | 889996 |
| 3 | 3183600 | 2673012 | 374110 | 839619 |
| 4 | 4374616 | 3465105 | 288591 | 792093 |
| 5 | 5637093 | 4212363 | 237396 | 747258 |
| 6 | 6975318 | 4917324 | 203363 | 704960 |
| 7 | 8393837 | 5582381 | 179135 | 665057 |
| 8 | 9897467 | 6209792 | 161036 | 627412 |
| 9 | 11491315 | 6801691 | 147022 | 591898 |
| 10 | 13180794 | 7360086 | 135868 | 558394 |
| 11 | 14971642 | 7886873 | 126793 | 526787 |
| 12 | 16869940 | 8383843 | 119277 | 496969 |
| 13 | 18882137 | 8852682 | 112960 | 468839 |
| 14 | 21015065 | 9294983 | 107585 | 442301 |
| 15 | 23275969 | 9712248 | 102963 | 417265 |
| 16 | 25672527 | 10105894 | 98952 | 393646 |
| 17 | 28212879 | 10477258 | 95445 | 371364 |
| 18 | 30905651 | 10827602 | 92356 | 350343 |
| 19 | 33759990 | 11158115 | 89621 | 330513 |
| 20 | 36785590 | 11469920 | 87184 | 311804 |
| 21 | 39992725 | 11764075 | 85004 | 294155 |
| 22 | 43392289 | 12041580 | 83045 | 277505 |
| 23 | 46995826 | 12303377 | 81278 | 261797 |
| 24 | 50815575 | 12550356 | 79679 | 246978 |
| 25 | 54864510 | 12783354 | 78227 | 232998 |
| 26 | 59156381 | 13003164 | 76904 | 219810 |
| 27 | 63705763 | 13210532 | 75697 | 207368 |
| 28 | 68528109 | 13406162 | 74592 | 195630 |
| 29 | 73639796 | 13592719 | 73579 | 184556 |
| 30 | 79058184 | 13764829 | 72649 | 174110 |
| 31 | 84801675 | 13929084 | 71792 | 164254 |
| 32 | 90889775 | 14084041 | 71002 | 154957 |
| 33 | 97343162 | 14230227 | 70273 | 146186 |
| 34 | 104183752 | 14368158 | 69598 | 137930 |
| 35 | 111434777 | 14498363 | 68974 | 130105 |
| 36 | 119120864 | 14621003 | 68395 | 122740 |
| 37 | 127268116 | 14736797 | 67857 | 115793 |
| 38 | 135904203 | 14846035 | 67358 | 109238 |
| 39 | 145058455 | 14949097 | 66894 | 103055 |
| 40 | 154761962 | 15046313 | 66461 | 97222 |

*THE RATES OF*

# POST-LETTERS,

Both Inland and Outland,

ESTABLISHED

*Anno XII. Car. II. Regis.*

WITH

*The Times for sending and receiving them:*
*And also the POST-STAGES.*

| | s. | d. |
|---|---|---|
| 1. THe Carriage of every single Letter not exceeding one Sheet, to or from any place not exceeding fourscore Miles. —— | 0 | 2 |
| The like Carriage of every double Letter not exceeding two Sheets ———— | 0 | 4 |
| The like Carriage of every Pacquet of Letters proportionable to these Rates. | | |
| The like Carriage of every Pacquet of Writs, Deeds, and other things, for every Ounce —— | 0 | 8 |
| 2. The Carriage of every single Letter, above fourscore Miles ———— | 0 | 3 |
| The like Carriage of every double Letter | 0 | 6 |
| And after these Rates for all Pacquets of Letters. | | |
| The like Carriage of every other Pacquet for every Ounce ———— | 1 | 4 |

3. The

## *The Rates of Poſt-Letters.*

| | s. | d. |
|---|---|---|
| 3. The Carriage of every ſingle Letter from *London* to *Berwick*, or from *Berwick* to *London* — | 0 | 3 |
| The like Carriage of every double Letter — | 0 | 6 |
| And after theſe Rates for all Pacquets of Letters. | | |
| The like Carriage of every other Pacquet, for every Ounce — | 1 | 6 |
| 4. The Carriage of every ſingle Letter from *Berwick* unto any place within 40 Miles diſtance- | 0 | 2 |
| The like Carriage of every double Letter - | 0 | 4 |
| And after theſe Rates for every Pacquet of Letters. | | |
| The Carriage of every other Pacquet, for every Ounce — | 0 | 8 |
| The Carriage of every ſingle Letter a greater diſtance than 40 Miles — | 0 | 4 |
| The like Carriage of every double Letter— | 0 | 8 |
| And after theſe Rates for every Pacquet of Letters. | | |
| The like Carriage for things of greater bulk, by the Ounce — | 1 | 0 |
| 5. The Carriage of every ſingle Letter from *England* to *Dublin* in *Ireland*, or from *Dublin* into *England* — | 0 | 6 |
| The like Carriage of every double Letter— | 1 | 0 |
| And after theſe Rates for every Pacquet of Letters. | | |
| The like Carriage of every other Pacquet, for every Ounce — | 2 | 0 |
| 6. The Carriage of every ſingle Letter from *Dublin* to any place within 40 Miles diſtance, or from any place within the like diſtance to *Dublin* — | 0 | 2 |
| The like Carriage of every double Letter — | 0 | 4 |
| And after theſe Rates for every Pacquet of Letters. | | |

The

## *The Rates of Post-Letters.*

| | s. | d. |
|---|---|---|
| The like Carriage of every other Pacquet, for every Ounce ——————— | 0 | 8 |
| The Carriage of every Letter a farther distance than 40 Miles ——————— | 0 | 4 |
| The like Carriage of every double Letter — | 0 | 8 |

And after these Rates for every Pacquet of Letters.

| | | |
|---|---|---|
| The like Carriage of every other Pacquet, for every Ounce ——————— | 1 | 0 |

The several Rates that now are and have been taken for the Carriage of Letters, Pacquets, and Parcels, to or from any of His Majesties said Dominions, to or from any other Parts or Places beyond the Seas, are as follow, that is to say,

| | | s. | d. |
|---|---|---|---|
| *Morlaix*, St. *Maloes*, *Caen*, *New-haven*, and Places of like distance, Carriage paid to *Rouen*, is for ——— | Single | 0 | 6 |
| | Double | 1 | 0 |
| | Treble | 1 | 6 |
| | Ounce | 1 | 6 |
| *Hamburgh*, *Colen*, *Frankfurt*, Carriage paid to *Antwerp*, is ——— | Single | 0 | 8 |
| | Double | 1 | 4 |
| | Treble | 2 | 0 |
| | Ounce | 2 | 0 |
| *Venice*, *Geneva*, *Legorn*, *Rome*, *Naples*, *Messina*, and all other Parts of *Italy* by way of *Venice*, *franct pro Mantua* ——— | Single | 0 | 9 |
| | Double | 1 | 6 |
| | Treble | 2 | 3 |
| | Ounce | 2 | 8 |
| *Marcelia*, *Smirna*, *Constantinople*, *Aleppo*, and all parts of *Turkie*, Carriage paid to *Marcelia* ——— | Single | 1 | 0 |
| | Double | 2 | 0 |
| | $\frac{1}{4}$ Ounce | 2 | 9 |
| | Ounce | 3 | 9 |
| And for Letters brought from the said places to *England* ——— | Single | 0 | 8 |
| | Double | 1 | 4 |
| | Treble | 2 | 0 |
| | Ounce | 2 | 0 |

*The*

# *The Rates of Post-Letters.*

The Carriage of Letters brought into *England*, from

| | | s. | d. |
|---|---|---|---|
| *Calice*, *Diep*, *Bulloign*, *Abbeville*, *Amiens*, St. *Omers*, *Montrell* —— | Single | 0 | 4 |
| | Double | 0 | 8 |
| | Treble | 1 | 0 |
| | Ounce | 1 | 0 |
| *Roven* —————— | Single | 0 | 6 |
| | Double | 1 | 0 |
| | Treble | 1 | 6 |
| | Ounce | 1 | 6 |
| *Genqua*, *Legorn*, *Rome*, and other parts of *Italy* by way of *Lyons*, *franct pro Lyons* —————— | Single | 1 | 0 |
| | Double | 2 | 0 |
| | ¾ Ounce | 2 | 9 |
| | Ounce | 3 | 9 |

The Carriage of Letters outwards,

| | | s. | d. |
|---|---|---|---|
| To *Bourdeaux*, *Rochel*, *Nantes*, *Orleans*, *Bayon*, *Tours*, and places of like distance, Carriage paid to *Paris* —— | Single | 0 | 9 |
| | Double | 1 | 6 |
| | Treble | 2 | 3 |
| | Ounce | 2 | 0 |
| Letters brought from the same places into *England* —————— | Single | 1 | 0 |
| | Double | 2 | 0 |
| | ¾ Ounce | 3 | 0 |
| | Ounce | 4 | 0 |

The Carriage of Letters outwards,

| | | s. | d. |
|---|---|---|---|
| To *Norembourgh*, *Bremen*, *Dantzick*, *Lubeck*, *Lipswick*, and other places of like distance, Carriage paid to *Hamburgh* —————— | Single | 1 | 0 |
| | Double | 2 | 0 |
| | ¾ Ounce | 3 | 0 |
| | Ounce | 4 | 0 |
| *Paris* —————— | Single | 0 | 9 |
| | Double | 1 | 6 |
| | Treble | 2 | 3 |
| | Ounce | 2 | 0 |

*Dunkirk*,

## *The Rates of Post-Letters.*

| | | s. | d. |
|---|---|---|---|
| *Dunkirk*, *Ostend*, *Lisle*, *Ipres*, *Cambray*, *Ghent*, *Bruxels*, *Bruges*, *Antwerp*, and all other parts of *Flanders*. *Sluce*, *Flushing*, *Middleburgh*, *Amsterdam*, *Rotterdam*, *Delph*, *Hague*, and all other parts of *Holland* and *Zealand* — | Single | 0 | 8 |
| | Double | 1 | 4 |
| | Treble | 2 | 0 |
| | Ounce | 2 | 0 |

All Merchants Accompts, not exceeding a Sheet, Bills of Exchange, Invoices, Bills of Lading, shall be allowed without rate in the price of the Letters, and also the Covers of the Letters not exceeding a Sheet, to *Marseils*, *Venice*, or *Legorn*, towards *Turkie*.

The Hire of Post-Horses is after the Rate of 3 *d.* for every *English* Mile, and 4 *d.* every Stage for a Guide.

---

## POST-LETTERS *may be sent from* LONDON,

*On* Mondays,

TO *France*, *Spain*, *Italy*, *Germany*, *Flanders* and *Sweedland*, *Denmark*, *Kent* and the *Downs*.

*On* Tuesdays,

To *Holland*, *Germany*, *Sweedland*, *Denmark*, *Ireland*, *Scotland*, all parts of *England* and *Wales*.

*On* Wednesdays,

To all parts of *Kent* and the *Downs*.

*On* Thursdays,

To *France*, *Spain*, *Italy*, all parts of *England* and *Scotland*.

*On* Fridays,

To *Flanders*, *Germany*, *Italy*, *Sweedland*, *Denmark*, *Holland*, *Kent* and the *Downs*.

*On* Saturdays,

All parts of *England*, *Wales*, *Scotland*, and *Ireland*.

Letters are returned from all parts of *England* and *Scotland*, certainly every *Monday*, *Wednesday*, and *Friday*; from *Wales* every *Monday* and *Friday*; and from *Kent* and the *Downs* every day: But from other parts more uncertainly, in regard of the Sea.

POST-

# *The* Poſt-Stages, *ſhewing the Length of each Stage, and the Total of Miles from* LONDON.

## *Northern* Road from *London.*

| | Mil. | Tot. | | Mil. | Tot. |
|---|---|---|---|---|---|
| WAltham-croſs | 12 | 12 | Tadcaſter | 9 | 144 |
| Ware | 8 | 20 | York | 8 | 152 |
| Royſton | 13 | 33 | Burrowbrigg | 12 | 164 |
| Caxton | 8 | 41 | North-allerton | 12 | 176 |
| Huntington | 9 | 50 | Darlington | 10 | 186 |
| Stilton | 9 | 59 | Durham | 14 | 200 |
| Stamford | 12 | 71 | Newcaſtle | 12 | 212 |
| Southwitham | 8 | 79 | Morpeth | 12 | 224 |
| Grantham | 8 | 87 | Alnwik | 12 | 236 |
| Newark | 10 | 97 | Belford | 12 | 248 |
| Tuxford | 10 | 107 | Berwick | 12 | 260 |
| Bautry | 12 | 119 | Cockburnſpeth | 14 | 274 |
| Doncaſter | 6 | 125 | Haddington | 14 | 288 |
| Ferrybrigg | 10 | 135 | Edenbrough | 12 | 300 |

## *Norwich* Road from *London.*

| | | | | | |
|---|---|---|---|---|---|
| Royſton | 33 | 33 | Thetford | 10 | 73 |
| Cambridge | 10 | 43 | Attlebrough | 10 | 83 |
| Newmarket | 10 | 53 | Norwich | 12 | 95 |
| Bury | 10 | 63 | | | |

## *Cheſter* Road from *London.*

| | | | | | |
|---|---|---|---|---|---|
| Barnet | 10 | 10 | Stone | 16 | 110 |
| *St.* Albans | 10 | 20 | Namptwich | 16 | 126 |
| Dunſtable | 10 | 30 | Cheſter | 14 | 140 |
| Feniſtratford | 8 | 38 | Northope | 18 | 158 |
| Toſſeter | 12 | 50 | Denbeigh | 12 | 170 |
| Daintry | 10 | 60 | Conway | 14 | 184 |
| Coventry | 14 | 74 | Blewmorris | 10 | 194 |
| Coſhall | 8 | 82 | Hollyhead | 24 | 218 |
| Litchfield | 12 | 94 | | | |

*Darby*

# *The Poſt-Stages.*

## *Darby* Road from *London.*

| | Mil. | Tot. | | Mil. | Tot. |
|---|---|---|---|---|---|
| Toſſeter | 50 | 50 | Leiceſter | 12 | 80 |
| Northampton | 6 | 56 | Loubrough | 8 | 88 |
| Harborough | 12 | 68 | Darby | 12 | 100 |

## *Weſtern* Road from *London.*

| | | | | | |
|---|---|---|---|---|---|
| Stanes | 16 | 16 | Hunniton | 19 | 142 |
| Hartford-Bridge | 16 | 32 | Exeter | 15 | 157 |
| Baſingſtoke | 9 | 41 | Aſhburton | 20 | 177 |
| Andover | 18 | 59 | Plymouth | 24 | 201 |
| Salisbury | 16 | 75 | Foye | | |
| Shaftsbury | 19 | 94 | Trowro | | |
| Sherborn | 16 | 110 | Merkejew | | |
| Crookhorn | 13 | 123 | | | |

## *Portſmouth* Road from *London.*

| | | | | | |
|---|---|---|---|---|---|
| Stanes | 16 | 16 | Petersfield | 10 | 42 |
| Hartford-Bridge | 16 | 32 | Portsmouth | 24 | 66 |

## *Yarmouth* Road from *London.*

| | | | | | |
|---|---|---|---|---|---|
| Burntwood | 16 | 16 | Saxmundum | 16 | 78 |
| VVitham | 18 | 34 | Beckles | 16 | 94 |
| Colcheſter | 12 | 46 | Yarmouth | 10 | 104 |
| Ipſwich | 16 | 62 | | | |

## *Briſtol* Road from *London.*

| | | | | | |
|---|---|---|---|---|---|
| Huntſlo | 10 | 10 | Malbrough | 15 | 69 |
| Maidenhead | 16 | 26 | Chippenham | 15 | 84 |
| Reading | 12 | 38 | Briſtol | 20 | 104 |
| Newberry | 16 | 54 | | | |

## *Gloceſter* Road from *London.*

| | | | | | |
|---|---|---|---|---|---|
| Maidenhead | 26 | 26 | Cirenciſter | 15 | 72 |
| Abbington | 16 | 42 | Gloceſter | 18 | 90 |
| Farrington | 15 | 57 | | | |

## *Kentiſh* Road from *London.*

| | | | | | |
|---|---|---|---|---|---|
| Dartford | 14 | 14 | Canterbury | 15 | 55 |
| Rocheſter | 14 | 28 | Deal, or Dover | 15 | 70 |
| Sittingburn | 12 | 40 | | | |

# THE RATES and ORDERS OF *COACH-MEN.*

BY an Act of Parliament made in the Fourteenth Year of Our Soveraign Lord King *CHARLES* the Second, it is appointed, That no person or persons after *May* 1. 1662. shall presume to drive, (except Stage-Coaches) or let to Hire by the hour or day, or otherwise, any Hackney-Coach or Coach-Horses within the Parishes comprised within the Bills of Mortality, without an especial License from the Commissioners appointed by His Majesty for Licensing and regulating Hackney-Coaches. That no Horse, Gelding, or Mare, to be used with such Coaches, be under 14 hands high, according to the Standard. That the Number of Coaches to be Licensed shall not exceed 400. That every Coach so Licensed shall have a Mark of distinction by Figure, or otherwise, as the Commissioners shall think fit, to the end they may be known, if any complaint shall be made of them. That no person shall be Licensed to keep more than two Coaches, which Coaches shall have several Figures or Marks of distinction, as if belonging to several persons. That no person shall put that Figure or Mark upon his Coach which is appointed for any other, under the forfeiture of five pounds. That no person shall be Licensed to drive or keep a Hackney-

## *Rates and Orders of Coach-men.*

Hackney-Coach, or Coach-Horſes, that uſes any other Trade or Occupation. That firſt ſuch as have been ancient Coach-men, or ſuch Coach-men as have ſuffered for their Service to His Majeſty or his Father, or the Widows of ſuch (that have Coaches of their own) be Licenſed. That the Commiſſioners forfeit one hundred pounds for every Coach they Licenſe above the Number of 400.

That no Hackney-Coach-man ſo Licenſed ſhall preſume to take for his Hire in or about the Cities of *London* and *Weſtminſter* above Ten ſhillings for a day, reckoning 12 hours to the day; and by the hour, not above Eighteen-pence for the firſt hour, and 12 pence for every hour after; nor for his Hire from any of the *Inns of Court*, or thereabouts, to any part of St. *James's* or *Weſtminſter*, (except beyond *Tuttle-Street*) above 12 pence, and the like from the ſame places to the *Inns of Court*, or places thereabouts; nor from the *Inns of Court*, or thereabouts, to the *Royal Exchange*, more than 12 pence; but if to the *Tower*, *Biſhopſgate-Street*, *Aldgate*, or places thereabouts, 18 pence; and ſo from the ſame places to the ſaid *Inns of Court* as aforeſaid. That the like Rates be obſerved from or to any place, at the like diſtance with the places before named. That if any Coach-man ſhall refuſe to go at, or exact more for his Hire than theſe Rates, he ſhall for every Offence forfeit Ten ſhillings.

---

*The*

# *The* RATES *and* ORDERS *for* CARR-MEN.

*At a General Quarter-Seſſions of the Peace holden for the City of* London (*the* 10th *of* October, *in the Twenty ninth year of His Majeſties Reign, Sir* Thomas Davies *then Lord Mayor*) *at* Juſtice-Hall *in the* Old-Baily, *the following Rates and Orders were appointed for Carr-men.*

## *RATES for* CARR-MEN.

ALL Carr-men Trading or Working with Carrs in the City of *London*, and Liberties thereof, ſhall and may demand and take for every Carriage or Load of the Commodities under-mentioned, the Rates hereafter following, that is to ſay,

| | *s.* | *d.* |
|---|---|---|
| From any the Wharfs between the *Tower* and *London-Bridge*, to *Tower-ſtreet*, *Grace-Church-ſtreet*, *Fan-Church-ſtreet*, *Biſhopſgate-ſtreet* within, *Cornhill*, and places of like diſtance up the Hill, with 15 Hundred Weight, not exceeding 20 Hundred Weight ———— | 2 | 2 |
| And being above 20 Hundred Weight, for every Hundred ———— | 0 | 2 |
| *In which may be included*, | | |
| Two Puncheons of *Prunes*, 2 Bales of *Mather*, 20 Barrels of *Figs*, 2 Fats of *Fuſtians*, 6 ordinary Sacks of *Cotton Wools* of *Smyrna*, and 3 *Cyprus Bags*, a Butt of *Currans*, a great Butt of Oyls, 3 Cheſts of *Sugar*, 8 Bags of *Alums*, 1 Laſt of *Flax*, 1 Laſt of *Hemp*, and any other Goods herein not named of the like Weight, for every Load— | 2 | 2 |

And

## *Rates for Carr-men:*

| | s. | d. |
|---|---|---|
| And for *Sea-Coals*, 14 pence the Load, every Load to be half a Chaldron; and for one Hundred Fagots the like Rate ——— | 1 | 2 |
| And from any the Wharfs aforeſaid, to *Broad-ſtreet, Lothbury, Old Jury, Baſſiſhaw, Coleman-ſtreet, Ironmonger-Lane,* St. *Lawrence-Lane, Milk-ſtreet, Aldermanbury, Cheapſide, Wood-ſtreet, Friday-ſtreet, Bread-ſtreet,* and places of like diſtance, for the like Weight of 18 Hundred, not exceeding 20 Hundred Weight, for the Goods aforeſaid, and other Goods herein not named, of the like Weight, for every Load ——— | 2 | 6 |
| And being above 20 Hundred Weight, for every Hundred ——— | 0 | 2 |
| And for *Sea-Coals*, 16 pence the Load, every Load to be half a Chaldron; and for one Hundred Fagots the like Rate ——— | 1 | 4 |
| Alſo from any the Wharfs aforeſaid, to *Smithfield-Bars, Holborn-Bars, Temple-Bar,* or any of the Bars on the North-ſide of the City, and places of like diſtance up the Hill, with 18 Hundred Weight, not exceeding 20 Hundred Weight, for every Load ——— | 3 | 4 |

And going beyond the ſaid places, the parties to agree with the Carr-men.

| | s. | d. |
|---|---|---|
| Alſo from any the Wharfs aforeſaid, to *Tower-ſtreet, Biſhopſgate* within, *Cornhill,* and other places of like diſtance up the Hill, with 14 Hundred Weight, not exceeding 18 Hundred Weight— | 1 | 10 |

*In which may be included.*

| | s. | d. |
|---|---|---|
| Twenty pieces of *Raiſins*, a Load of *Raiſins* of the *Sun*, 6 Bags of *Pepper*, 6 ordinary Bags of *Galls*, 3 great Bags of *Galls*, 6 Bales and Barrels of *Indico*, 6 Bales of *Grogram Yarn*, 6 Bales of *Turkie Silk*, 5 Hogſheads of *Cloves*, 4 Bales of *Callicoes*, 3 Hogſheads of *Wines*, 2 Cheſts of *Sugar*, or any other Goods of the like Weight, 5 Hogſheads of *Tobacco*, not exceeding 18 *C.* Weight- | 1 | 10 |

Alſo

## *Rates of Carr-men.*

| | s. | d. |
|---|---|---|
| Alſo from any the Wharfs aforeſaid, to *Broad-ſtreet, Lothbury, Old Jury, Baſſiſhaw, Coleman-ſtreet, Ironmonger-Lane,* St. *Lawrence-Lane, Milk-Street, Aldermanbury, Cheapſide, Wood-ſtreet, Friday-ſtreet, Bread-ſtreet,* and places of the like diſtance for any of the ſaid Goods of the ſame quantity and Weight, for every Load ——— | 2 | 0 |
| Alſo from any the Wharfs aforeſaid, to *Tower-ſtreet, Grace-Church-ſtreet, Fan-Church-Street, Biſhopſgate-ſtreet* within, *Cornhill,* and other places of like diſtance up the Hill, with 8 Hundred Weight, not exceeding 14 Hundred Weight ——— | 1 | 6 |
| *In which may be included,* | | |
| All Buts and Pipes of *Wine,* or a Pipe of *Oil,* Packs of *Canvas,* 2 Hogſheads, or 3 Terces, a Fat of *Fuſtians,* and all other Goods of the like Bulk and Weight, for every Load ——— | 1 | 6 |
| And from any the Wharfs aforeſaid, to *Broad-ſtreet, Lothbury, Old Jury, Baſſiſhaw, Coleman-ſtreet, Ironmonger-Lane,* St. *Lawrence-Lane, Milk-ſtreet, Aldermanbury, Cheap-ſide, Wood-ſtreet, Friday-ſtreet,* and other places of like diſtance, for any other Goods of like Load, or Weight, for every Load - | 1 | 8 |
| Alſo from *London-Bridge-foot,* Weſtward to the *Old Swan, Cole Harbor,* the 3 *Cranes, Queenhith, Broken Wharf, Paul's Wharf, Puddle Wharf,* the *Wardrobe,* and to all other places not exceeding the *Poultry, Cheapſide,* or *Newgate-Market,* for 13 Hundred Weight, not exceeding 18*C.* Weight - | 1 | 10 |
| And for *Sea-Coals,* 14 pence the Load, every Load to be half a Chaldron; and for one Hundred Fagots the like Rate ——— | 1 | 2 |
| And from all other Wharfs, and places between *London-Bridge* and *Temple-Bar,* to the ſame, and places of like diſtance, for every Load of Coals 14 pence, every Load to be half a Chaldron; and 100 of Fagots the like Rate ——— | 1 | 2 |

And

## *Orders for Carr-men.*

| | s. | d. |
|---|---|---|
| And to all places Northwards of the *Poultry*, *Cheapſide*, *Newgate-Market*, *Holborn-Bridge*, and *Fleet-ſtreet*, for 14 Hundred Weight, not exceeding 18 Hundred Weight ———————— | 2 | 2 |
| And from *Tower-ſtreet*, *Grace-Church-ſtreet*, *Fan-Church-ſtreet*, *Biſhopſgate-ſtreet* within, *Cornhill*, and other places of like diſtance, for every Pack of 20 *Cloths*, for 6 Bales of *Cloths* and *Kerſeys*, 6 Bales of *Pepper*, 6 Barrels of *Indico*, 5 Hogſheads of *Cloves*, and for other Goods not herein mentioned, of like Weight, to the Water-ſide — | 1 | 4 |
| And from *Broad-ſtreet*, *Lothbury*, *Old Jury*, *Baſſiſhaw*, *Coleman-ſtreet*, *Ironmonger-Lane*, St. *Lawrence-Lane*, *Milk-ſtreet*, *Aldermanbury*, *Cheapſide*, *Wood-ſtreet*, *Friday-ſtreet*, *Bread-ſtreet*, and other places of like diſtance, to the Water-ſide, for the like Weight ———————————— | 1 | 8 |

And for places nearer, or of leſs diſtance, the parties hiring, and to be hired, are to make Agreement anſwerable or proportionable to the Rates before-mentioned.

## *ORDERS for* CARR-MEN.

THe *Carr-men* for the foregoing Rates are to help load and unload their *Carrs*.

If a *Carr-man* exact more than theſe Rates, upon due proof before the Lord Mayor, or any two Juſtices of the Peace, he ſhall ſuffer Impriſonment for the ſpace of 21 days, without Bayl or Mainpriſe.

If any Merchant, or other perſon, ſhall refuſe to pay a *Carr-man* for his Hire after theſe Rates, upon Complaint made by the *Carr-man* to the Preſident of *Chriſt-Hoſpital*, or any Juſtice of the Peace, the Preſident or Juſtice may oblige them to do it.

All Merchants, or others, may chuſe what *Carr* they pleaſe, except ſuch as ſtand for Wharf-work, Tackle-work,

*Orders for Carr-men.*

work, Crane-work, Shop and Merchants Houſes, which are to be taken in turn.

Every *Carr-man* ſtanding with his empty *Carr* next to any Goods to be loaden, ſhall upon the firſt demand load the ſame, without bargaining for any other Wages than the Rates before-mentioned.

If a Merchant, or other perſon, ſhall cauſe a *Carr-man* to attend at his Houſe, Shop, Ware-houſe, or Cellar, with his loaden *Carr*, above half an hour before he unloads, (the *Carr-man* being willing to help unload the ſame) he ſhall pay the *Carr-man* after the rate of Twelve pence for every hour after the firſt half hour, for his Attendance.

Every Licenſed *Carr-man* is to have a piece of Braſs fixed upon his *Carr*, upon which is to be ſet a certain Number, which Number (together with the *Carr-man*'s Name) is Regiſtred in a Regiſter kept in *Chriſt-Hoſpital*; ſo that if any *Carr-man* offends, it is but taking notice of the Number of his *Carr*, and ſearch for that in the ſaid Regiſter, and you will find his Name.

Every *Carr-man* that ſhall not conform to theſe Rules, or Work without a Numbred Piece of Braſs fixed on his *Carr*, may be ſuſpended from his Employment.

Complaints of the Abuſes of *Carr-men* may be made every *Tueſday*, at Two of the Clock in the Afternoon, to the Court ſitting in *Chriſt-Hoſpital*.

*The*

# The RATES or FARES OF WATER-MEN.

*As they were set forth by the Lord Mayor, and Court of Aldermen*, Sept. 7. 1671.

| | Oars. | | Skuller. | |
|---|---|---|---|---|
| | s. | d. | s. | d. |
| From *London* to *Lime-house*, *New-Crane*, *Shadwell-Dock*, *Bell-Wharf*, *Ratcliff-Cross* | 1 | 0 | 0 | 6 |
| To *Wapping-Dock*, *Wapping New*, and *Wapping Old Stairs*, the *Hermitage*, *Rotherhith* Church Stairs, and *Rotherhith* Stairs | 0 | 6 | 0 | 3 |
| From St. *Olaves* to *Rotherhith* Church Stairs, and *Rotherhith* Stairs | 0 | 6 | 0 | 3 |
| From *Billinsgate* and St. *Olaves* to St. *Saviour*'s Mill | 0 | 6 | 0 | 3 |
| All the Stairs between *London-Bridge* and *Westminster* | 0 | 6 | 0 | 3 |
| From either side above *London-Bridge* to *Lambeth* and *Fox-Hall* | 1 | 0 | 0 | 6 |
| From *White-hall* to *Lambeth* and *Fox-Hall* | 0 | 6 | 0 | 3 |
| From *Temple*, *Dorset*, *Black-Fryers* Stairs, and *Paul's Wharf*, to *Lambeth* | 0 | 8 | 0 | 4 |
| Over the Water directly in the next Skuller between *London-Bridge* and *Lime-house*, or *London-Bridge* and *Fox-Hall* | 0 | 0 | 0 | 2 |

## *OARS*,

| | Whole Fare | | Company. | |
|---|---|---|---|---|
| | s. | d. | s. | d. |
| From *London* to *Gravesend* | 4 | 6 | 0 | 9 |
| *Graise*, or *Greenhive* | 4 | 0 | 0 | 8 |
| *Purfleet*, or *Eriff* | 3 | 0 | 0 | 6 |
| *Woolwich* | 2 | 6 | 0 | 4 |
| *Black-wall* | 2 | 0 | 0 | 4 |
| *Greenwich*, or *Deptford* | 1 | 6 | 0 | 3 |

From

# *The Rates of Water-men.*

## *OARS,*

| From London to | Whole Fare. s. | Whole Fare. d. | Company. s. | Company. d. |
|---|---|---|---|---|
| *Chelſey, Batterſey, Wanſworth* | 1 | 6 | 0 | 3 |
| *Putney, Fulham, Barn-Elms* | 2 | 0 | 0 | 4 |
| *Hamerſmith, Chiſwick, Mortlack* | 2 | 6 | 0 | 6 |
| *Brentford, Iſleworth, Richmond* | 3 | 6 | 0 | 6 |
| *Twickenham* | 4 | 0 | 0 | 6 |
| *Kingſton* | 5 | 0 | 0 | 9 |
| *Hampton-Court* | 6 | 0 | 1 | 0 |
| *Hampton Town, Sunbury,* and *Walton* | 7 | 0 | 1 | 0 |
| *Weybridge* and *Chertſey* | 10 | 0 | 1 | 0 |
| *Stanes* | 12 | 0 | 1 | 0 |
| *Windſor* | 14 | 0 | 2 | 0 |

## *Rates for carrying of Goods in the Tilt-Boat between* Graveſend *and* London.

| | s. | d. | | s. | d. |
|---|---|---|---|---|---|
| A Half Firkin | 0 | 1 | An ordinary Cheſt or Trunk | 0 | 6 |
| Whole Firkin | 0 | 2 | An ordinary Hamper | 0 | 6 |
| Hogſhead | 2 | 0 | The Hire of the whole Tilt-Boat | 22 | 6 |
| Hundred Weight of Cheeſe, Iron, or any heavy Goods | 0 | 4 | Every ſingle Perſon in the ordinary paſſage | 0 | 6 |
| Sack of Salt, or Corn | 0 | 6 | | | |

What Waterman takes and demands more than theſe Rates, lies liable to pay Forty Shillings, and ſuffer half a Years Impriſonment.

And if he refuſe to carry any Paſſenger or Goods at theſe Rates, upon Complaint made to the Lord Mayor, and Court of Aldermen, he ſhall be ſuſpended from his Employ for Twelve Months.

For Product Safety Concerns and Information please contact our EU representative GPSR@taylorandfrancis.com
Taylor & Francis Verlag GmbH, Kaufingerstraße 24, 80331 München, Germany

www.ingramcontent.com/pod-product-compliance
Lightning Source LLC
LaVergne TN
LVHW020002031026
849161LV00023B/833
* 9 7 8 1 1 3 8 7 6 0 6 9 1 *